SAYONARA, ZETSUBOU-SENSEI

# The Power of Negative Thinking

1

# Koji Kumeta

Translated and adapted by Joyce Aurino
Lettered by Foltz Design

BALLANTINE BOOKS · NEW YORK

A Del Rey Manga/Kodansha Trade Paperback Original

*Sayonara, Zetsubou-sensei: The Power of Negative Thinking*
volume 1 copyright © 2005 by Koji Kumeta.
English translation copyright © 2009 by Koji Kumeta.

Published in the United States by Del Rey, an imprint of The Random House Publishing Group, a division of Random House, Inc., New York.

DEL REY is a registered trademark and the Del Rey colophon is a trademark of Random House, Inc.

Publication rights arranged through Kodansha Ltd.

First published in Japan in 2005 by Kodansha Ltd., Tokyo

ISBN 978-0-345-50893-5

Printed in the United States of America

www.delreymanga.com

4 5 6 7 8 9

Translator/Adapter: Joyce Aurino
Lettering: Foltz Design

# SAYONARA, ZETSUBOU-SENSEI

## The Power of Negative Thinking

## CONTENTS

# Honorifics Explained

Throughout the Del Rey Manga books, you will find Japanese honorifics left intact in the translations. For those not familiar with how the Japanese use honorifics and, more important, how they differ from American honorifics, we present this brief overview.

Politeness has always been a critical facet of Japanese culture. Ever since the feudal era, when Japan was a highly stratified society, use of honorifics—which can be defined as polite speech that indicates relationship or status—has played an essential role in the Japanese language. When you address someone in Japanese, an honorific usually takes the form of a suffix attached to one's name (example: "Asuna-san"), is used as a title at the end of one's name, or appears in place of the name itself (example: "Negi-sensei," or simply "Sensei!").

Honorifics can be expressions of respect or endearment. In the context of manga and anime, honorifics give insight into the nature of the relationship between characters. Many English translations leave out these important honorifics and therefore distort the feel of the original Japanese. Because Japanese honorifics contain nuances that English honorifics lack, it is our policy at Del Rey not to translate them. Here, instead, is a guide to some of the honorifics you may encounter in Del Rey Manga.

**-san:** This is the most common honorific and is equivalent to Mr., Miss, Ms., or Mrs. It is the all-purpose honorific and can be used in any situation where politeness is required.

**-sama:** This is one level higher than "-san" and is used to confer great respect.

**-dono:** This comes from the word "tono," which means "lord." It is an even higher level than "-sama" and confers utmost respect.

**-kun:** This suffix is used at the end of boys' names to express familiarity or endearment. It is also sometimes used by men among friends, or when addressing someone younger or of a lower station.

**-chan:** This is used to express endearment, mostly toward girls. It is also used for little boys, pets, and even among lovers. It gives a sense of childish cuteness.

**Bozu:** This is an informal way to refer to a boy, similar to the English terms "kid" and "squirt."

**Sempai/**
**Senpai:** This title suggests that the addressee is one's senior in a group or organization. It is most often used in a school setting, where underclassmen refer to their upperclassmen as "sempai." It can also be used in the workplace, such as when a newer employee addresses an employee who has seniority in the company.

**Kohai:** This is the opposite of "sempai" and is used toward underclassmen in school or newcomers in the workplace. It connotes that the addressee is of a lower station.

**Sensei:** Literally meaning "one who has come before," this title is used for teachers, doctors, or masters of any profession or art.

**-[blank]:** This is usually forgotten in these lists, but it is perhaps the most significant difference between Japanese and English. The lack of honorific, known as *yobisute,* means that the speaker has permission to address the person in a very intimate way. Usually only family, spouses, or very close friends have this kind of permission. It can be gratifying when someone who has earned the intimacy starts to call one by one's name without an honorific. But when that intimacy hasn't been earned, it can be very insulting.

# Koji Kumeta

# SAYONARA, ZETSUBOU-SENSEI

**1**

## The Power of Negative Thinking

# Contents



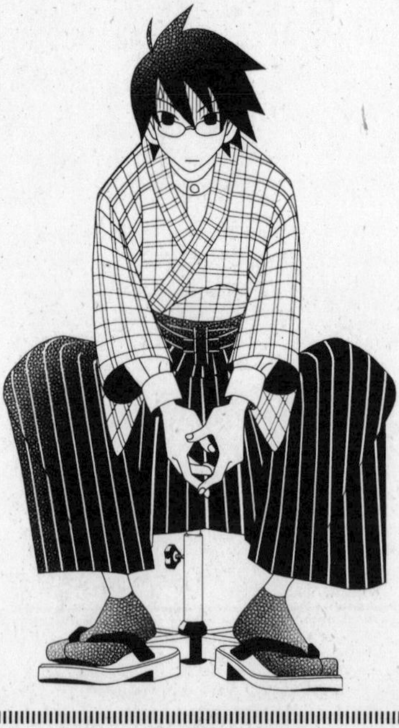


The stories, characters, and incidents mentioned in this publication are entirely fictional. Originally published in 2005 in *Weekly Shônen Magazine* #22/23 (double issue) to #31.

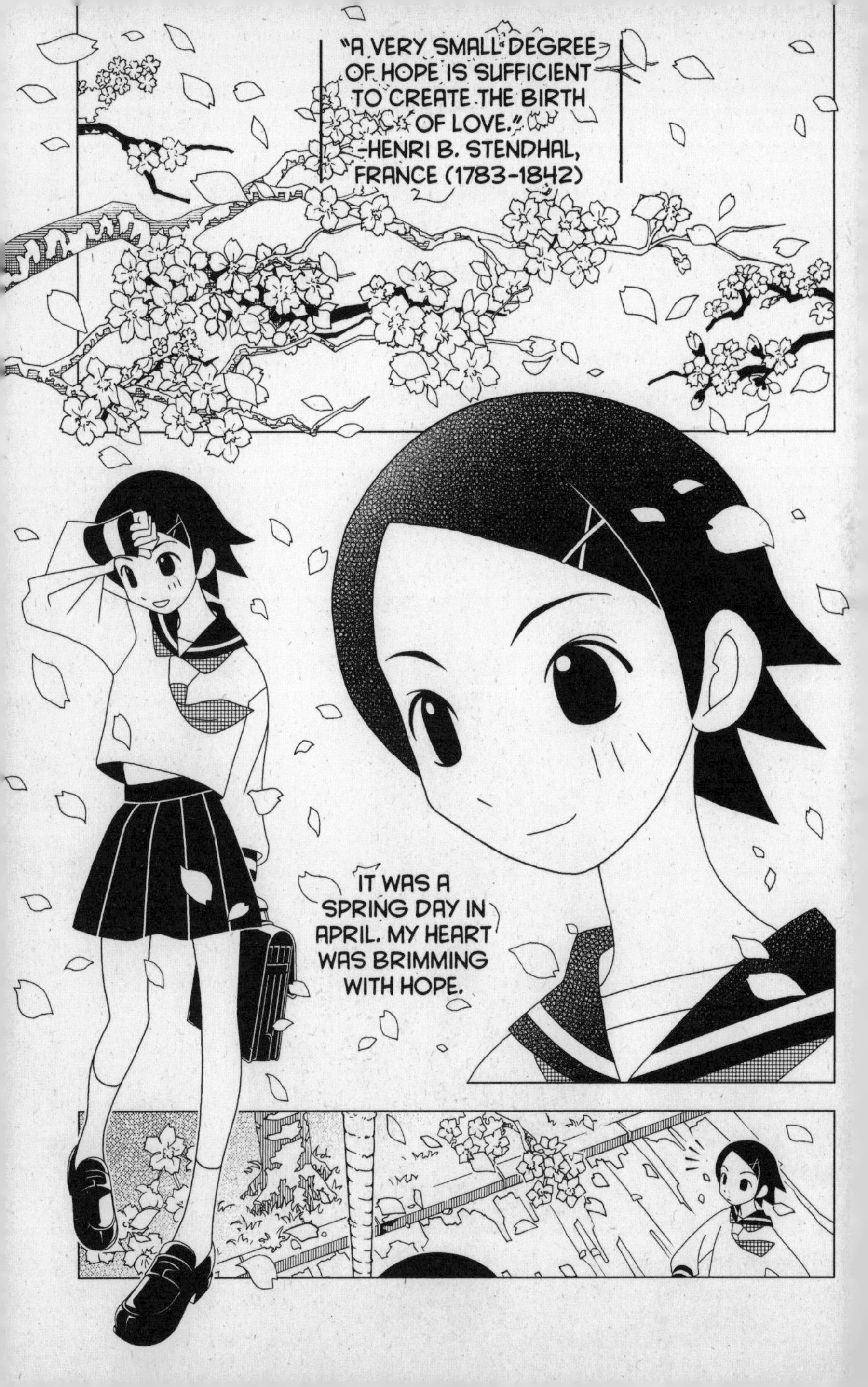
"A VERY SMALL DEGREE OF HOPE IS SUFFICIENT TO CREATE THE BIRTH OF LOVE."
-HENRI B. STENDHAL, FRANCE (1783-1842)
IT WAS A SPRING DAY IN APRIL. MY HEART WAS BRIMMING WITH HOPE.

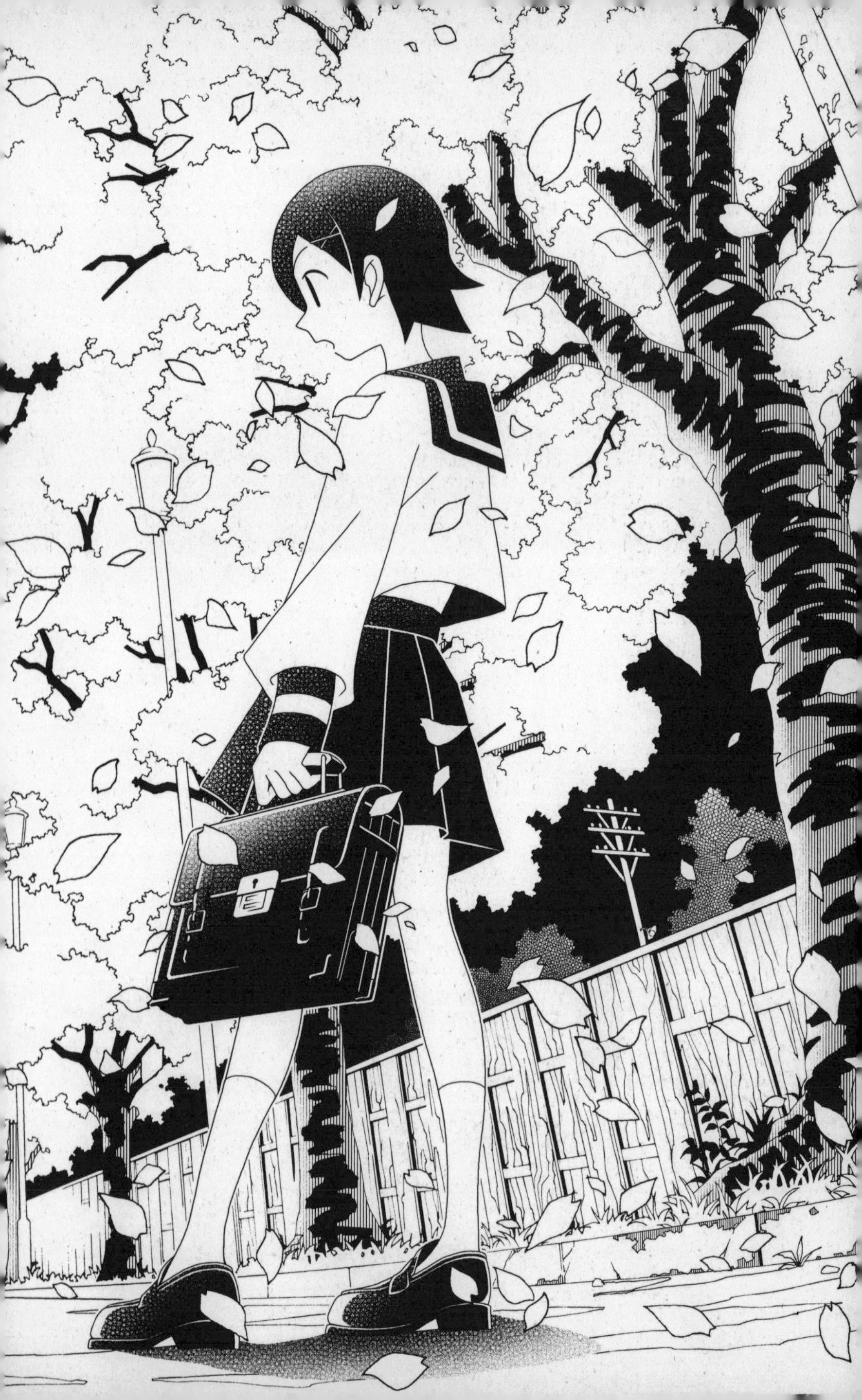

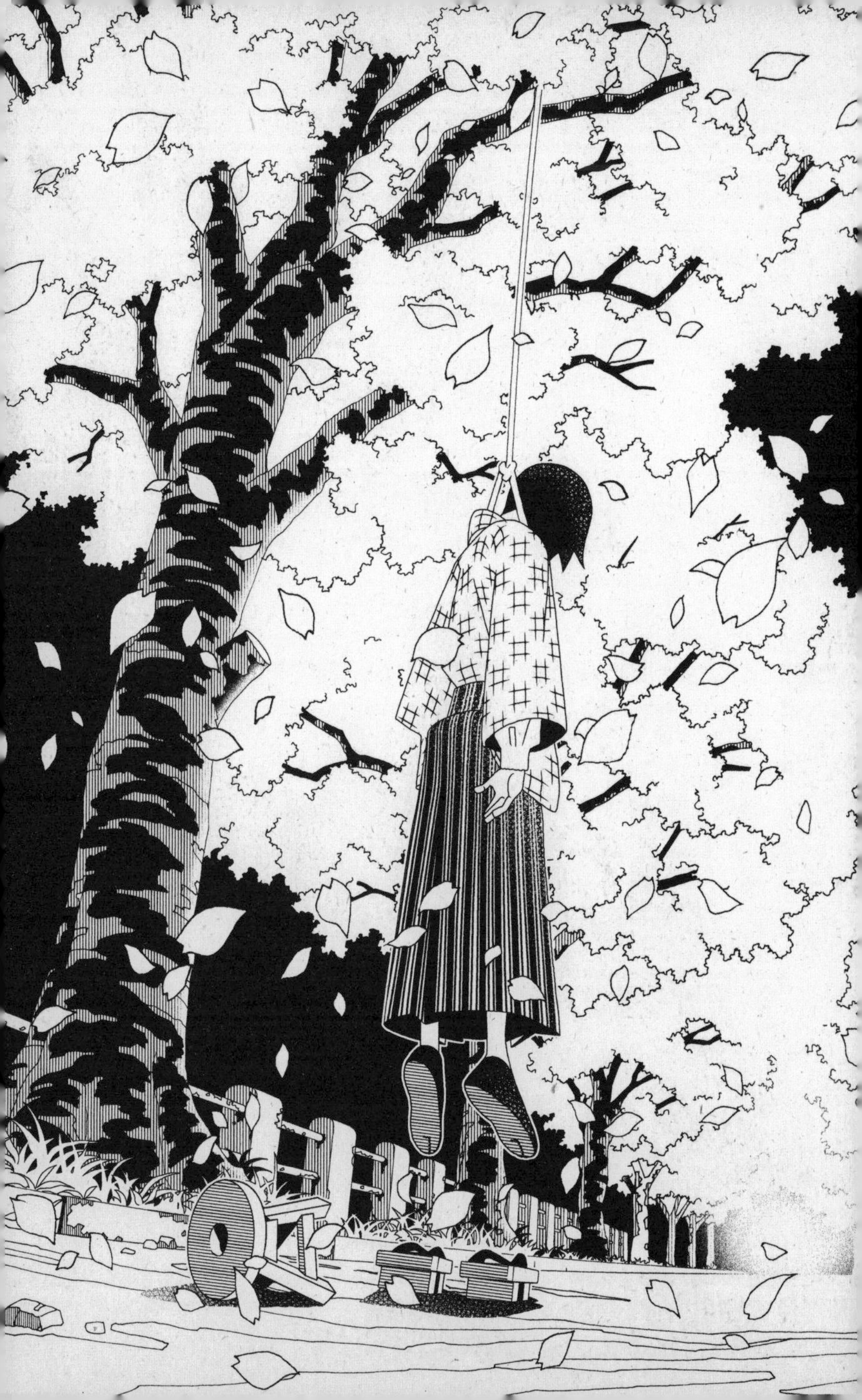

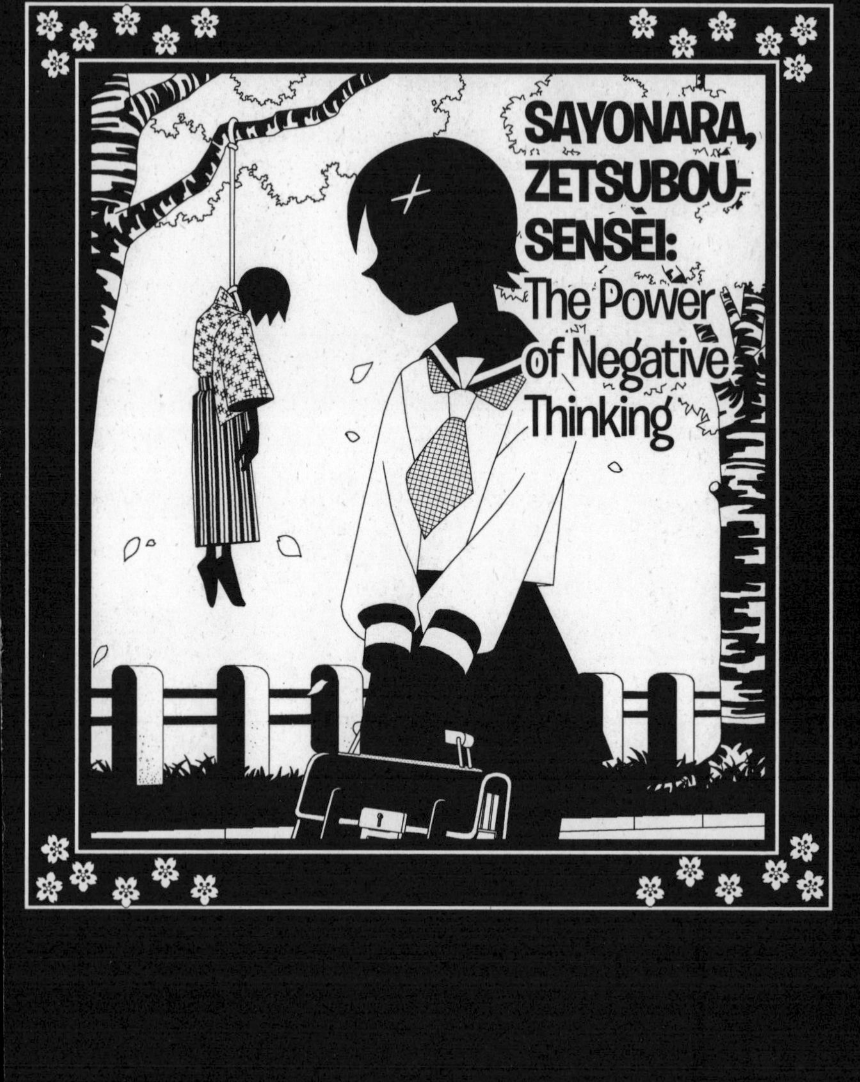
SAYONARA, ZETSUBOU-SENSEI:
The Power of Negative Thinking

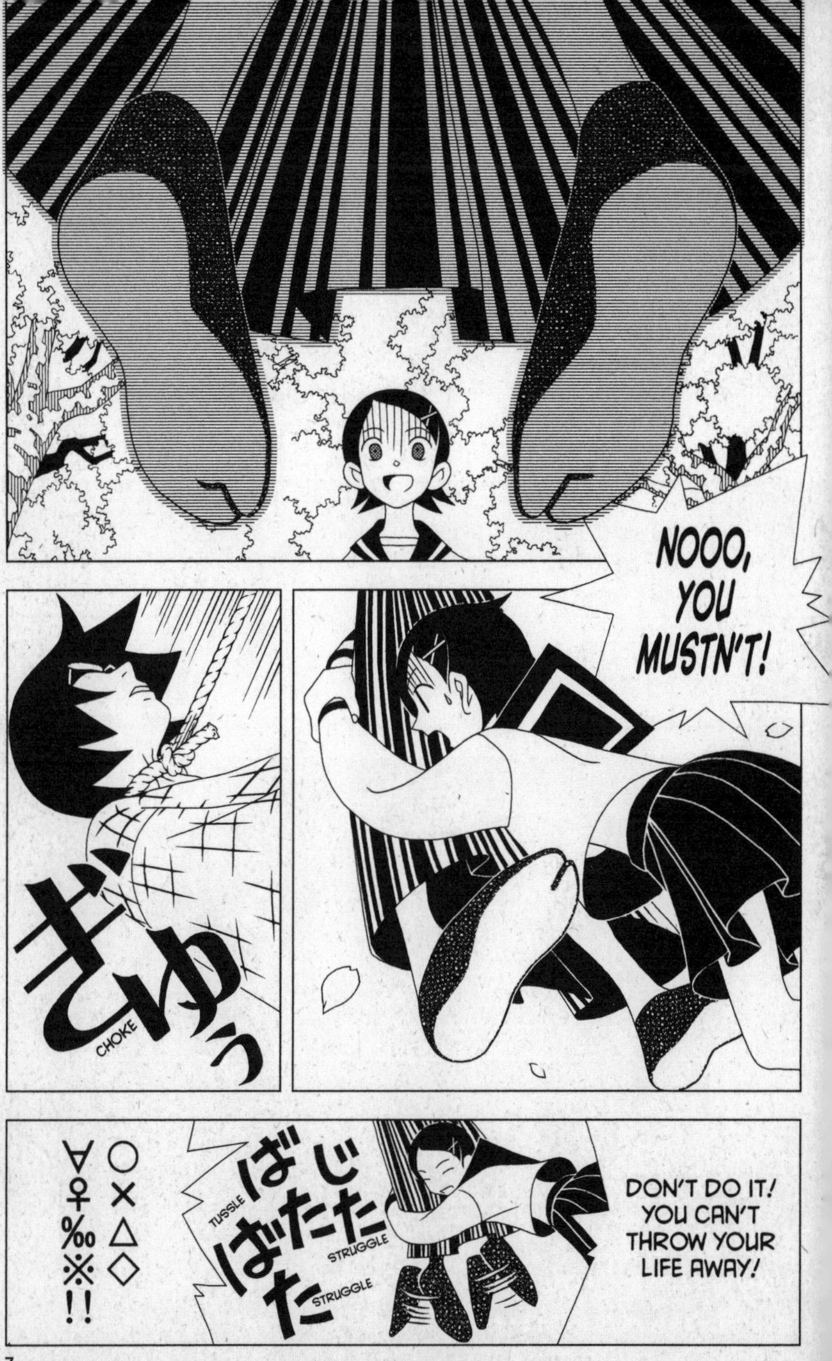
NOOO, YOU MUSTN'T!
CHOKE
DON'T DO IT! YOU CAN'T THROW YOUR LIFE AWAY!
TUSSLE
STRUGGLE
STRUGGLE
○×△◇∀♀‰※!!

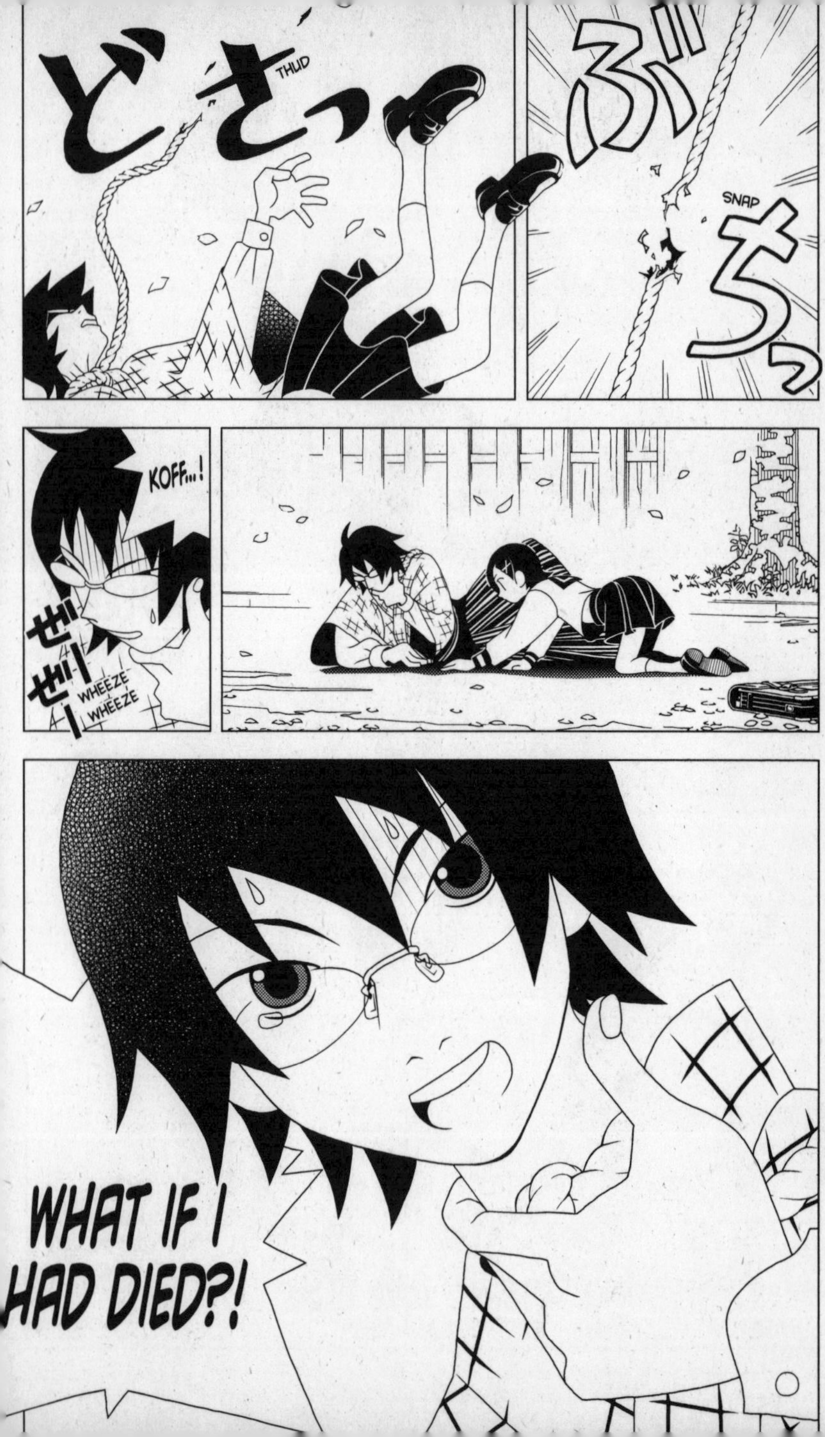
ぶちっ
SNAP
どさっ
THUD
KOFF...!
ぜーぜー
WHEEZE WHEEZE
WHAT IF I HAD DIED?!

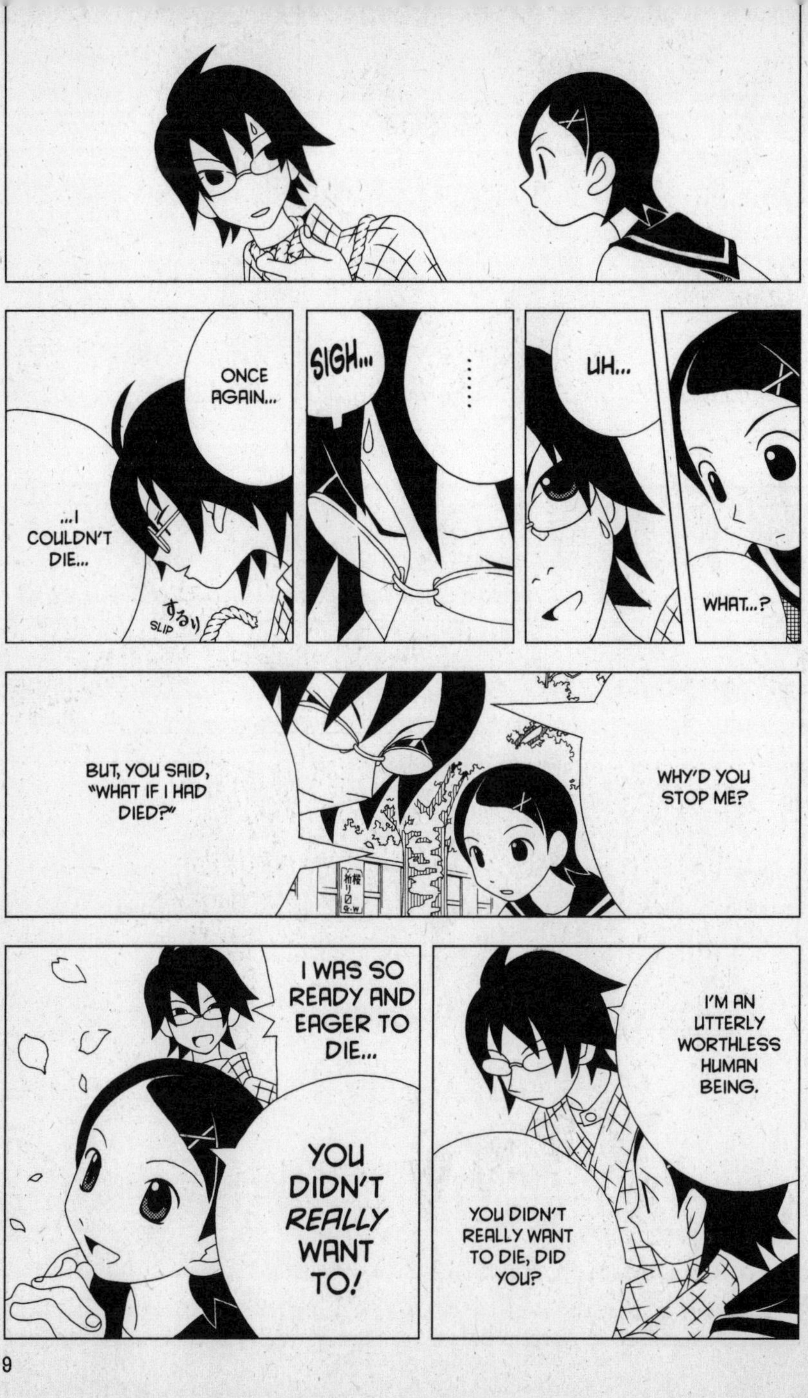
WHAT...?
UH...
SIGH...
......
ONCE AGAIN...
...I COULDN'T DIE...
するり SLIP
WHY'D YOU STOP ME?
BUT, YOU SAID, "WHAT IF I HAD DIED?"
I'M AN UTTERLY WORTHLESS HUMAN BEING.
YOU DIDN'T REALLY WANT TO DIE, DID YOU?
I WAS SO READY AND EAGER TO DIE...
YOU DIDN'T *REALLY* WANT TO!

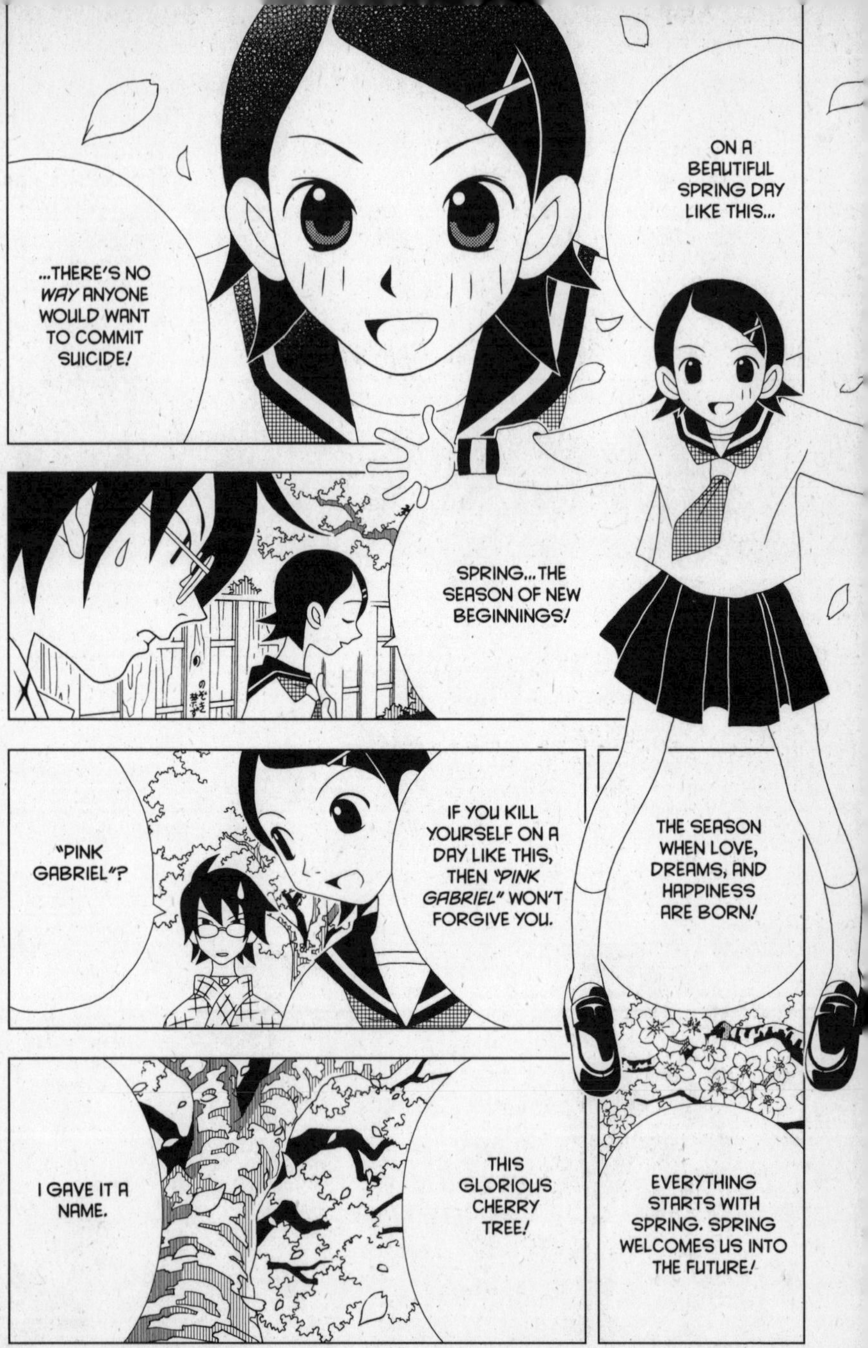
ON A BEAUTIFUL SPRING DAY LIKE THIS...
...THERE'S NO *WAY* ANYONE WOULD WANT TO COMMIT SUICIDE!
SPRING...THE SEASON OF NEW BEGINNINGS!
THE SEASON WHEN LOVE, DREAMS, AND HAPPINESS ARE BORN!
EVERYTHING STARTS WITH SPRING. SPRING WELCOMES US INTO THE FUTURE!
IF YOU KILL YOURSELF ON A DAY LIKE THIS, THEN *"PINK GABRIEL"* WON'T FORGIVE YOU.
"PINK GABRIEL"?
THIS GLORIOUS CHERRY TREE!
I GAVE IT A NAME.

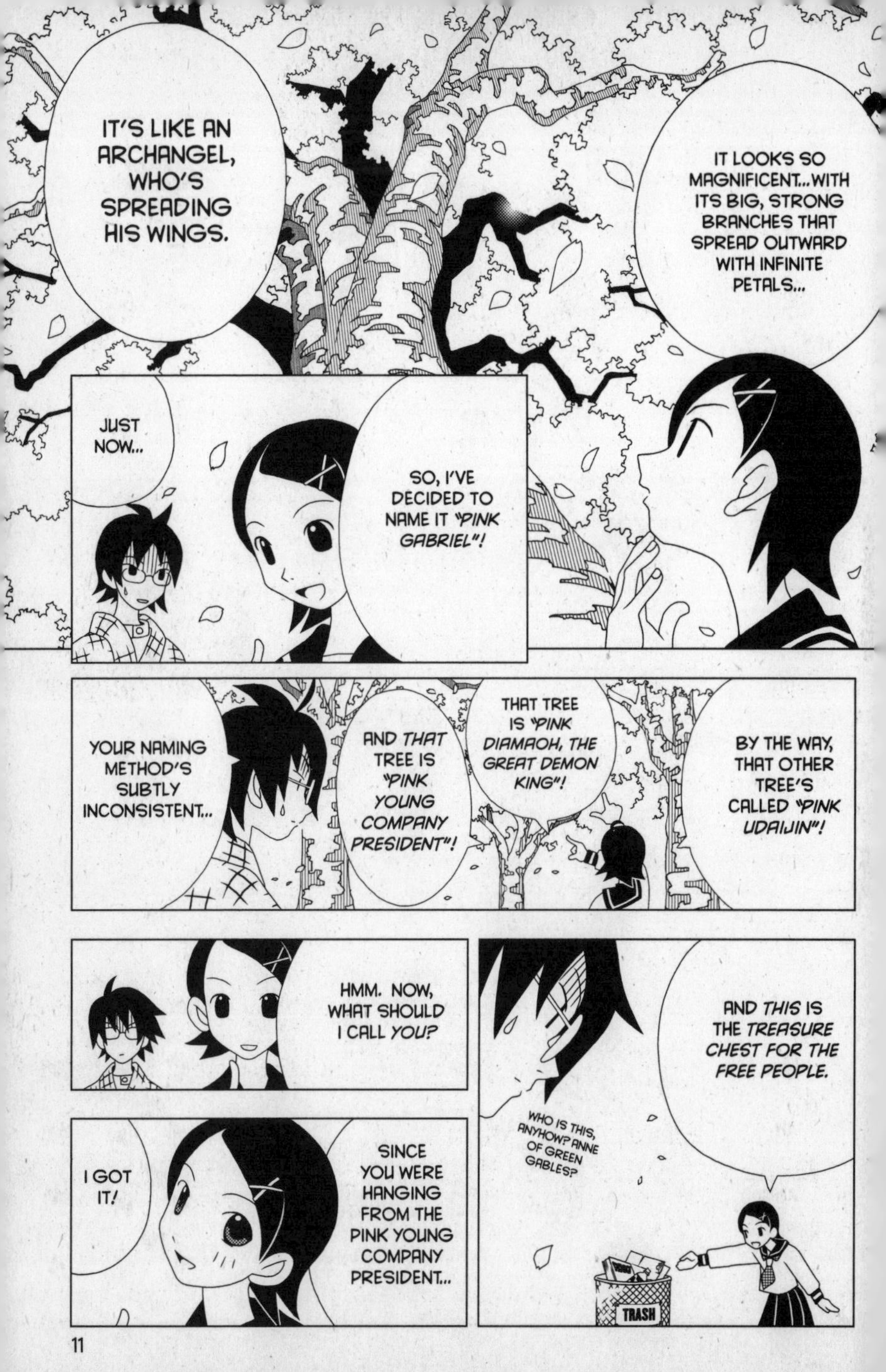
IT LOOKS SO MAGNIFICENT...WITH ITS BIG, STRONG BRANCHES THAT SPREAD OUTWARD WITH INFINITE PETALS...
IT'S LIKE AN ARCHANGEL, WHO'S SPREADING HIS WINGS.
SO, I'VE DECIDED TO NAME IT "PINK GABRIEL"!
JUST NOW...
BY THE WAY, THAT OTHER TREE'S CALLED "PINK UDAIJIN"!
THAT TREE IS "PINK DIAMAOH, THE GREAT DEMON KING"!
AND THAT TREE IS "PINK YOUNG COMPANY PRESIDENT"!
YOUR NAMING METHOD'S SUBTLY INCONSISTENT...
AND THIS IS THE TREASURE CHEST FOR THE FREE PEOPLE.
WHO IS THIS, ANYHOW? ANNE OF GREEN GABLES?
TRASH
HMM. NOW, WHAT SHOULD I CALL YOU?
SINCE YOU WERE HANGING FROM THE PINK YOUNG COMPANY PRESIDENT...
I GOT IT!

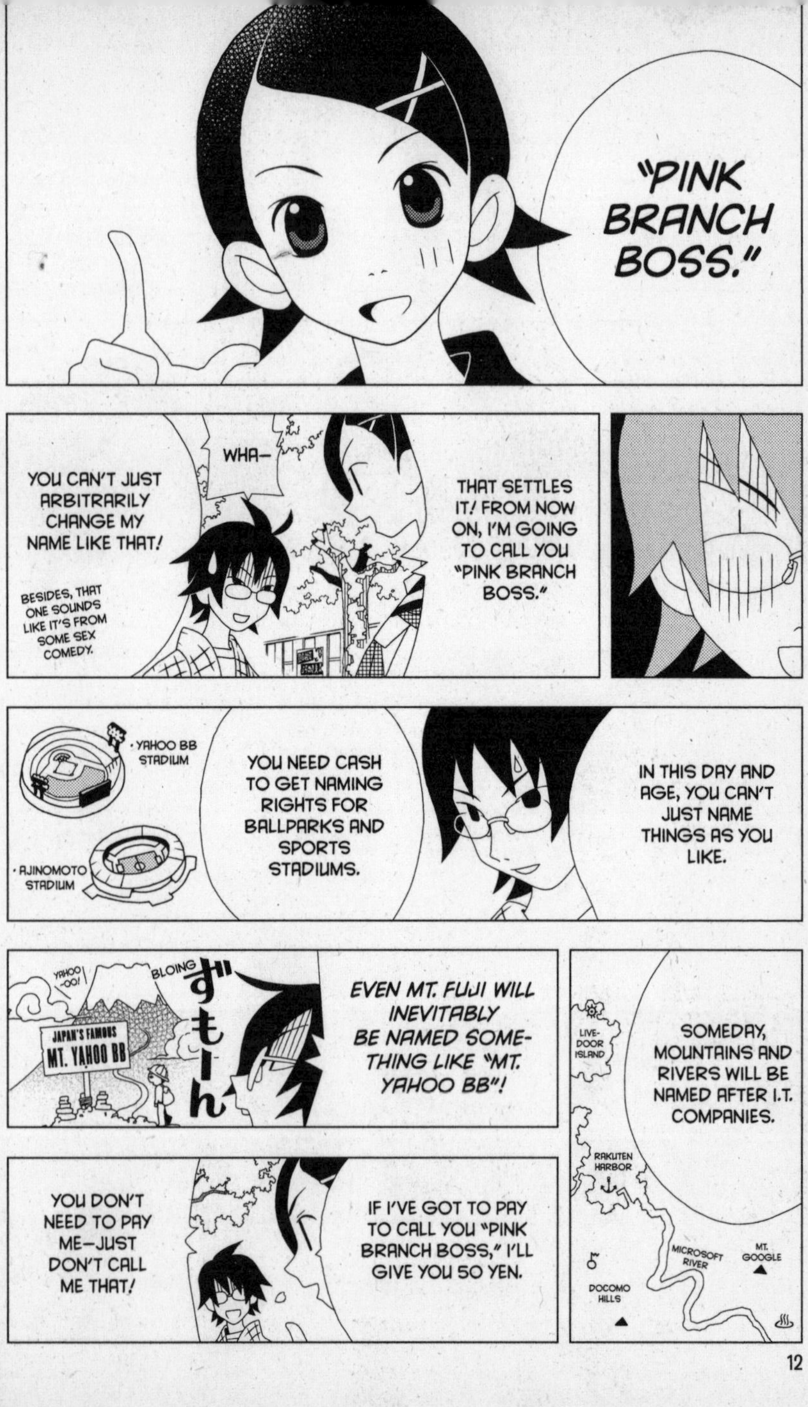
"PINK BRANCH BOSS."
THAT SETTLES IT! FROM NOW ON, I'M GOING TO CALL YOU "PINK BRANCH BOSS."
WHA-
YOU CAN'T JUST ARBITRARILY CHANGE MY NAME LIKE THAT!
BESIDES, THAT ONE SOUNDS LIKE IT'S FROM SOME SEX COMEDY.
IN THIS DAY AND AGE, YOU CAN'T JUST NAME THINGS AS YOU LIKE.
YOU NEED CASH TO GET NAMING RIGHTS FOR BALLPARKS AND SPORTS STADIUMS.
• YAHOO BB STADIUM
• AJINOMOTO STADIUM
SOMEDAY, MOUNTAINS AND RIVERS WILL BE NAMED AFTER I.T. COMPANIES.
LIVE-DOOR ISLAND
RAKUTEN HARBOR
MT. GOOGLE
MICROSOFT RIVER
DOCOMO HILLS
EVEN MT. FUJI WILL INEVITABLY BE NAMED SOMETHING LIKE "MT. YAHOO BB"!
ずもーん
BLOING
YAHOO-OO!
JAPAN'S FAMOUS MT. YAHOO BB
IF I'VE GOT TO PAY TO CALL YOU "PINK BRANCH BOSS," I'LL GIVE YOU 50 YEN.
YOU DON'T NEED TO PAY ME—JUST DON'T CALL ME THAT!

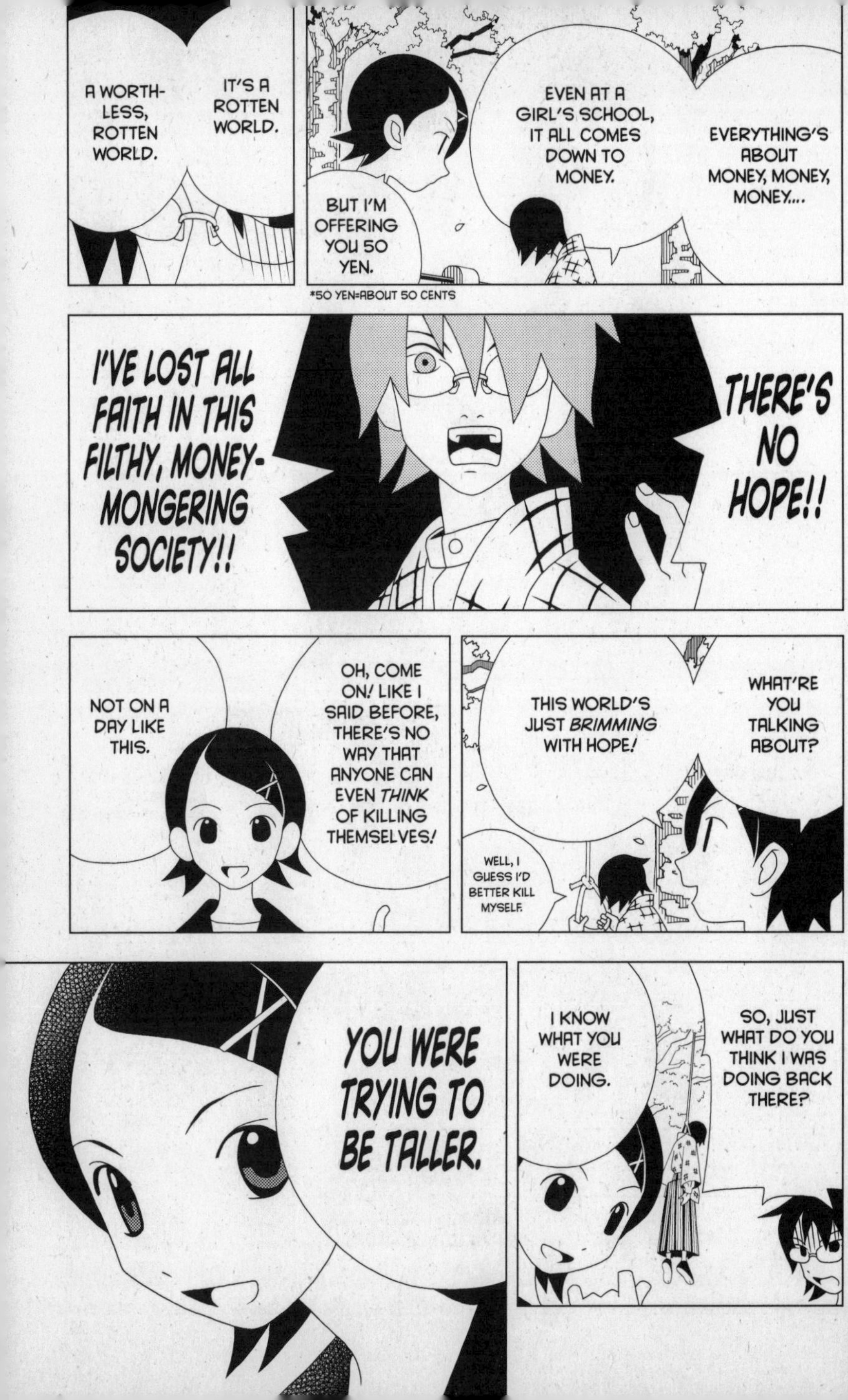
EVERYTHING'S ABOUT MONEY, MONEY, MONEY....
EVEN AT A GIRL'S SCHOOL, IT ALL COMES DOWN TO MONEY.
BUT I'M OFFERING YOU 50 YEN.
IT'S A ROTTEN WORLD.
A WORTHLESS, ROTTEN WORLD.
*50 YEN=ABOUT 50 CENTS
THERE'S NO HOPE!!
I'VE LOST ALL FAITH IN THIS FILTHY, MONEY-MONGERING SOCIETY!!
WHAT'RE YOU TALKING ABOUT?
THIS WORLD'S JUST *BRIMMING* WITH HOPE!
WELL, I GUESS I'D BETTER KILL MYSELF.
OH, COME ON! LIKE I SAID BEFORE, THERE'S NO WAY THAT ANYONE CAN EVEN *THINK* OF KILLING THEMSELVES!
NOT ON A DAY LIKE THIS.
SO, JUST WHAT DO YOU THINK I WAS DOING BACK THERE?
I KNOW WHAT YOU WERE DOING.
YOU WERE TRYING TO BE TALLER.

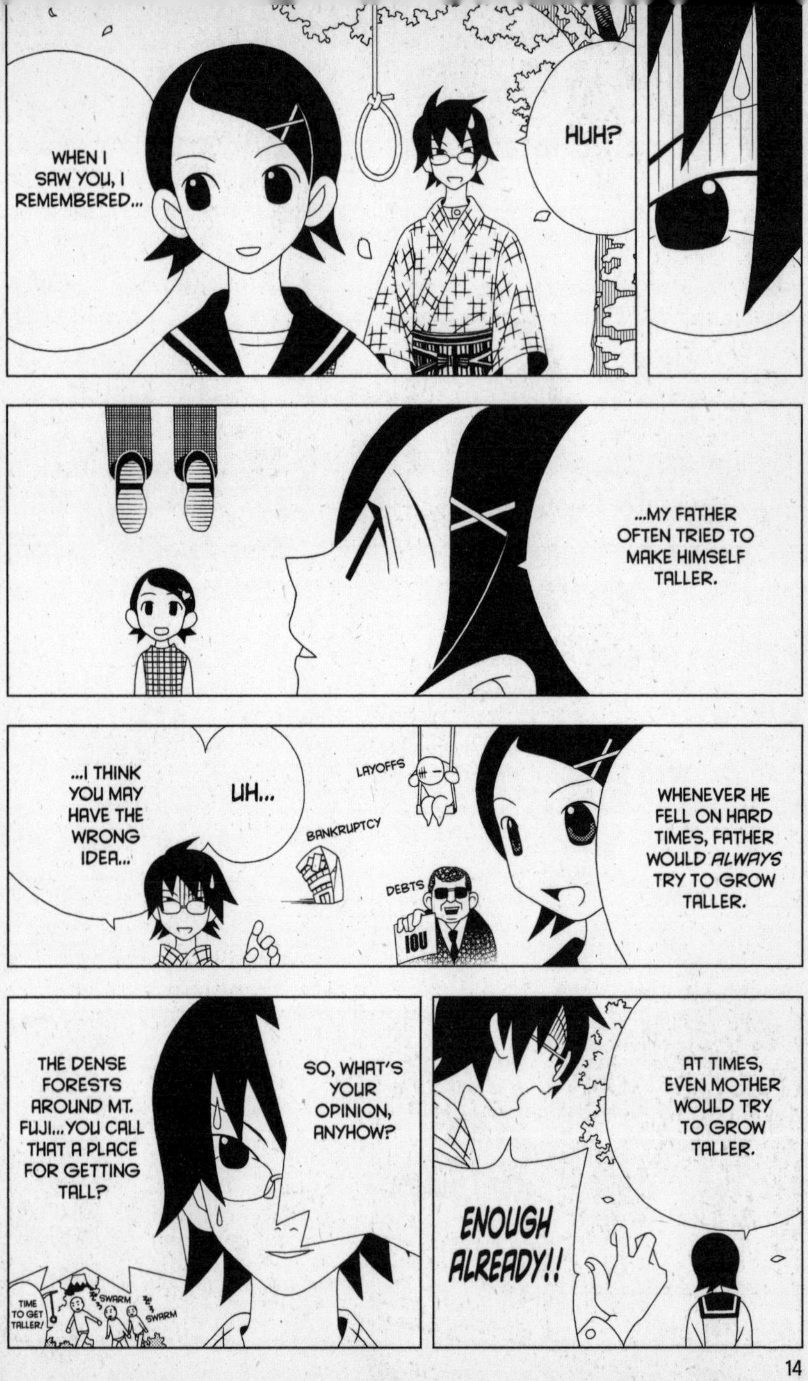
HUH?
WHEN I SAW YOU, I REMEMBERED...
...MY FATHER OFTEN TRIED TO MAKE HIMSELF TALLER.
WHENEVER HE FELL ON HARD TIMES, FATHER WOULD *ALWAYS* TRY TO GROW TALLER.
LAYOFFS
BANKRUPTCY
DEBTS
IOU
UH...
...I THINK YOU MAY HAVE THE WRONG IDEA...
AT TIMES, EVEN MOTHER WOULD TRY TO GROW TALLER.
ENOUGH ALREADY!!
SO, WHAT'S YOUR OPINION, ANYHOW?
THE DENSE FORESTS AROUND MT. FUJI...YOU CALL THAT A PLACE FOR GETTING TALL?
TIME TO GET TALLER!
SWARM
SWARM

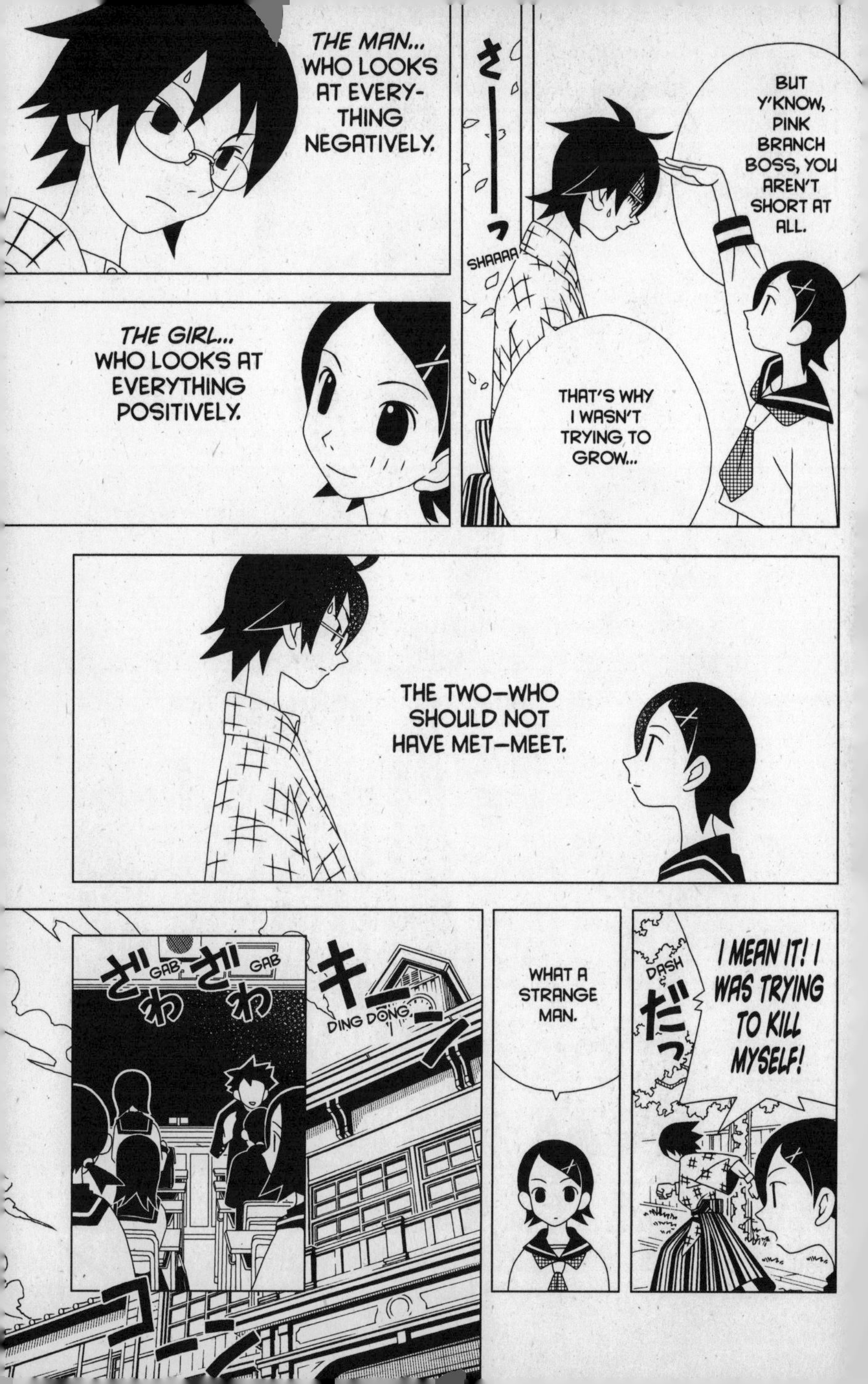
BUT Y'KNOW, PINK BRANCH BOSS, YOU AREN'T SHORT AT ALL.
さーっ
SHAAAA
THAT'S WHY I WASN'T TRYING TO GROW...
THE MAN... WHO LOOKS AT EVERY-THING NEGATIVELY.
THE GIRL... WHO LOOKS AT EVERYTHING POSITIVELY.
THE TWO—WHO SHOULD NOT HAVE MET—MEET.
I MEAN IT! I WAS TRYING TO KILL MYSELF!
だっ
DASH
WHAT A STRANGE MAN.
キーンコーン
DING DONG
ざわ ざわ
GAB GAB

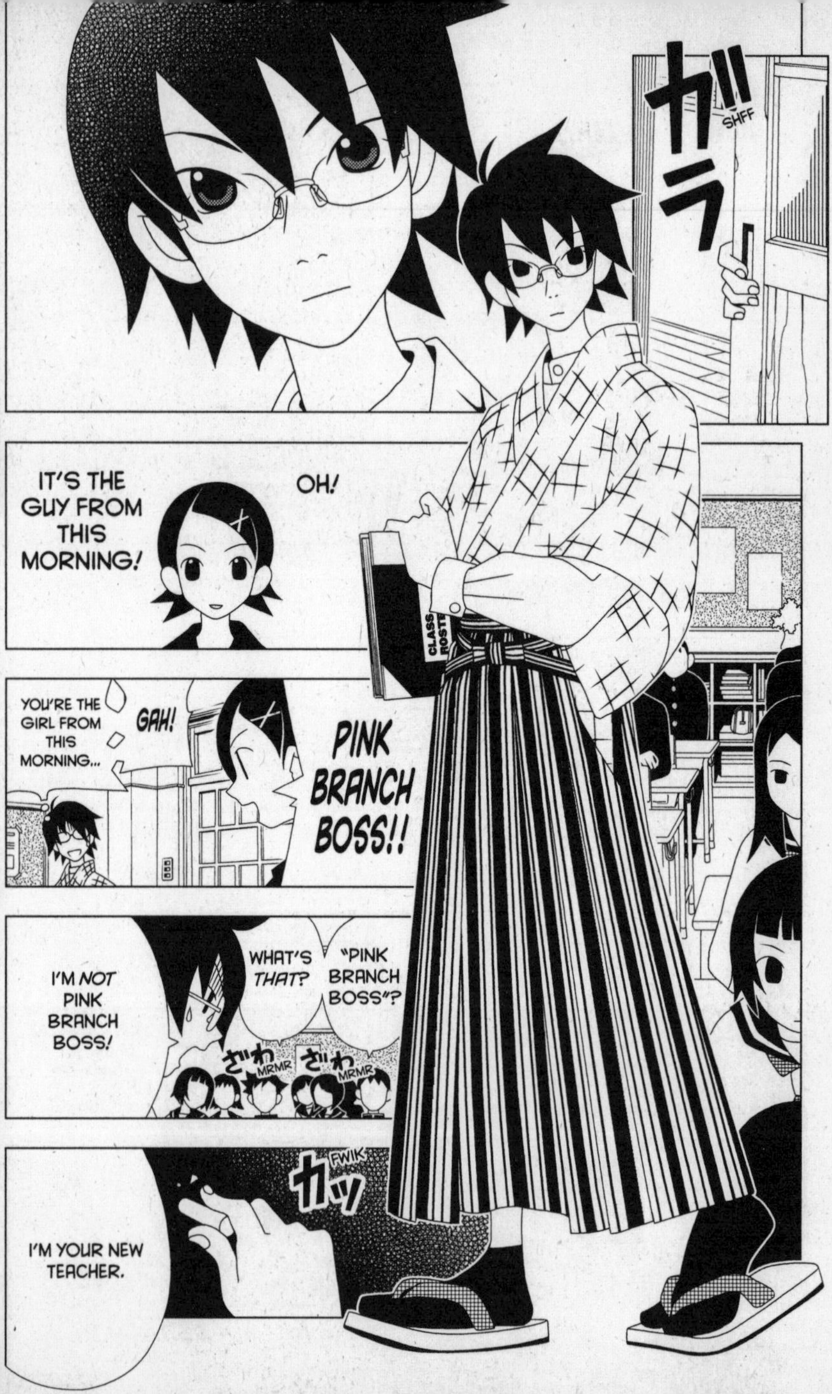

ガラ
SHFF
OH!
IT'S THE GUY FROM THIS MORNING!
CLASS ROSTE
PINK BRANCH BOSS!!
GAH!
YOU'RE THE GIRL FROM THIS MORNING...
"PINK BRANCH BOSS"?
WHAT'S *THAT*?
ざわ MRMR ざわ MRMR
I'M *NOT* PINK BRANCH BOSS!
カッ
FWIK
I'M YOUR NEW TEACHER.

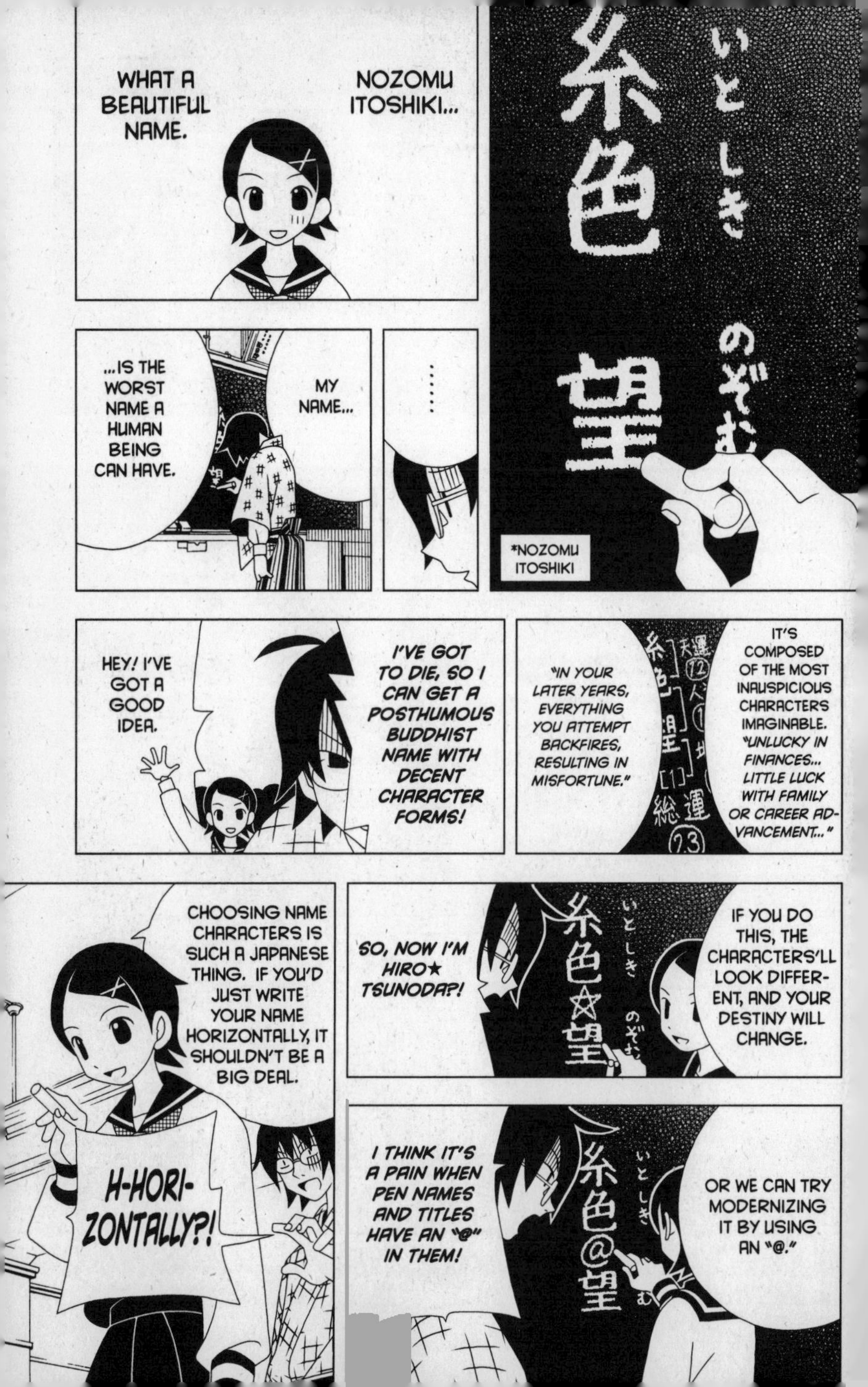
いとしき
糸色
のぞむ
望
*NOZOMU ITOSHIKI
NOZOMU ITOSHIKI...
WHAT A BEAUTIFUL NAME.
......
MY NAME...
...IS THE WORST NAME A HUMAN BEING CAN HAVE.
IT'S COMPOSED OF THE MOST INAUSPICIOUS CHARACTERS IMAGINABLE. "UNLUCKY IN FINANCES... LITTLE LUCK WITH FAMILY OR CAREER ADVANCEMENT..."
"IN YOUR LATER YEARS, EVERYTHING YOU ATTEMPT BACKFIRES, RESULTING IN MISFORTUNE."
I'VE GOT TO DIE, SO I CAN GET A POSTHUMOUS BUDDHIST NAME WITH DECENT CHARACTER FORMS!
HEY! I'VE GOT A GOOD IDEA.
IF YOU DO THIS, THE CHARACTERS'LL LOOK DIFFERENT, AND YOUR DESTINY WILL CHANGE.
いとしき
糸色☆望
のぞむ
SO, NOW I'M HIRO★ TSUNODA?!
OR WE CAN TRY MODERNIZING IT BY USING AN "@."
いとしき
糸色@望
I THINK IT'S A PAIN WHEN PEN NAMES AND TITLES HAVE AN "@" IN THEM!
CHOOSING NAME CHARACTERS IS SUCH A JAPANESE THING. IF YOU'D JUST WRITE YOUR NAME HORIZONTALLY, IT SHOULDN'T BE A BIG DEAL.
H-HORIZONTALLY?!

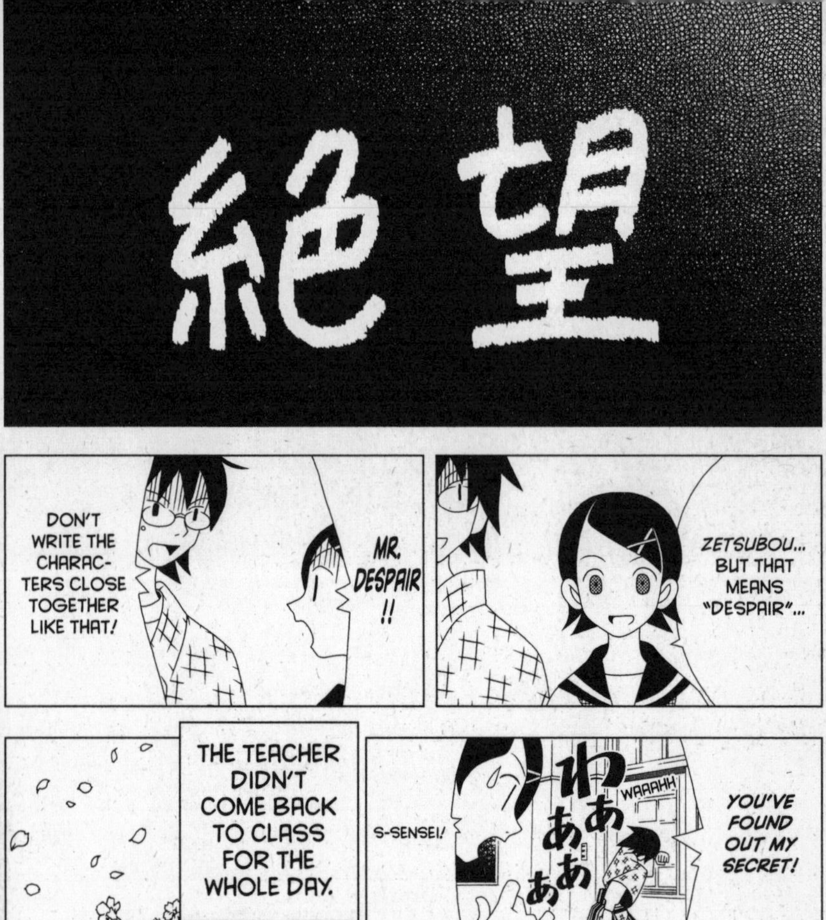
絶望
ZETSUBOU... BUT THAT MEANS "DESPAIR"...
MR. DESPAIR!!
DON'T WRITE THE CHARAC-TERS CLOSE TOGETHER LIKE THAT!
YOU'VE FOUND OUT MY SECRET!
わあああああ
WAAAHH
S-SENSEI!
THE TEACHER DIDN'T COME BACK TO CLASS FOR THE WHOLE DAY.
OUR TEACHER'S PRETTY SENSITIVE FOR A GROWN-UP.
YEAH, SENSI-TIVE...
AFTER THAT, WHEN ANYONE WROTE THE TEACHER'S NAME, THEY MADE SURE TO PUT PLENTY OF SPACE BETWEEN THE CHARACTERS.
糸 色望
I THINK YOU'RE TRYING TOO HARD TO PLEASE.

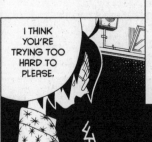

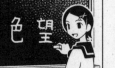

# ATTENDANCE LIST
## CLASS 2-F

**HOMEROOM TEACHER**
## NOZOMU ITOSHIKI
**SUPER-NEGATIVE MAN**

2005·04·27

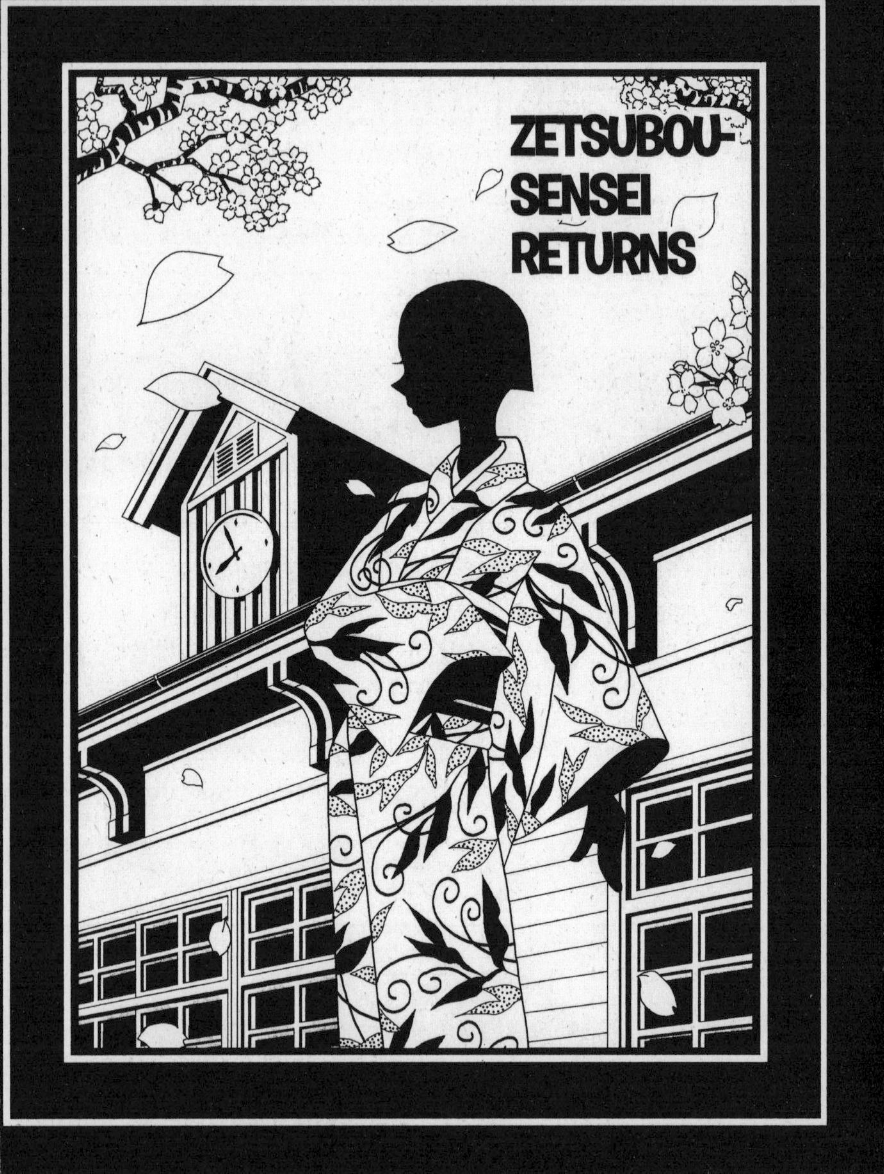
ZETSUBOU-
SENSEI
RETURNS

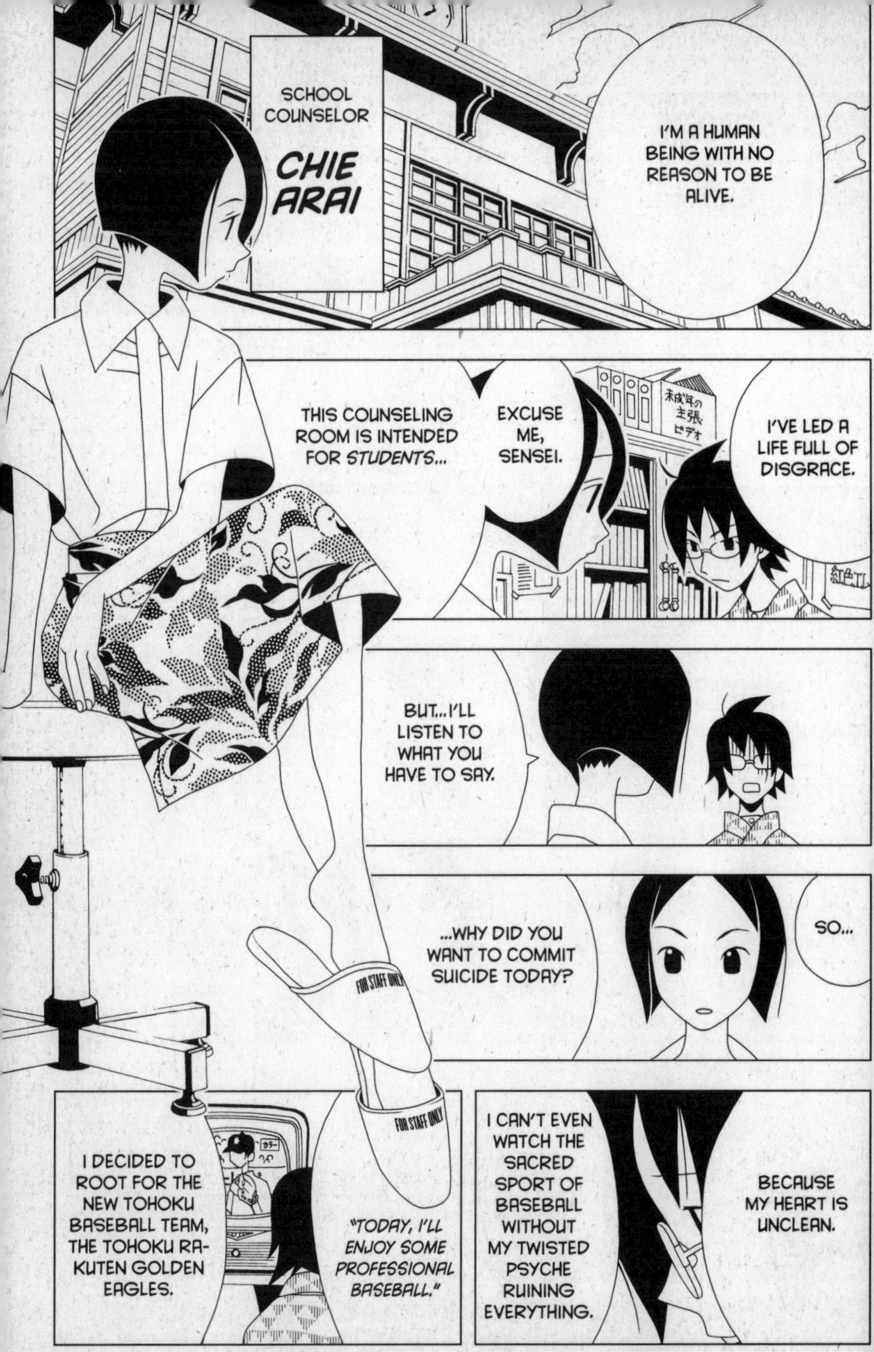
I'M A HUMAN BEING WITH NO REASON TO BE ALIVE.
SCHOOL COUNSELOR
CHIE ARAI
I'VE LED A LIFE FULL OF DISGRACE.
未成年の主張 ビデオ
EXCUSE ME, SENSEI.
THIS COUNSELING ROOM IS INTENDED FOR *STUDENTS*...
BUT...I'LL LISTEN TO WHAT YOU HAVE TO SAY.
SO...
...WHY DID YOU WANT TO COMMIT SUICIDE TODAY?
FOR STAFF ONLY
FOR STAFF ONLY
BECAUSE MY HEART IS UNCLEAN.
I CAN'T EVEN WATCH THE SACRED SPORT OF BASEBALL WITHOUT MY TWISTED PSYCHE RUINING EVERYTHING.
*"TODAY, I'LL ENJOY SOME PROFESSIONAL BASEBALL."*
I DECIDED TO ROOT FOR THE NEW TOHOKU BASEBALL TEAM, THE TOHOKU RAKUTEN GOLDEN EAGLES.

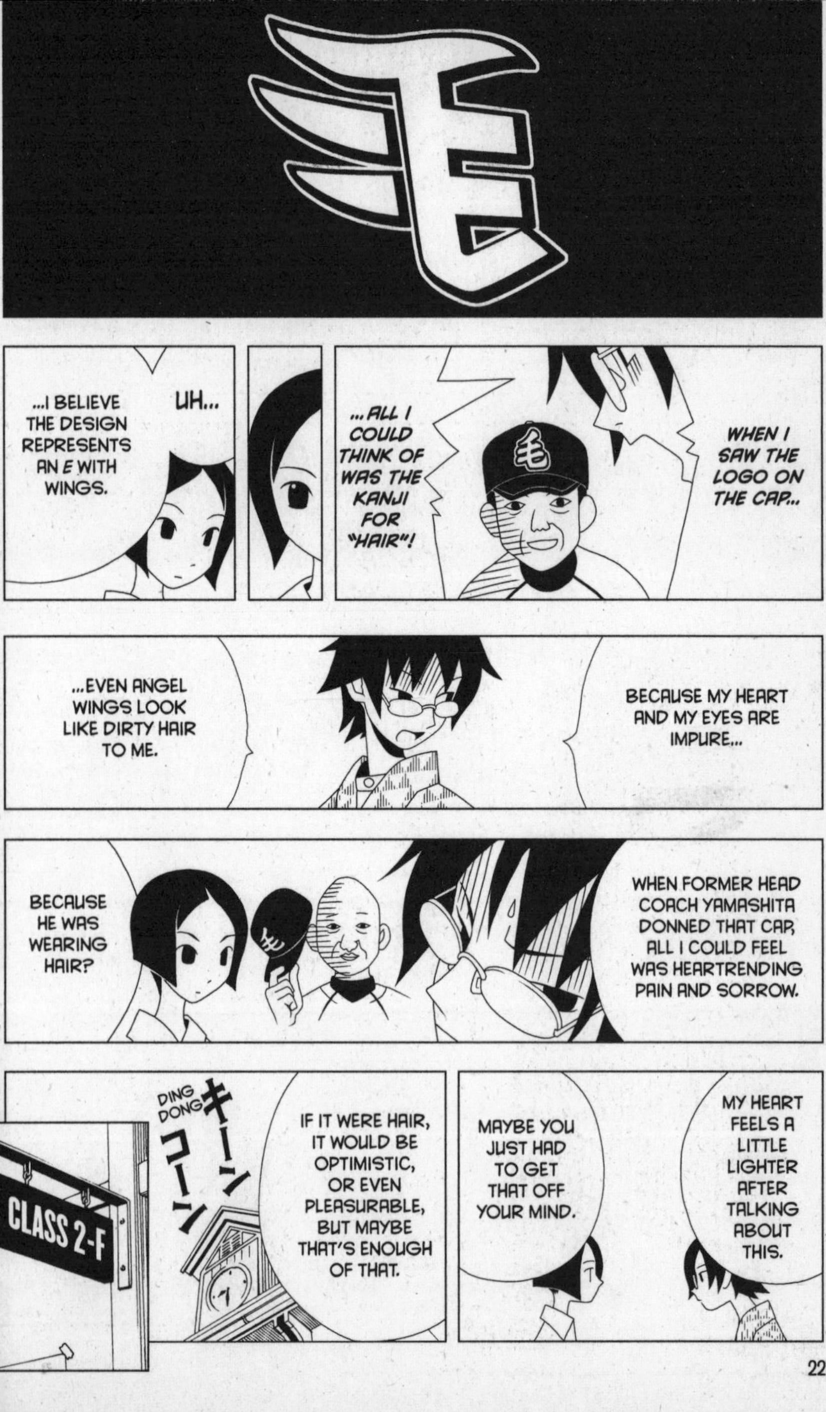
WHEN I SAW THE LOGO ON THE CAP...
...ALL I COULD THINK OF WAS THE KANJI FOR "HAIR"!
UH...
...I BELIEVE THE DESIGN REPRESENTS AN *E* WITH WINGS.
BECAUSE MY HEART AND MY EYES ARE IMPURE...
...EVEN ANGEL WINGS LOOK LIKE DIRTY HAIR TO ME.
WHEN FORMER HEAD COACH YAMASHITA DONNED THAT CAP, ALL I COULD FEEL WAS HEARTRENDING PAIN AND SORROW.
BECAUSE HE WAS WEARING HAIR?
MY HEART FEELS A LITTLE LIGHTER AFTER TALKING ABOUT THIS.
MAYBE YOU JUST HAD TO GET THAT OFF YOUR MIND.
IF IT WERE HAIR, IT WOULD BE OPTIMISTIC, OR EVEN PLEASURABLE, BUT MAYBE THAT'S ENOUGH OF THAT.
DING DONG
キーンコーン
CLASS 2-F

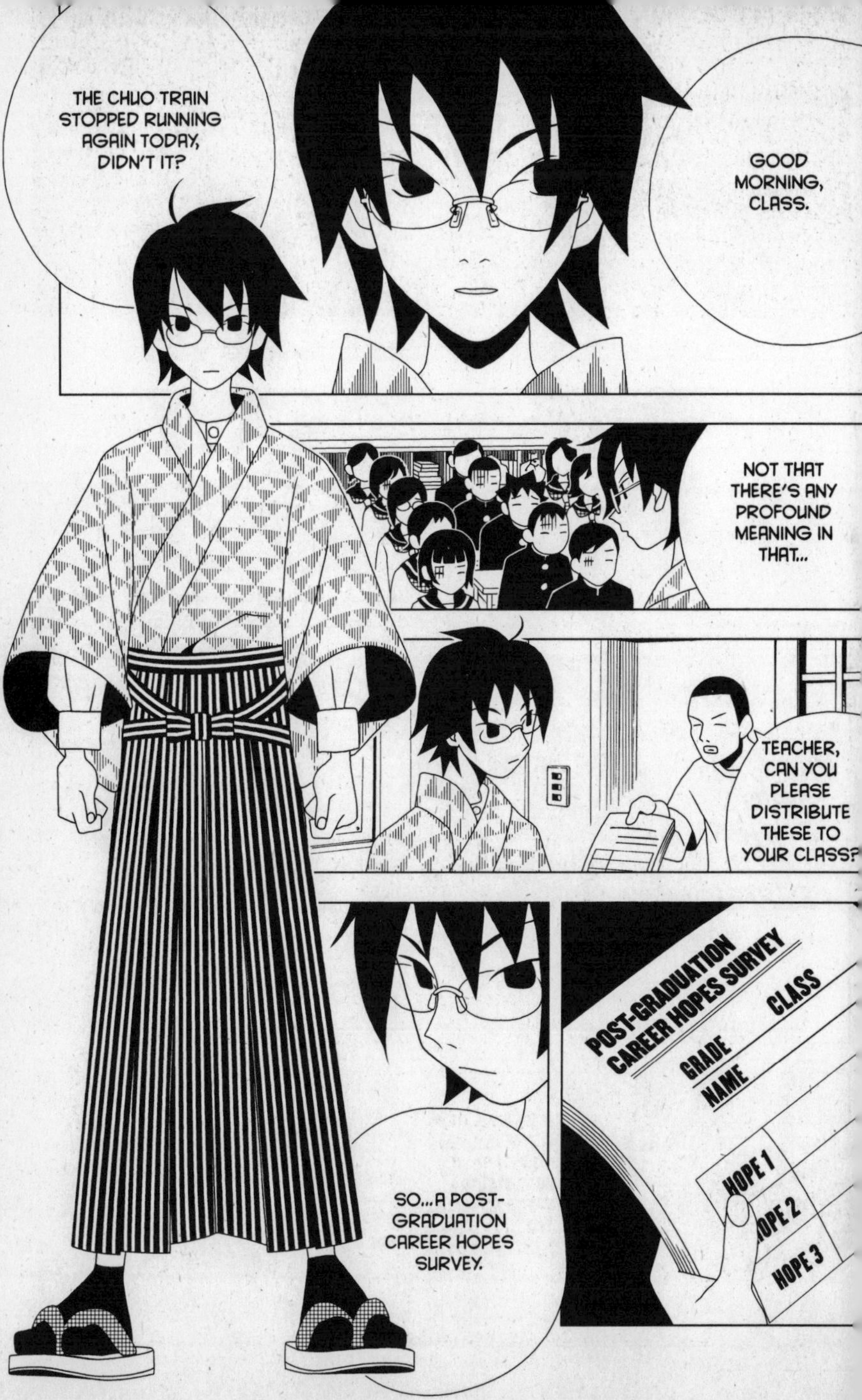
GOOD MORNING, CLASS.
THE CHUO TRAIN STOPPED RUNNING AGAIN TODAY, DIDN'T IT?
NOT THAT THERE'S ANY PROFOUND MEANING IN THAT...
TEACHER, CAN YOU PLEASE DISTRIBUTE THESE TO YOUR CLASS?
POST-GRADUATION CAREER HOPES SURVEY
CLASS
GRADE
NAME
HOPE 1
HOPE 3
SO... A POST-GRADUATION CAREER HOPES SURVEY.

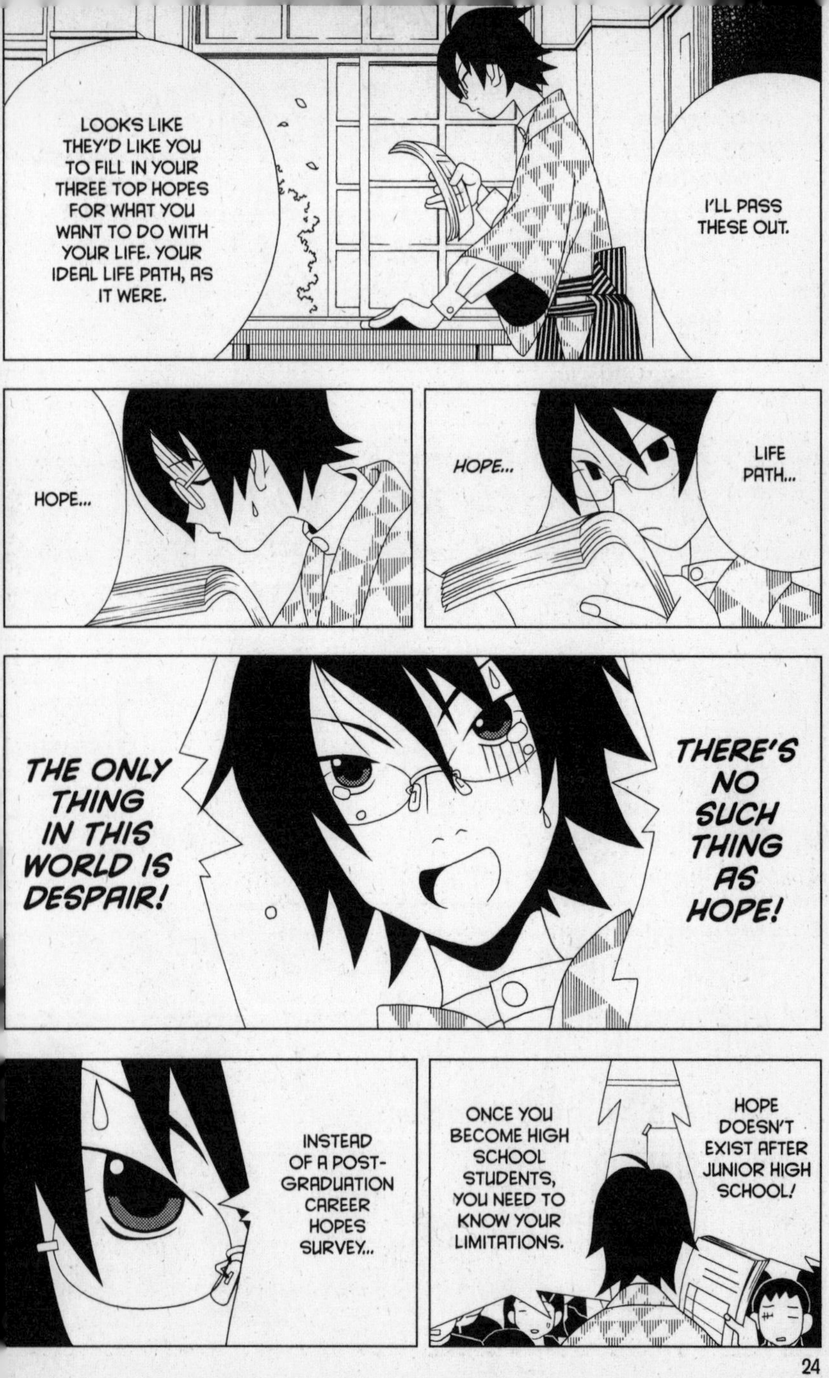
I'LL PASS THESE OUT.
LOOKS LIKE THEY'D LIKE YOU TO FILL IN YOUR THREE TOP HOPES FOR WHAT YOU WANT TO DO WITH YOUR LIFE. YOUR IDEAL LIFE PATH, AS IT WERE.
LIFE PATH...
HOPE...
HOPE...
THERE'S NO SUCH THING AS HOPE!
THE ONLY THING IN THIS WORLD IS DESPAIR!
HOPE DOESN'T EXIST AFTER JUNIOR HIGH SCHOOL!
ONCE YOU BECOME HIGH SCHOOL STUDENTS, YOU NEED TO KNOW YOUR LIMITATIONS.
INSTEAD OF A POST-GRADUATION CAREER HOPES SURVEY...

WRITE DOWN THREE THINGS YOU CAN NEVER HOPE TO ACHIEVE!

WE'LL DO A POST-GRADUATION CAREER DESPAIR SURVEY!

ALL YOU HAVE TO DO IS WRITE DOWN YOUR THREE MOST IMPOSSIBLE, HOPELESS FUTURE PATHS, AND RANK THEM FROM MOST HOPELESS TO LEAST HOPELESS (BUT STILL HOPELESS).

UH...WHAT SHOULD WE DO AGAIN...?

NAME Usui

| | |
|---|---|
| HOPE 1 | Tokyo University |
| HOPE 2 | Kyoto University |
| HOPE 3 | Ichihashi University |

ion deadline: April 27

YOU LOOK LIKE YOU'RE PROBABLY THE BEST STUDENT IN THIS CLASS, BUT...

TAKE YOU, FOR EXAMPLE.

YOU'RE RIGHT, IT IS PRETTY HOPELESS.

YOU MEAN TO SAY YOU CAN ENTER TOKYO UNIVERSITY, THE MOST PRESTIGIOUS SCHOOL IN JAPAN?

THAT'S MEAN.

THIS IS HOPE-LESS!

THEN WRITE IT DOWN.

NOT A CHANCE.

...

COULD YOU GET INTO THE J. LEAGUE, JAPAN'S TOP PROFESSIONAL SOCCER TEAM?

YOU LOOK LIKE YOU'RE ON THE SOCCER TEAM.

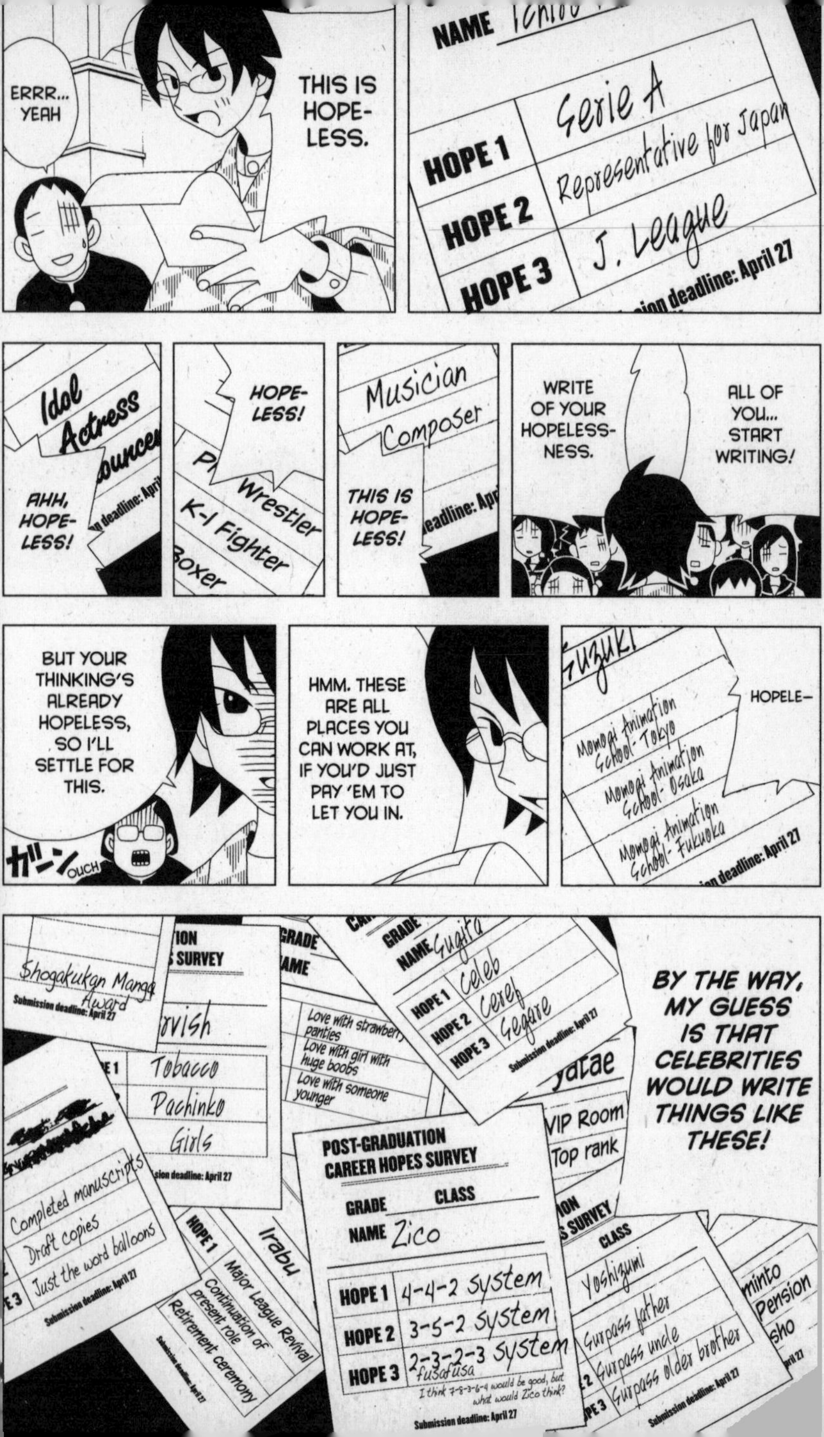

NAME Ichiro
HOPE 1 Serie A
HOPE 2 Representative for Japan
HOPE 3 J. League
Submission deadline: April 27
THIS IS HOPELESS.
ERRR... YEAH
ALL OF YOU... START WRITING!
WRITE OF YOUR HOPELESSNESS.
Musician
Composer
THIS IS HOPELESS!
HOPELESS!
Wrestler
K-1 Fighter
Boxer
Idol
Actress
AHH, HOPELESS!
Suzuki
Momoai Animation School- Tokyo
Momoai Animation School- Osaka
Momoai Animation School- Fukuoka
Submission deadline: April 27
HOPELE—
HMM. THESE ARE ALL PLACES YOU CAN WORK AT, IF YOU'D JUST PAY 'EM TO LET YOU IN.
BUT YOUR THINKING'S ALREADY HOPELESS, SO I'LL SETTLE FOR THIS.
ガーン
OUCH
BY THE WAY, MY GUESS IS THAT CELEBRITIES WOULD WRITE THINGS LIKE THESE!
GRADE
NAME Sugita
HOPE 1 Celeb
HOPE 2 Ceref
HOPE 3 Segare
Submission deadline: April 27
Shogakukan Manga Award
Submission deadline: April 27
Love with strawberry panties
Love with girl with huge boobs
Love with someone younger
Tobacco
Pachinko
Girls
Submission deadline: April 27
Yatae
VIP Room
Top rank
Completed manuscripts
Draft copies
Just the word balloons
Submission deadline: April 27
Irabu
HOPE 1
Major League Revival
Continuation of present role
Retirement ceremony
Submission deadline: April 27
POST-GRADUATION CAREER HOPES SURVEY
GRADE CLASS
NAME Zico
HOPE 1 4-4-2 System
HOPE 2 3-5-2 System
HOPE 3 2-3-2-3 System
fusafusa
I think 7-8-3-6-4 would be good, but what would Zico think?
Submission deadline: April 27
CLASS
Yoshizumi
Surpass father
Surpass uncle
Surpass older brother
Submission deadline: April 27
Pension
Submission deadline: April 27

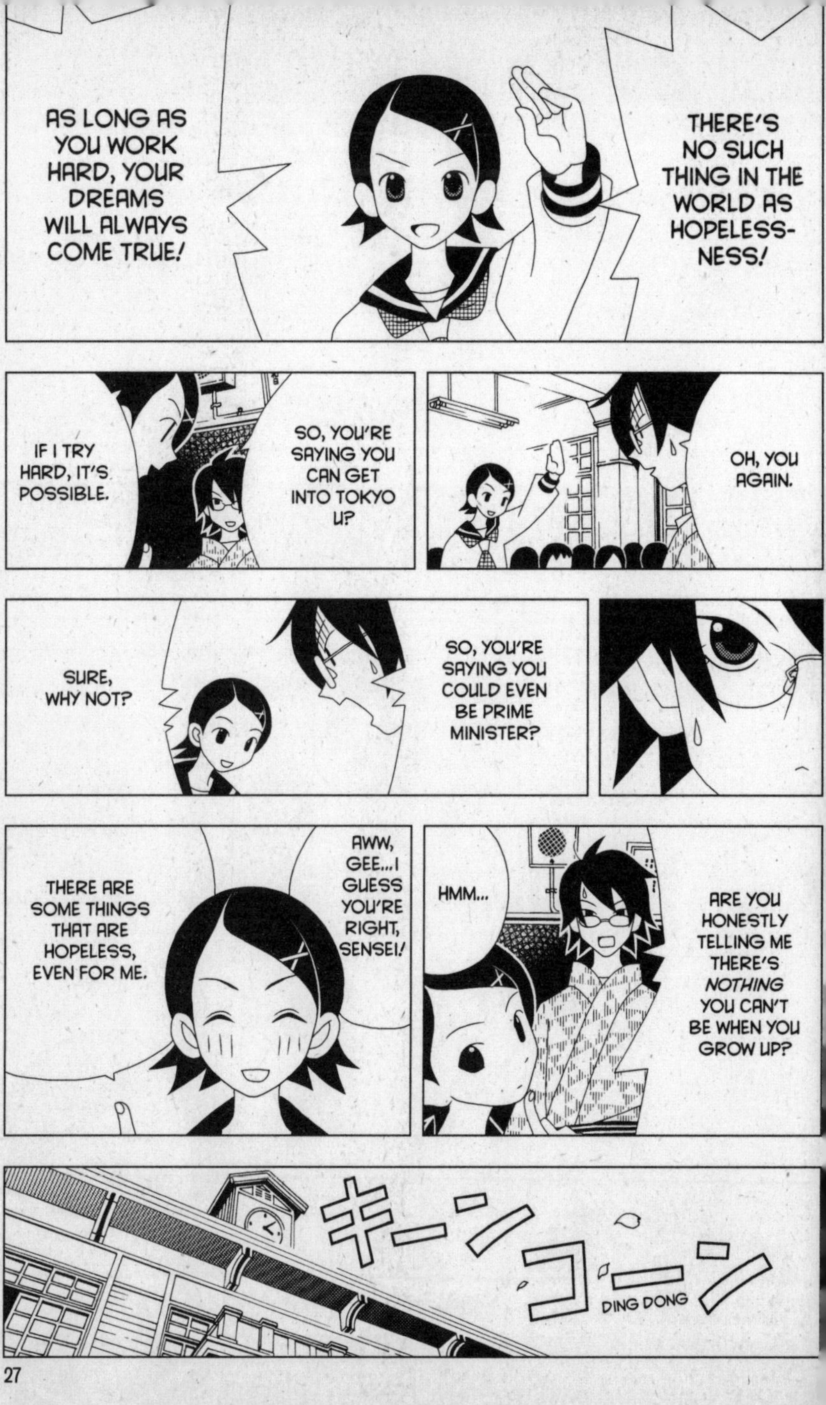
THERE'S NO SUCH THING IN THE WORLD AS HOPELESS-NESS!
AS LONG AS YOU WORK HARD, YOUR DREAMS WILL ALWAYS COME TRUE!
OH, YOU AGAIN.
SO, YOU'RE SAYING YOU CAN GET INTO TOKYO U?
IF I TRY HARD, IT'S POSSIBLE.
SO, YOU'RE SAYING YOU COULD EVEN BE PRIME MINISTER?
SURE, WHY NOT?
ARE YOU HONESTLY TELLING ME THERE'S *NOTHING* YOU CAN'T BE WHEN YOU GROW UP?
HMM...
AWW, GEE...I GUESS YOU'RE RIGHT, SENSEI!
THERE ARE SOME THINGS THAT ARE HOPELESS, EVEN FOR ME.
キーンコーン
DING DONG

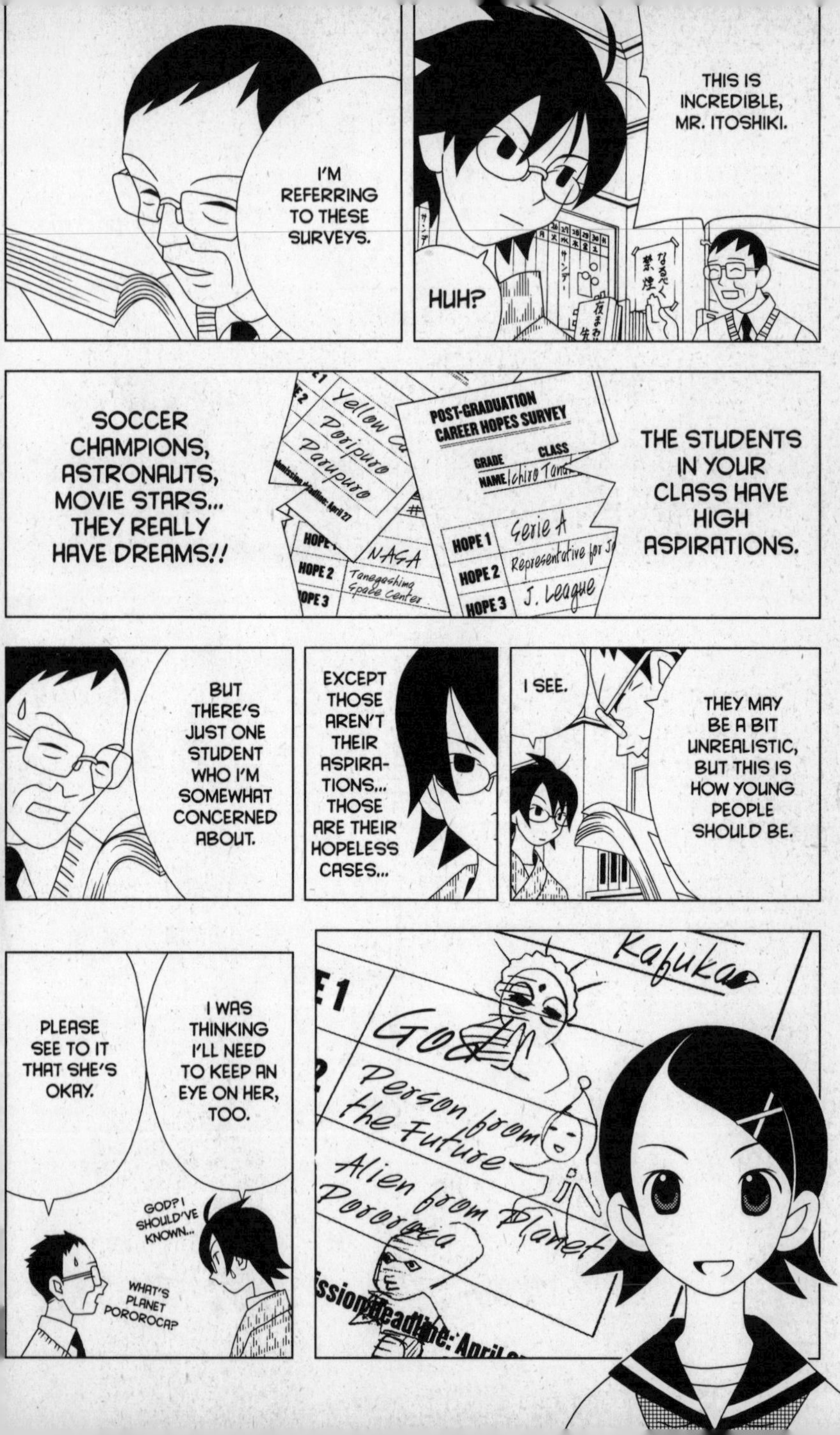

THIS IS INCREDIBLE, MR. ITOSHIKI.
HUH?
I'M REFERRING TO THESE SURVEYS.
THE STUDENTS IN YOUR CLASS HAVE HIGH ASPIRATIONS.
POST-GRADUATION CAREER HOPES SURVEY
GRADE
CLASS
NAME Ichiro Tana
HOPE 1 Serie A
HOPE 2 Representative for J
HOPE 3 J. League
Yellow Ca
Poripuro
Parupuro
Submission deadline: April 27
HOPE 1 NASA
HOPE 2 Tanegashima Space Center
HOPE 3
SOCCER CHAMPIONS, ASTRONAUTS, MOVIE STARS... THEY REALLY HAVE DREAMS!!
THEY MAY BE A BIT UNREALISTIC, BUT THIS IS HOW YOUNG PEOPLE SHOULD BE.
I SEE.
EXCEPT THOSE AREN'T THEIR ASPIRATIONS... THOSE ARE THEIR HOPELESS CASES...
BUT THERE'S JUST ONE STUDENT WHO I'M SOMEWHAT CONCERNED ABOUT.
Kafuka
God
Person from the Future
Alien from Planet Pororoca
Submission deadline: April
I WAS THINKING I'LL NEED TO KEEP AN EYE ON HER, TOO.
PLEASE SEE TO IT THAT SHE'S OKAY.
GOD? I SHOULD'VE KNOWN...
WHAT'S PLANET POROROCA?

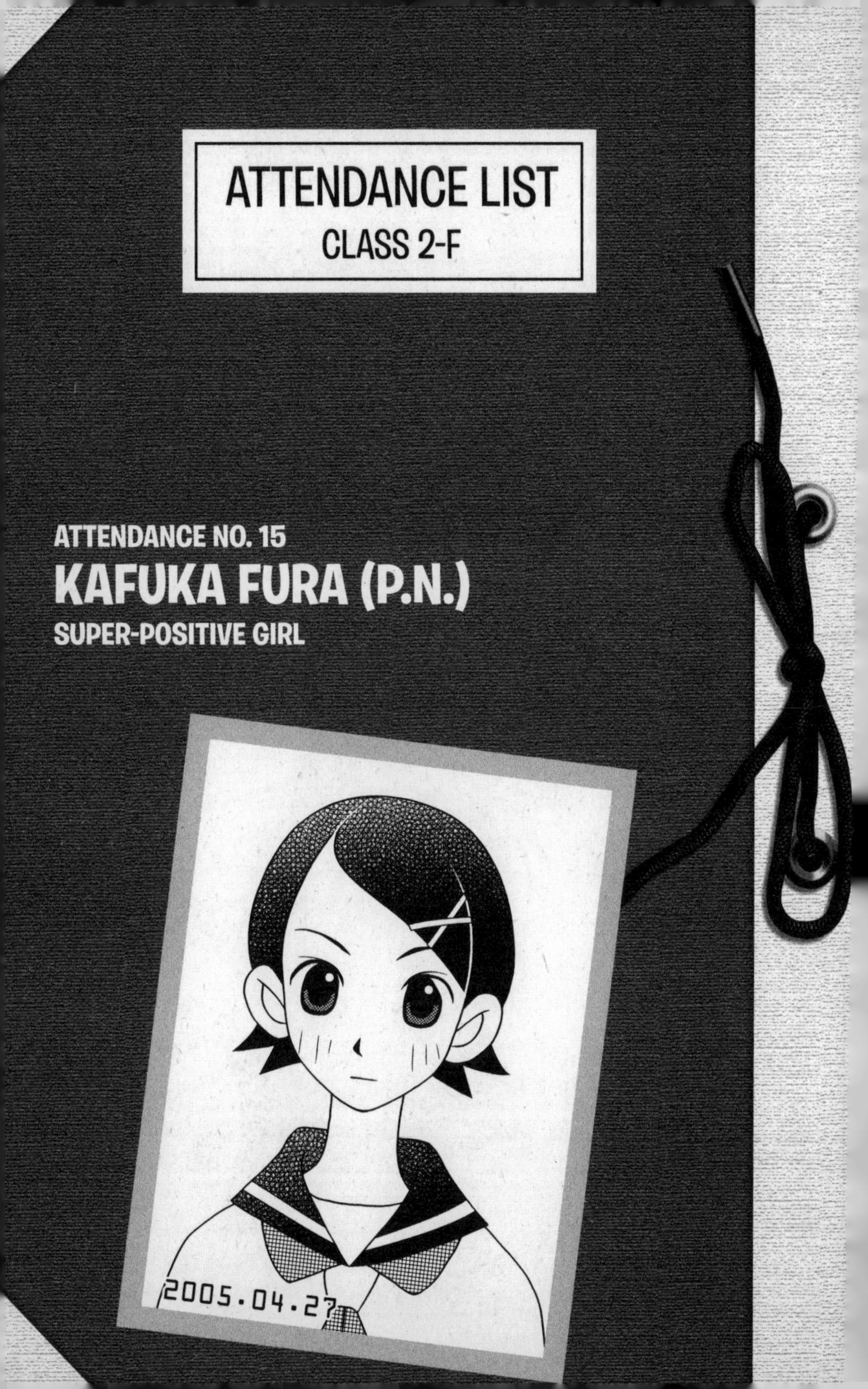
ATTENDANCE LIST
CLASS 2-F
ATTENDANCE NO. 15
KAFUKA FURA (P.N.)
SUPER-POSITIVE GIRL
2005.04.27

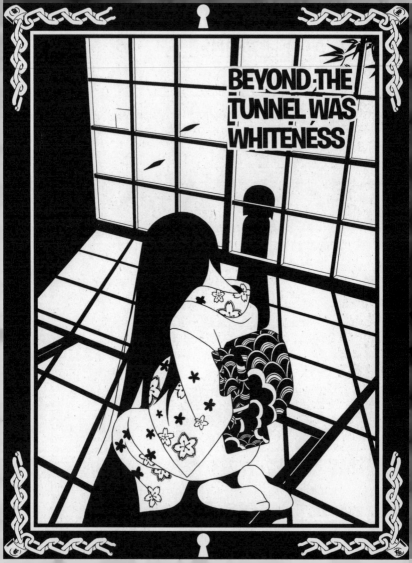

BEYOND THE TUNNEL WAS WHITENESS

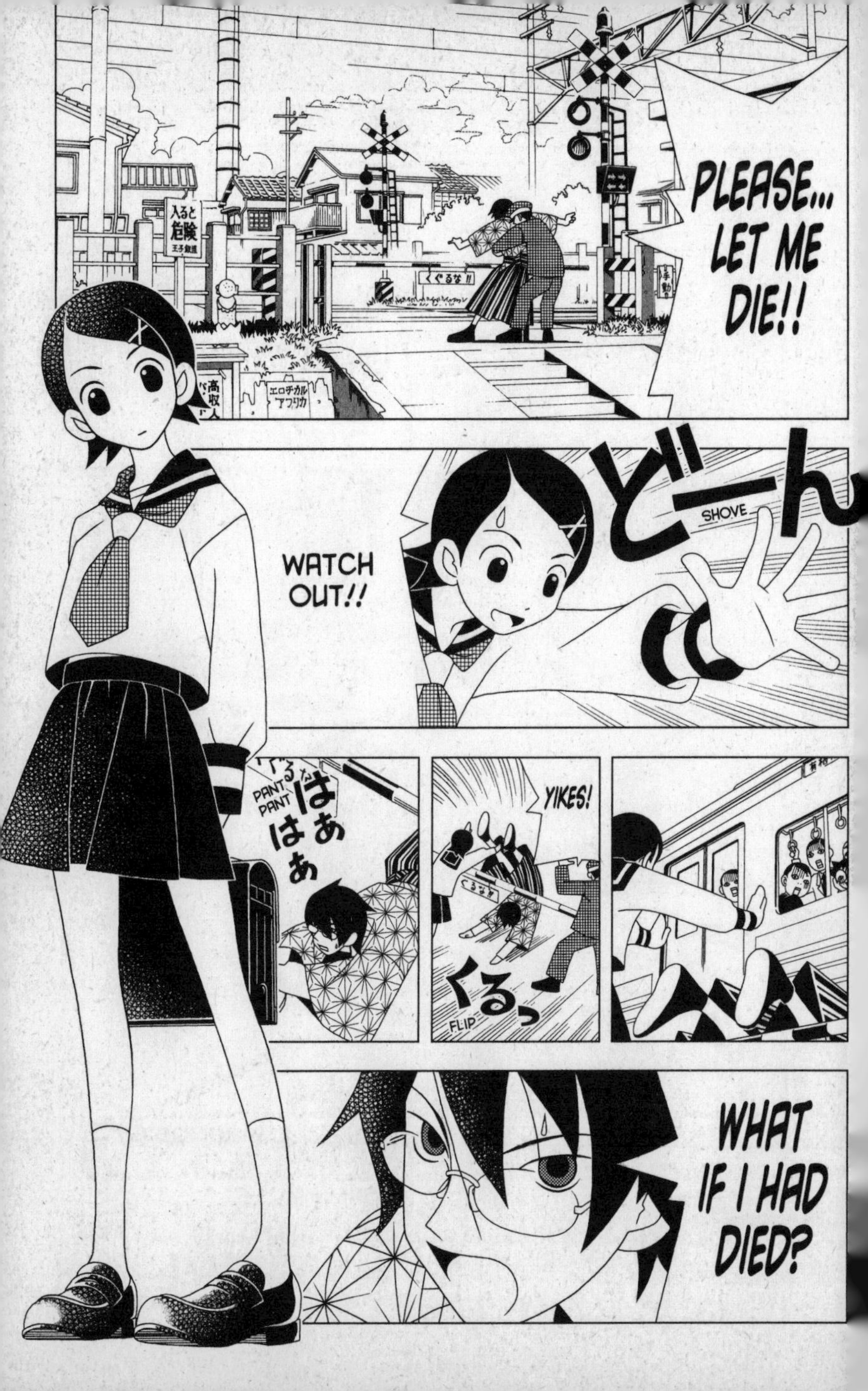
PLEASE... LET ME DIE!!
入ると危険
くぐるな!!
どーん
SHOVE
WATCH OUT!!
YIKES!
くるっ
FLIP
はあ はあ
PANT PANT
WHAT IF I HAD DIED?

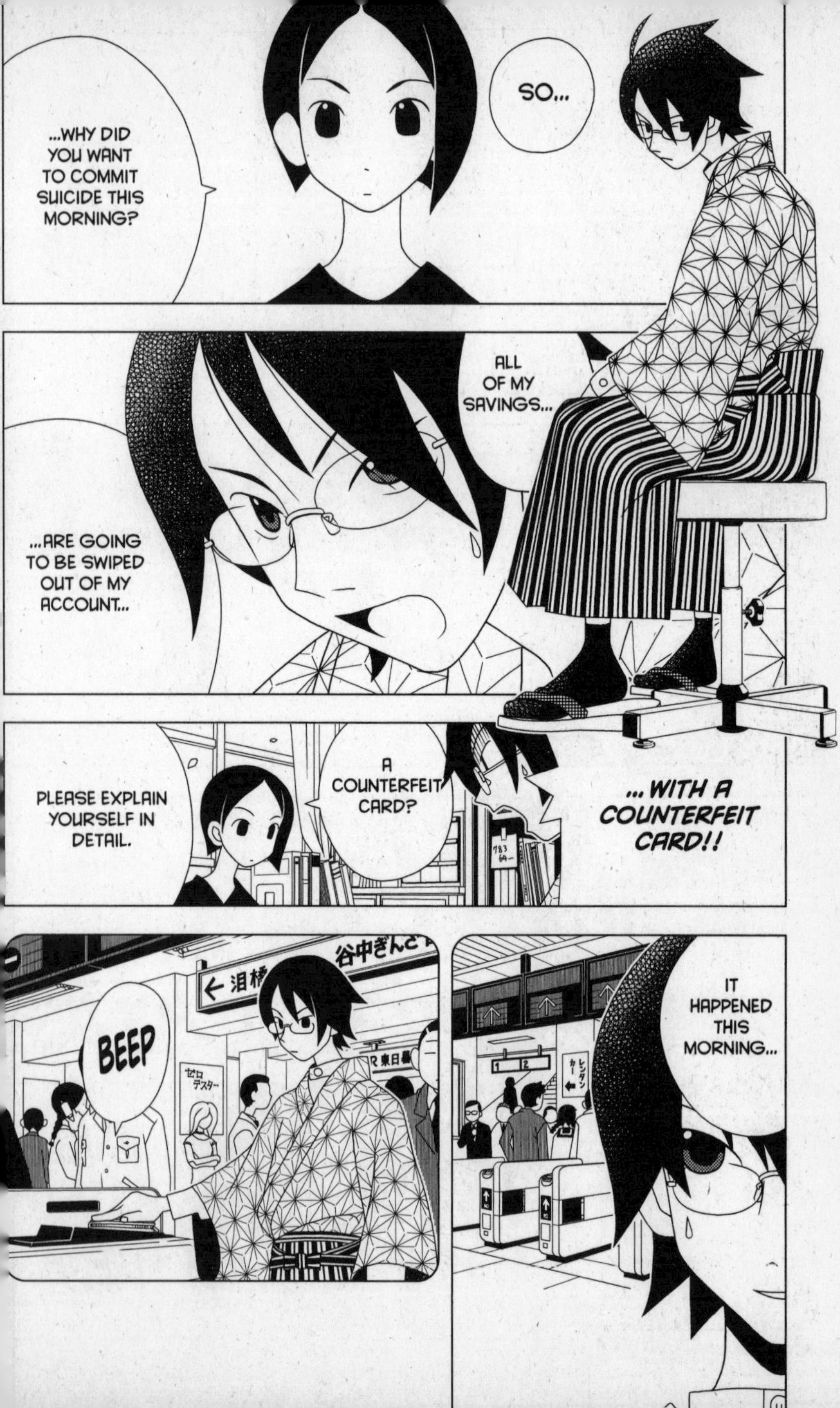
SO...
...WHY DID YOU WANT TO COMMIT SUICIDE THIS MORNING?
ALL OF MY SAVINGS...
...ARE GOING TO BE SWIPED OUT OF MY ACCOUNT...
...WITH A COUNTERFEIT CARD!!
A COUNTERFEIT CARD?
PLEASE EXPLAIN YOURSELF IN DETAIL.
IT HAPPENED THIS MORNING...
BEEP

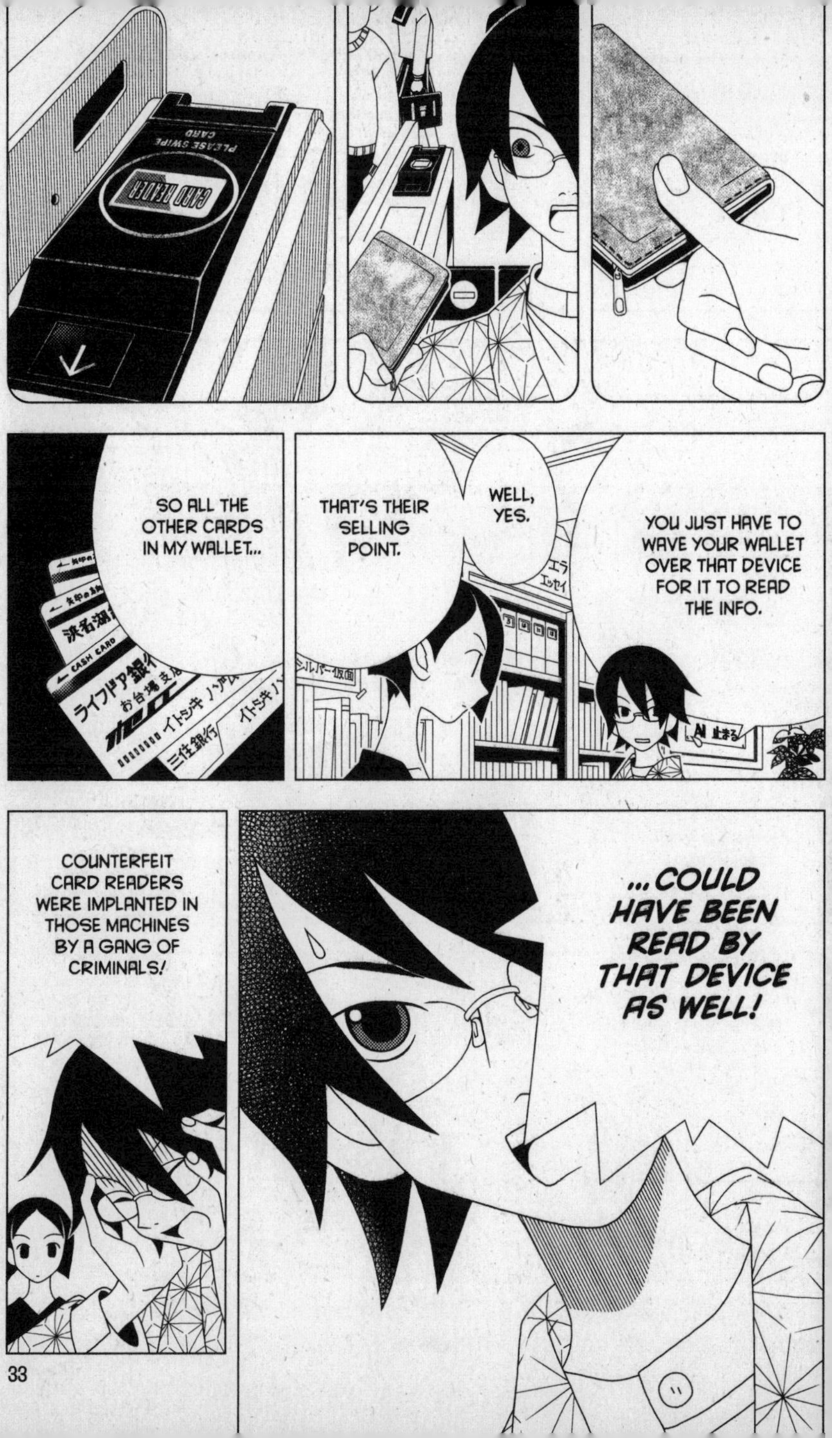
YOU JUST HAVE TO WAVE YOUR WALLET OVER THAT DEVICE FOR IT TO READ THE INFO.
WELL, YES.
THAT'S THEIR SELLING POINT.
SO ALL THE OTHER CARDS IN MY WALLET...
CASH CARD
...COULD HAVE BEEN READ BY THAT DEVICE AS WELL!
COUNTERFEIT CARD READERS WERE IMPLANTED IN THOSE MACHINES BY A GANG OF CRIMINALS!

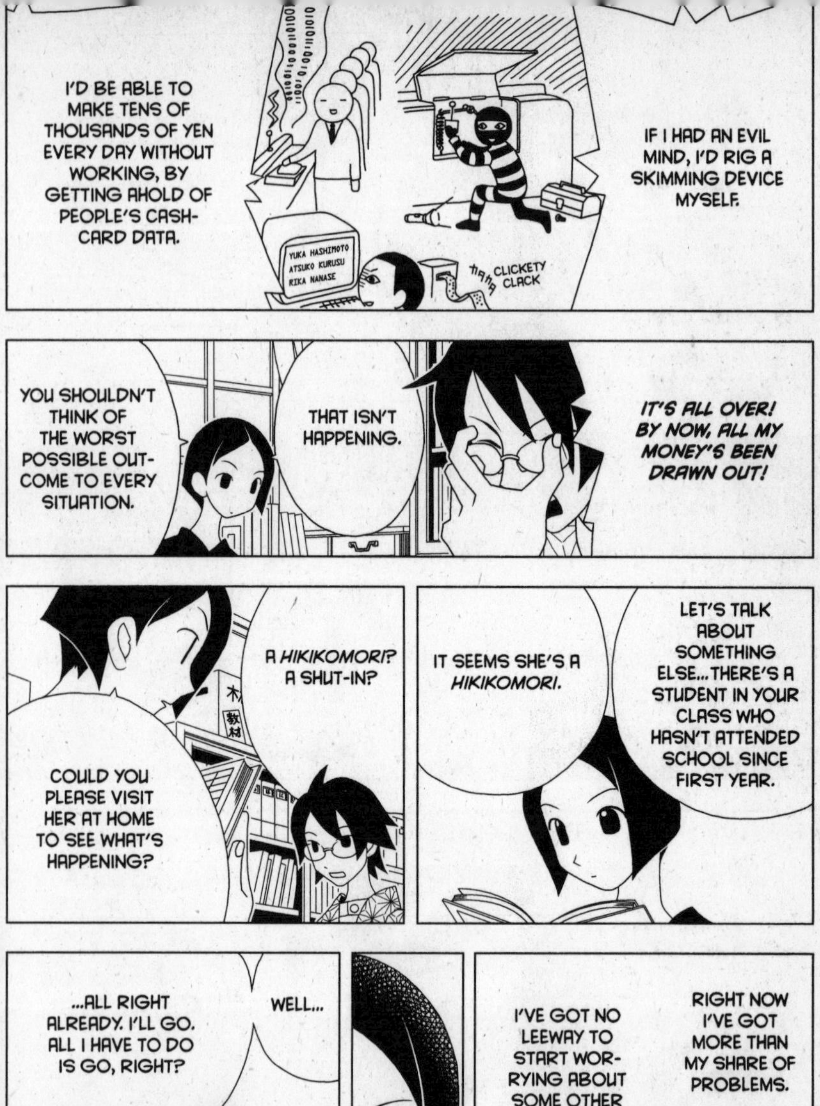
IF I HAD AN EVIL MIND, I'D RIG A SKIMMING DEVICE MYSELF.
I'D BE ABLE TO MAKE TENS OF THOUSANDS OF YEN EVERY DAY WITHOUT WORKING, BY GETTING AHOLD OF PEOPLE'S CASH-CARD DATA.
YUKA HASHIMOTO
ATSUKO KURUSU
RIKA NANASE
カタカタ
CLICKETY CLACK
*IT'S ALL OVER! BY NOW, ALL MY MONEY'S BEEN DRAWN OUT!*
THAT ISN'T HAPPENING.
YOU SHOULDN'T THINK OF THE WORST POSSIBLE OUT-COME TO EVERY SITUATION.
LET'S TALK ABOUT SOMETHING ELSE...THERE'S A STUDENT IN YOUR CLASS WHO HASN'T ATTENDED SCHOOL SINCE FIRST YEAR.
IT SEEMS SHE'S A *HIKIKOMORI*.
A *HIKIKOMORI*? A SHUT-IN?
COULD YOU PLEASE VISIT HER AT HOME TO SEE WHAT'S HAPPENING?
RIGHT NOW I'VE GOT MORE THAN MY SHARE OF PROBLEMS.
I'VE GOT NO LEEWAY TO START WOR-RYING ABOUT SOME OTHER STUDENT'S PROBLEMS.
WELL...
...ALL RIGHT ALREADY. I'LL GO. ALL I HAVE TO DO IS GO, RIGHT?

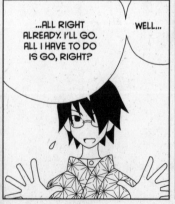

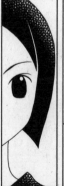

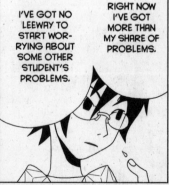

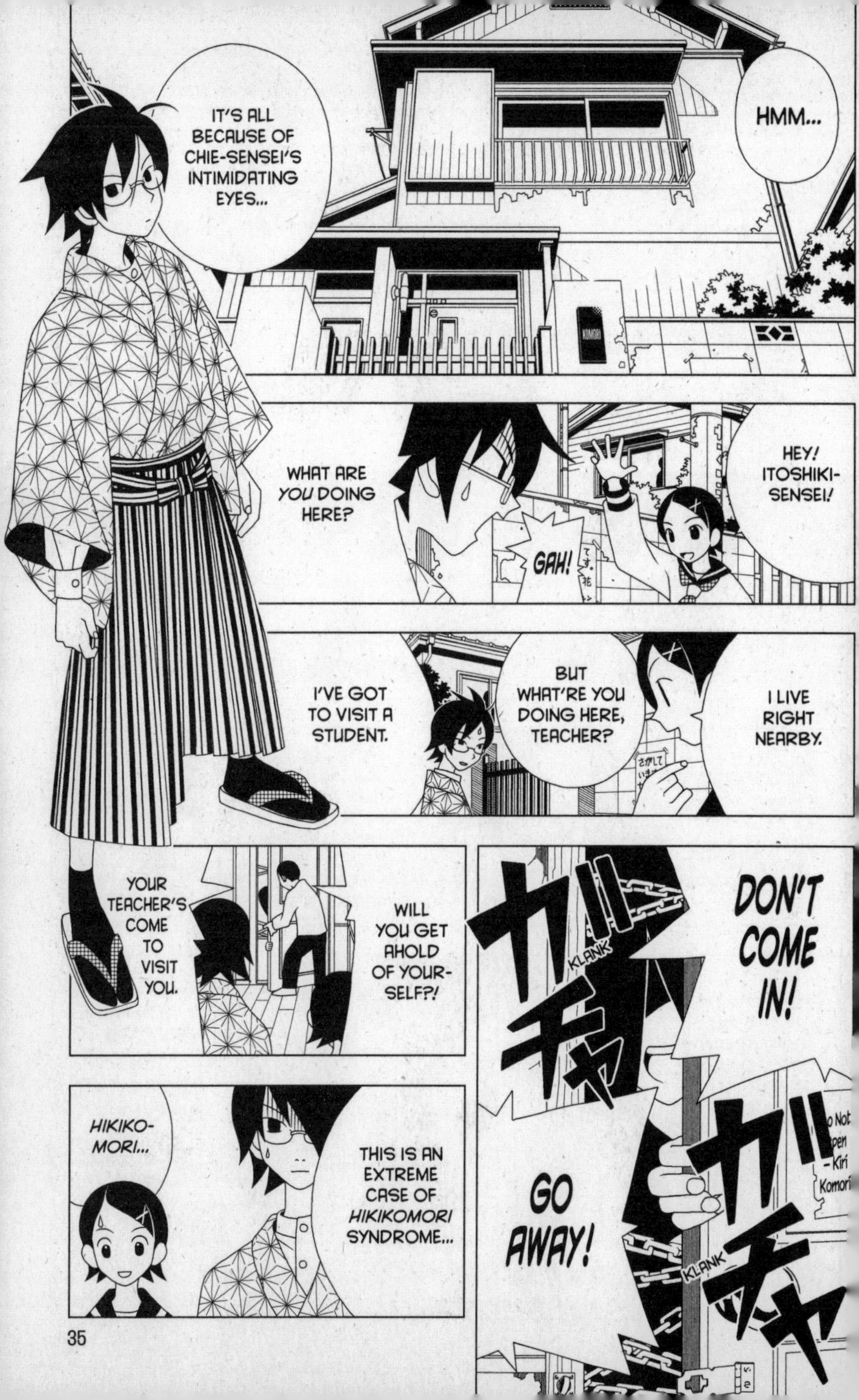
HMM...
IT'S ALL BECAUSE OF CHIE-SENSEI'S INTIMIDATING EYES...
KOMORI
HEY! ITOSHIKI-SENSEI!
GAH!
WHAT ARE *YOU* DOING HERE?
I LIVE RIGHT NEARBY.
BUT WHAT'RE YOU DOING HERE, TEACHER?
I'VE GOT TO VISIT A STUDENT.
DON'T COME IN!
ガチャ
KLANK
GO AWAY!
ガチャ
KLANK
WILL YOU GET AHOLD OF YOURSELF?!
YOUR TEACHER'S COME TO VISIT YOU.
THIS IS AN EXTREME CASE OF *HIKIKOMORI* SYNDROME...
*HIKIKO-MORI...*

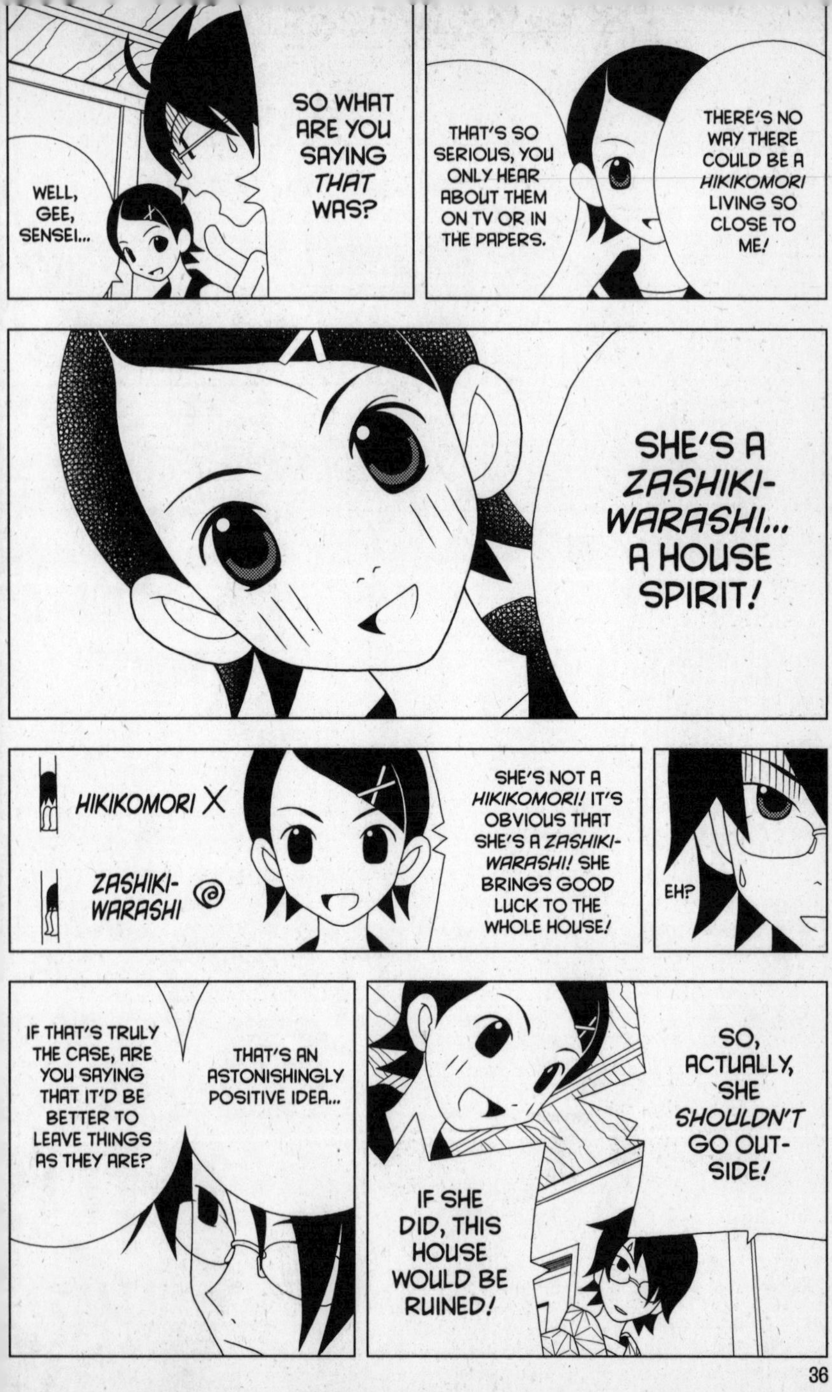
THERE'S NO WAY THERE COULD BE A *HIKIKOMORI* LIVING SO CLOSE TO ME!
THAT'S SO SERIOUS, YOU ONLY HEAR ABOUT THEM ON TV OR IN THE PAPERS.
SO WHAT ARE YOU SAYING *THAT* WAS?
WELL, GEE, SENSEI...
SHE'S A *ZASHIKI-WARASHI*... A HOUSE SPIRIT!
EH?
SHE'S NOT A *HIKIKOMORI!* IT'S OBVIOUS THAT SHE'S A *ZASHIKI-WARASHI!* SHE BRINGS GOOD LUCK TO THE WHOLE HOUSE!
*HIKIKOMORI* X
*ZASHIKI-WARASHI*
SO, ACTUALLY, SHE *SHOULDN'T* GO OUTSIDE!
IF SHE DID, THIS HOUSE WOULD BE RUINED!
THAT'S AN ASTONISHINGLY POSITIVE IDEA...
IF THAT'S TRULY THE CASE, ARE YOU SAYING THAT IT'D BE BETTER TO LEAVE THINGS AS THEY ARE?

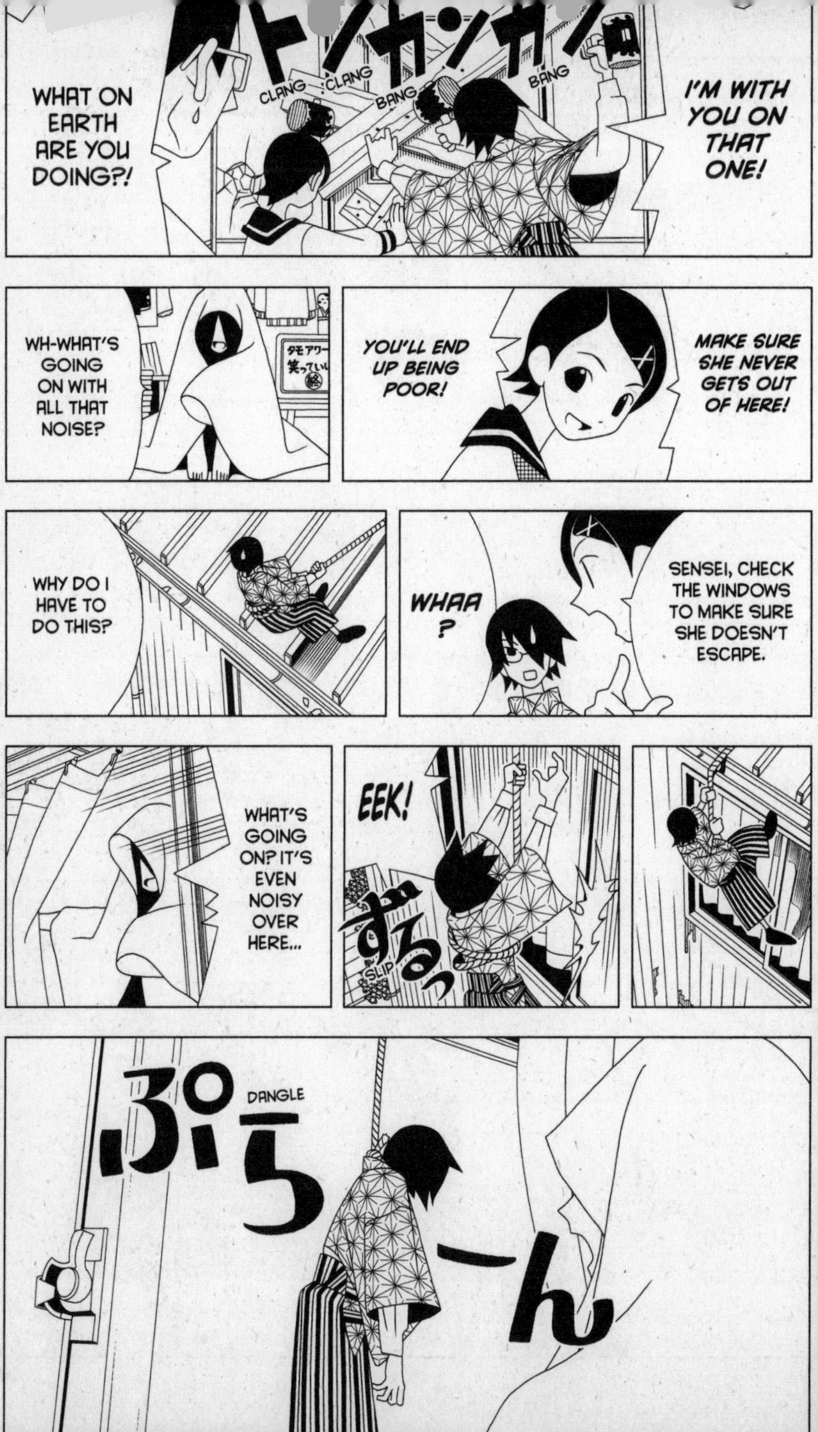
トンカンカン
I'M WITH YOU ON THAT ONE!
BANG
CLANG CLANG BANG
WHAT ON EARTH ARE YOU DOING?!
MAKE SURE SHE NEVER GETS OUT OF HERE!
YOU'LL END UP BEING POOR!
WH-WHAT'S GOING ON WITH ALL THAT NOISE?
SENSEI, CHECK THE WINDOWS TO MAKE SURE SHE DOESN'T ESCAPE.
WHAA ?
WHY DO I HAVE TO DO THIS?
EEK!
するっ
SLIP
WHAT'S GOING ON? IT'S EVEN NOISY OVER HERE...
ぶらーん
DANGLE

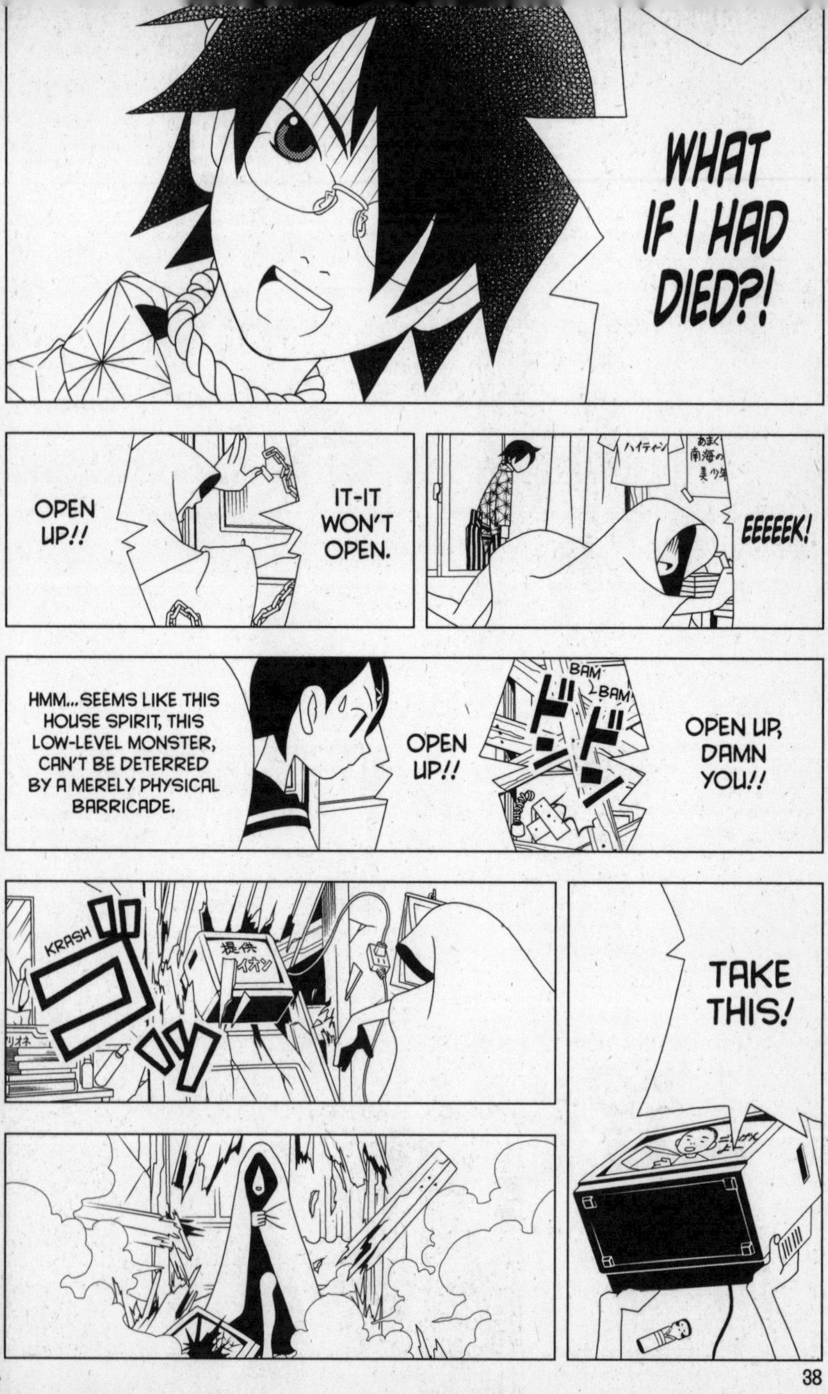
WHAT IF I HAD DIED?!
ハイティーン
あまく 南海の 美少年
EEEEEK!
IT-IT WON'T OPEN.
OPEN UP!!
OPEN UP, DAMN YOU!!
BAM BAM
ドドン
OPEN UP!!
HMM...SEEMS LIKE THIS HOUSE SPIRIT, THIS LOW-LEVEL MONSTER, CAN'T BE DETERRED BY A MERELY PHYSICAL BARRICADE.
TAKE THIS!
提供 イオン
KRASH

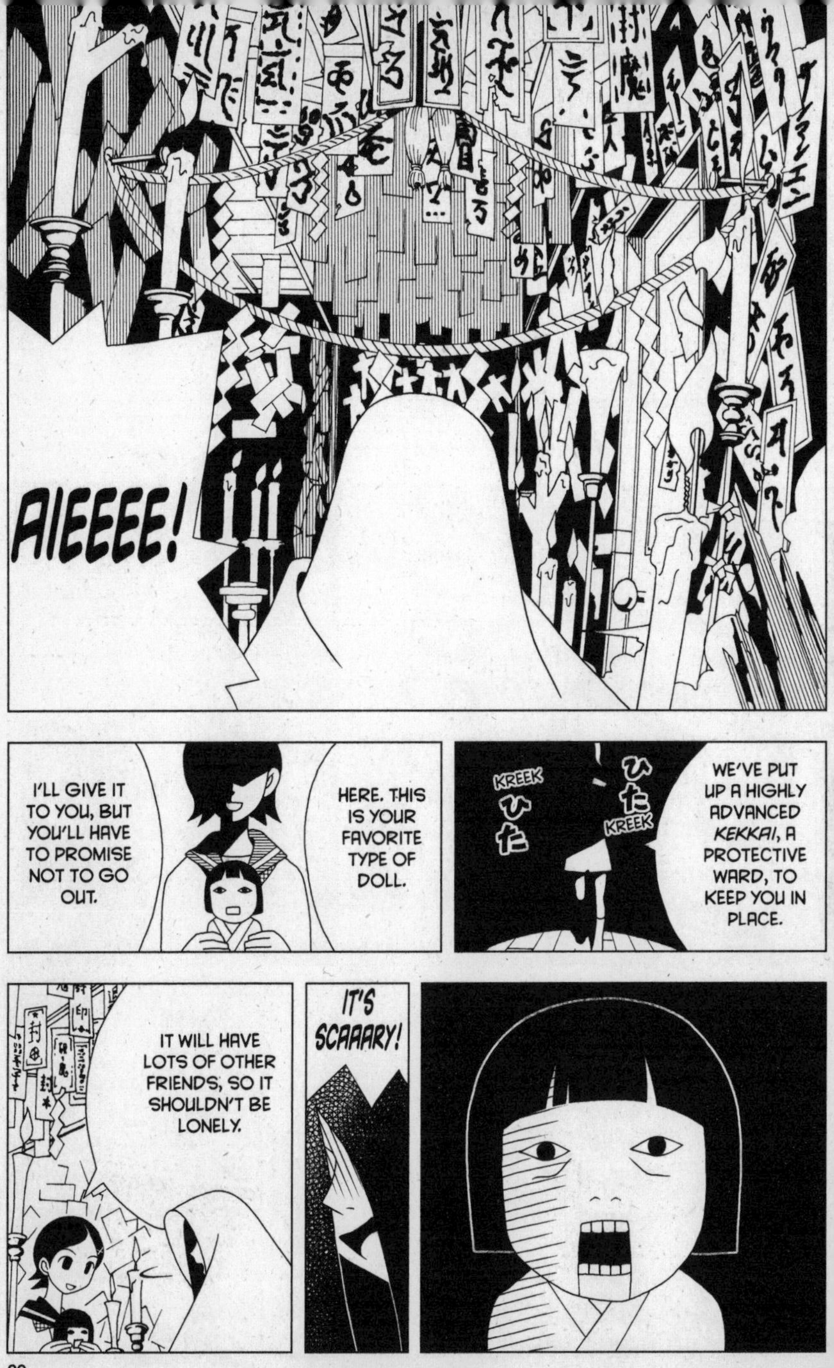
AIEEEE!
KREEK ひた ひた KREEK
WE'VE PUT UP A HIGHLY ADVANCED *KEKKAI*, A PROTECTIVE WARD, TO KEEP YOU IN PLACE.
HERE. THIS IS YOUR FAVORITE TYPE OF DOLL.
I'LL GIVE IT TO YOU, BUT YOU'LL HAVE TO PROMISE NOT TO GO OUT.
IT'S SCAAARY!
IT WILL HAVE LOTS OF OTHER FRIENDS, SO IT SHOULDN'T BE LONELY.

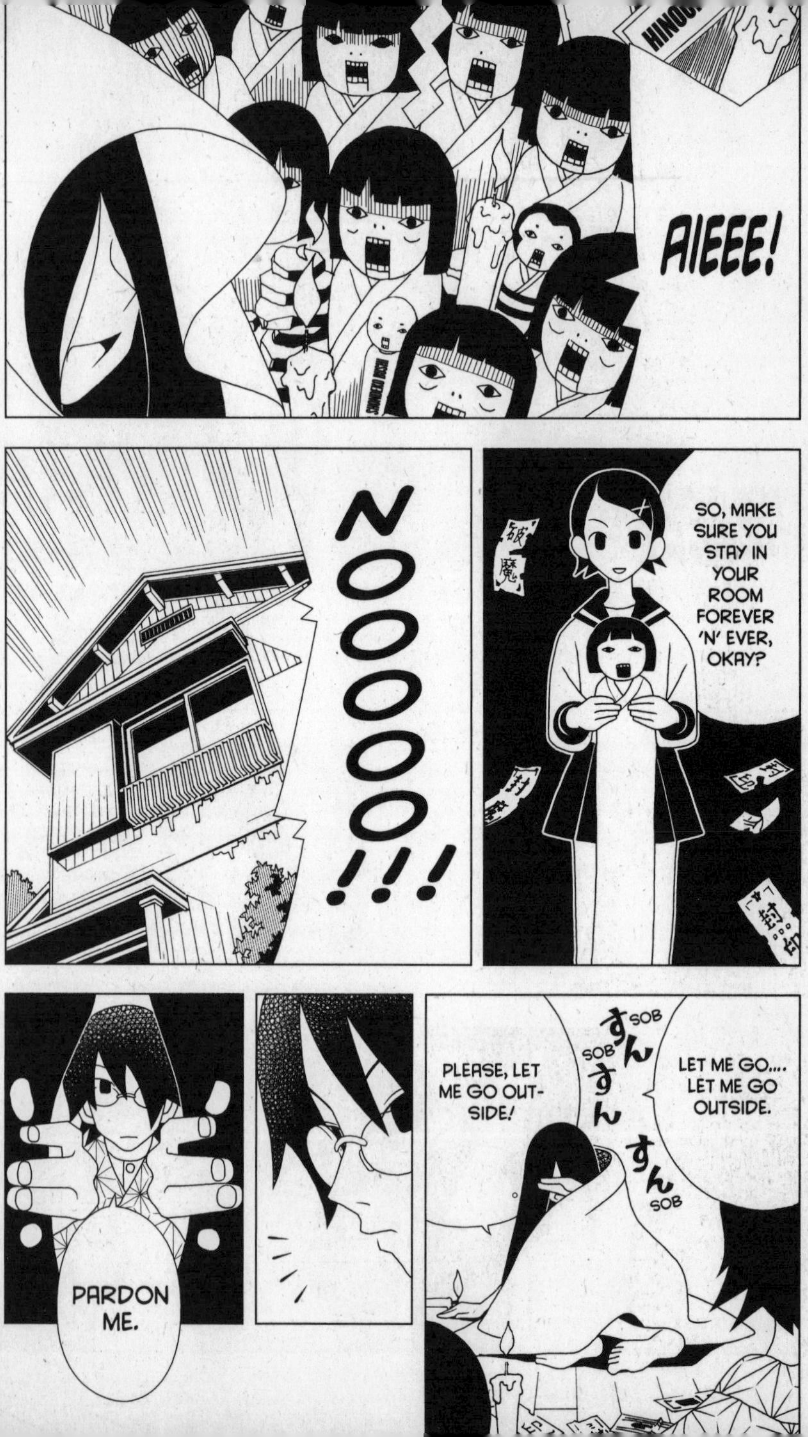
AIEEE!
SO, MAKE SURE YOU STAY IN YOUR ROOM FOREVER 'N' EVER, OKAY?
破魔
NOOOOOO!!!
LET ME GO.... LET ME GO OUTSIDE.
すん SOB すん SOB すん SOB
PLEASE, LET ME GO OUT-SIDE!
PARDON ME.

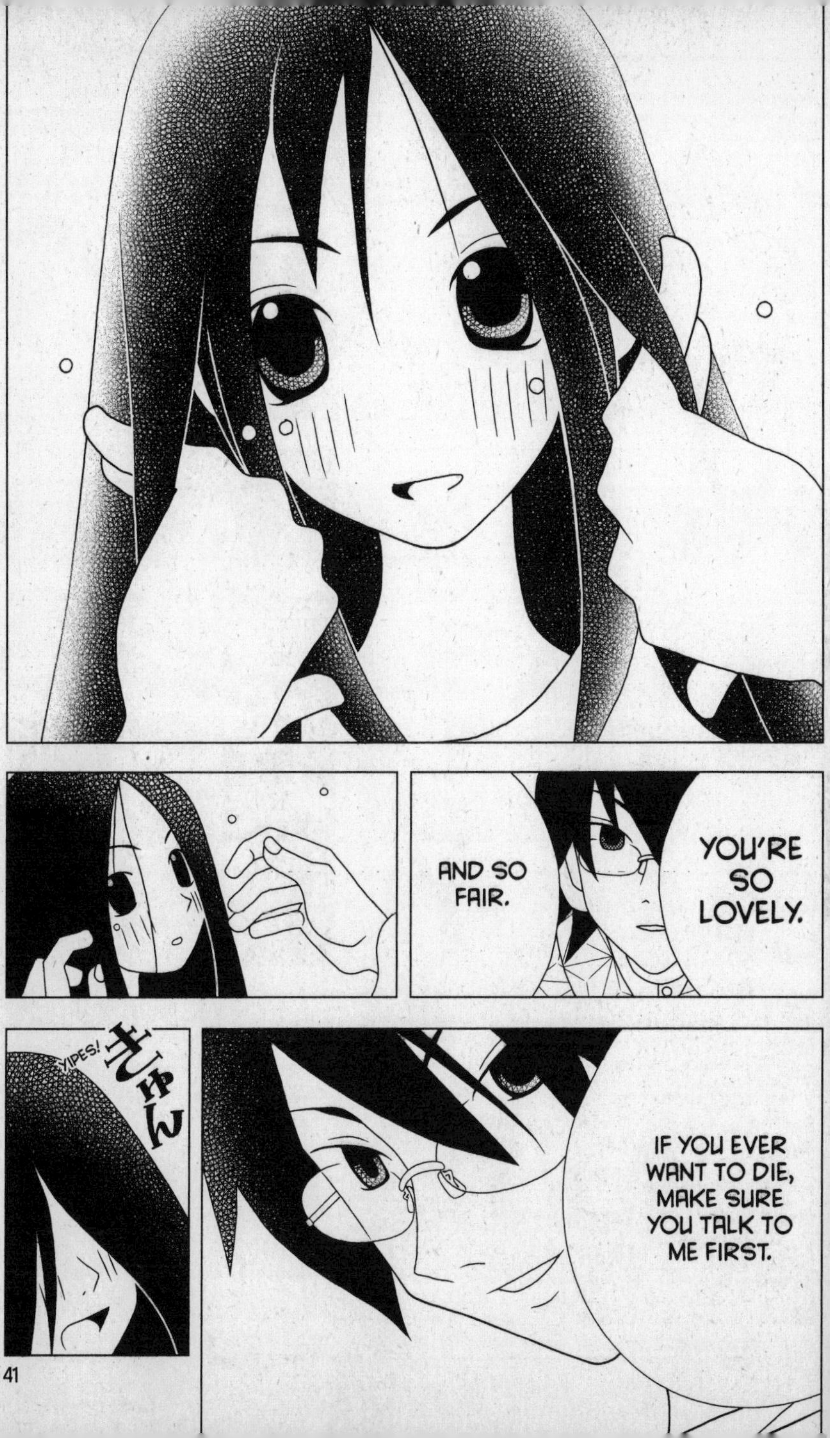
YOU'RE SO LOVELY.
AND SO FAIR.
IF YOU EVER WANT TO DIE, MAKE SURE YOU TALK TO ME FIRST.
きゅん
YIPES!

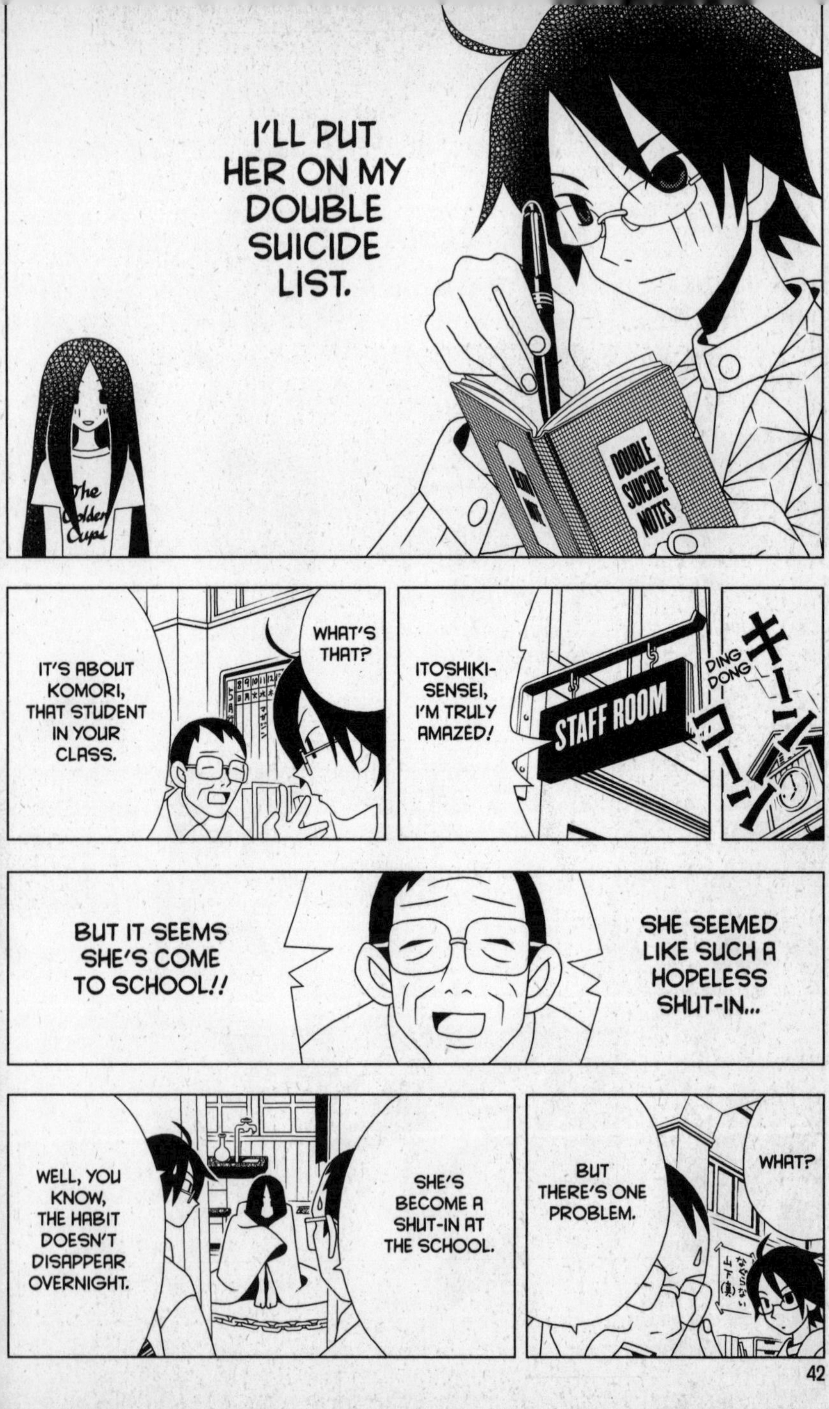
I'LL PUT HER ON MY DOUBLE SUICIDE LIST.
DOUBLE SUICIDE NOTES
キーンコーン
DING DONG
STAFF ROOM
ITOSHIKI-SENSEI, I'M TRULY AMAZED!
WHAT'S THAT?
IT'S ABOUT KOMORI, THAT STUDENT IN YOUR CLASS.
SHE SEEMED LIKE SUCH A HOPELESS SHUT-IN...
BUT IT SEEMS SHE'S COME TO SCHOOL!!
WHAT?
BUT THERE'S ONE PROBLEM.
SHE'S BECOME A SHUT-IN AT THE SCHOOL.
WELL, YOU KNOW, THE HABIT DOESN'T DISAPPEAR OVERNIGHT.

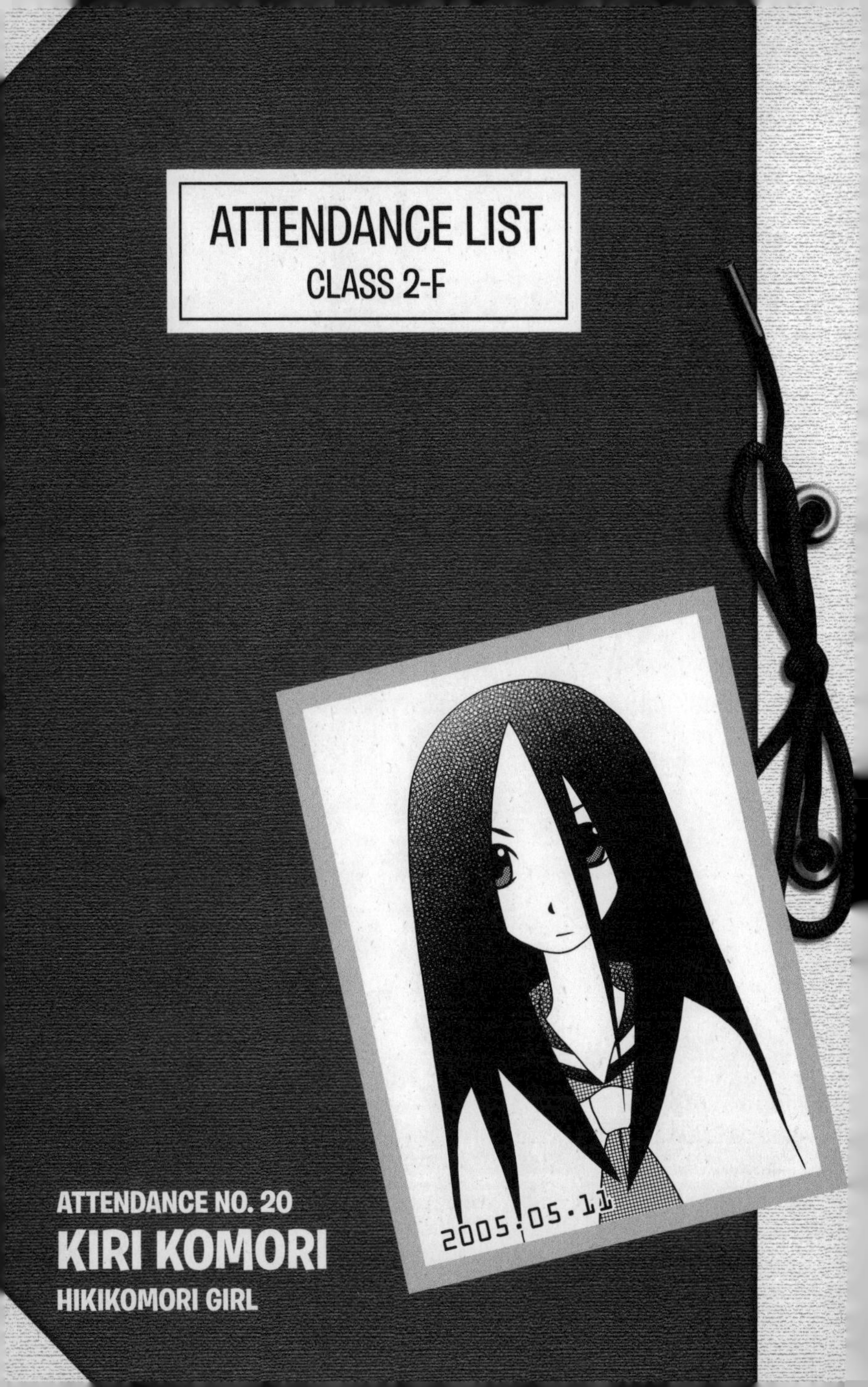
ATTENDANCE LIST
CLASS 2-F
2005.05.11
ATTENDANCE NO. 20
KIRI KOMORI
HIKIKOMORI GIRL

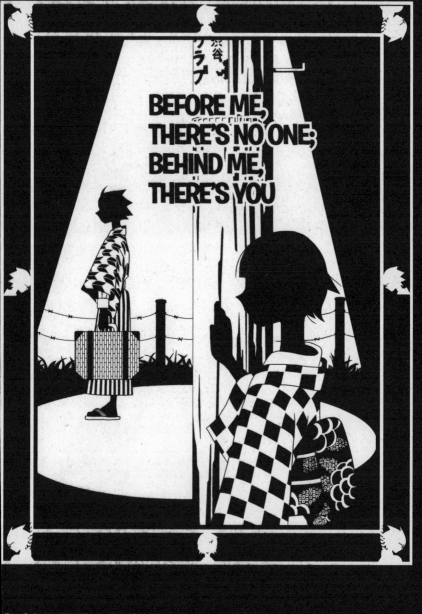

BEFORE ME,
THERE'S NO ONE;
BEHIND ME,
THERE'S YOU

CHAPTER 4

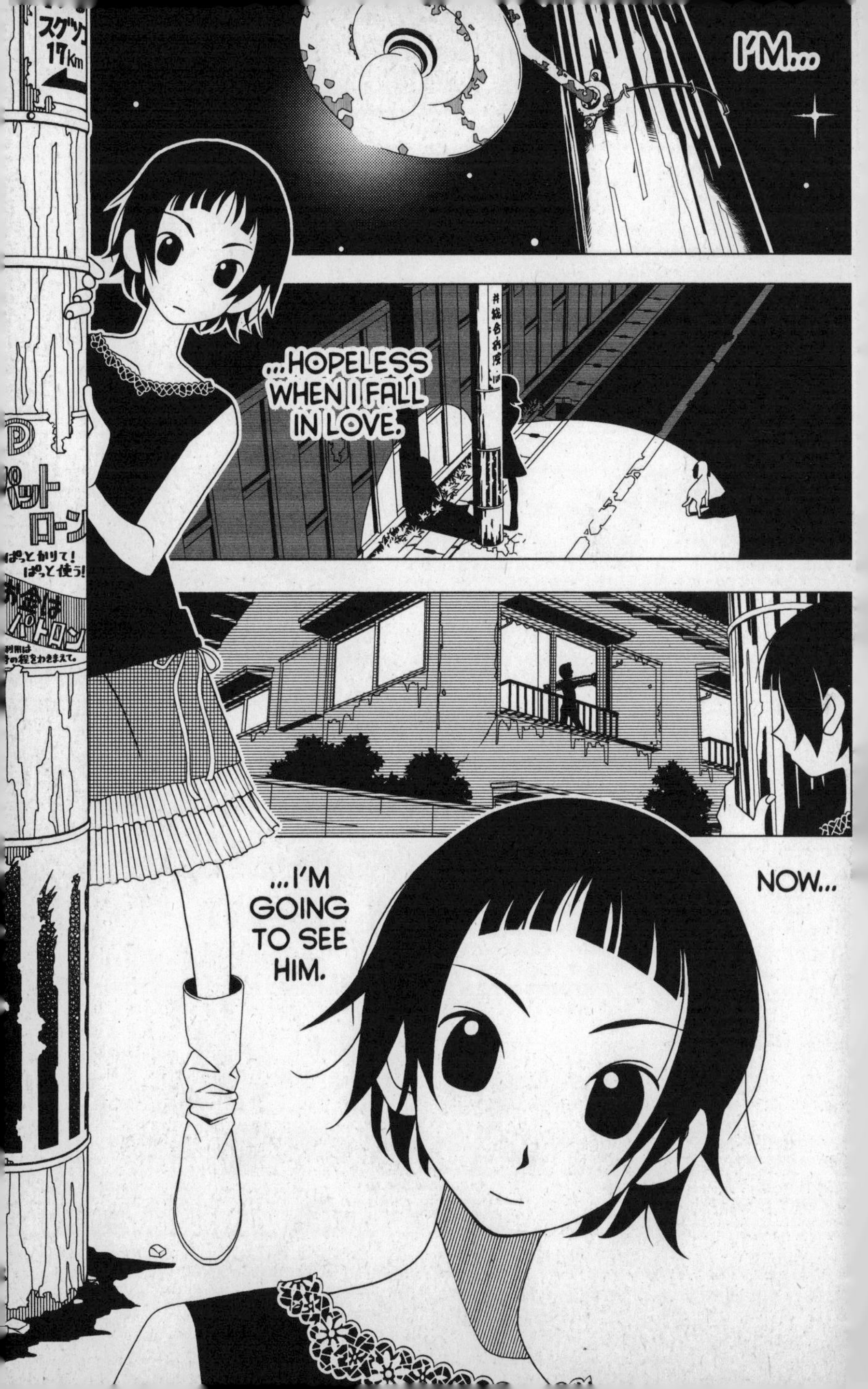
I'M...
...HOPELESS WHEN I FALL IN LOVE.
NOW...
...I'M GOING TO SEE HIM.
17Km
パットローン
ぱっとかりて！
ぱっと使う！
お金はパトロン

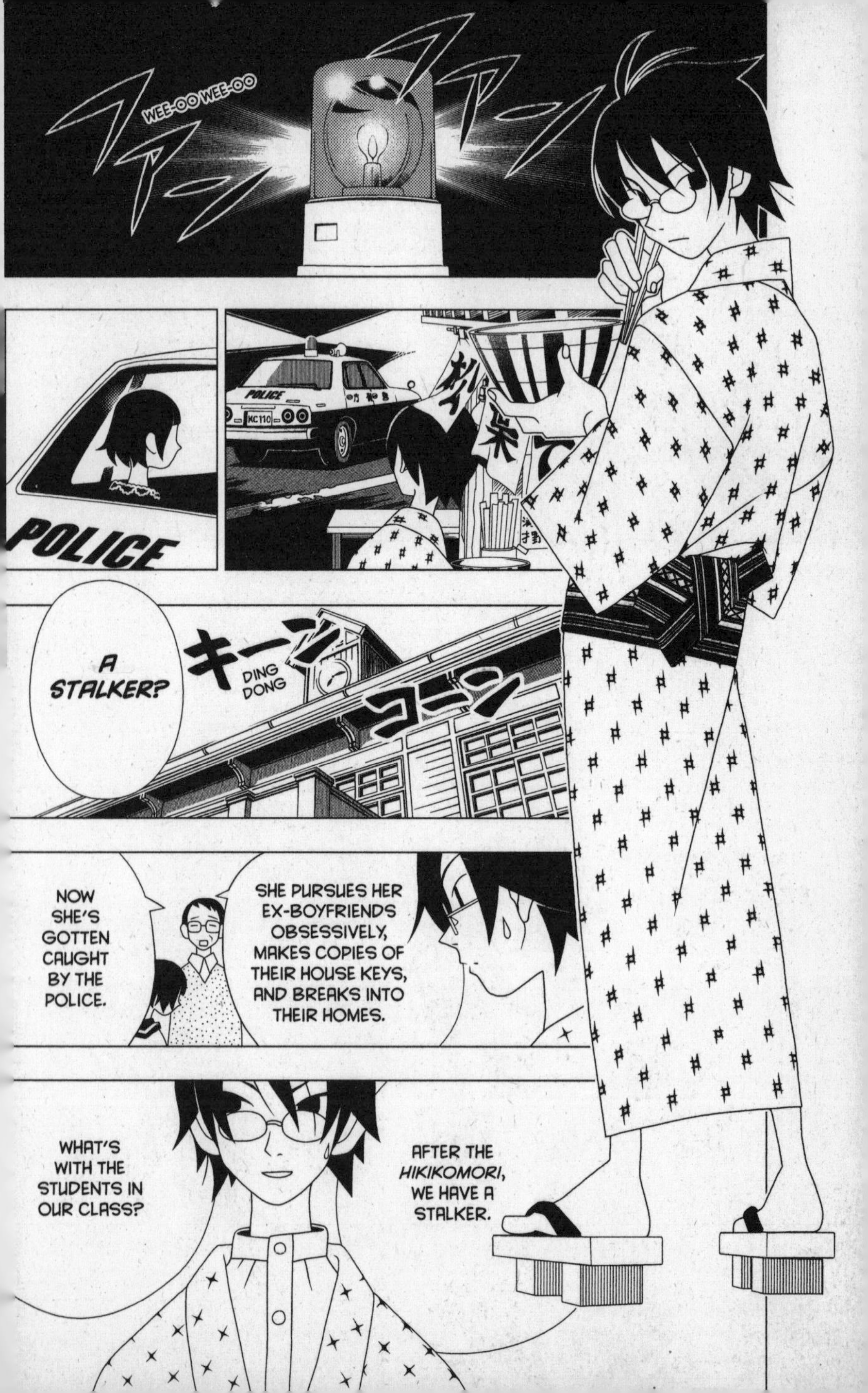
WEE-OO WEE-OO
DING DONG
A STALKER?
SHE PURSUES HER EX-BOYFRIENDS OBSESSIVELY, MAKES COPIES OF THEIR HOUSE KEYS, AND BREAKS INTO THEIR HOMES.
NOW SHE'S GOTTEN CAUGHT BY THE POLICE.
AFTER THE *HIKIKOMORI*, WE HAVE A STALKER.
WHAT'S WITH THE STUDENTS IN OUR CLASS?

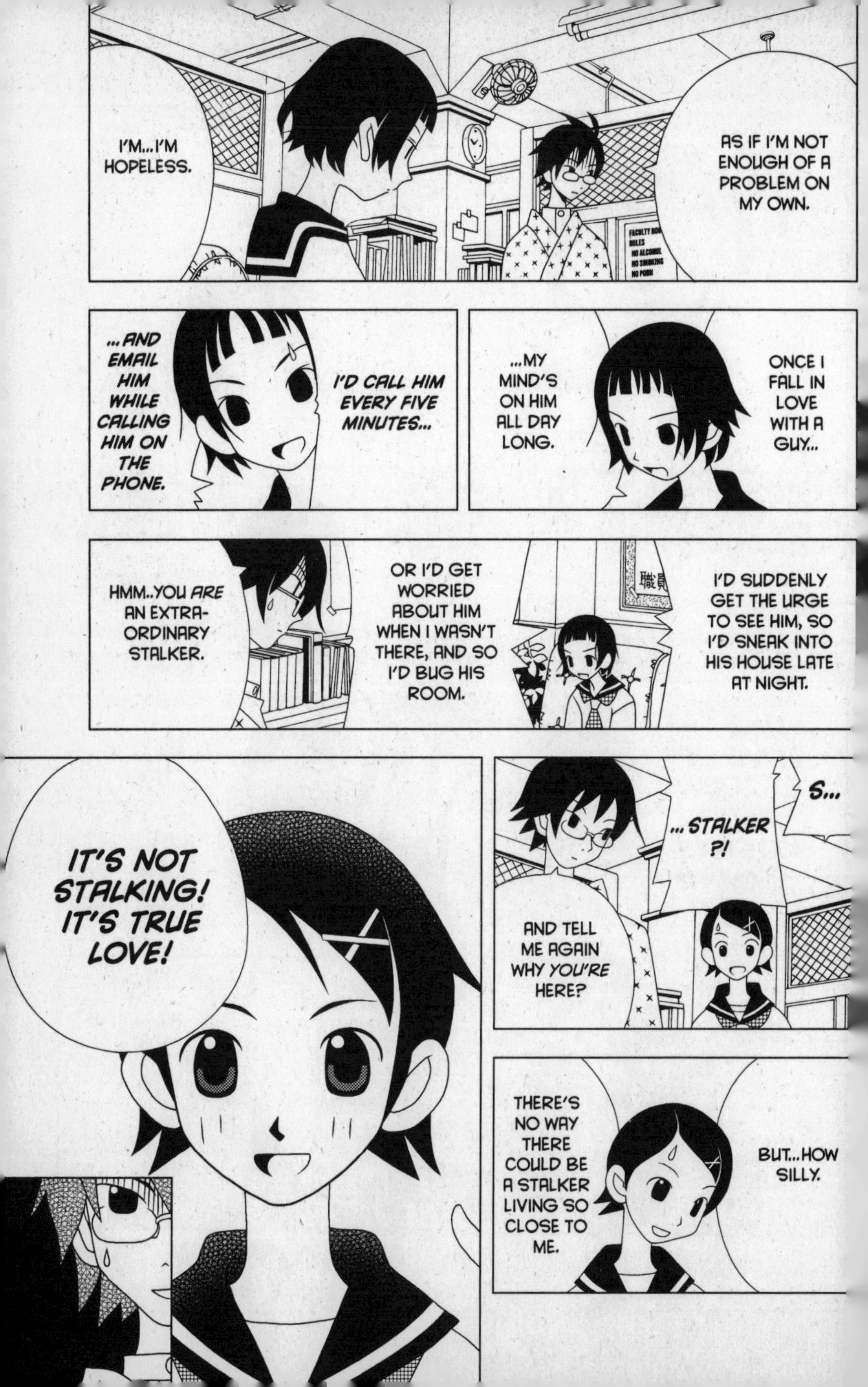
AS IF I'M NOT ENOUGH OF A PROBLEM ON MY OWN.
NO ALCOHOL
NO SMOKING
NO PORN
I'M...I'M HOPELESS.
ONCE I FALL IN LOVE WITH A GUY...
...MY MIND'S ON HIM ALL DAY LONG.
I'D CALL HIM EVERY FIVE MINUTES...
...AND EMAIL HIM WHILE CALLING HIM ON THE PHONE.
I'D SUDDENLY GET THE URGE TO SEE HIM, SO I'D SNEAK INTO HIS HOUSE LATE AT NIGHT.
OR I'D GET WORRIED ABOUT HIM WHEN I WASN'T THERE, AND SO I'D BUG HIS ROOM.
HMM..YOU ARE AN EXTRA-ORDINARY STALKER.
S...
...STALKER?!
AND TELL ME AGAIN WHY YOU'RE HERE?
BUT...HOW SILLY.
THERE'S NO WAY THERE COULD BE A STALKER LIVING SO CLOSE TO ME.
IT'S NOT STALKING! IT'S TRUE LOVE!

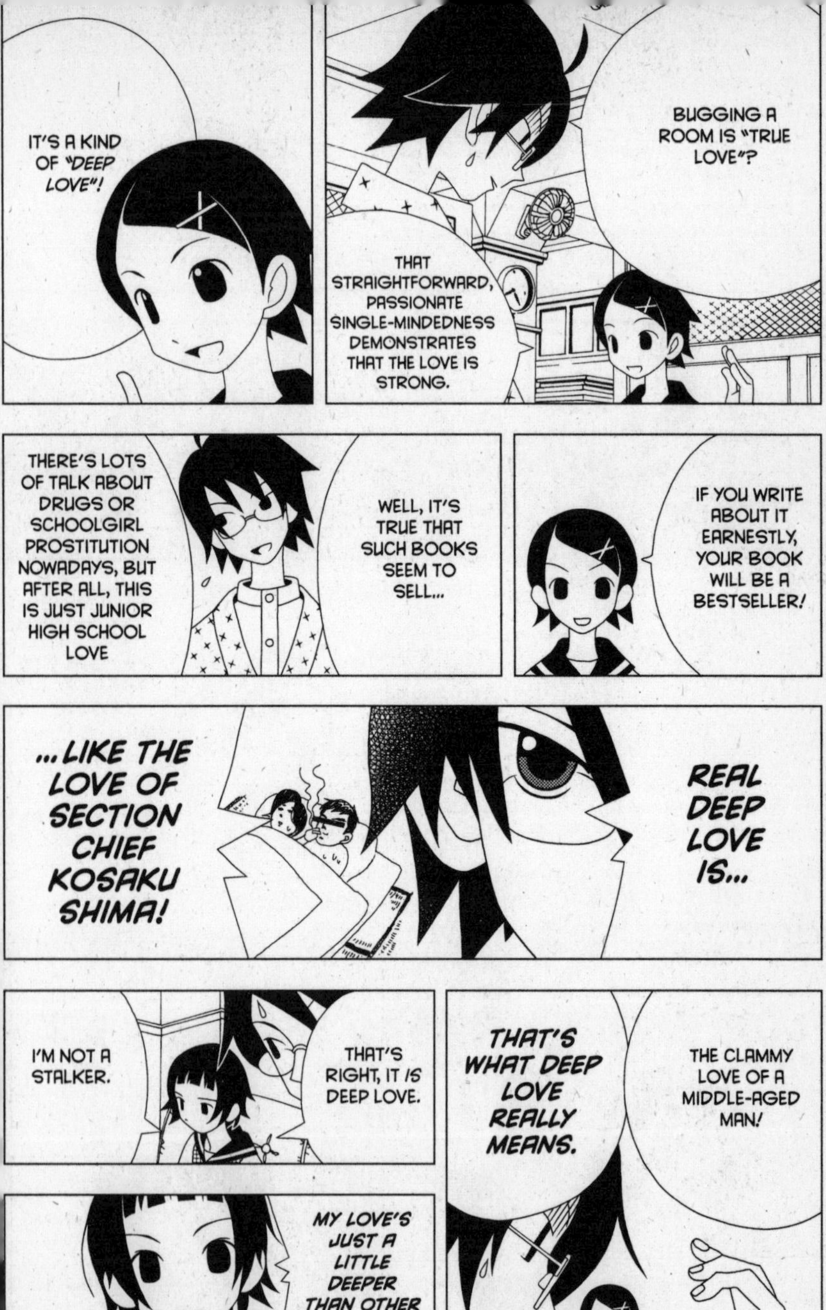
BUGGING A ROOM IS "TRUE LOVE"?
THAT STRAIGHTFORWARD, PASSIONATE SINGLE-MINDEDNESS DEMONSTRATES THAT THE LOVE IS STRONG.
IT'S A KIND OF "DEEP LOVE"!
IF YOU WRITE ABOUT IT EARNESTLY, YOUR BOOK WILL BE A BESTSELLER!
WELL, IT'S TRUE THAT SUCH BOOKS SEEM TO SELL...
THERE'S LOTS OF TALK ABOUT DRUGS OR SCHOOLGIRL PROSTITUTION NOWADAYS, BUT AFTER ALL, THIS IS JUST JUNIOR HIGH SCHOOL LOVE
REAL DEEP LOVE IS...
...LIKE THE LOVE OF SECTION CHIEF KOSAKU SHIMA!
THE CLAMMY LOVE OF A MIDDLE-AGED MAN!
THAT'S WHAT DEEP LOVE REALLY MEANS.
?
THAT'S RIGHT, IT IS DEEP LOVE.
I'M NOT A STALKER.
MY LOVE'S JUST A LITTLE DEEPER THAN OTHER PEOPLE'S!

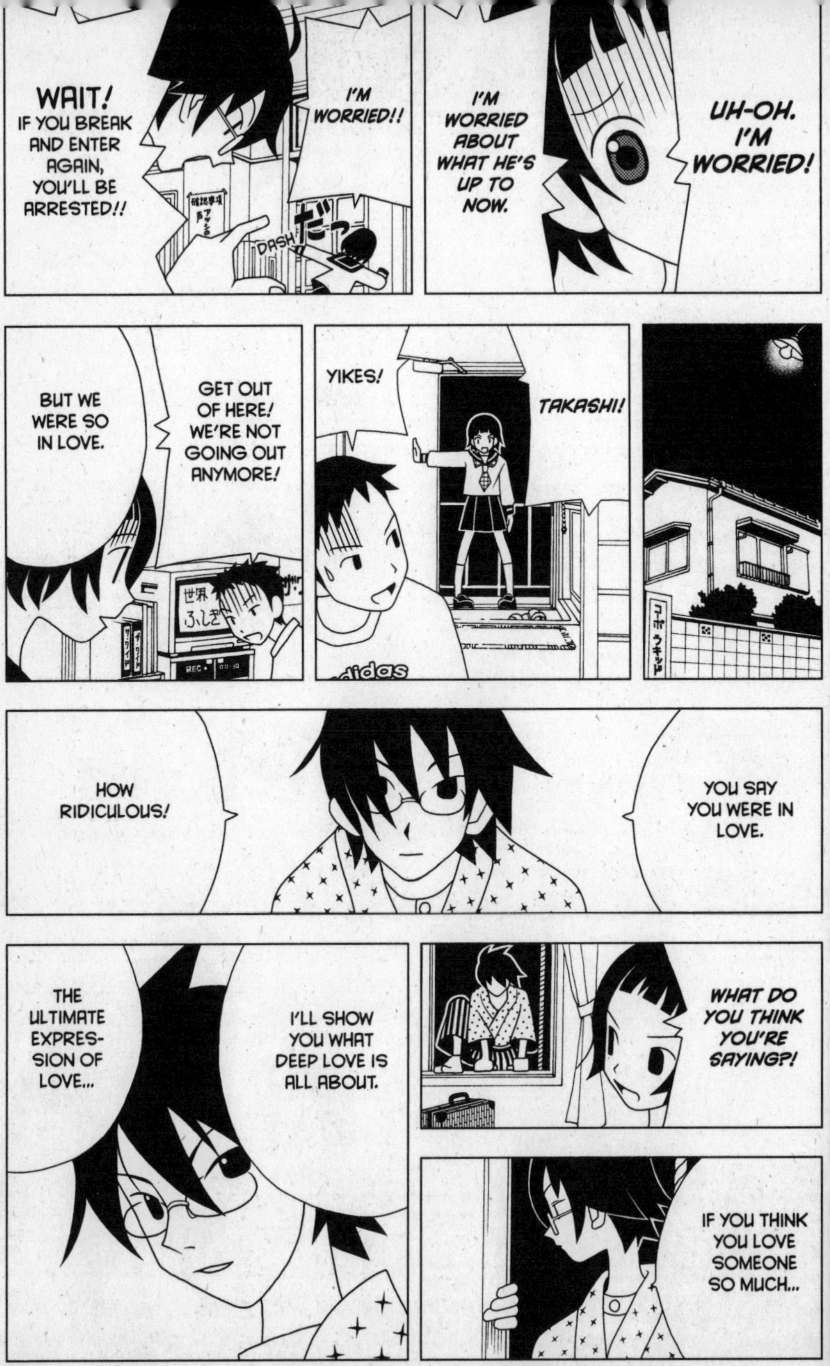
UH-OH. I'M WORRIED!
I'M WORRIED ABOUT WHAT HE'S UP TO NOW.
I'M WORRIED!!
WAIT! IF YOU BREAK AND ENTER AGAIN, YOU'LL BE ARRESTED!!
DASH
TAKASHI!
YIKES!
GET OUT OF HERE! WE'RE NOT GOING OUT ANYMORE!
BUT WE WERE SO IN LOVE.
世界ふしぎ
YOU SAY YOU WERE IN LOVE.
HOW RIDICULOUS!
WHAT DO YOU THINK YOU'RE SAYING?!
IF YOU THINK YOU LOVE SOMEONE SO MUCH...
I'LL SHOW YOU WHAT DEEP LOVE IS ALL ABOUT.
THE ULTIMATE EXPRES-SION OF LOVE...

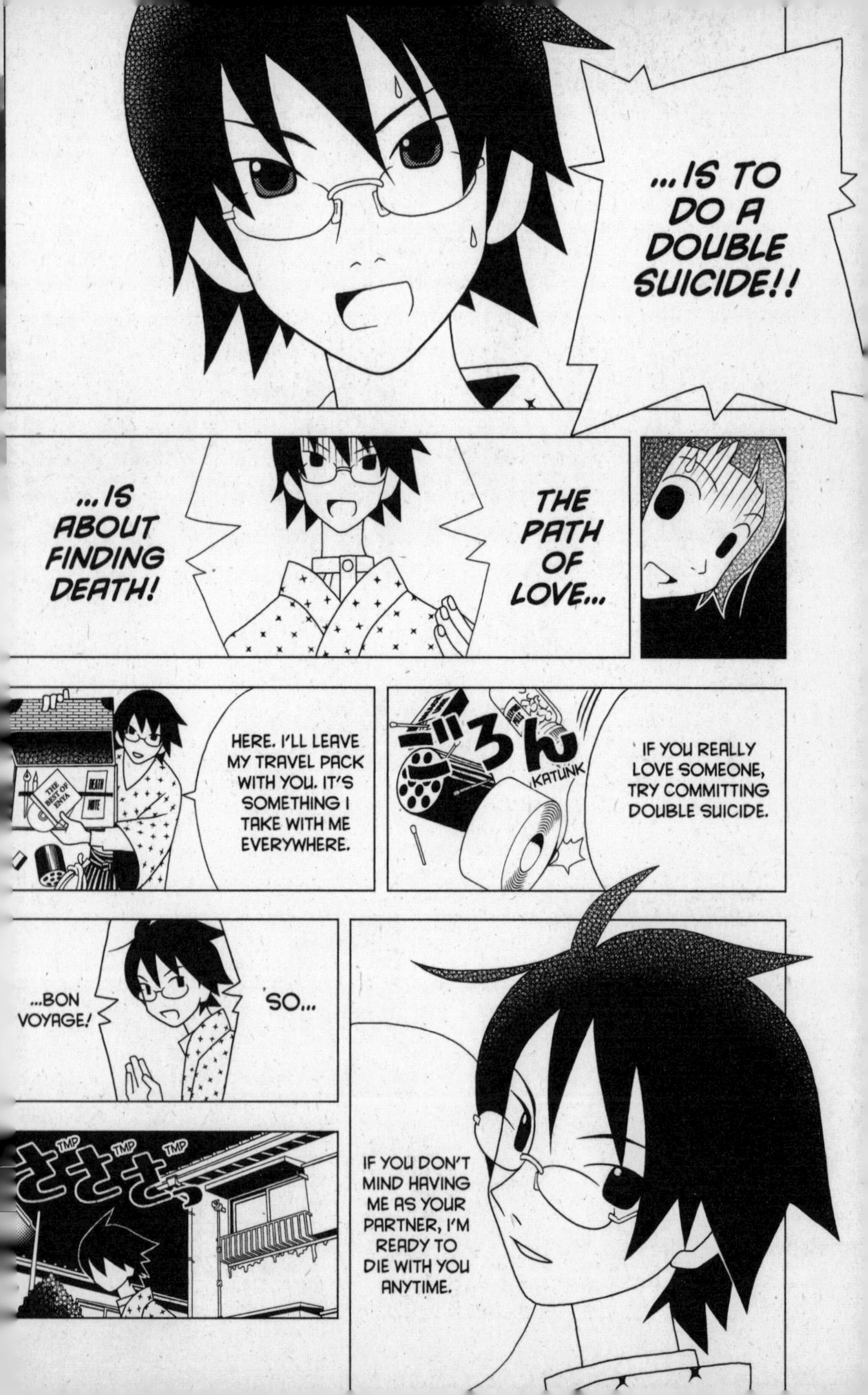
...IS TO DO A DOUBLE SUICIDE!!
THE PATH OF LOVE...
...IS ABOUT FINDING DEATH!
IF YOU REALLY LOVE SOMEONE, TRY COMMITTING DOUBLE SUICIDE.
ごろん
KATUNK
HERE. I'LL LEAVE MY TRAVEL PACK WITH YOU. IT'S SOMETHING I TAKE WITH ME EVERYWHERE.
DEATH NOTE
THE BEST OF ENYA
IF YOU DON'T MIND HAVING ME AS YOUR PARTNER, I'M READY TO DIE WITH YOU ANYTIME.
SO...
...BON VOYAGE!
TMP
TMP
TMP

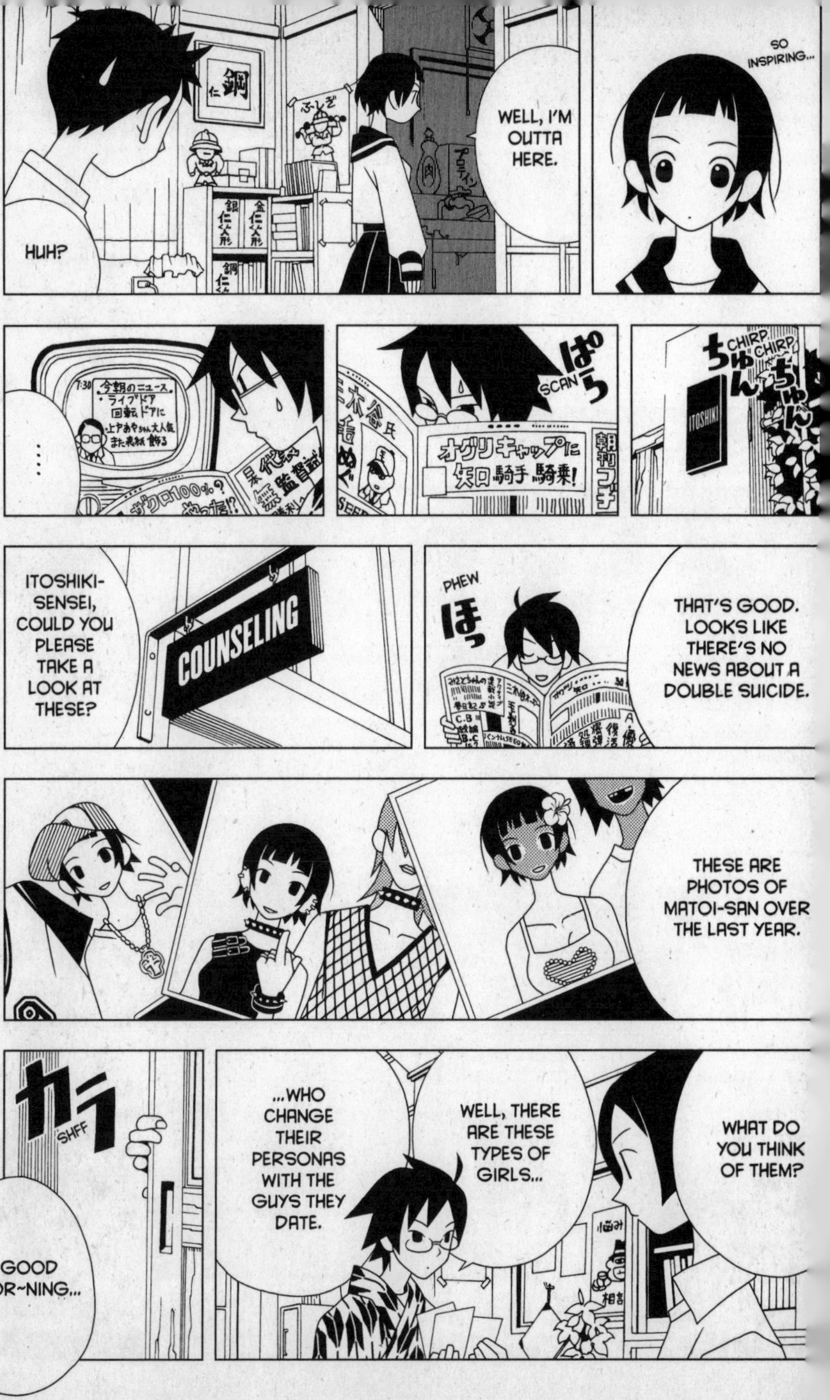
SO INSPIRING...
WELL, I'M OUTTA HERE.
HUH?
ちゅん ちゅん
CHIRP CHIRP
ITOSHIKI
ぱち
SCAN
オグリキャップに 矢口騎手騎乗!
今朝のニュース
....
THAT'S GOOD. LOOKS LIKE THERE'S NO NEWS ABOUT A DOUBLE SUICIDE.
ほっ
PHEW
COUNSELING
ITOSHIKI-SENSEI, COULD YOU PLEASE TAKE A LOOK AT THESE?
THESE ARE PHOTOS OF MATOI-SAN OVER THE LAST YEAR.
WHAT DO YOU THINK OF THEM?
WELL, THERE ARE THESE TYPES OF GIRLS...
...WHO CHANGE THEIR PERSONAS WITH THE GUYS THEY DATE.
カラ
SHFF
GOOD MOR~NING...

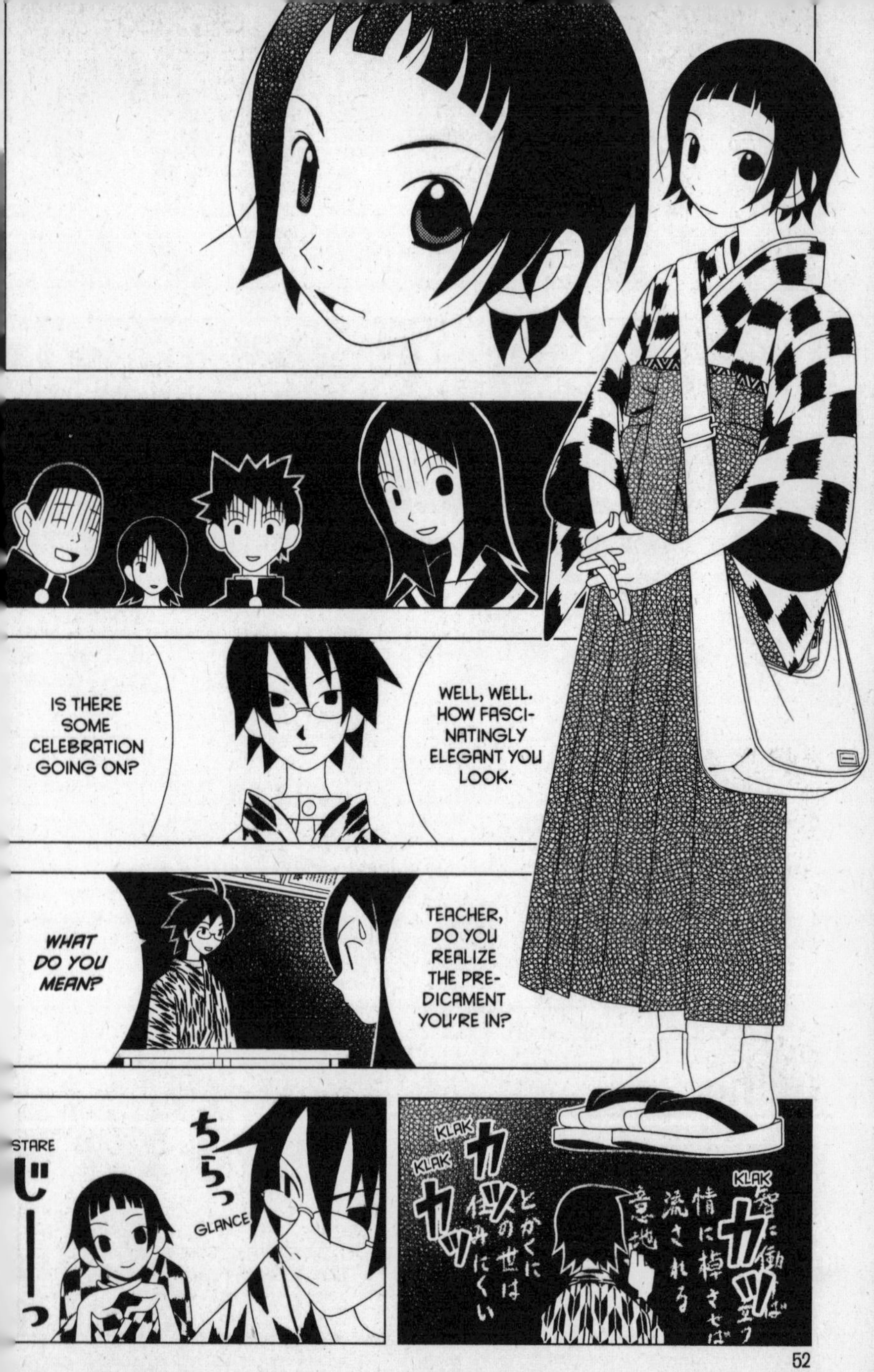
WELL, WELL. HOW FASCI-NATINGLY ELEGANT YOU LOOK.
IS THERE SOME CELEBRATION GOING ON?
TEACHER, DO YOU REALIZE THE PRE-DICAMENT YOU'RE IN?
WHAT DO YOU MEAN?
KLAK
カッ
智に働ば立つ
情に棹させば
流される
意地
とかくに
人の世は
住みにくい
KLAK
カッ
KLAK
カッ
ちらっ
GLANCE
STARE
じーっ

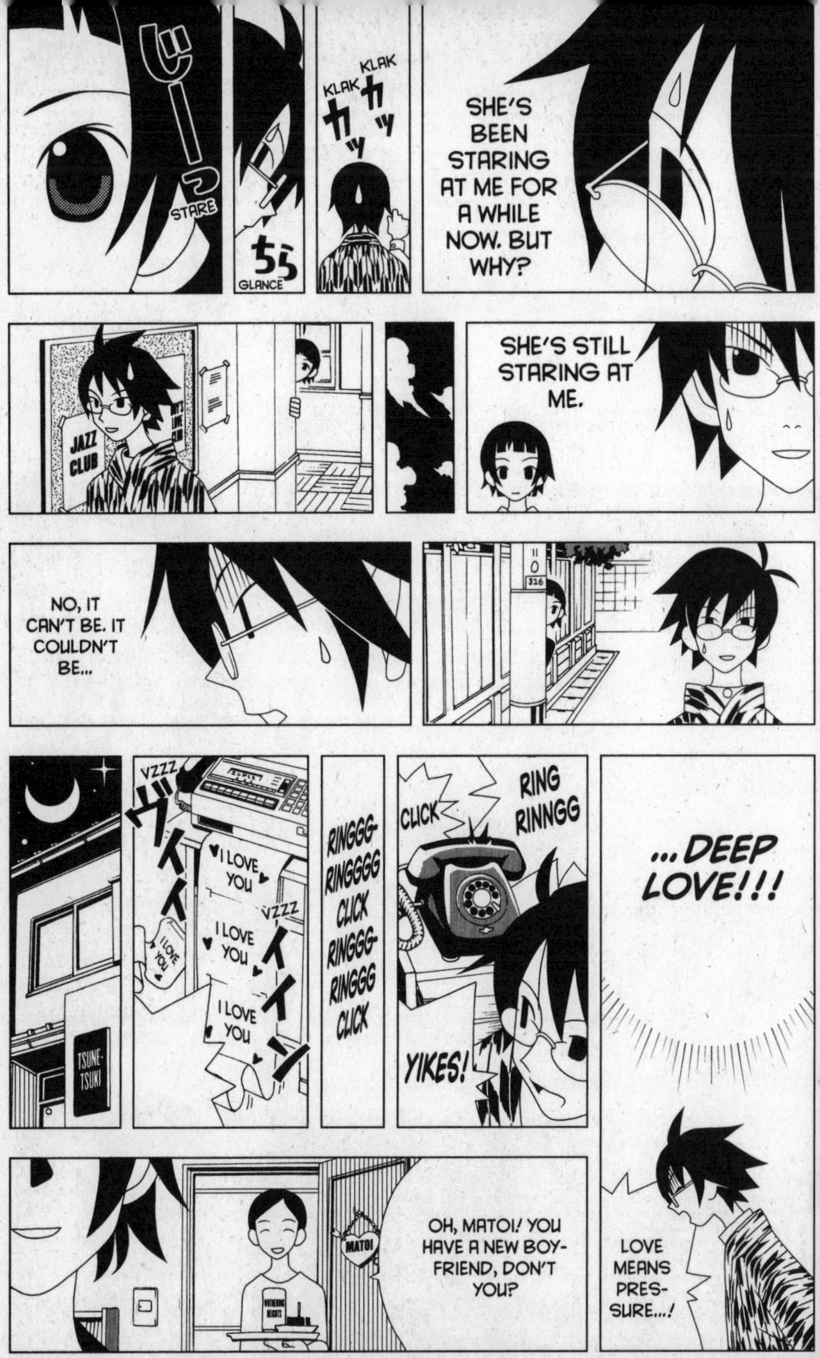
SHE'S BEEN STARING AT ME FOR A WHILE NOW. BUT WHY?
KLAK KLAK
カッカッ
ちら
GLANCE
じーっ
STARE
SHE'S STILL STARING AT ME.
JAZZ CLUB
NO, IT CAN'T BE. IT COULDN'T BE...
...DEEP LOVE!!!
LOVE MEANS PRES-SURE...!
RING RINNGG
CLICK
YIKES!
RINGGG-RINGGGG CLICK RINGGG-RINGGG CLICK
VZZZ
I LOVE YOU
I LOVE YOU
VZZZ
I LOVE YOU
I LOVE YOU
TSUNE-TSUKI
OH, MATOI! YOU HAVE A NEW BOY-FRIEND, DON'T YOU?
MATOI
WUTHERING HEIGHTS

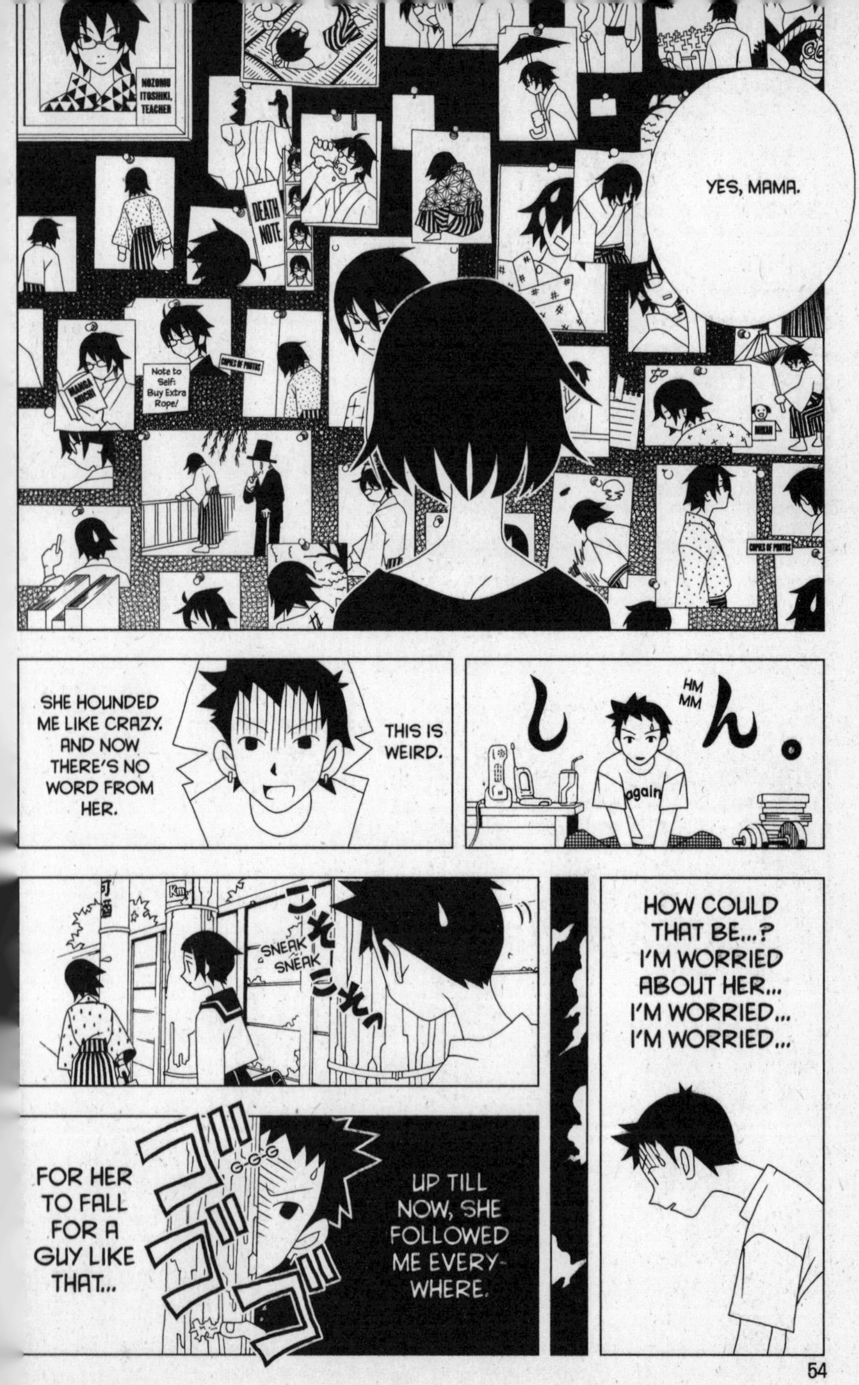
NOZOMU ITOSHIKI, TEACHER
DEATH NOTE
YES, MAMA.
COPIES OF PHOTOS
Note to Self: Buy Extra Rope!
MIKAN
HM MM
しん。
THIS IS WEIRD.
SHE HOUNDED ME LIKE CRAZY. AND NOW THERE'S NO WORD FROM HER.
HOW COULD THAT BE...? I'M WORRIED ABOUT HER... I'M WORRIED... I'M WORRIED...
こそこそ
SNEAK SNEAK
UP TILL NOW, SHE FOLLOWED ME EVERY-WHERE.
G-G-G
FOR HER TO FALL FOR A GUY LIKE THAT...

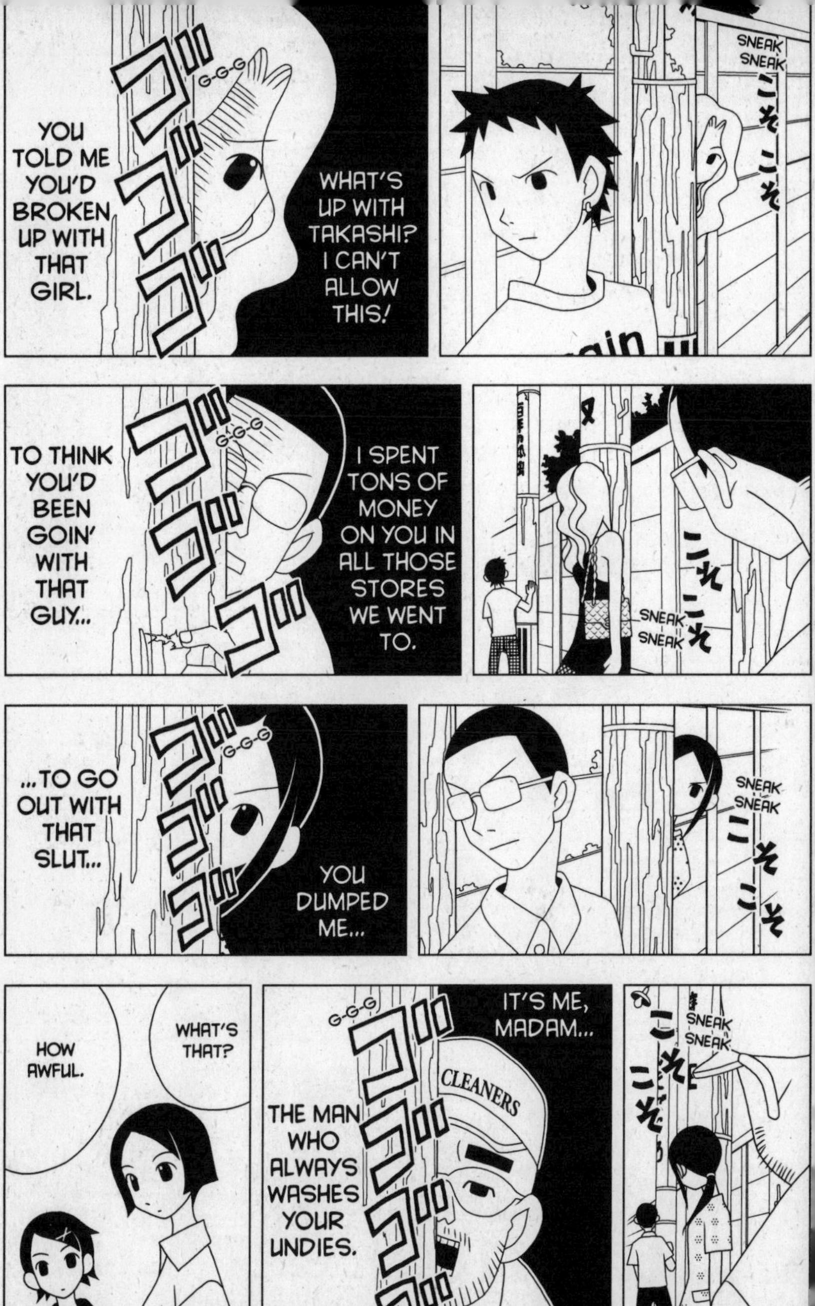
SNEAK SNEAK
こそこそ
WHAT'S UP WITH TAKASHI? I CAN'T ALLOW THIS!
YOU TOLD ME YOU'D BROKEN UP WITH THAT GIRL.
ゴゴゴ
G-G-G
SNEAK SNEAK
こそこそ
I SPENT TONS OF MONEY ON YOU IN ALL THOSE STORES WE WENT TO.
TO THINK YOU'D BEEN GOIN' WITH THAT GUY...
ゴゴゴゴ
G-G-G
SNEAK SNEAK
こそこそ
YOU DUMPED ME...
...TO GO OUT WITH THAT SLUT...
ゴゴゴゴ
G-G-G
SNEAK SNEAK
こそこそ
IT'S ME, MADAM...
THE MAN WHO ALWAYS WASHES YOUR UNDIES.
CLEANERS
ゴゴゴゴ
G-G-G
WHAT'S THAT?
HOW AWFUL.

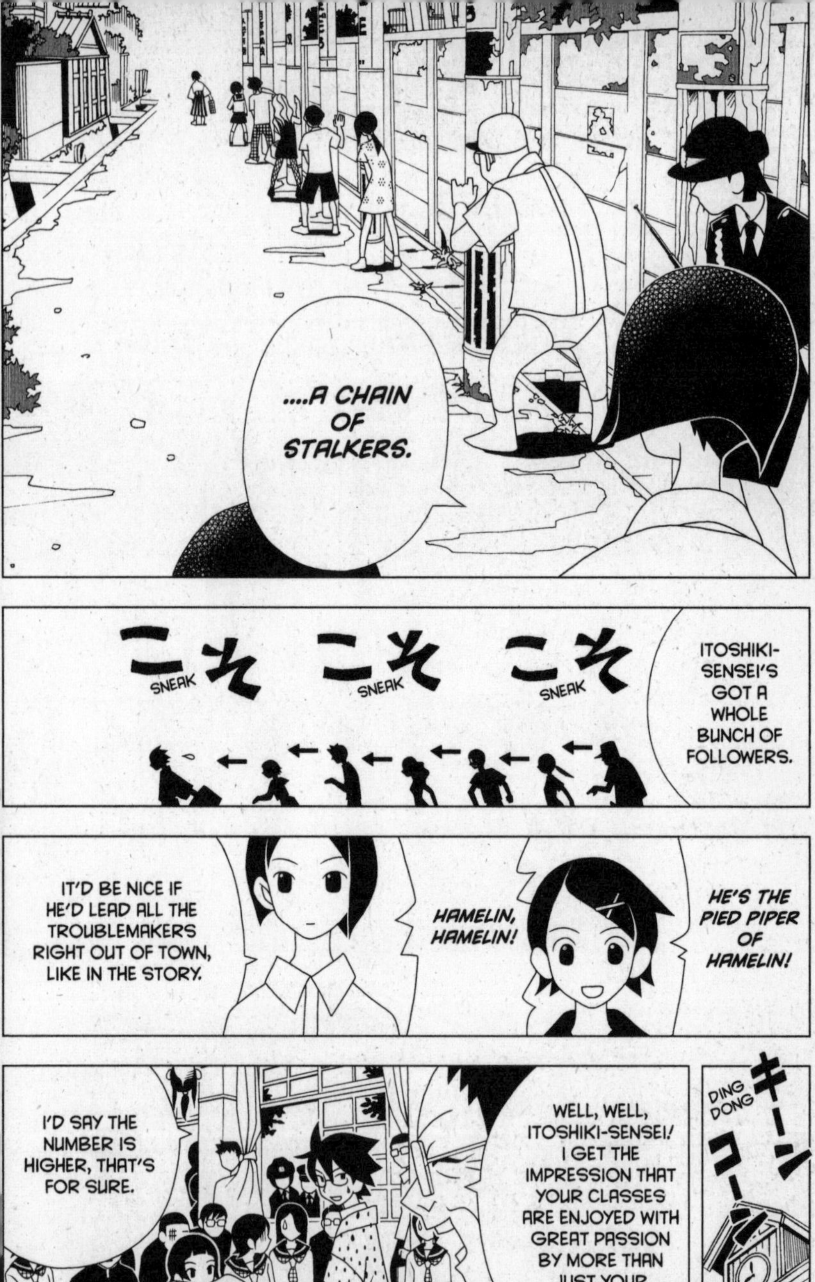
....A CHAIN OF STALKERS.
ITOSHIKI-SENSEI'S GOT A WHOLE BUNCH OF FOLLOWERS.
こそ SNEAK
こそ SNEAK
こそ SNEAK
HE'S THE PIED PIPER OF HAMELIN!
HAMELIN, HAMELIN!
IT'D BE NICE IF HE'D LEAD ALL THE TROUBLEMAKERS RIGHT OUT OF TOWN, LIKE IN THE STORY.
キーンコーン DING DONG
WELL, WELL, ITOSHIKI-SENSEI! I GET THE IMPRESSION THAT YOUR CLASSES ARE ENJOYED WITH GREAT PASSION BY MORE THAN JUST YOUR STUDENTS.
I'D SAY THE NUMBER IS HIGHER, THAT'S FOR SURE.

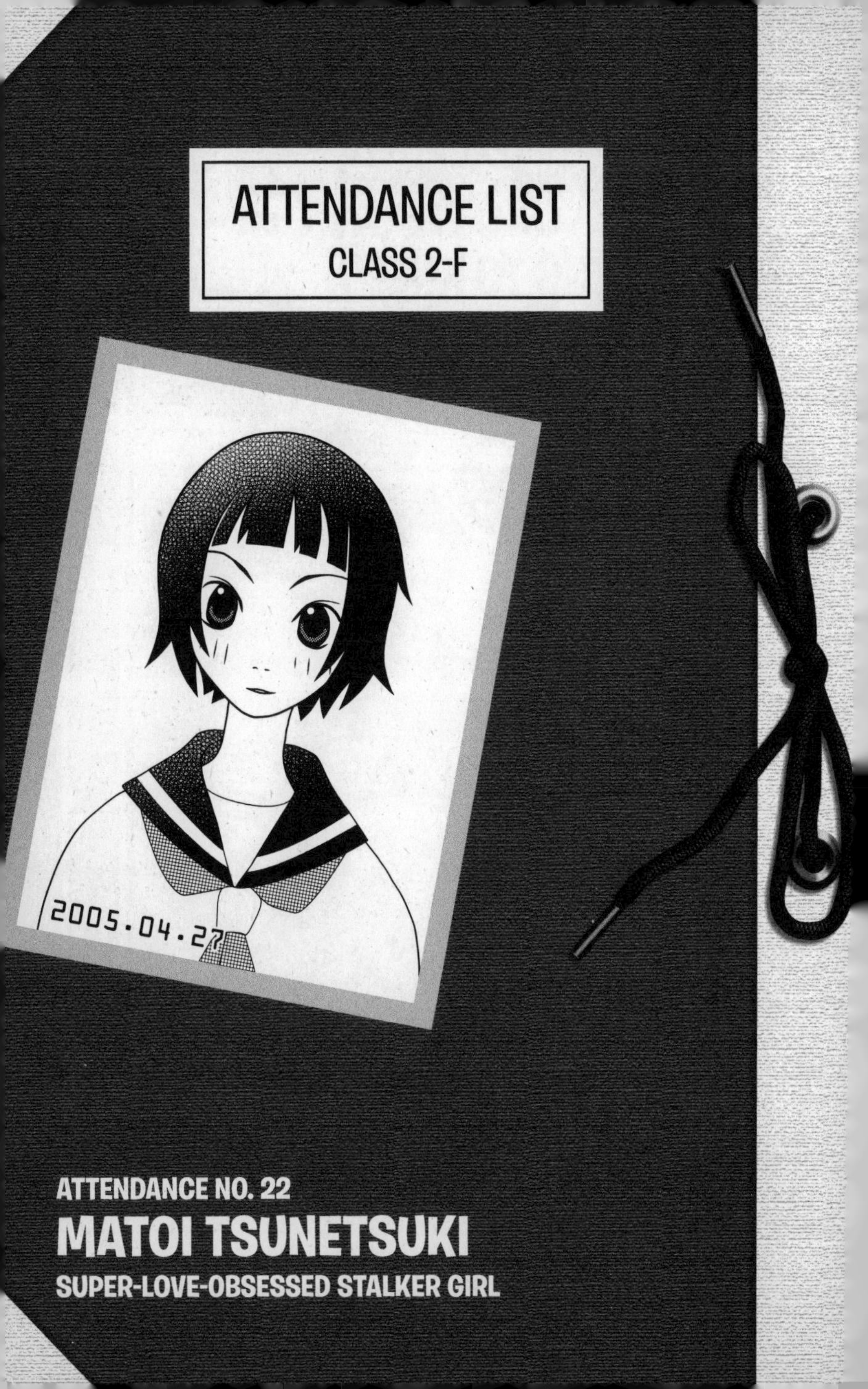
ATTENDANCE LIST
CLASS 2-F
2005.04.27
ATTENDANCE NO. 22
MATOI TSUNETSUKI
SUPER-LOVE-OBSESSED STALKER GIRL

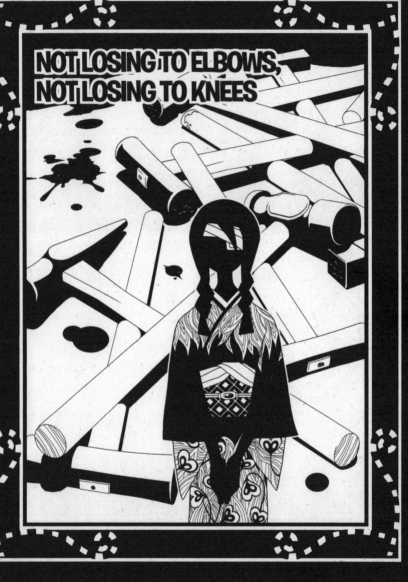

# NOT LOSING TO ELBOWS, NOT LOSING TO KNEES

CHAPTER 5

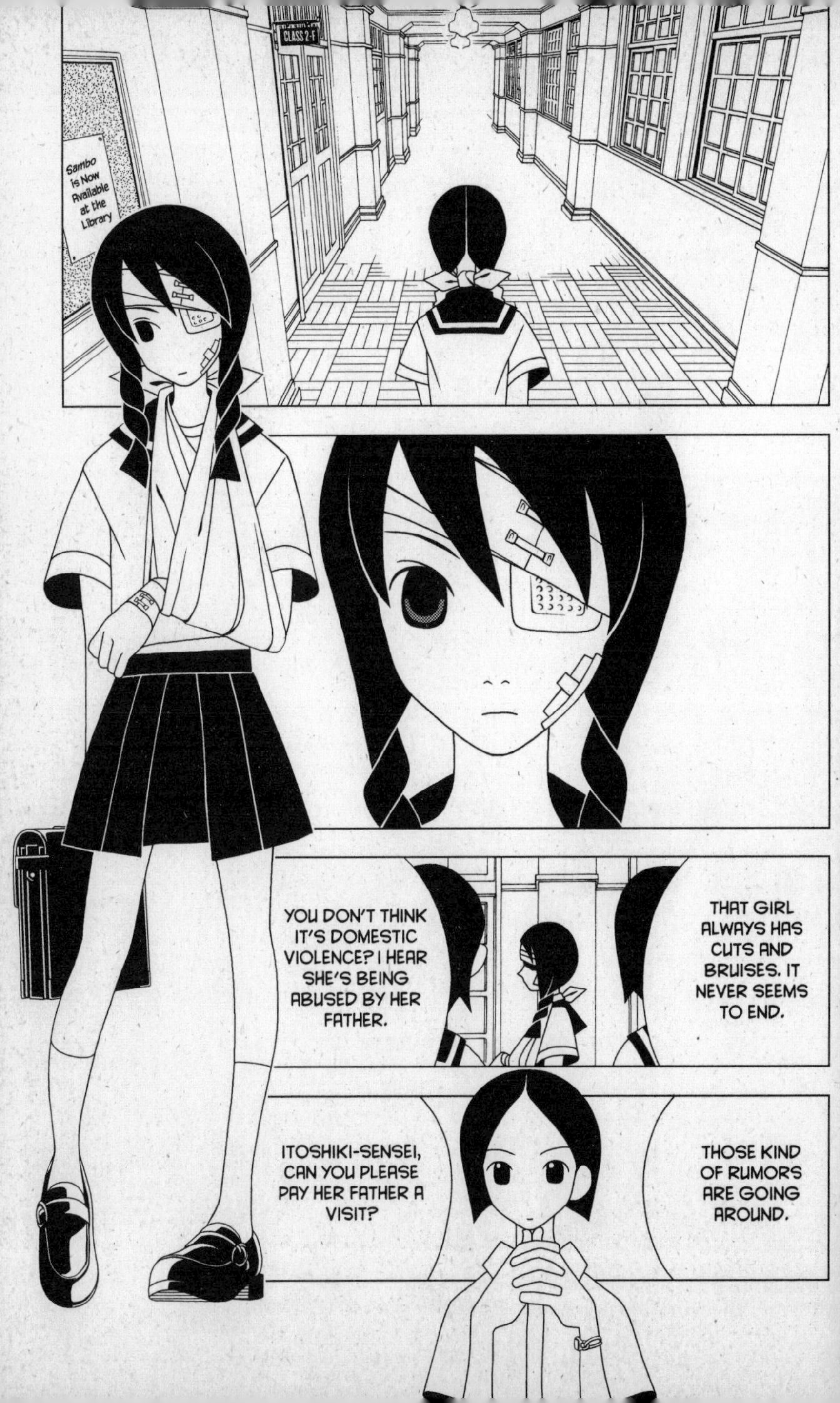
CLASS 2-F
Sambo is Now Available at the Library
THAT GIRL ALWAYS HAS CUTS AND BRUISES. IT NEVER SEEMS TO END.
YOU DON'T THINK IT'S DOMESTIC VIOLENCE? I HEAR SHE'S BEING ABUSED BY HER FATHER.
THOSE KIND OF RUMORS ARE GOING AROUND.
ITOSHIKI-SENSEI, CAN YOU PLEASE PAY HER FATHER A VISIT?

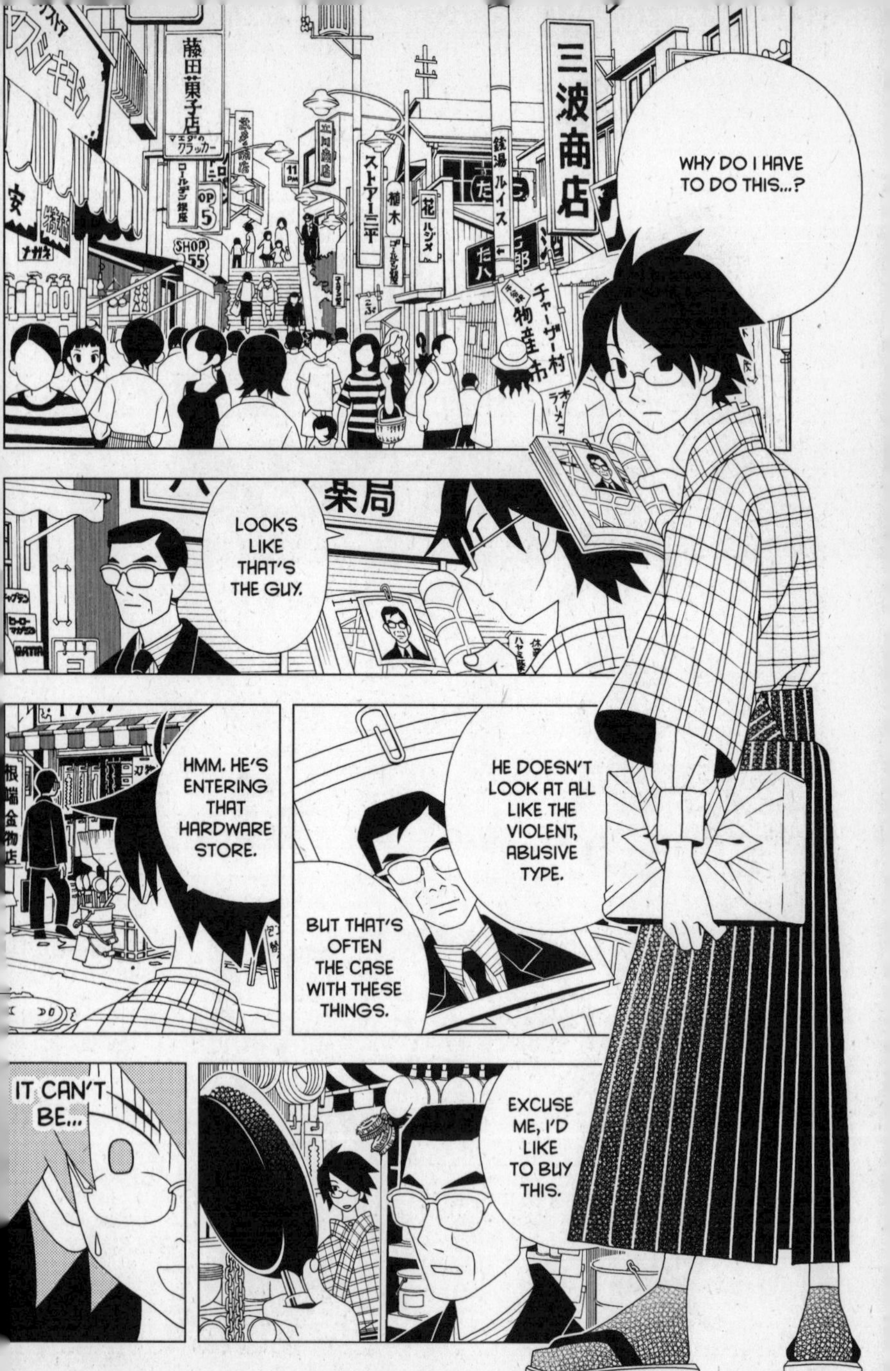
WHY DO I HAVE TO DO THIS...?
LOOKS LIKE THAT'S THE GUY.
HE DOESN'T LOOK AT ALL LIKE THE VIOLENT, ABUSIVE TYPE.
BUT THAT'S OFTEN THE CASE WITH THESE THINGS.
HMM. HE'S ENTERING THAT HARDWARE STORE.
EXCUSE ME, I'D LIKE TO BUY THIS.
IT CAN'T BE...

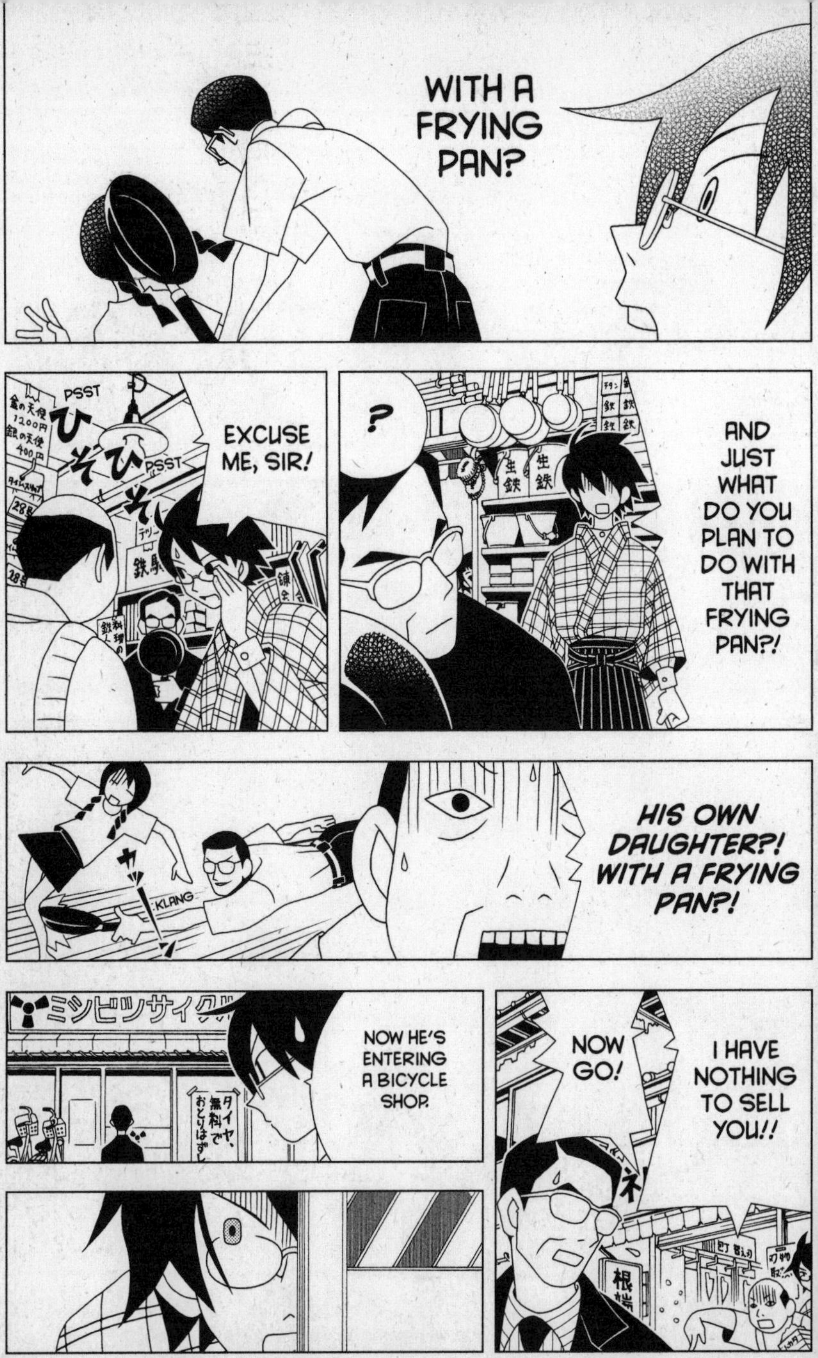
WITH A FRYING PAN?
?
AND JUST WHAT DO YOU PLAN TO DO WITH THAT FRYING PAN?!
生鉄
生鉄
EXCUSE ME, SIR!
PSST
ひそ
ひそ
PSST
金の天使 1200円
銀の天使 400円
HIS OWN DAUGHTER?! WITH A FRYING PAN?!
KLANG
I HAVE NOTHING TO SELL YOU!!
NOW GO!
NOW HE'S ENTERING A BICYCLE SHOP.
タイヤ、無料でおとりはずし

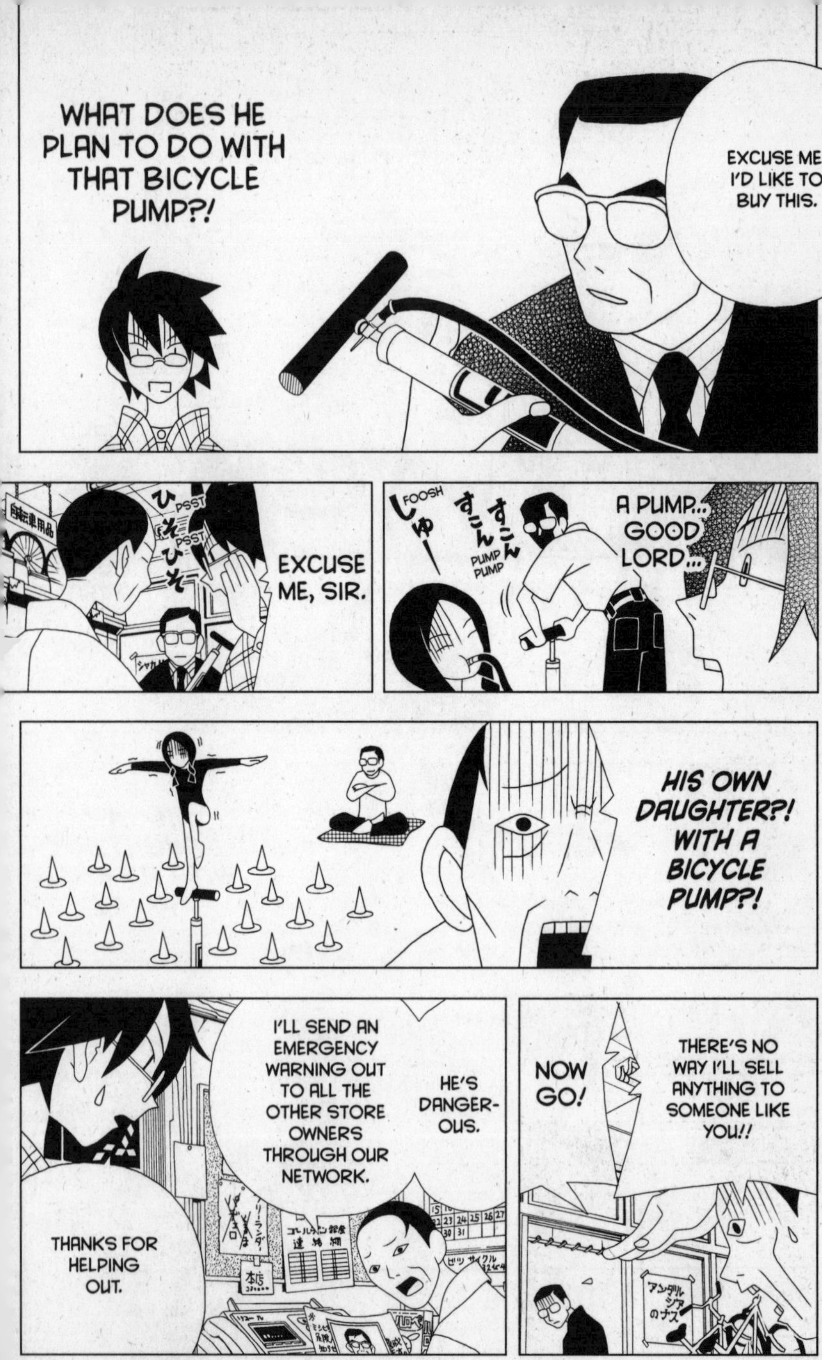
EXCUSE ME, I'D LIKE TO BUY THIS.
WHAT DOES HE PLAN TO DO WITH THAT BICYCLE PUMP?!
A PUMP... GOOD LORD...
すこんすこん PUMP PUMP
しゅー FOOSH
EXCUSE ME, SIR.
ひそひそ PSST PSST
自転車用品
HIS OWN DAUGHTER?! WITH A BICYCLE PUMP?!
THERE'S NO WAY I'LL SELL ANYTHING TO SOMEONE LIKE YOU!!
NOW GO!
HE'S DANGER-OUS.
I'LL SEND AN EMERGENCY WARNING OUT TO ALL THE OTHER STORE OWNERS THROUGH OUR NETWORK.
THANKS FOR HELPING OUT.

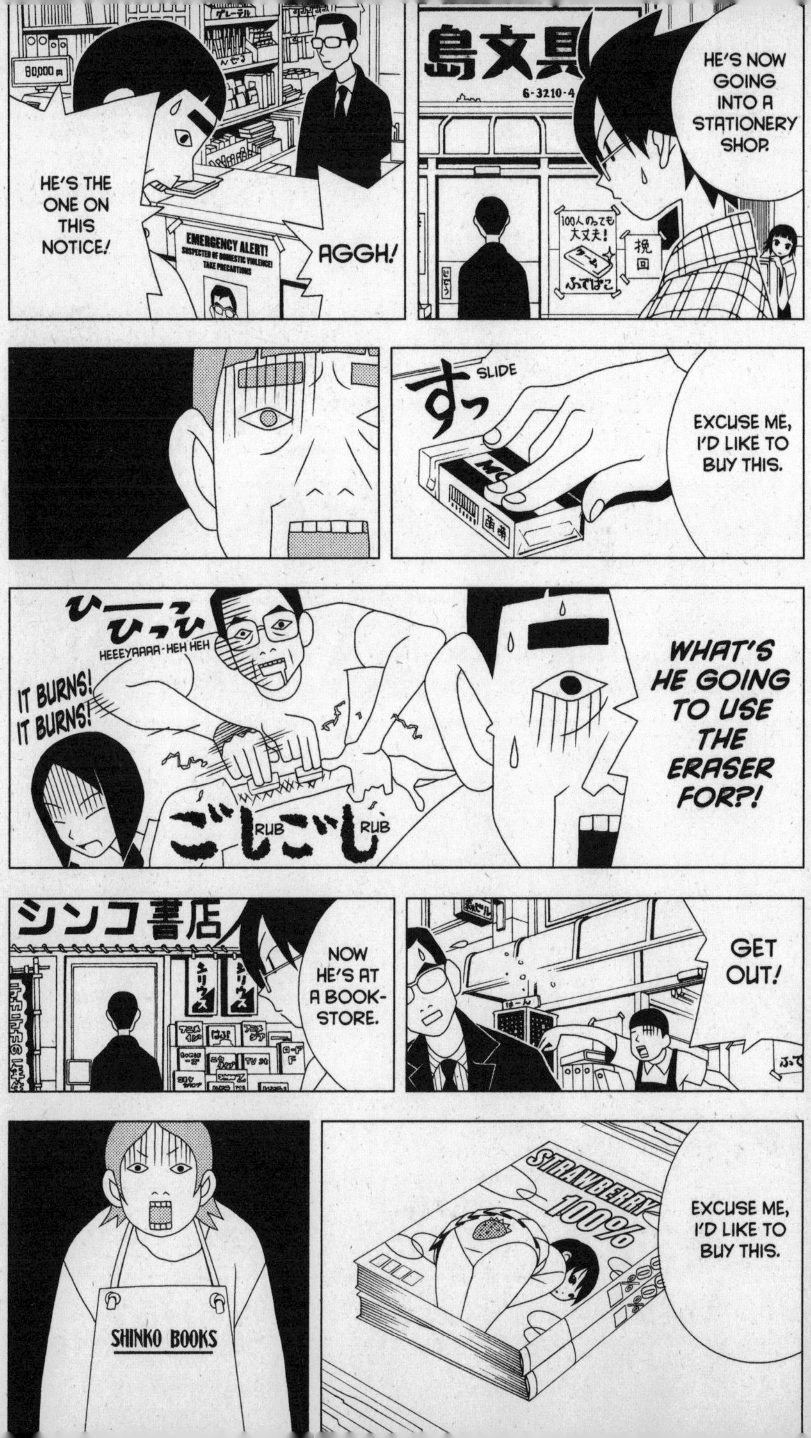
島文具
6-3210-4
HE'S NOW GOING INTO A STATIONERY SHOP.
100人のっても大丈夫!
ふでばこ
挽回
80,000円
AGGH!
HE'S THE ONE ON THIS NOTICE!
EMERGENCY ALERT!
SUSPECTED OF DOMESTIC VIOLENCE!
TAKE PRECAUTIONS
すっ
SLIDE
EXCUSE ME, I'D LIKE TO BUY THIS.
WHAT'S HE GOING TO USE THE ERASER FOR?!
ひーひっひ
HEEEYAAAA-HEH HEH
IT BURNS! IT BURNS!
ごしごし
RUB RUB
GET OUT!
シンコ書店
NOW HE'S AT A BOOK-STORE.
STRAWBERRY 100%
EXCUSE ME, I'D LIKE TO BUY THIS.
SHINKO BOOKS

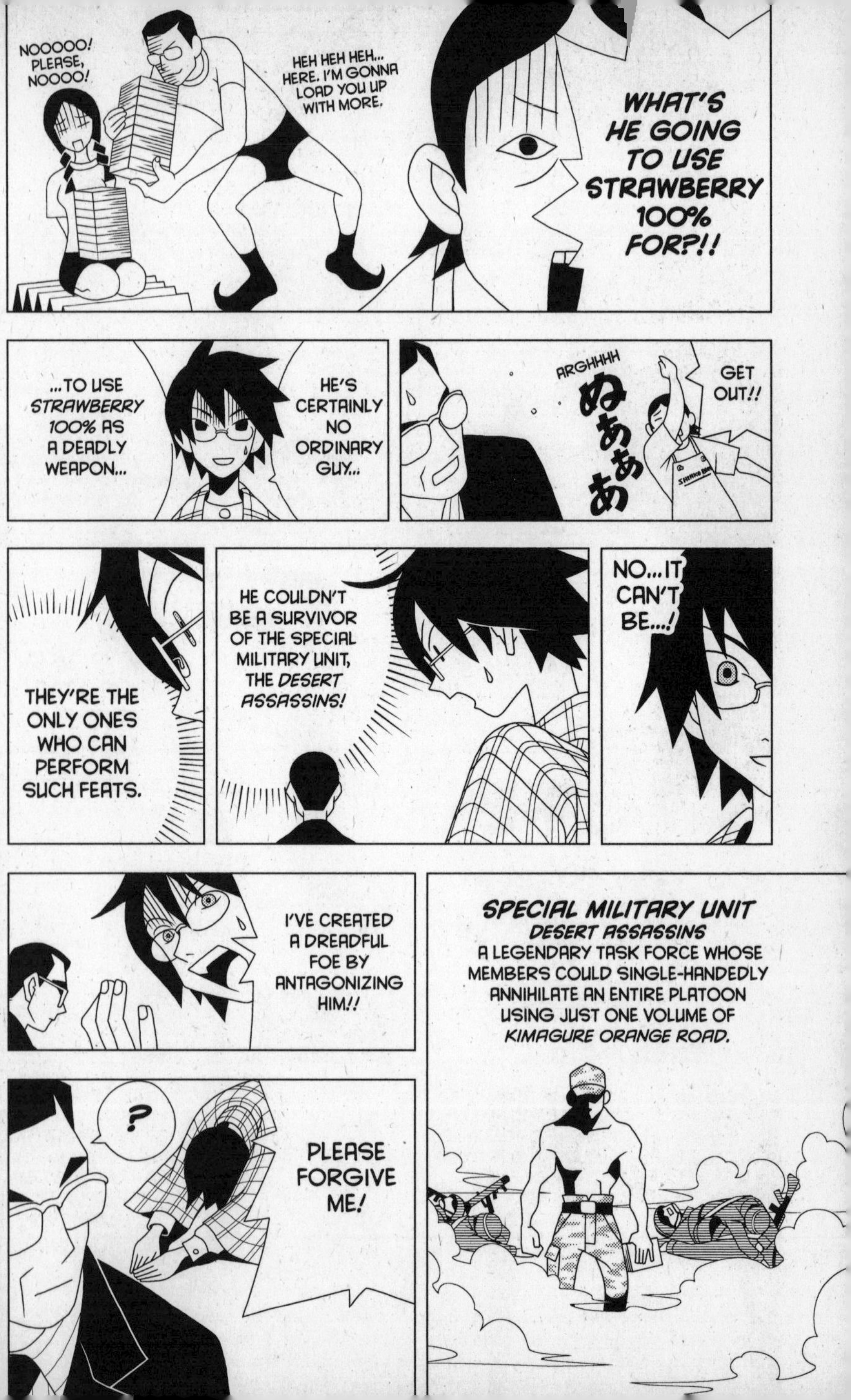
WHAT'S HE GOING TO USE STRAWBERRY 100% FOR?!!
HEH HEH HEH... HERE. I'M GONNA LOAD YOU UP WITH MORE.
NOOOOO! PLEASE, NOOOO!
GET OUT!!
ARGHHHH
ぬあぁあ
HE'S CERTAINLY NO ORDINARY GUY...
...TO USE STRAWBERRY 100% AS A DEADLY WEAPON...
NO...IT CAN'T BE...!
HE COULDN'T BE A SURVIVOR OF THE SPECIAL MILITARY UNIT, THE DESERT ASSASSINS!
THEY'RE THE ONLY ONES WHO CAN PERFORM SUCH FEATS.
SPECIAL MILITARY UNIT
DESERT ASSASSINS
A LEGENDARY TASK FORCE WHOSE MEMBERS COULD SINGLE-HANDEDLY ANNIHILATE AN ENTIRE PLATOON USING JUST ONE VOLUME OF KIMAGURE ORANGE ROAD.
I'VE CREATED A DREADFUL FOE BY ANTAGONIZING HIM!!
PLEASE FORGIVE ME!
?

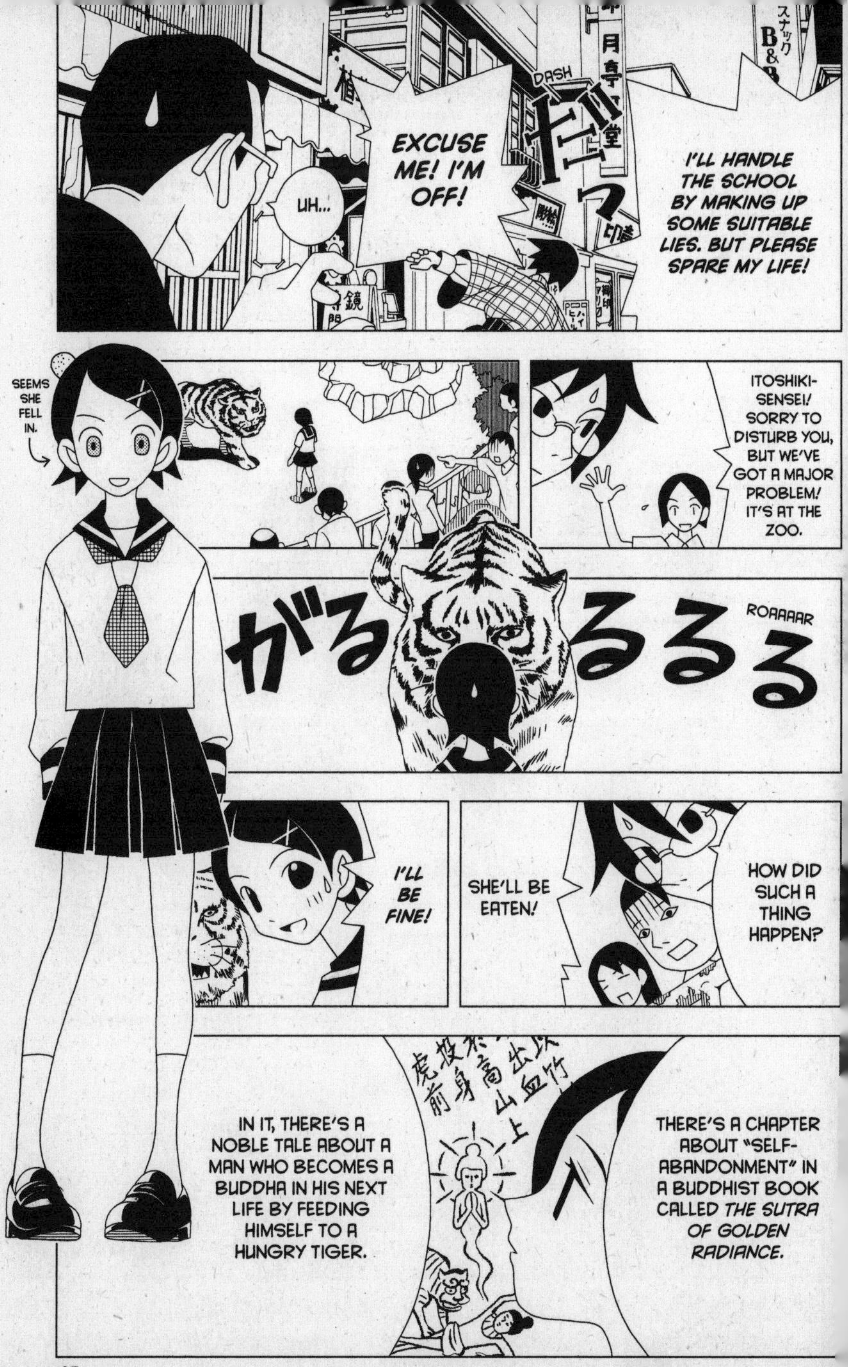
I'LL HANDLE THE SCHOOL BY MAKING UP SOME SUITABLE LIES. BUT PLEASE SPARE MY LIFE!
EXCUSE ME! I'M OFF!
DASH
UH...
ITOSHIKI-SENSEI! SORRY TO DISTURB YOU, BUT WE'VE GOT A MAJOR PROBLEM! IT'S AT THE ZOO.
がるるるる
ROAAAAR
HOW DID SUCH A THING HAPPEN?
SHE'LL BE EATEN!
I'LL BE FINE!
THERE'S A CHAPTER ABOUT "SELF-ABANDONMENT" IN A BUDDHIST BOOK CALLED *THE SUTRA OF GOLDEN RADIANCE.*
IN IT, THERE'S A NOBLE TALE ABOUT A MAN WHO BECOMES A BUDDHA IN HIS NEXT LIFE BY FEEDING HIMSELF TO A HUNGRY TIGER.
SEEMS SHE FELL IN.

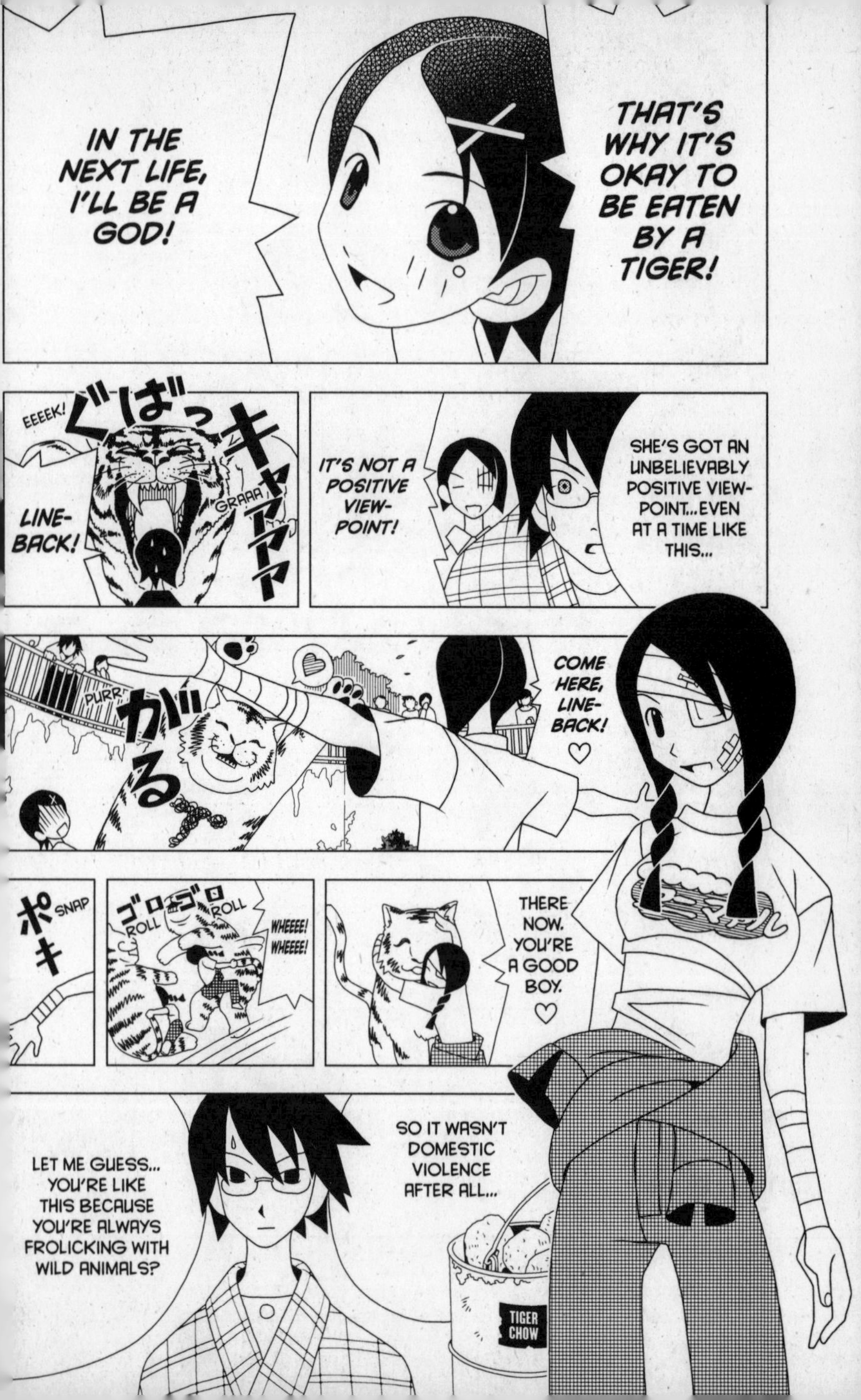
THAT'S WHY IT'S OKAY TO BE EATEN BY A TIGER!
IN THE NEXT LIFE, I'LL BE A GOD!
SHE'S GOT AN UNBELIEVABLY POSITIVE VIEW-POINT...EVEN AT A TIME LIKE THIS...
IT'S NOT A POSITIVE VIEW-POINT!
キャアアア
ぐばっ
EEEEK!
GRAAA
LINE-BACK!
COME HERE, LINE-BACK! ♡
がる
PURR
THERE NOW. YOU'RE A GOOD BOY. ♡
WHEEEE! WHEEEE!
ゴロゴロ
ROLL ROLL
ポキ
SNAP
SO IT WASN'T DOMESTIC VIOLENCE AFTER ALL...
TIGER CHOW
LET ME GUESS... YOU'RE LIKE THIS BECAUSE YOU'RE ALWAYS FROLICKING WITH WILD ANIMALS?

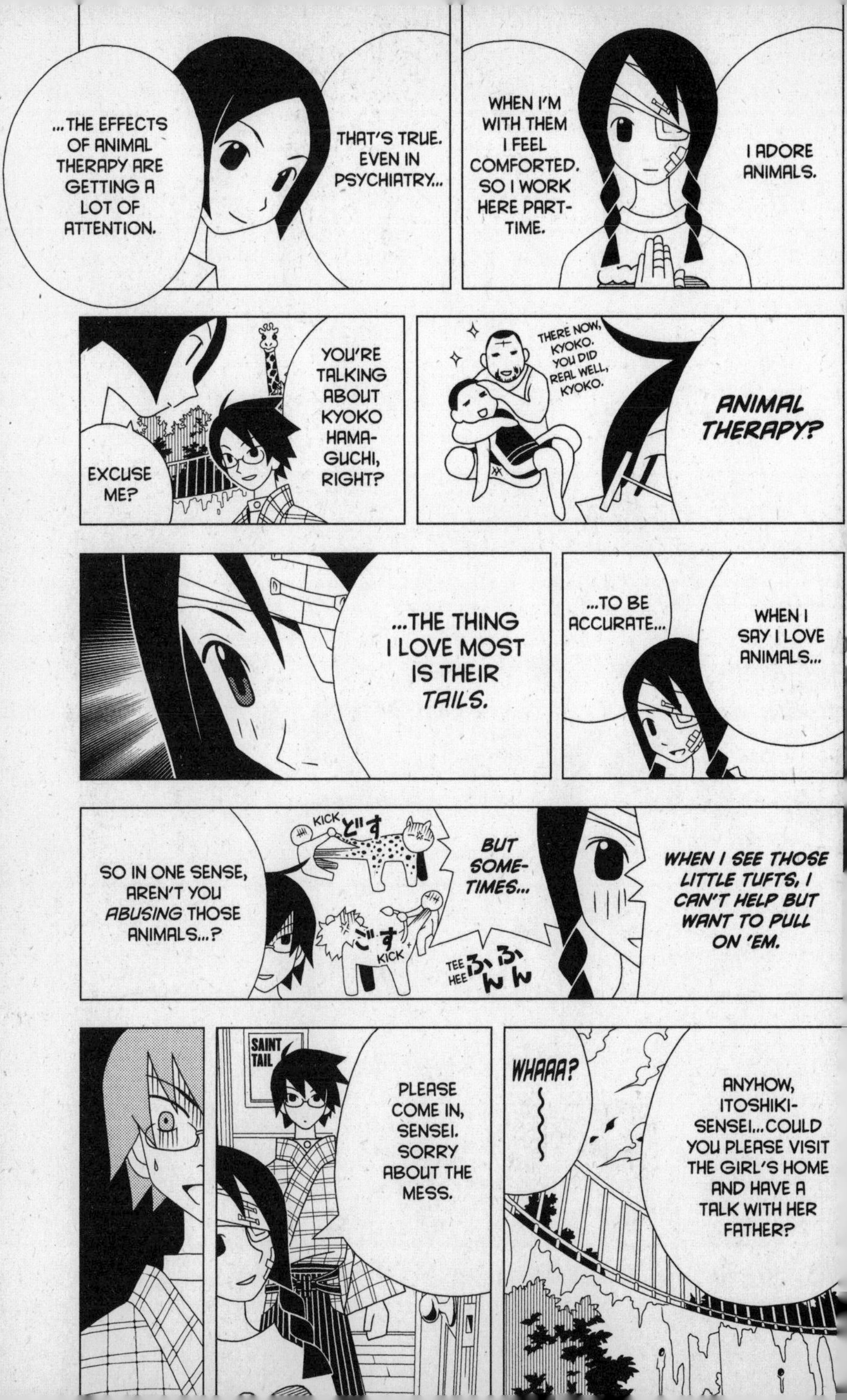
I ADORE ANIMALS.
WHEN I'M WITH THEM I FEEL COMFORTED. SO I WORK HERE PART-TIME.
THAT'S TRUE. EVEN IN PSYCHIATRY...
...THE EFFECTS OF ANIMAL THERAPY ARE GETTING A LOT OF ATTENTION.
ANIMAL THERAPY?
THERE NOW, KYOKO. YOU DID REAL WELL, KYOKO.
YOU'RE TALKING ABOUT KYOKO HAMA-GUCHI, RIGHT?
EXCUSE ME?
WHEN I SAY I LOVE ANIMALS...
...TO BE ACCURATE...
...THE THING I LOVE MOST IS THEIR TAILS.
WHEN I SEE THOSE LITTLE TUFTS, I CAN'T HELP BUT WANT TO PULL ON 'EM.
BUT SOMETIMES...
TEE HEE ふんふん
KICK どす
ごす KICK
SO IN ONE SENSE, AREN'T YOU ABUSING THOSE ANIMALS...?
ANYHOW, ITOSHIKI-SENSEI...COULD YOU PLEASE VISIT THE GIRL'S HOME AND HAVE A TALK WITH HER FATHER?
WHAAA?
SAINT TAIL
PLEASE COME IN, SENSEI. SORRY ABOUT THE MESS.

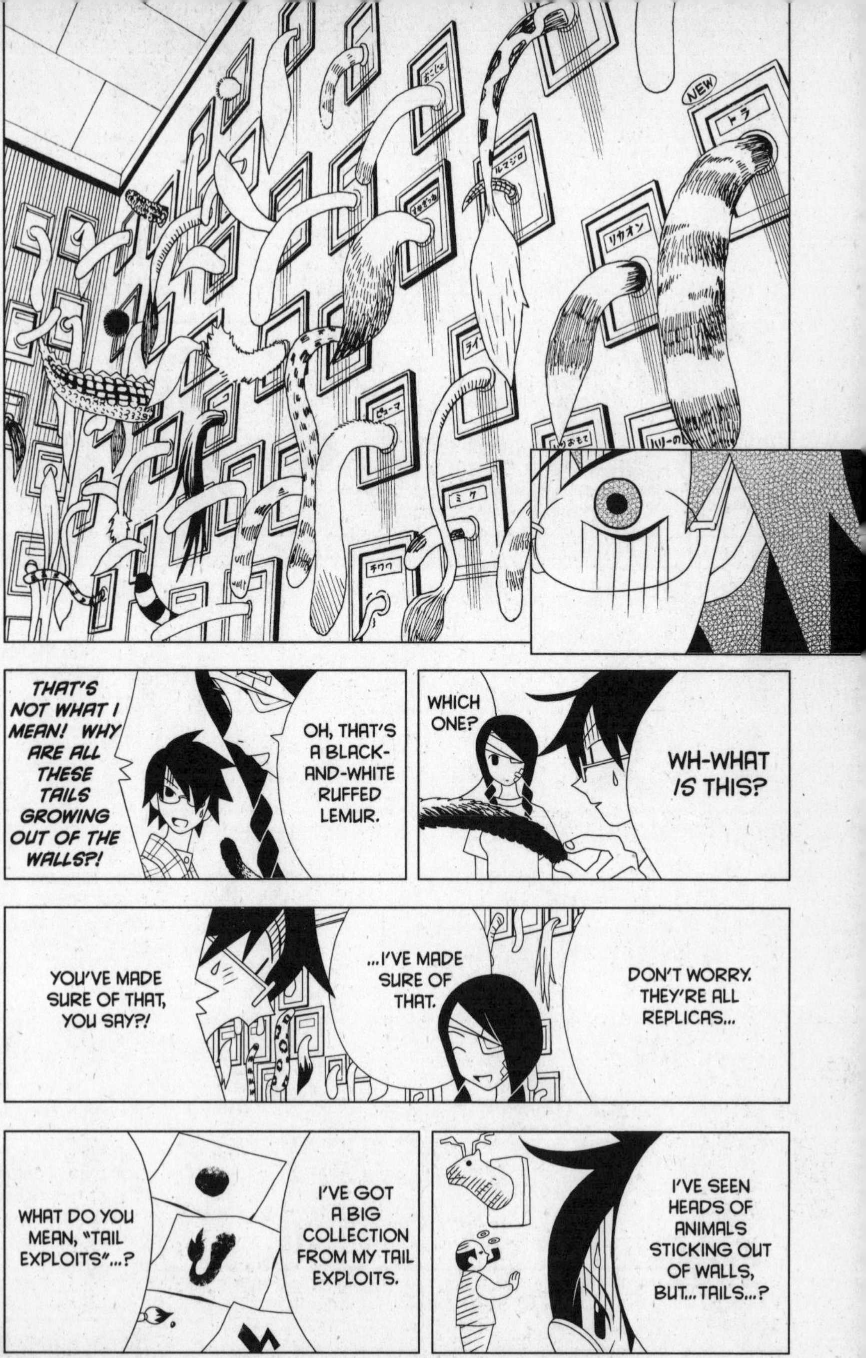
NEW
トラ
リカオン
ミケ
チワワ
WH-WHAT *IS* THIS?
WHICH ONE?
OH, THAT'S A BLACK-AND-WHITE RUFFED LEMUR.
THAT'S NOT WHAT I MEAN! WHY ARE ALL THESE TAILS GROWING OUT OF THE WALLS?!
DON'T WORRY. THEY'RE ALL REPLICAS...
...I'VE MADE SURE OF THAT.
YOU'VE MADE SURE OF THAT, YOU SAY?!
I'VE SEEN HEADS OF ANIMALS STICKING OUT OF WALLS, BUT...TAILS...?
I'VE GOT A BIG COLLECTION FROM MY TAIL EXPLOITS.
WHAT DO YOU MEAN, "TAIL EXPLOITS"...?

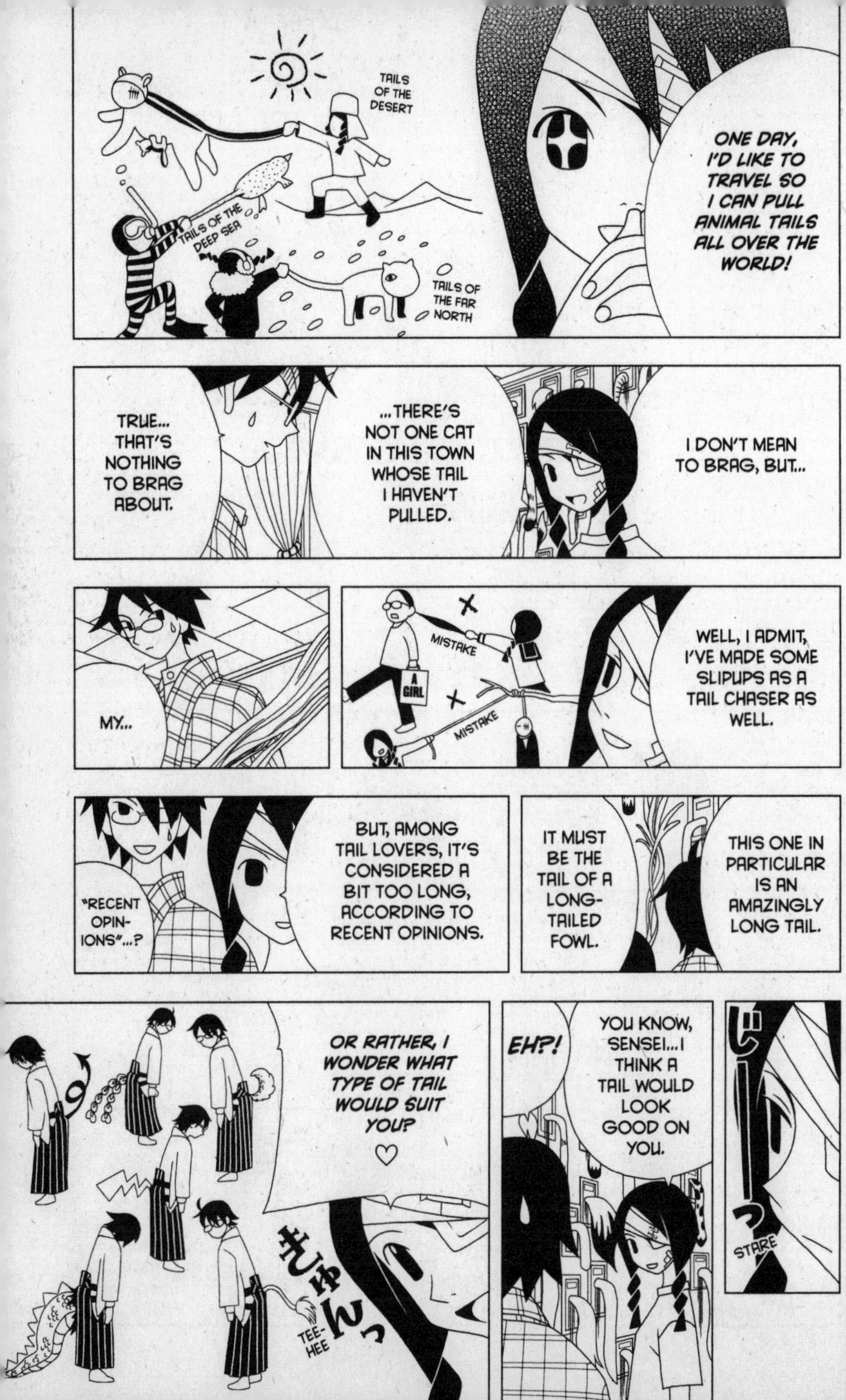
ONE DAY, I'D LIKE TO TRAVEL SO I CAN PULL ANIMAL TAILS ALL OVER THE WORLD!
TAILS OF THE DESERT
TAILS OF THE DEEP SEA
TAILS OF THE FAR NORTH
I DON'T MEAN TO BRAG, BUT...
...THERE'S NOT ONE CAT IN THIS TOWN WHOSE TAIL I HAVEN'T PULLED.
TRUE... THAT'S NOTHING TO BRAG ABOUT.
WELL, I ADMIT, I'VE MADE SOME SLIPUPS AS A TAIL CHASER AS WELL.
MISTAKE
A GIRL
MISTAKE
MY...
THIS ONE IN PARTICULAR IS AN AMAZINGLY LONG TAIL.
IT MUST BE THE TAIL OF A LONG-TAILED FOWL.
BUT, AMONG TAIL LOVERS, IT'S CONSIDERED A BIT TOO LONG, ACCORDING TO RECENT OPINIONS.
"RECENT OPINIONS"...?
じーっ
STARE
YOU KNOW, SENSEI...I THINK A TAIL WOULD LOOK GOOD ON YOU.
EH?!
OR RATHER, I WONDER WHAT TYPE OF TAIL WOULD SUIT YOU? ♡
きゅんっ
TEE-HEE

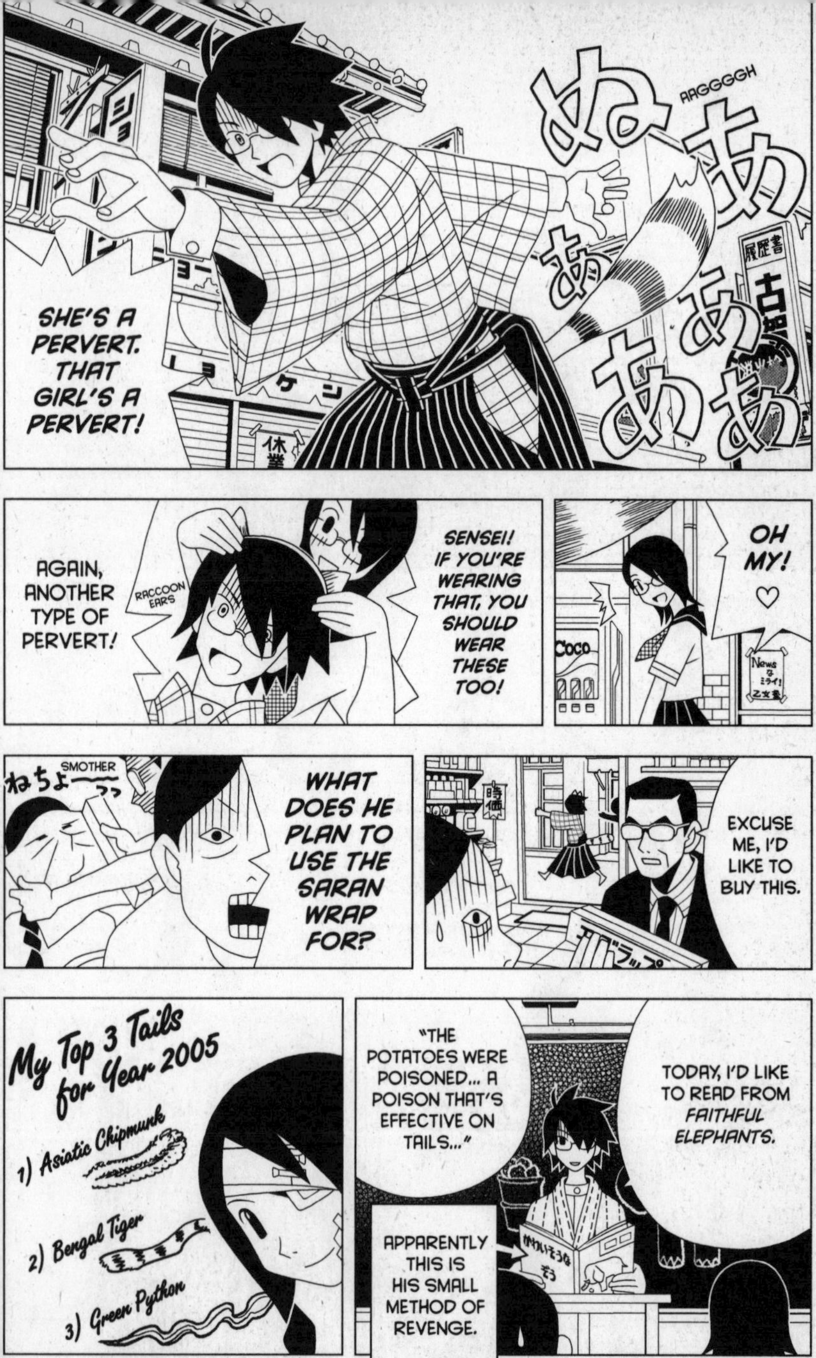
ぬあああああ
RAGGGGH
SHE'S A PERVERT. THAT GIRL'S A PERVERT!
履歴書
休業
OH MY! ♡
Coco
SENSEI! IF YOU'RE WEARING THAT, YOU SHOULD WEAR THESE TOO!
RACCOON EARS
AGAIN, ANOTHER TYPE OF PERVERT!
EXCUSE ME, I'D LIKE TO BUY THIS.
時価
WHAT DOES HE PLAN TO USE THE SARAN WRAP FOR?
ねちょーー
SMOTHER
TODAY, I'D LIKE TO READ FROM FAITHFUL ELEPHANTS.
"THE POTATOES WERE POISONED... A POISON THAT'S EFFECTIVE ON TAILS..."
かわいそうな ぞう
APPARENTLY THIS IS HIS SMALL METHOD OF REVENGE.
My Top 3 Tails for Year 2005
1) Asiatic Chipmunk
2) Bengal Tiger
3) Green Python

# ATTENDANCE LIST
## CLASS 2-F

**ATTENDANCE NO. 19**
## ABIRU KOBUSHI
**HAS TAIL FETISH, THOUGHT TO BE
VICTIM OF DOMESTIC VIOLENCE**

2005.05.25

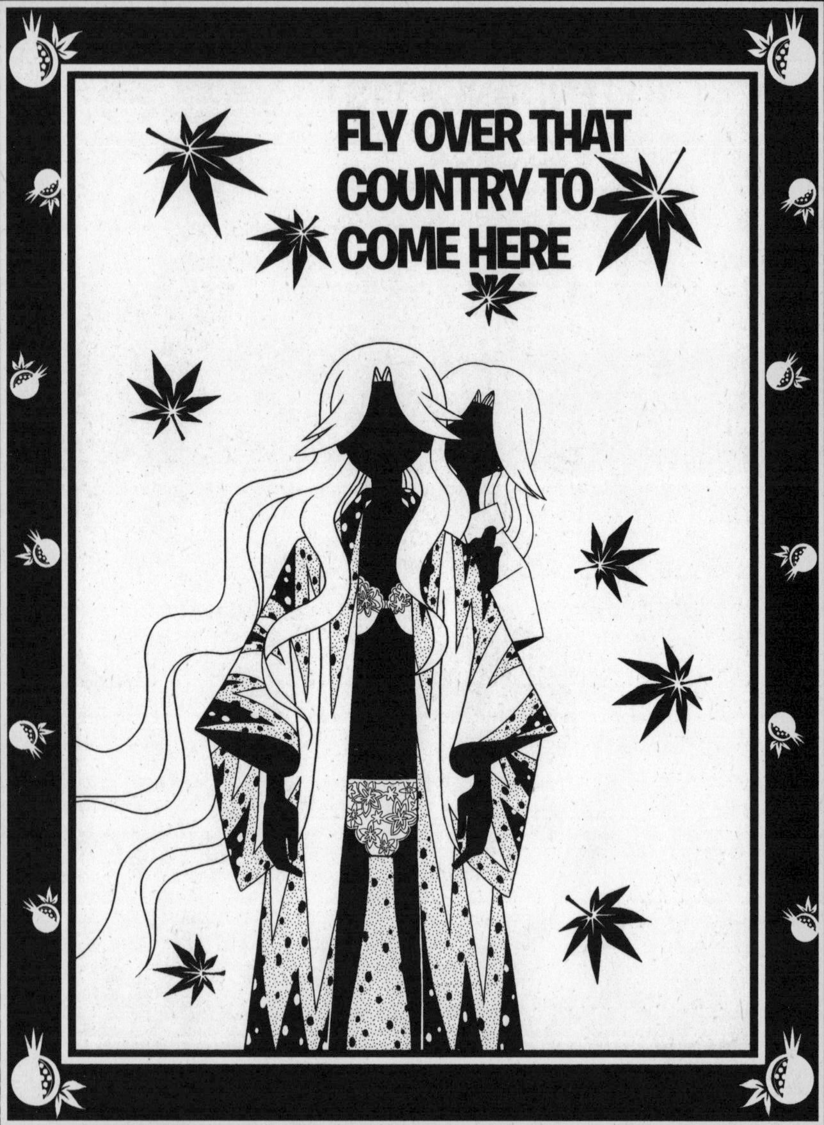
FLY OVER THAT
COUNTRY TO
COME HERE

# CHAPTER 6

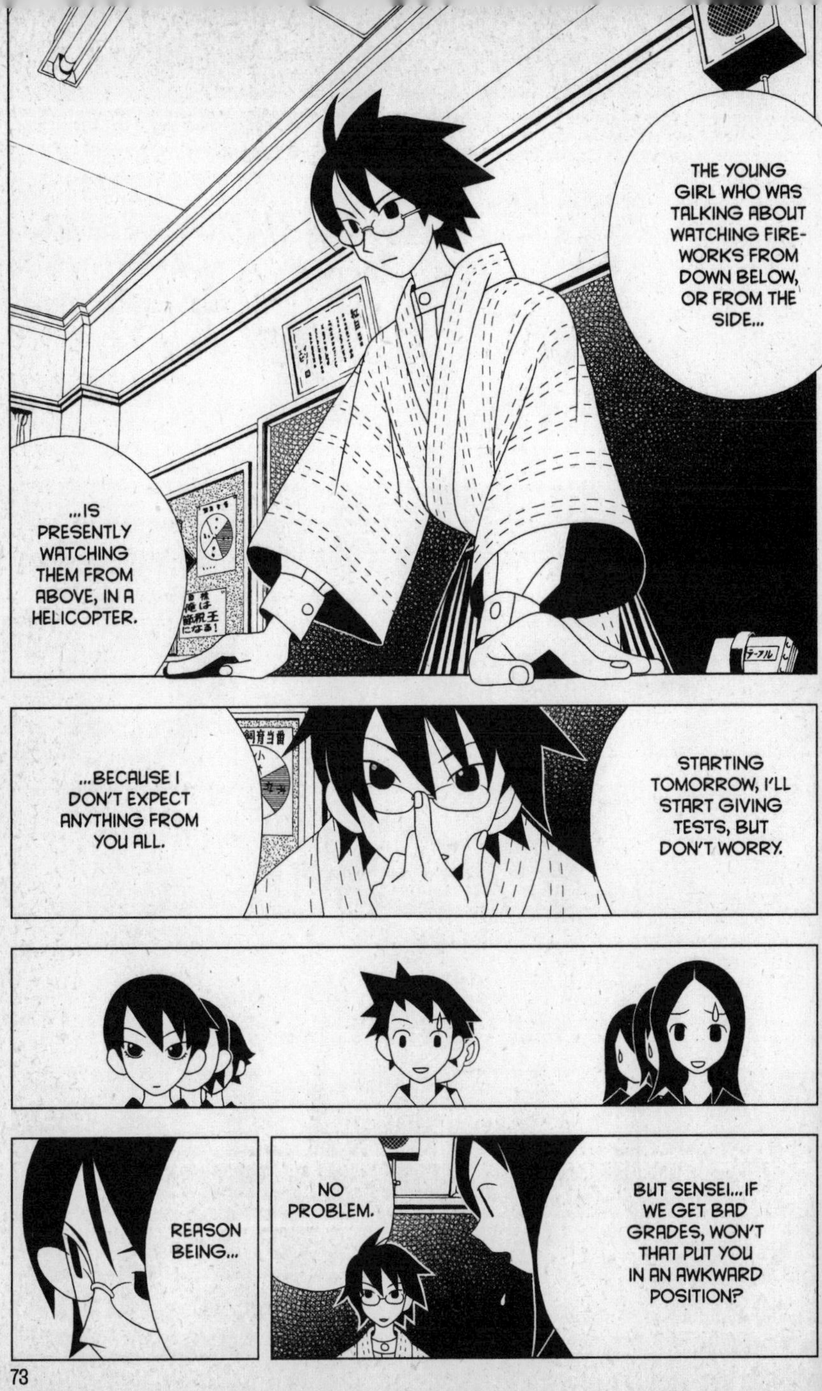
THE YOUNG GIRL WHO WAS TALKING ABOUT WATCHING FIRE-WORKS FROM DOWN BELOW, OR FROM THE SIDE...
...IS PRESENTLY WATCHING THEM FROM ABOVE, IN A HELICOPTER.
STARTING TOMORROW, I'LL START GIVING TESTS, BUT DON'T WORRY.
...BECAUSE I DON'T EXPECT ANYTHING FROM YOU ALL.
BUT SENSEI...IF WE GET BAD GRADES, WON'T THAT PUT YOU IN AN AWKWARD POSITION?
NO PROBLEM.
REASON BEING...

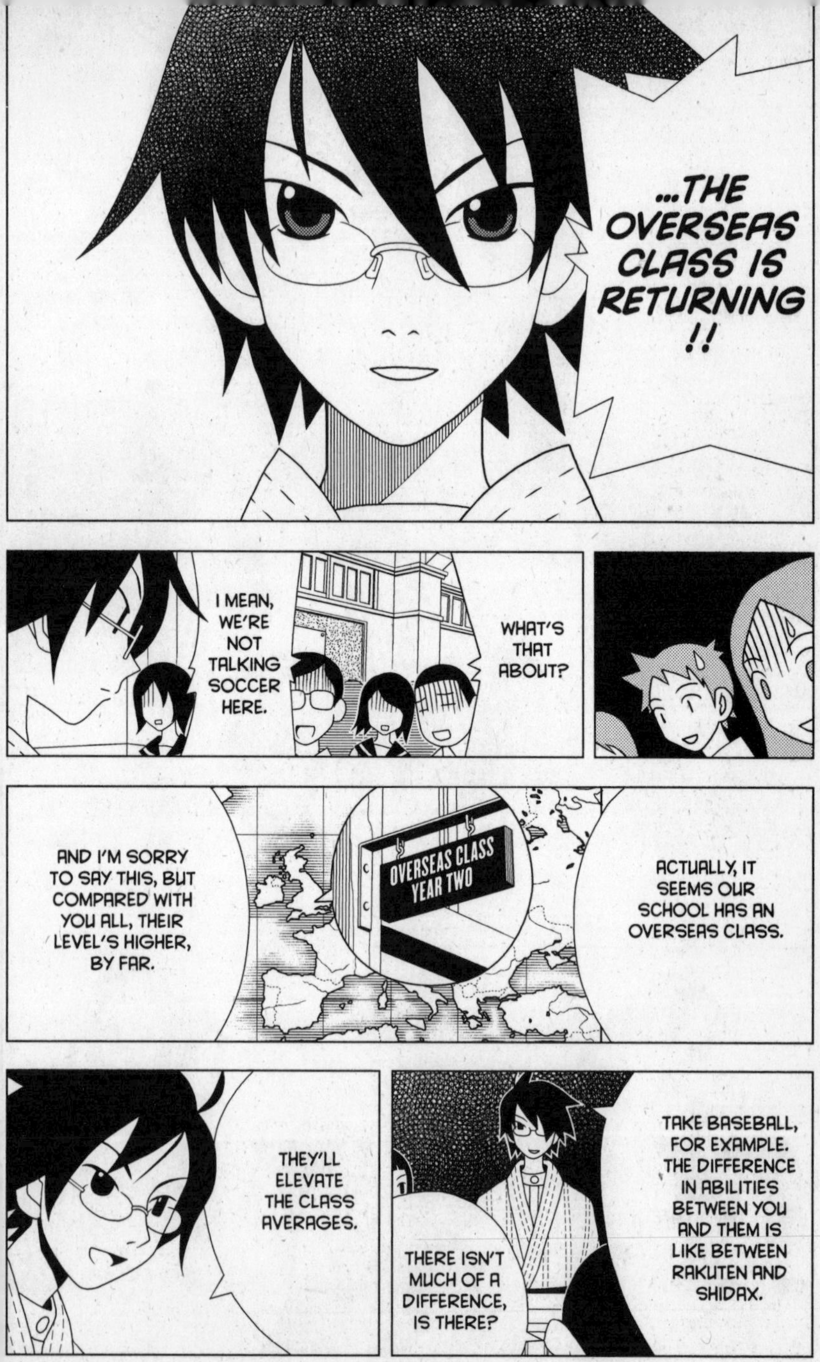

...THE OVERSEAS CLASS IS RETURNING !!
WHAT'S THAT ABOUT?
I MEAN, WE'RE NOT TALKING SOCCER HERE.
ACTUALLY, IT SEEMS OUR SCHOOL HAS AN OVERSEAS CLASS.
OVERSEAS CLASS YEAR TWO
AND I'M SORRY TO SAY THIS, BUT COMPARED WITH YOU ALL, THEIR LEVEL'S HIGHER, BY FAR.
TAKE BASEBALL, FOR EXAMPLE. THE DIFFERENCE IN ABILITIES BETWEEN YOU AND THEM IS LIKE BETWEEN RAKUTEN AND SHIDAX.
THERE ISN'T MUCH OF A DIFFERENCE, IS THERE?
THEY'LL ELEVATE THE CLASS AVERAGES.

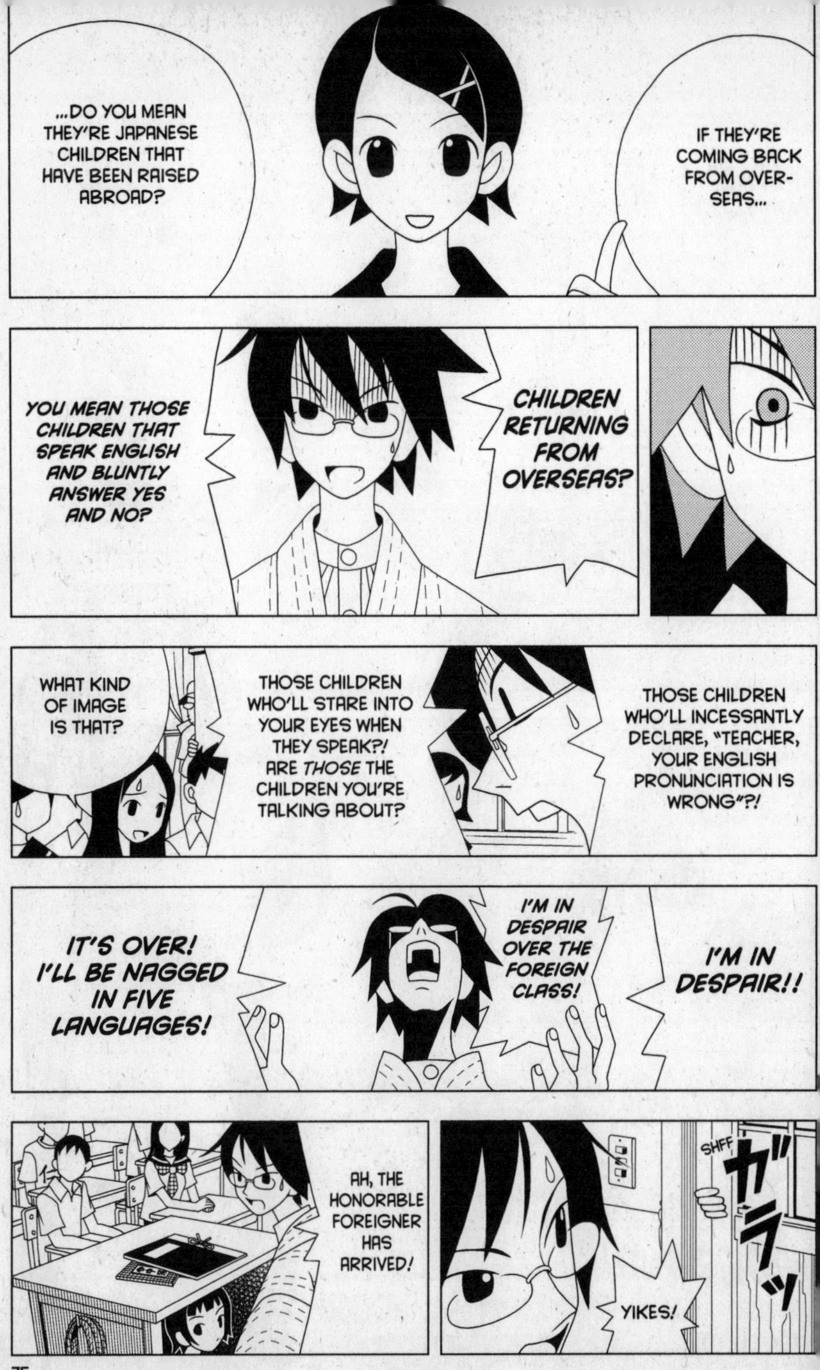
IF THEY'RE COMING BACK FROM OVER-SEAS...
...DO YOU MEAN THEY'RE JAPANESE CHILDREN THAT HAVE BEEN RAISED ABROAD?
CHILDREN RETURNING FROM OVERSEAS?
YOU MEAN THOSE CHILDREN THAT SPEAK ENGLISH AND BLUNTLY ANSWER YES AND NO?
THOSE CHILDREN WHO'LL INCESSANTLY DECLARE, "TEACHER, YOUR ENGLISH PRONUNCIATION IS WRONG"?!
THOSE CHILDREN WHO'LL STARE INTO YOUR EYES WHEN THEY SPEAK?! ARE *THOSE* THE CHILDREN YOU'RE TALKING ABOUT?
WHAT KIND OF IMAGE IS THAT?
I'M IN DESPAIR!!
I'M IN DESPAIR OVER THE FOREIGN CLASS!
IT'S OVER! I'LL BE NAGGED IN FIVE LANGUAGES!
SHFF
ガラッ
YIKES!
AH, THE HONORABLE FOREIGNER HAS ARRIVED!

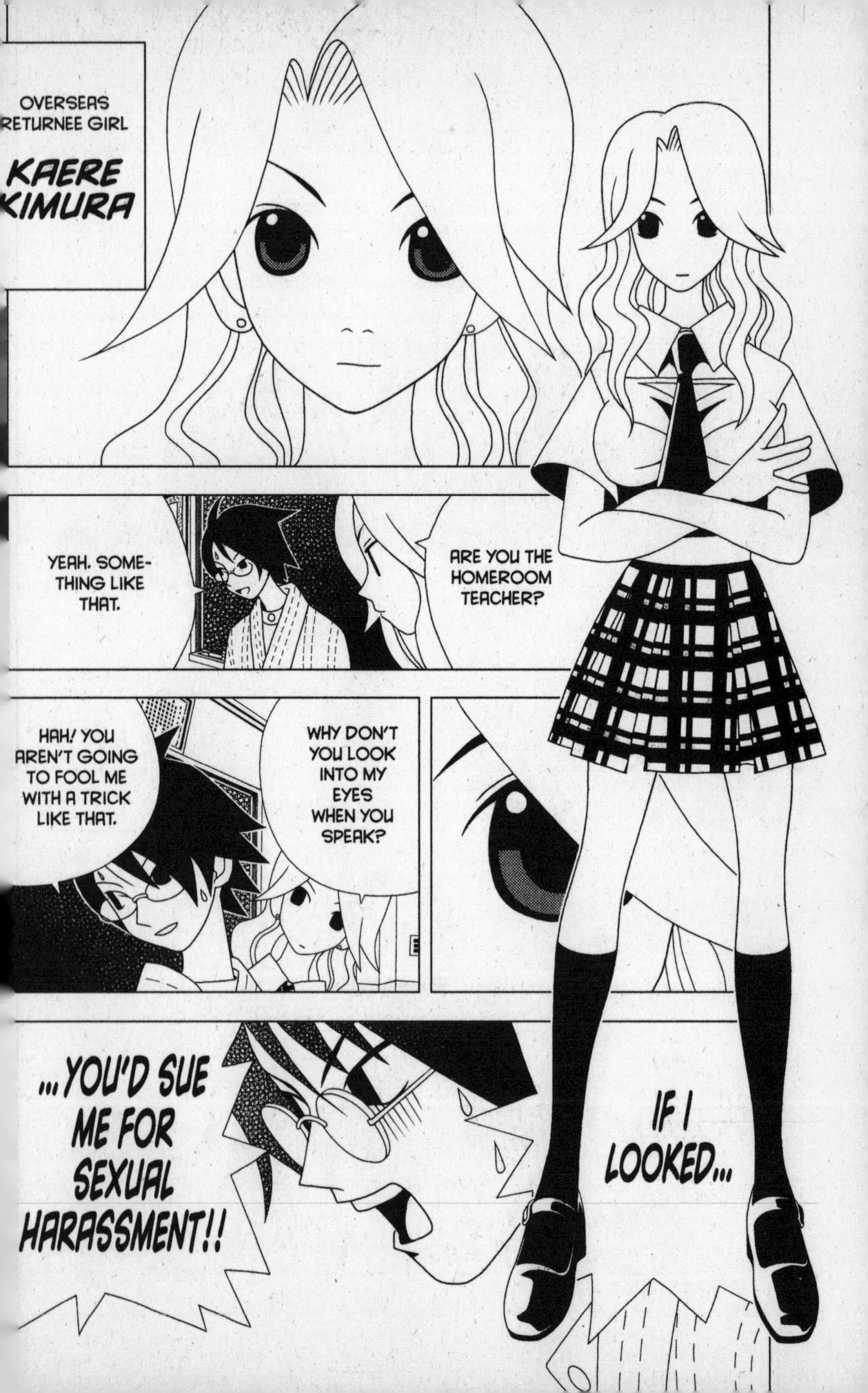
OVERSEAS RETURNEE GIRL
KAERE KIMURA
ARE YOU THE HOMEROOM TEACHER?
YEAH. SOME-THING LIKE THAT.
WHY DON'T YOU LOOK INTO MY EYES WHEN YOU SPEAK?
HAH! YOU AREN'T GOING TO FOOL ME WITH A TRICK LIKE THAT.
IF I LOOKED...
...YOU'D SUE ME FOR SEXUAL HARASSMENT!!

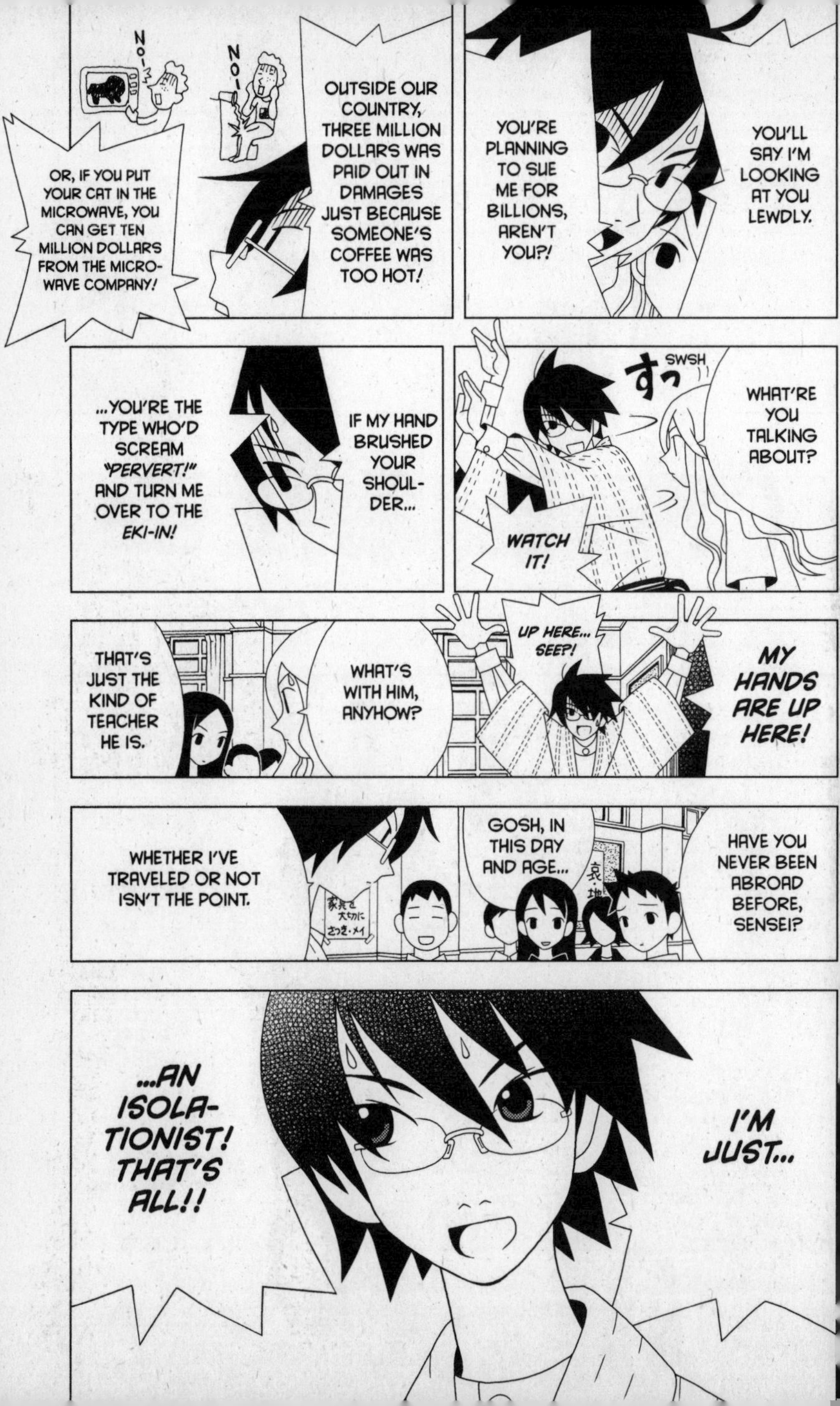
YOU'LL SAY I'M LOOKING AT YOU LEWDLY.
YOU'RE PLANNING TO SUE ME FOR BILLIONS, AREN'T YOU?!
OUTSIDE OUR COUNTRY, THREE MILLION DOLLARS WAS PAID OUT IN DAMAGES JUST BECAUSE SOMEONE'S COFFEE WAS TOO HOT!
OR, IF YOU PUT YOUR CAT IN THE MICROWAVE, YOU CAN GET TEN MILLION DOLLARS FROM THE MICRO-WAVE COMPANY!
WHAT'RE YOU TALKING ABOUT?
すっ SWSH
WATCH IT!
IF MY HAND BRUSHED YOUR SHOUL-DER...
...YOU'RE THE TYPE WHO'D SCREAM *"PERVERT!"* AND TURN ME OVER TO THE *EKI-IN!*
MY HANDS ARE UP HERE!
UP HERE... SEE?!
WHAT'S WITH HIM, ANYHOW?
THAT'S JUST THE KIND OF TEACHER HE IS.
HAVE YOU NEVER BEEN ABROAD BEFORE, SENSEI?
GOSH, IN THIS DAY AND AGE...
WHETHER I'VE TRAVELED OR NOT ISN'T THE POINT.
I'M JUST...
...AN ISOLATIONIST! THAT'S ALL!!

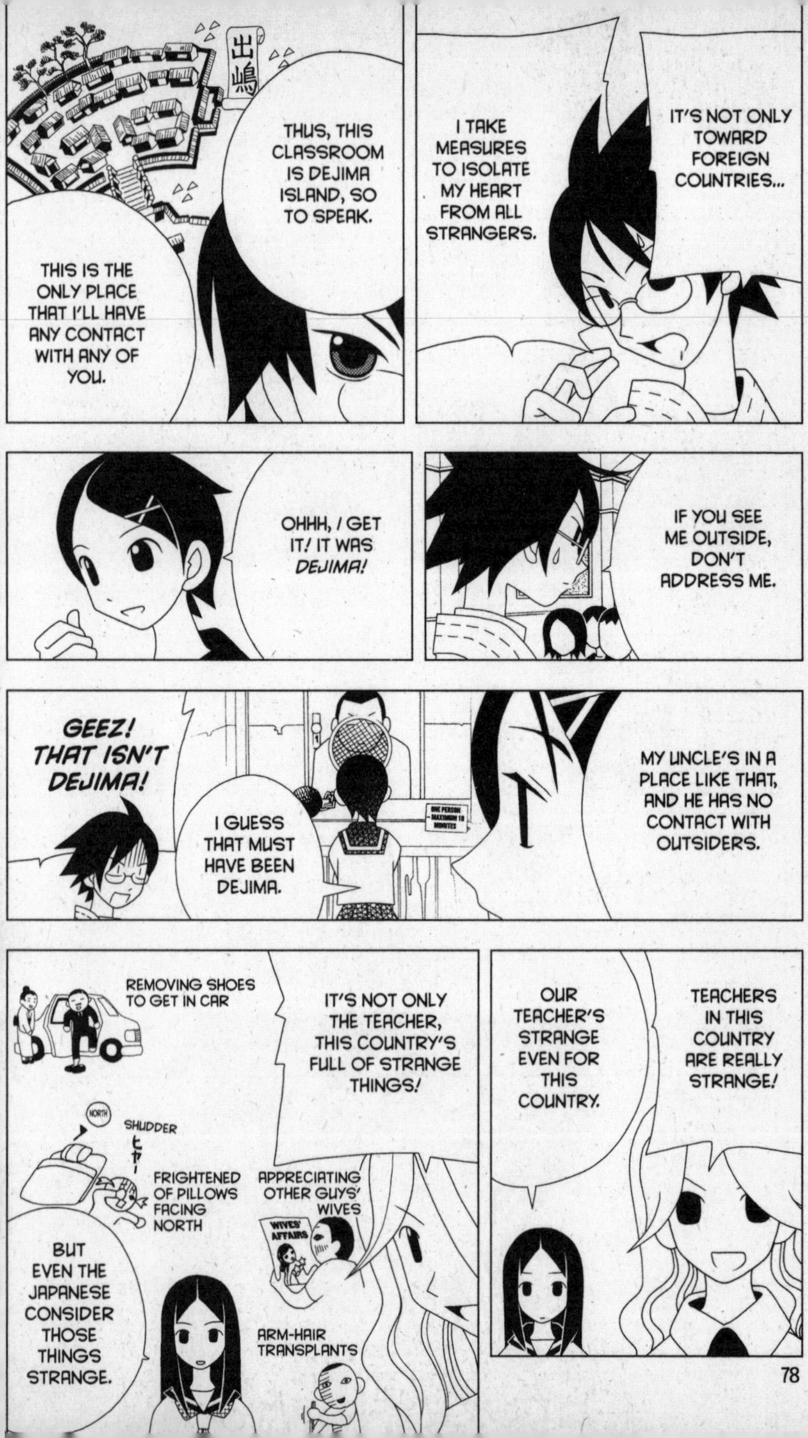
IT'S NOT ONLY TOWARD FOREIGN COUNTRIES...
I TAKE MEASURES TO ISOLATE MY HEART FROM ALL STRANGERS.
出嶋
THUS, THIS CLASSROOM IS DEJIMA ISLAND, SO TO SPEAK.
THIS IS THE ONLY PLACE THAT I'LL HAVE ANY CONTACT WITH ANY OF YOU.
IF YOU SEE ME OUTSIDE, DON'T ADDRESS ME.
OHHH, I GET IT! IT WAS *DEJIMA!*
MY UNCLE'S IN A PLACE LIKE THAT, AND HE HAS NO CONTACT WITH OUTSIDERS.
ONE PERSON MAXIMUM 10 MINUTES
I GUESS THAT MUST HAVE BEEN DEJIMA.
*GEEZ! THAT ISN'T DEJIMA!*
TEACHERS IN THIS COUNTRY ARE REALLY STRANGE!
OUR TEACHER'S STRANGE EVEN FOR THIS COUNTRY.
IT'S NOT ONLY THE TEACHER, THIS COUNTRY'S FULL OF STRANGE THINGS!
REMOVING SHOES TO GET IN CAR
NORTH
SHUDDER
FRIGHTENED OF PILLOWS FACING NORTH
APPRECIATING OTHER GUYS' WIVES
WIVES' AFFAIRS
ARM-HAIR TRANSPLANTS
BUT EVEN THE JAPANESE CONSIDER THOSE THINGS STRANGE.

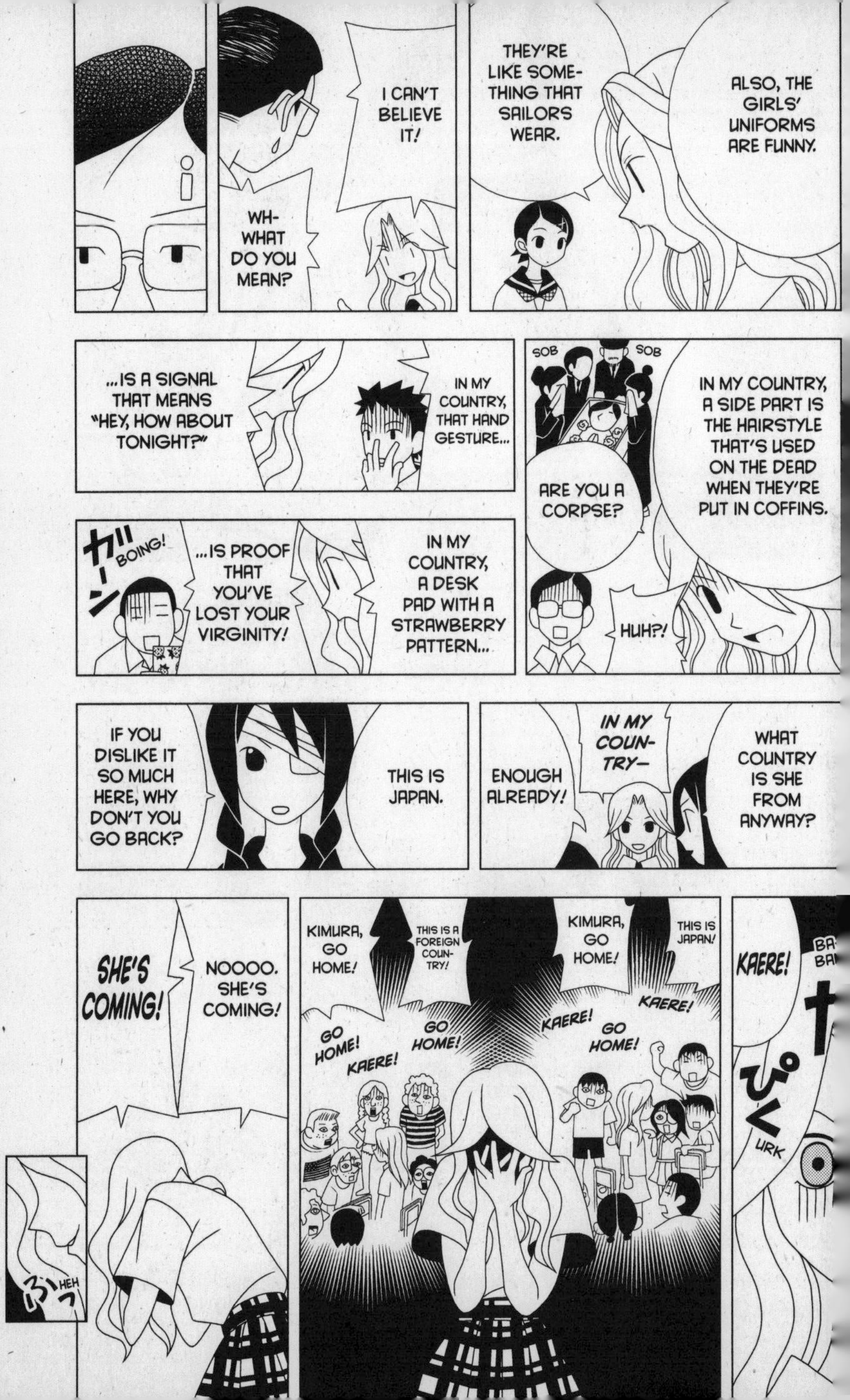

ALSO, THE GIRLS' UNIFORMS ARE FUNNY.
THEY'RE LIKE SOME-THING THAT SAILORS WEAR.
I CAN'T BELIEVE IT!
WH- WHAT DO YOU MEAN?
IN MY COUNTRY, A SIDE PART IS THE HAIRSTYLE THAT'S USED ON THE DEAD WHEN THEY'RE PUT IN COFFINS.
SOB
SOB
ARE YOU A CORPSE?
HUH?!
IN MY COUNTRY, THAT HAND GESTURE...
...IS A SIGNAL THAT MEANS "HEY, HOW ABOUT TONIGHT?"
IN MY COUNTRY, A DESK PAD WITH A STRAWBERRY PATTERN...
...IS PROOF THAT YOU'VE LOST YOUR VIRGINITY!
BOING!
WHAT COUNTRY IS SHE FROM ANYWAY?
IN MY COUN-TRY—
ENOUGH ALREADY!
THIS IS JAPAN.
IF YOU DISLIKE IT SO MUCH HERE, WHY DON'T YOU GO BACK?
KAERE!
URK
THIS IS JAPAN!
KIMURA, GO HOME!
THIS IS A FOREIGN COUN-TRY!
KIMURA, GO HOME!
KAERE!
KAERE!
GO HOME!
GO HOME!
GO HOME!
KAERE!
NOOOO. SHE'S COMING!
SHE'S COMING!
HEH

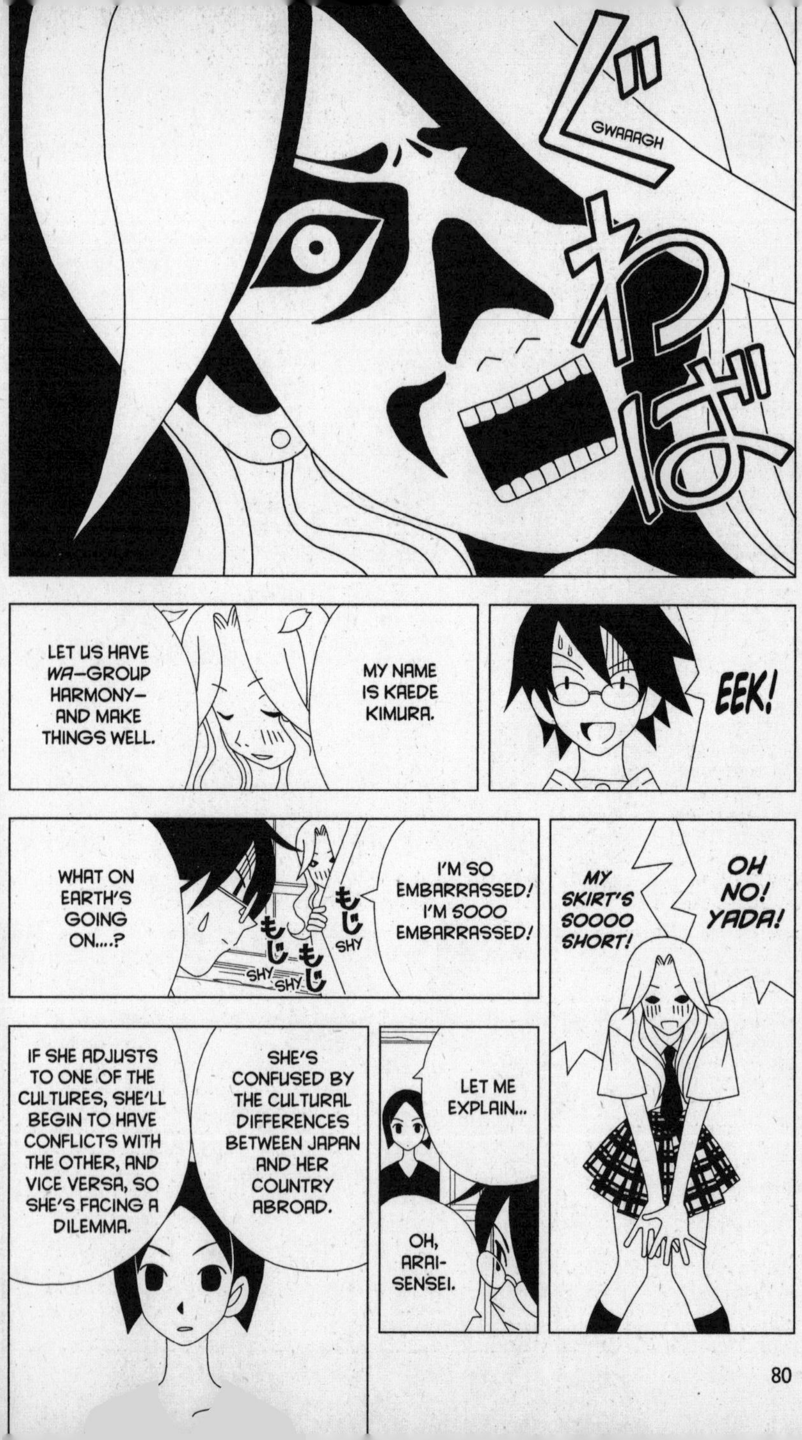
GWAAAGH
EEK!
MY NAME IS KAEDE KIMURA.
LET US HAVE *WA*—GROUP HARMONY—AND MAKE THINGS WELL.
OH NO! YADA!
MY SKIRT'S SOOOO SHORT!
I'M SO EMBARRASSED! I'M SOOO EMBARRASSED!
SHY
SHY
SHY
WHAT ON EARTH'S GOING ON....?
LET ME EXPLAIN...
OH, ARAI-SENSEI.
SHE'S CONFUSED BY THE CULTURAL DIFFERENCES BETWEEN JAPAN AND HER COUNTRY ABROAD.
IF SHE ADJUSTS TO ONE OF THE CULTURES, SHE'LL BEGIN TO HAVE CONFLICTS WITH THE OTHER, AND VICE VERSA, SO SHE'S FACING A DILEMMA.

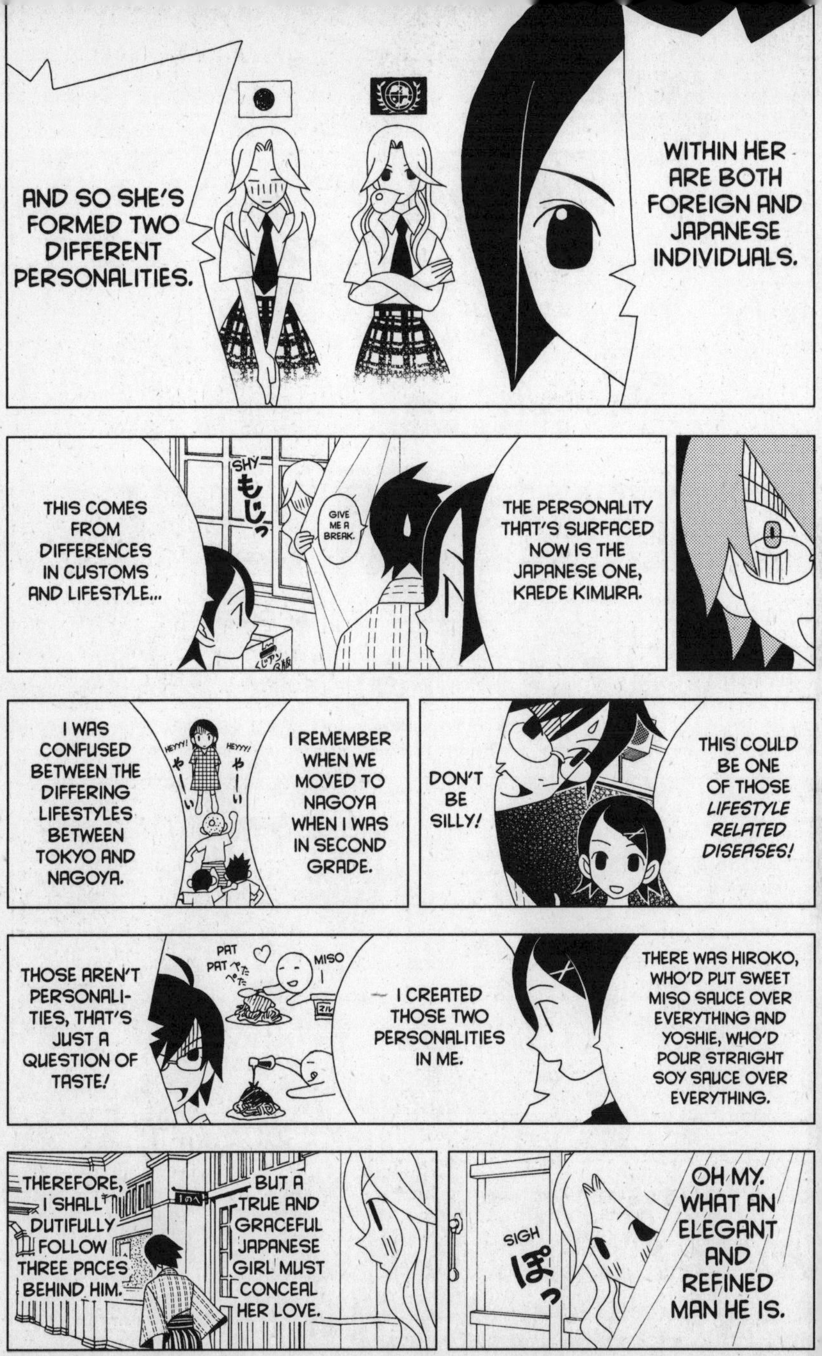
WITHIN HER ARE BOTH FOREIGN AND JAPANESE INDIVIDUALS.
AND SO SHE'S FORMED TWO DIFFERENT PERSONALITIES.
THE PERSONALITY THAT'S SURFACED NOW IS THE JAPANESE ONE, KAEDE KIMURA.
GIVE ME A BREAK.
SHY もじっ
THIS COMES FROM DIFFERENCES IN CUSTOMS AND LIFESTYLE...
THIS COULD BE ONE OF THOSE *LIFESTYLE RELATED DISEASES!*
DON'T BE SILLY!
I REMEMBER WHEN WE MOVED TO NAGOYA WHEN I WAS IN SECOND GRADE.
HEYYY! やーい
HEYYY! やーい
I WAS CONFUSED BETWEEN THE DIFFERING LIFESTYLES BETWEEN TOKYO AND NAGOYA.
THERE WAS HIROKO, WHO'D PUT SWEET MISO SAUCE OVER EVERYTHING AND YOSHIE, WHO'D POUR STRAIGHT SOY SAUCE OVER EVERYTHING.
I CREATED THOSE TWO PERSONALITIES IN ME.
MISO
PAT PAT ぺたぺた
THOSE AREN'T PERSONALITIES, THAT'S JUST A QUESTION OF TASTE!
OH MY. WHAT AN ELEGANT AND REFINED MAN HE IS.
SIGH ぽっ
BUT A TRUE AND GRACEFUL JAPANESE GIRL MUST CONCEAL HER LOVE.
THEREFORE, I SHALL DUTIFULLY FOLLOW THREE PACES BEHIND HIM.

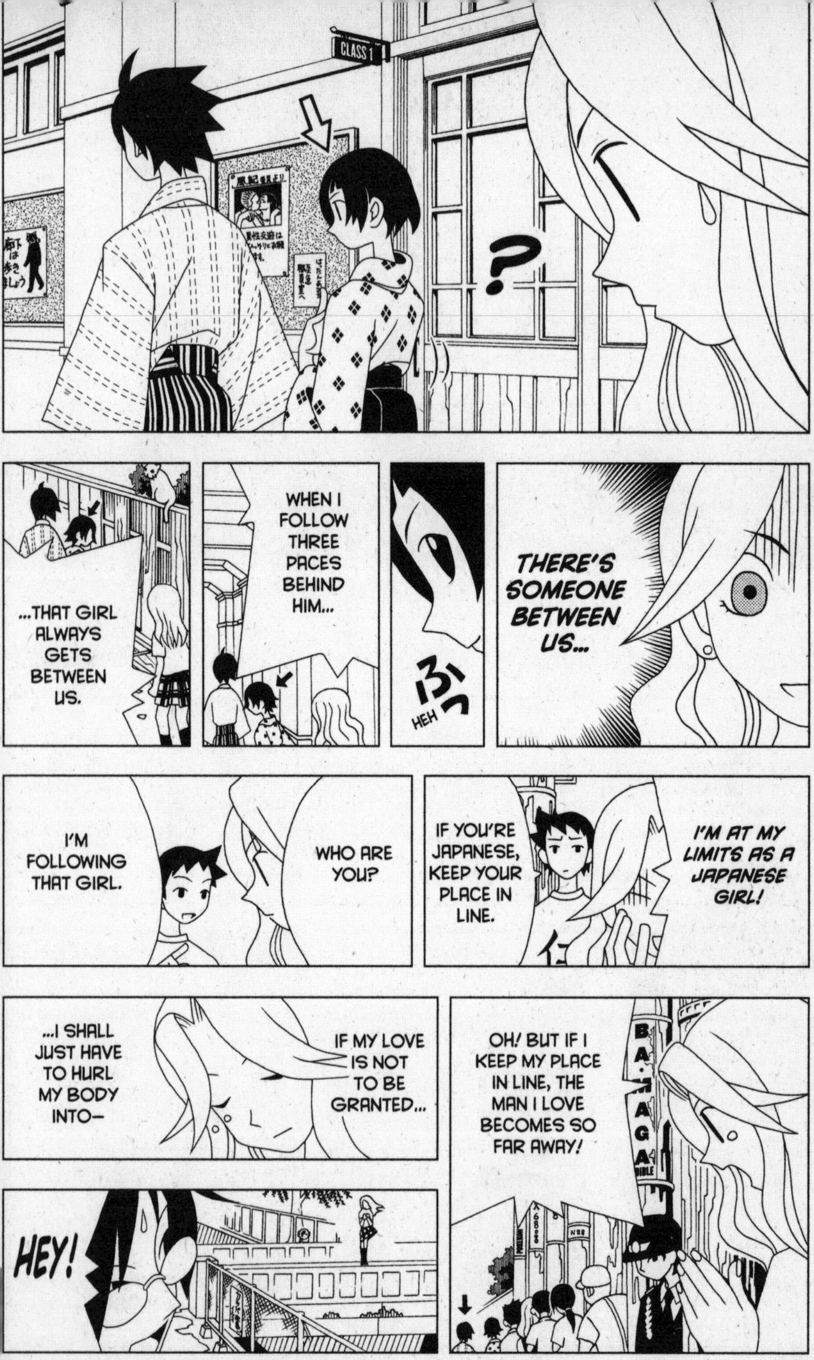
CLASS 1
?
THERE'S SOMEONE BETWEEN US...
ふっ
HEH
WHEN I FOLLOW THREE PACES BEHIND HIM...
...THAT GIRL ALWAYS GETS BETWEEN US.
I'M AT MY LIMITS AS A JAPANESE GIRL!
IF YOU'RE JAPANESE, KEEP YOUR PLACE IN LINE.
WHO ARE YOU?
I'M FOLLOWING THAT GIRL.
OH! BUT IF I KEEP MY PLACE IN LINE, THE MAN I LOVE BECOMES SO FAR AWAY!
IF MY LOVE IS NOT TO BE GRANTED...
...I SHALL JUST HAVE TO HURL MY BODY INTO–
HEY!

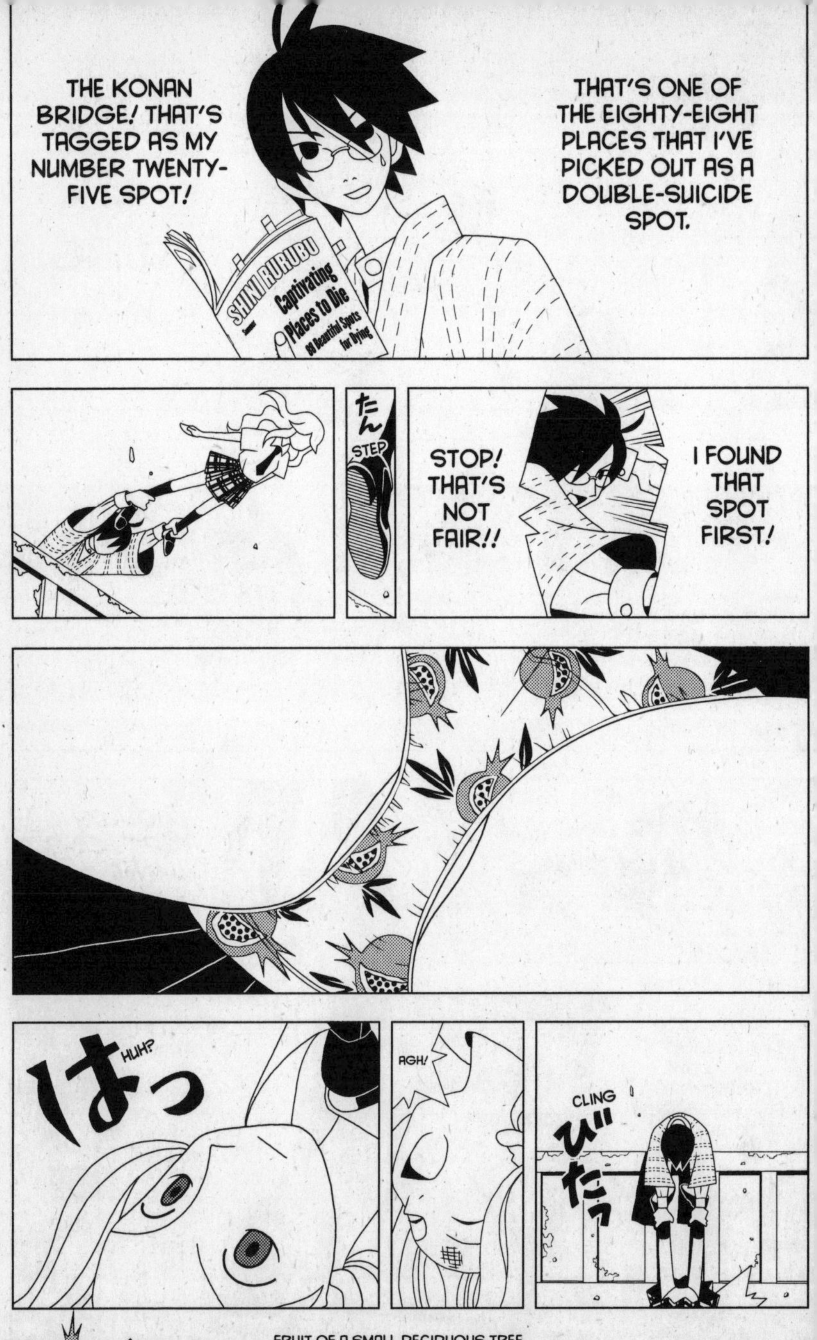
THE KONAN BRIDGE! THAT'S TAGGED AS MY NUMBER TWENTY-FIVE SPOT!
THAT'S ONE OF THE EIGHTY-EIGHT PLACES THAT I'VE PICKED OUT AS A DOUBLE-SUICIDE SPOT.
SHINI RURUBU
Captivating Places to Die
88 Beautiful Spots for Dying
たん
STEP
STOP! THAT'S NOT FAIR!!
I FOUND THAT SPOT FIRST!
はっ
HUH?
AGH!
びたっ
CLING

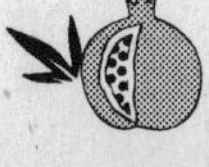
← POMEGRANATE FRUIT OF A SMALL DECIDUOUS TREE. RICHER IN CALCIUM THAN STRAWBERRIES.

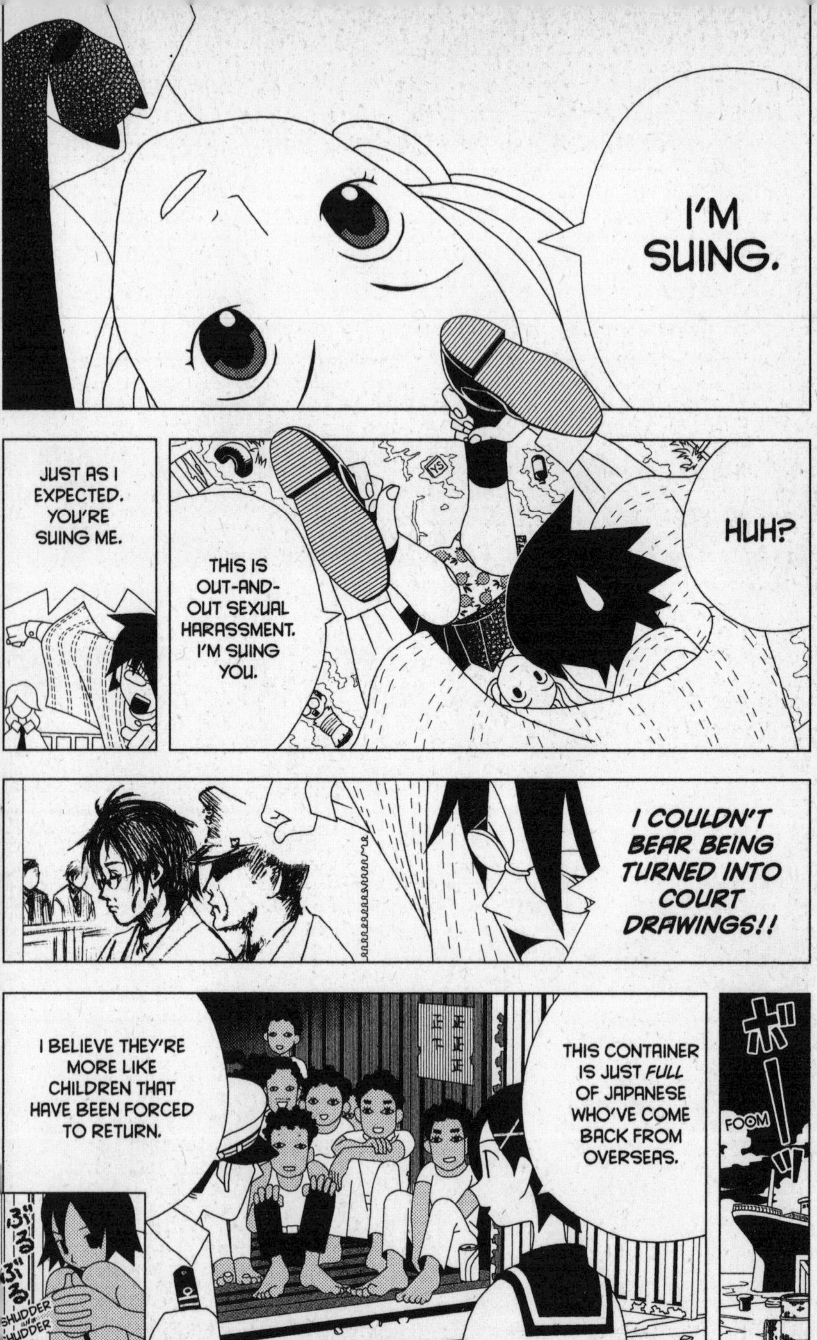

I'M SUING.
HUH?
THIS IS OUT-AND-OUT SEXUAL HARASSMENT. I'M SUING YOU.
JUST AS I EXPECTED. YOU'RE SUING ME.
I COULDN'T BEAR BEING TURNED INTO COURT DRAWINGS!!
ボーッ
FOOM
THIS CONTAINER IS JUST *FULL* OF JAPANESE WHO'VE COME BACK FROM OVERSEAS.
I BELIEVE THEY'RE MORE LIKE CHILDREN THAT HAVE BEEN FORCED TO RETURN.
ぶるぶる
SHUDDER SHUDDER

# ATTENDANCE LIST
## CLASS 2-F

ATTENDANCE NO. 18
# KAERE KIMURA
BILINGUAL GIRL

2005.06.

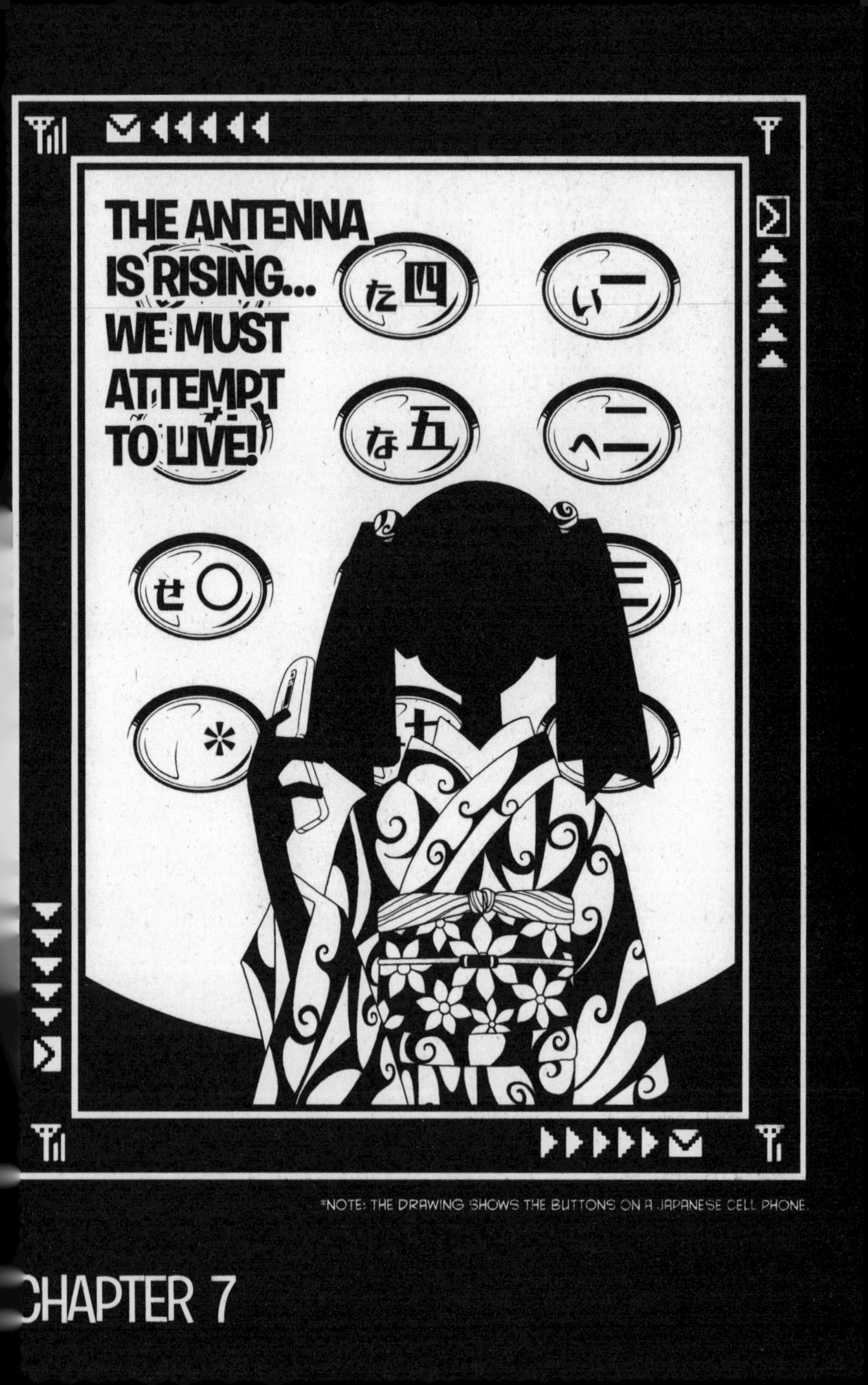
THE ANTENNA IS RISING... WE MUST ATTEMPT TO LIVE!
い一
た四
へ二
な五
三
せ〇
*

*NOTE: THE DRAWING SHOWS THE BUTTONS ON A JAPANESE CELL PHONE.

# CHAPTER 7

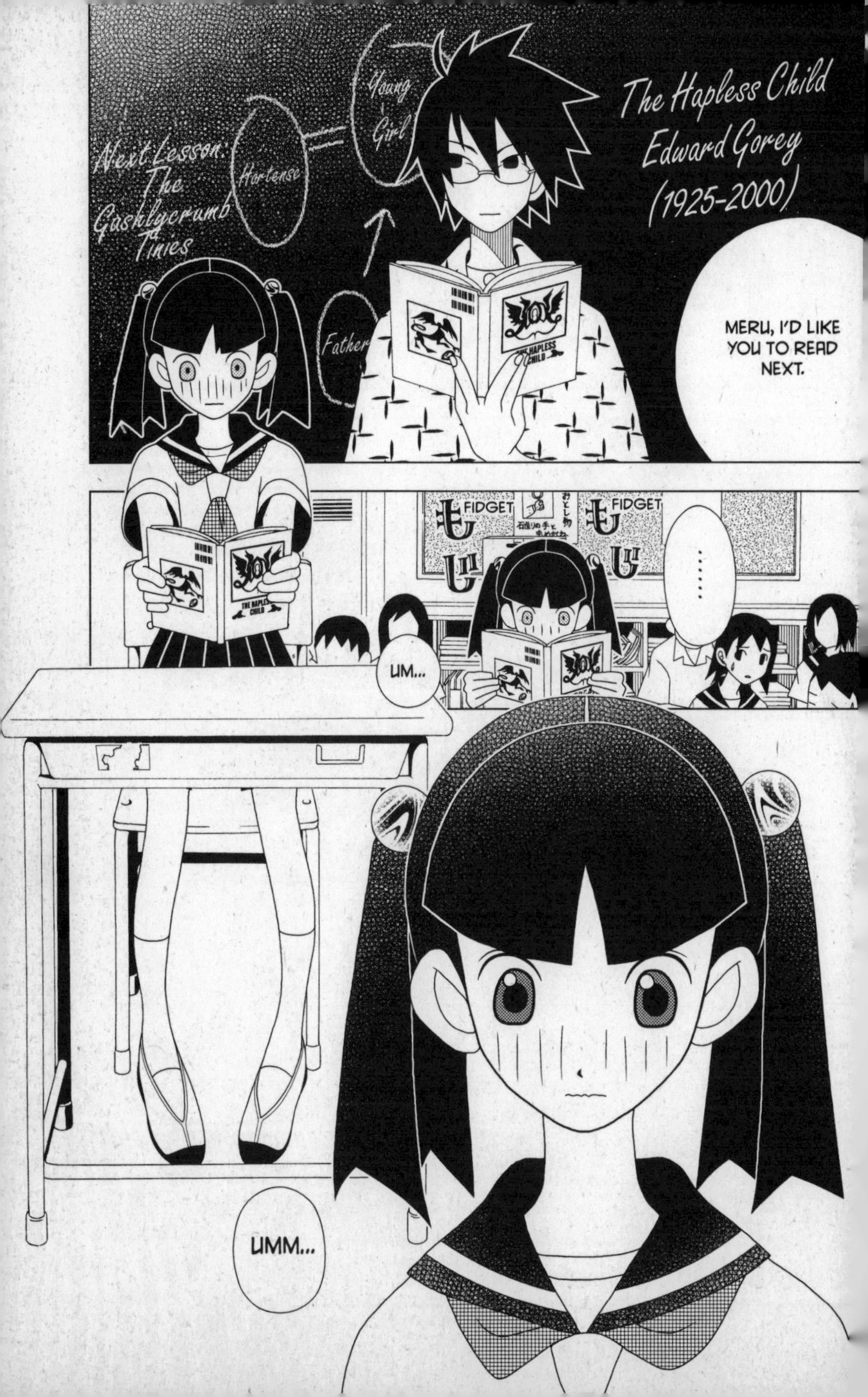
The Hapless Child
Edward Gorey
(1925-2000)
Young Girl
Hortense
Father
Next Lesson: The Gashlycrumb Tinies
THE HAPLESS CHILD
MERU, I'D LIKE YOU TO READ NEXT.
FIDGET
FIDGET
......
UM...
UMM...

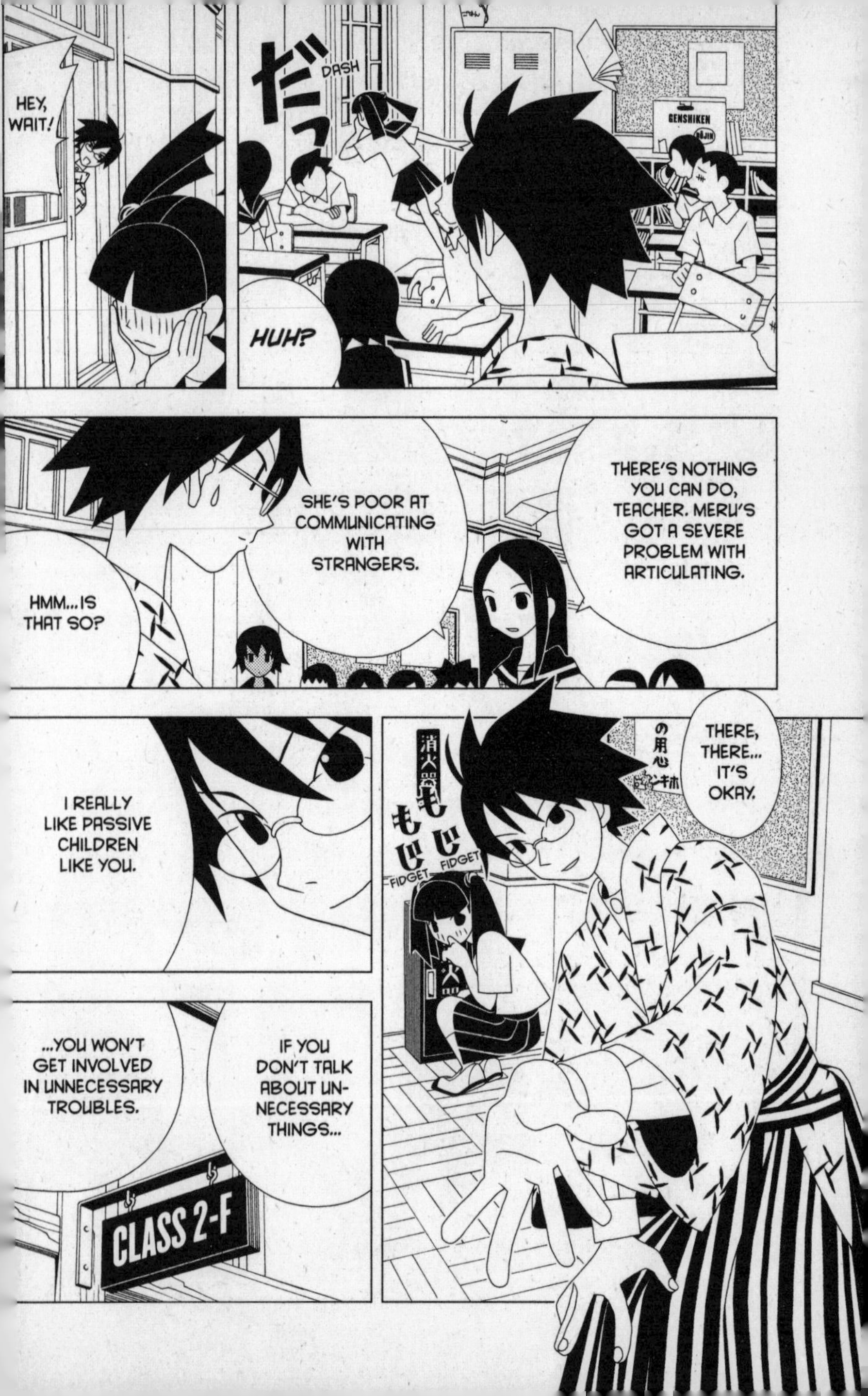
だっ
DASH
GENSHIKEN
DŌJIN
HUH?
HEY, WAIT!
THERE'S NOTHING YOU CAN DO, TEACHER. MERU'S GOT A SEVERE PROBLEM WITH ARTICULATING.
SHE'S POOR AT COMMUNICATING WITH STRANGERS.
HMM...IS THAT SO?
THERE, THERE... IT'S OKAY.
消火器
の用心
FIDGET
FIDGET
I REALLY LIKE PASSIVE CHILDREN LIKE YOU.
IF YOU DON'T TALK ABOUT UN-NECESSARY THINGS...
...YOU WON'T GET INVOLVED IN UNNECESSARY TROUBLES.
CLASS 2-F

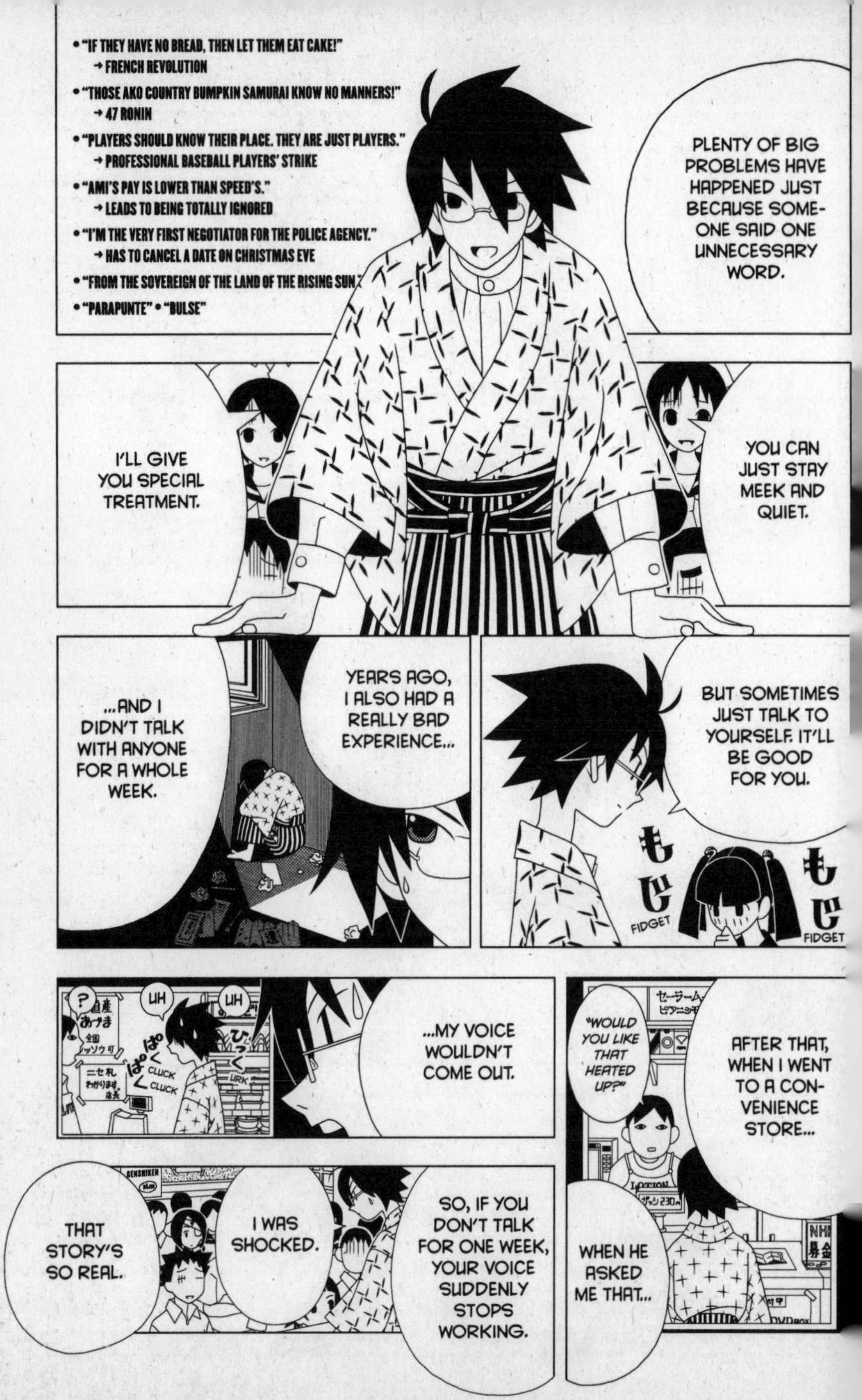
PLENTY OF BIG PROBLEMS HAVE HAPPENED JUST BECAUSE SOMEONE SAID ONE UNNECESSARY WORD.
• "IF THEY HAVE NO BREAD, THEN LET THEM EAT CAKE!" → FRENCH REVOLUTION
• "THOSE AKO COUNTRY BUMPKIN SAMURAI KNOW NO MANNERS!" → 47 RONIN
• "PLAYERS SHOULD KNOW THEIR PLACE. THEY ARE JUST PLAYERS." → PROFESSIONAL BASEBALL PLAYERS' STRIKE
• "AMI'S PAY IS LOWER THAN SPEED'S." → LEADS TO BEING TOTALLY IGNORED
• "I'M THE VERY FIRST NEGOTIATOR FOR THE POLICE AGENCY." → HAS TO CANCEL A DATE ON CHRISTMAS EVE
• "FROM THE SOVEREIGN OF THE LAND OF THE RISING SUN."
• "PARAPUNTE" • "BULSE"
YOU CAN JUST STAY MEEK AND QUIET.
I'LL GIVE YOU SPECIAL TREATMENT.
BUT SOMETIMES JUST TALK TO YOURSELF. IT'LL BE GOOD FOR YOU.
もじ FIDGET
もじ FIDGET
YEARS AGO, I ALSO HAD A REALLY BAD EXPERIENCE...
...AND I DIDN'T TALK WITH ANYONE FOR A WHOLE WEEK.
AFTER THAT, WHEN I WENT TO A CONVENIENCE STORE...
"WOULD YOU LIKE THAT HEATED UP?"
WHEN HE ASKED ME THAT...
...MY VOICE WOULDN'T COME OUT.
UH
UH
?
URK
ぱく CLICK
ぱく CLICK
SO, IF YOU DON'T TALK FOR ONE WEEK, YOUR VOICE SUDDENLY STOPS WORKING.
I WAS SHOCKED.
THAT STORY'S SO REAL.

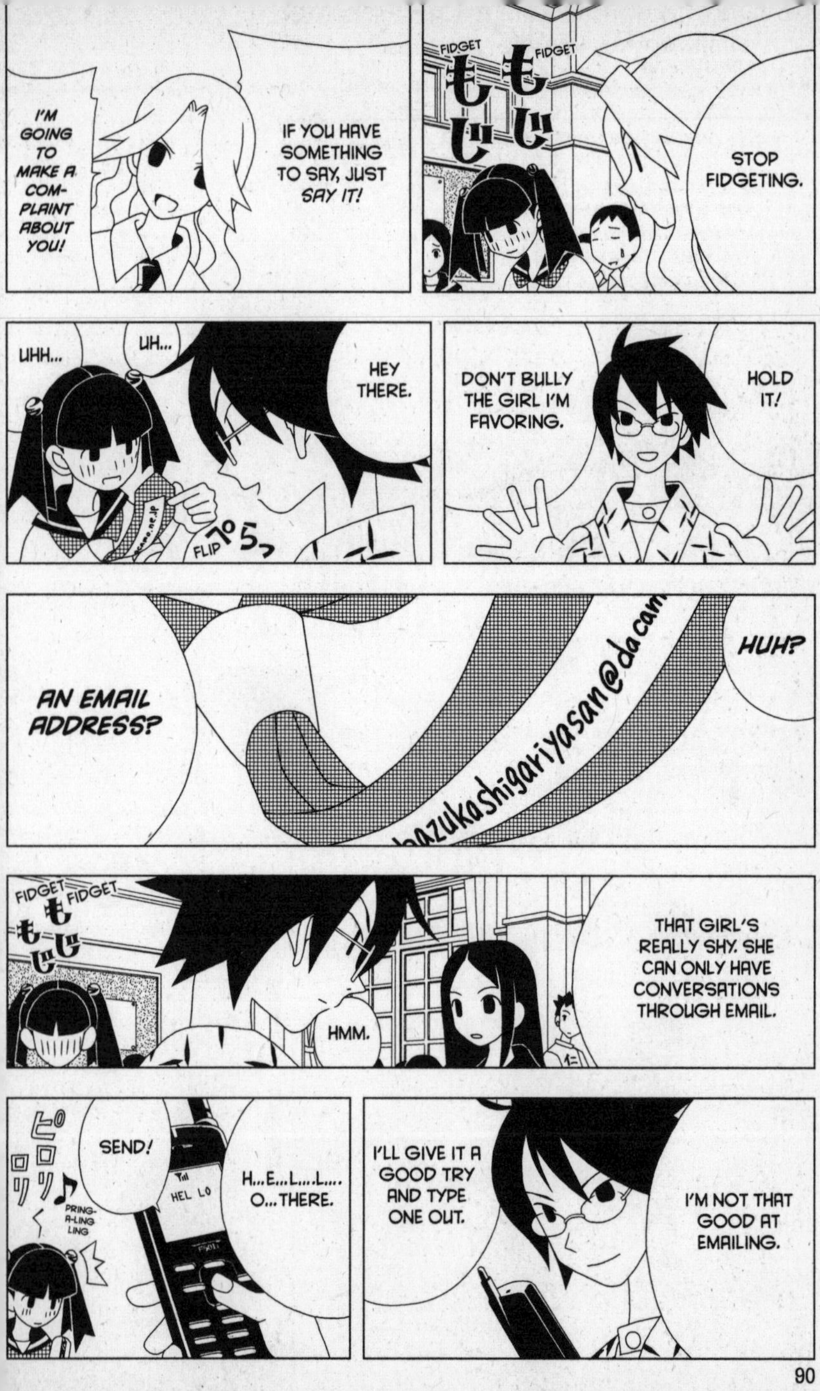
FIDGET
もじ
FIDGET
もじ
STOP FIDGETING.
IF YOU HAVE SOMETHING TO SAY, JUST SAY IT!
I'M GOING TO MAKE A COM-PLAINT ABOUT YOU!
HOLD IT!
DON'T BULLY THE GIRL I'M FAVORING.
HEY THERE.
UH...
UHH...
FLIP ぺらっ
HUH?
hazukashigariyasan@dacam
AN EMAIL ADDRESS?
THAT GIRL'S REALLY SHY. SHE CAN ONLY HAVE CONVERSATIONS THROUGH EMAIL.
HMM.
FIDGET FIDGET
もじもじ
I'M NOT THAT GOOD AT EMAILING.
I'LL GIVE IT A GOOD TRY AND TYPE ONE OUT.
H...E...L...L... O...THERE.
HEL LO
SEND!
ピロリロリ♪
PRING-A-LING LING

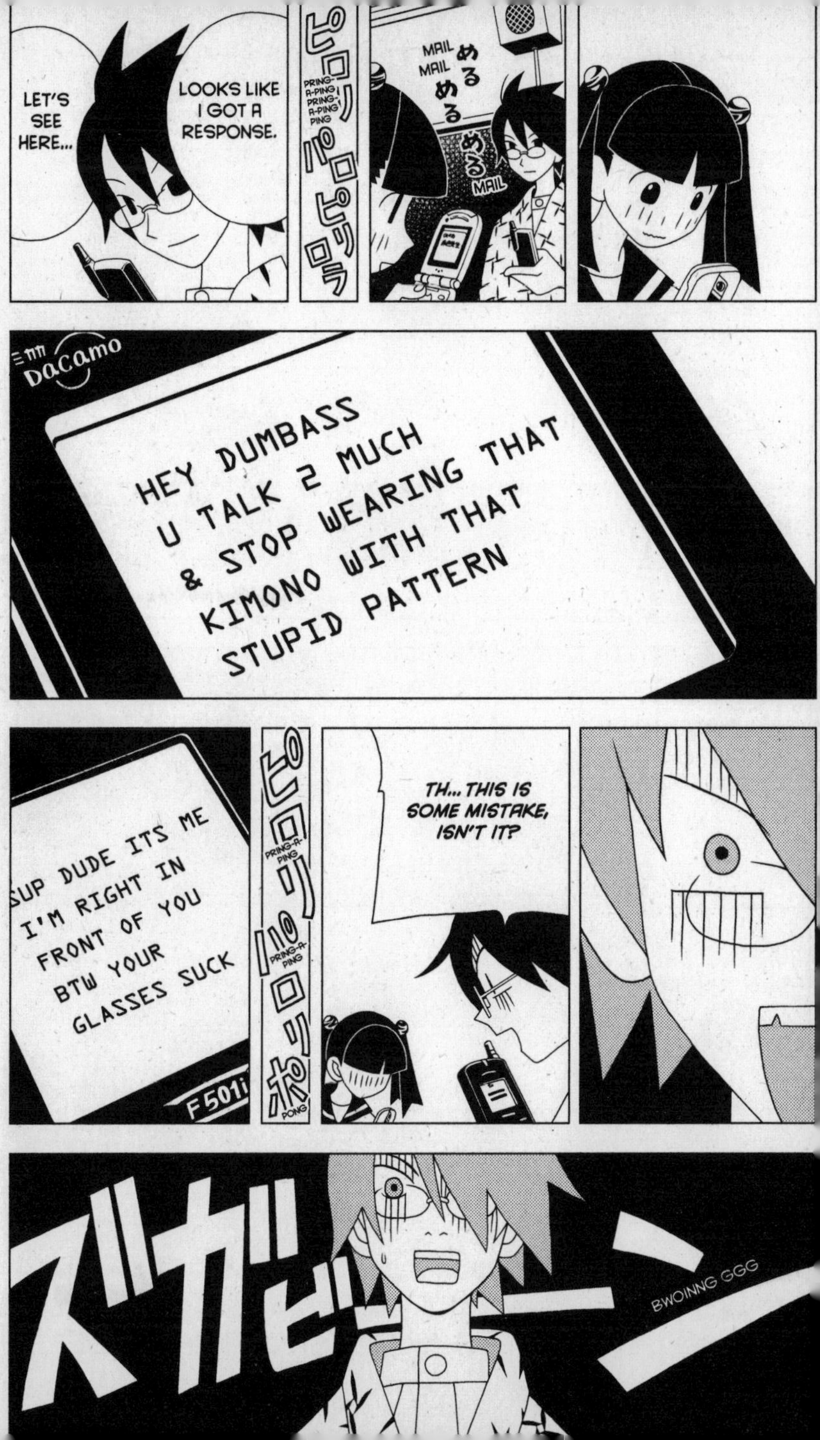
めるめる
MAIL
MAIL
める
MAIL
ピロリ パロピリロラ
PRING-A-PING PRING-A-PING PING
LOOKS LIKE I GOT A RESPONSE.
LET'S SEE HERE...
DaCamo
HEY DUMBASS
U TALK 2 MUCH
& STOP WEARING THAT
KIMONO WITH THAT
STUPID PATTERN
TH... THIS IS SOME MISTAKE, ISN'T IT?
ピロリ パロリポ
PRING-A-PING PRING-A-PING PONG
SUP DUDE ITS ME
I'M RIGHT IN
FRONT OF YOU
BTW YOUR
GLASSES SUCK
F501i
ズガビーン
BWOINNG GGG

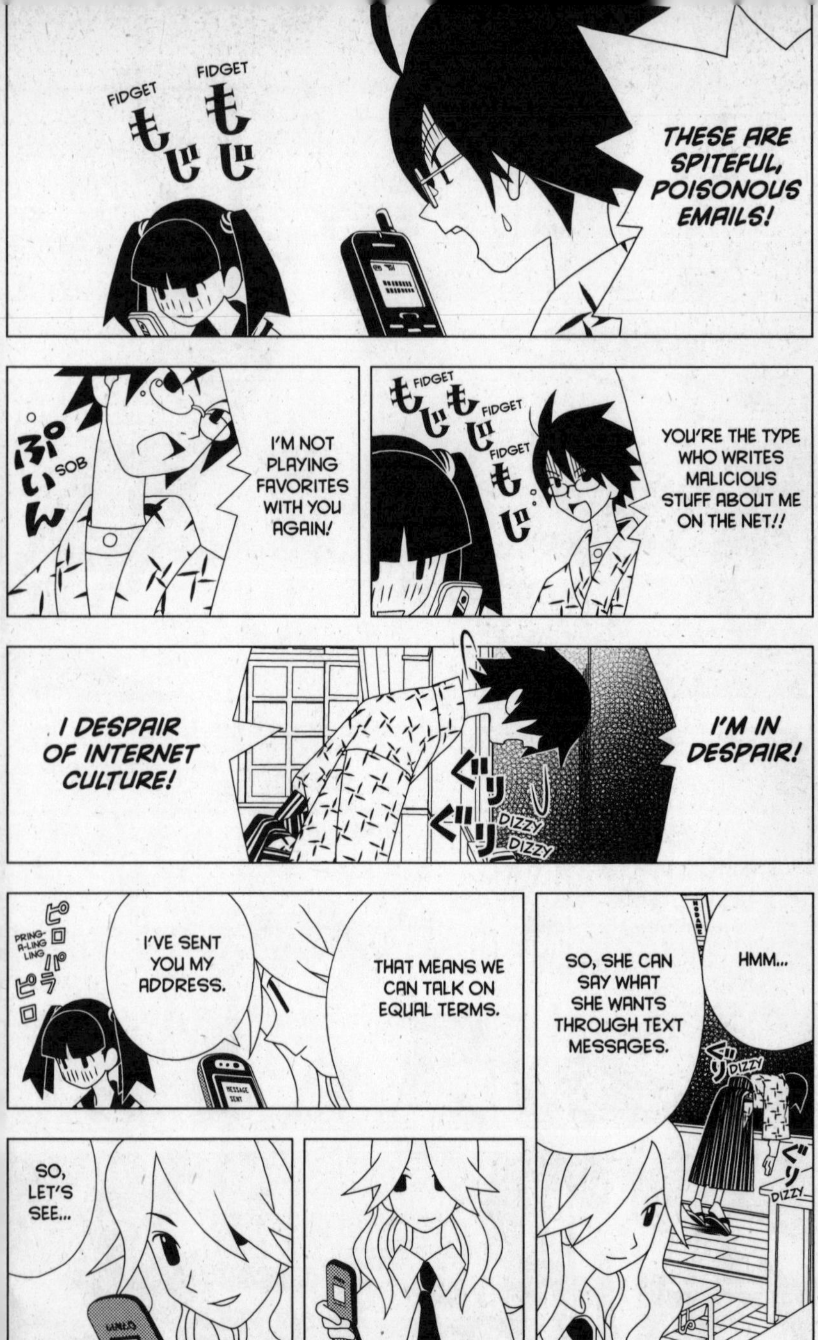
THESE ARE SPITEFUL, POISONOUS EMAILS!
FIDGET
もじ
FIDGET
もじ
YOU'RE THE TYPE WHO WRITES MALICIOUS STUFF ABOUT ME ON THE NET!!
もじもじもじ
FIDGET
FIDGET
FIDGET
I'M NOT PLAYING FAVORITES WITH YOU AGAIN!
ぷいん
SOB
I'M IN DESPAIR!
ぐり
ぐり
DIZZY
DIZZY
I DESPAIR OF INTERNET CULTURE!
HMM...
SO, SHE CAN SAY WHAT SHE WANTS THROUGH TEXT MESSAGES.
ぐり
DIZZY
ぐり
DIZZY
THAT MEANS WE CAN TALK ON EQUAL TERMS.
I'VE SENT YOU MY ADDRESS.
ピロパラピロ
PRING-A-LING LING
MESSAGE SENT
SO, LET'S SEE...

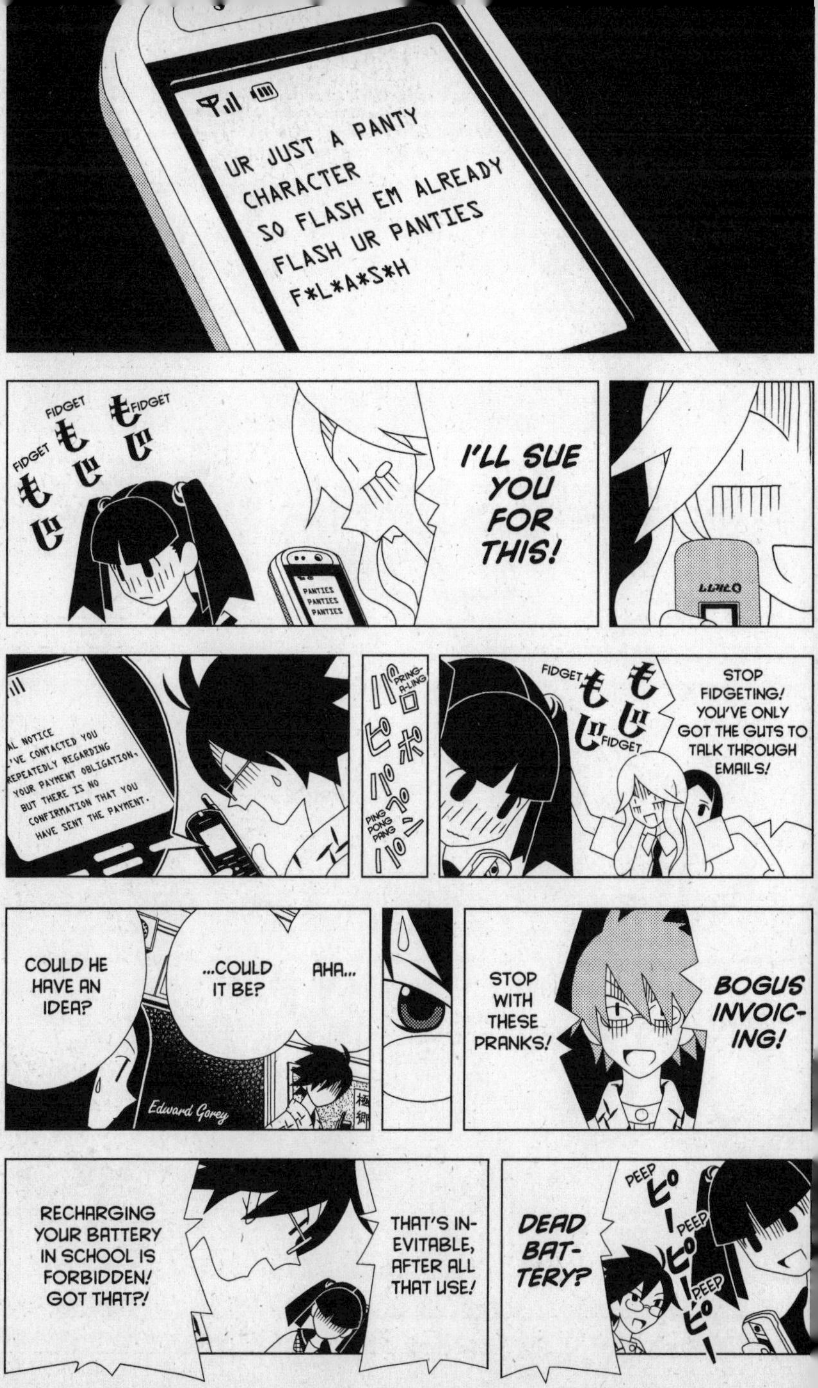
UR JUST A PANTY
CHARACTER
SO FLASH EM ALREADY
FLASH UR PANTIES
F*L*A*S*H
I'LL SUE YOU FOR THIS!
FIDGET
FIDGET
FIDGET
PANTIES
PANTIES
PANTIES
FIDGET
FIDGET
STOP FIDGETING! YOU'VE ONLY GOT THE GUTS TO TALK THROUGH EMAILS!
PRING-A-LING
PING PONG PANG
AL NOTICE
'VE CONTACTED YOU
REPEATEDLY REGARDING
YOUR PAYMENT OBLIGATION,
BUT THERE IS NO
CONFIRMATION THAT YOU
HAVE SENT THE PAYMENT.
BOGUS INVOICING!
STOP WITH THESE PRANKS!
AHA...
...COULD IT BE?
COULD HE HAVE AN IDEA?
Edward Gorey
PEEP
PEEP
PEEP
DEAD BATTERY?
THAT'S INEVITABLE, AFTER ALL THAT USE!
RECHARGING YOUR BATTERY IN SCHOOL IS FORBIDDEN! GOT THAT?!

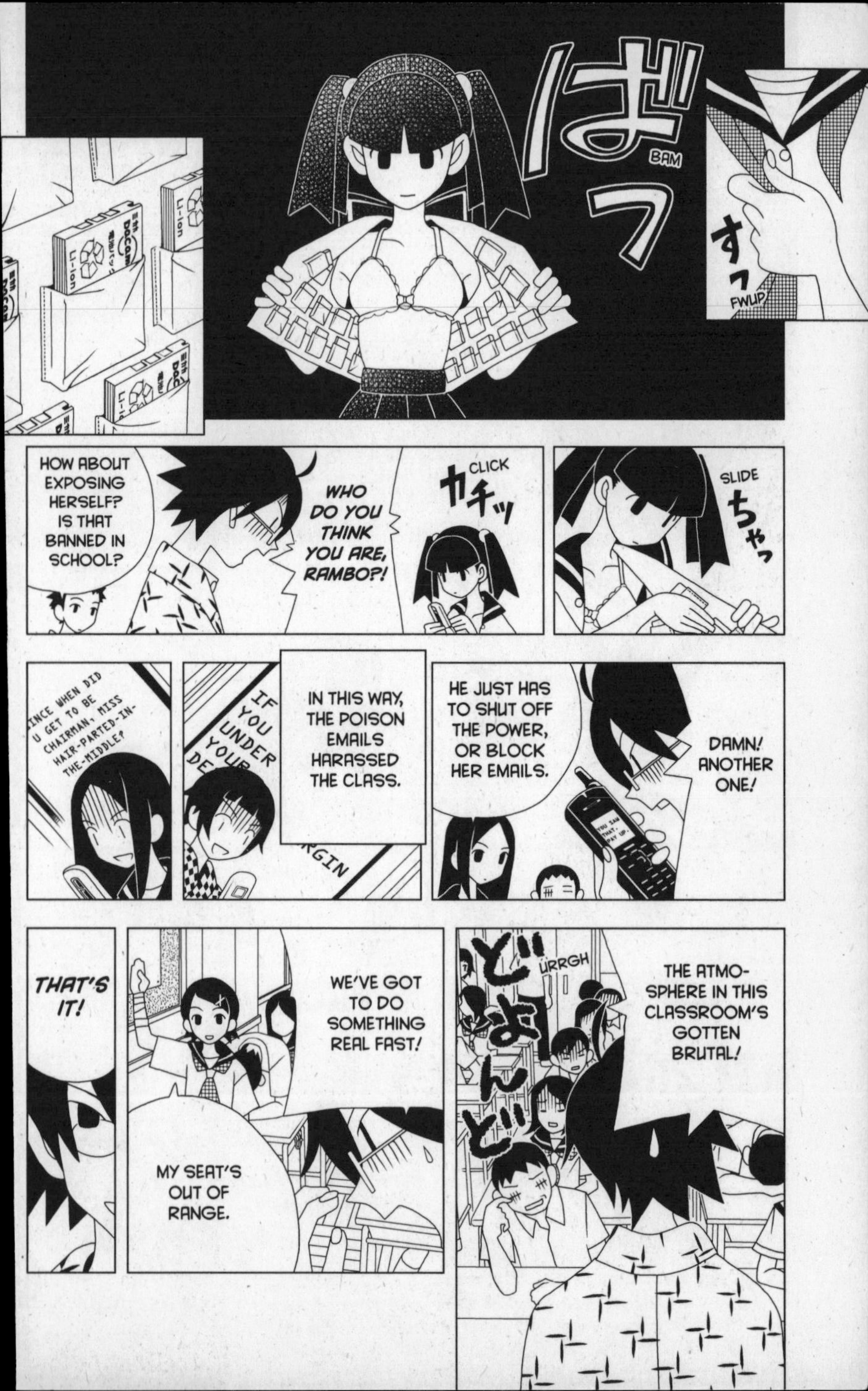
すっ
FWUP
ぱっ
BAM
Li-ion
カチッ
CLICK
WHO DO YOU THINK YOU ARE, RAMBO?!
HOW ABOUT EXPOSING HERSELF? IS THAT BANNED IN SCHOOL?
ちゃっ
SLIDE
DAMN! ANOTHER ONE!
HE JUST HAS TO SHUT OFF THE POWER, OR BLOCK HER EMAILS.
YOU SAW THAT. PAY UP.
IN THIS WAY, THE POISON EMAILS HARASSED THE CLASS.
SINCE WHEN DID U GET TO BE CHAIRMAN, MISS HAIR-PARTED-IN-THE-MIDDLE?
THE ATMOSPHERE IN THIS CLASSROOM'S GOTTEN BRUTAL!
URRGH
WE'VE GOT TO DO SOMETHING REAL FAST!
MY SEAT'S OUT OF RANGE.
THAT'S IT!

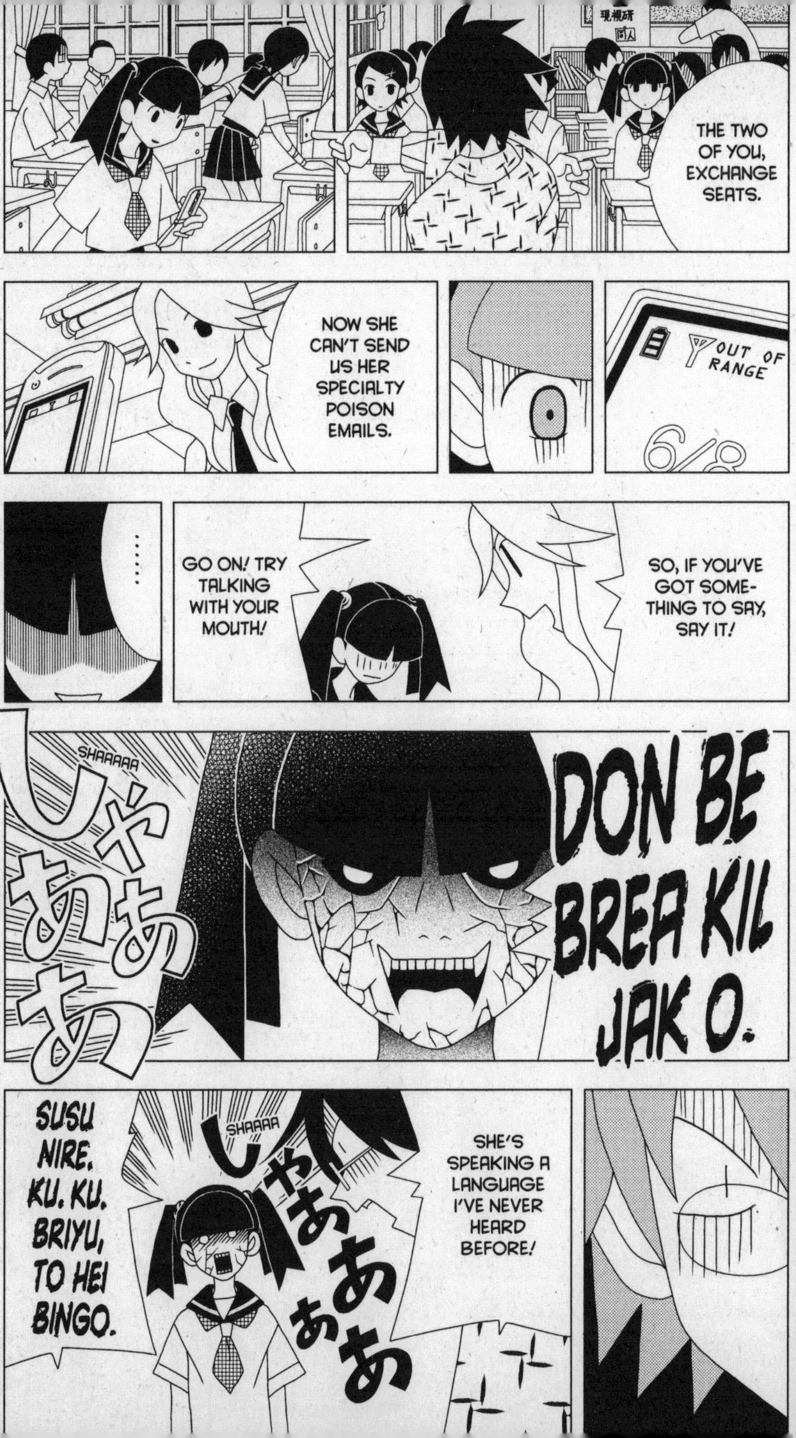
THE TWO OF YOU, EXCHANGE SEATS.
OUT OF RANGE
6/8
NOW SHE CAN'T SEND US HER SPECIALTY POISON EMAILS.
SO, IF YOU'VE GOT SOME-THING TO SAY, SAY IT!
GO ON! TRY TALKING WITH YOUR MOUTH!
......
DON BE BREA KIL JAK O.
しゃあああ
SHAAAAA
SHE'S SPEAKING A LANGUAGE I'VE NEVER HEARD BEFORE!
しゃあああ
SHAAAA
SUSU NIRE. KU. KU. BRIYU, TO HEI BINGO.

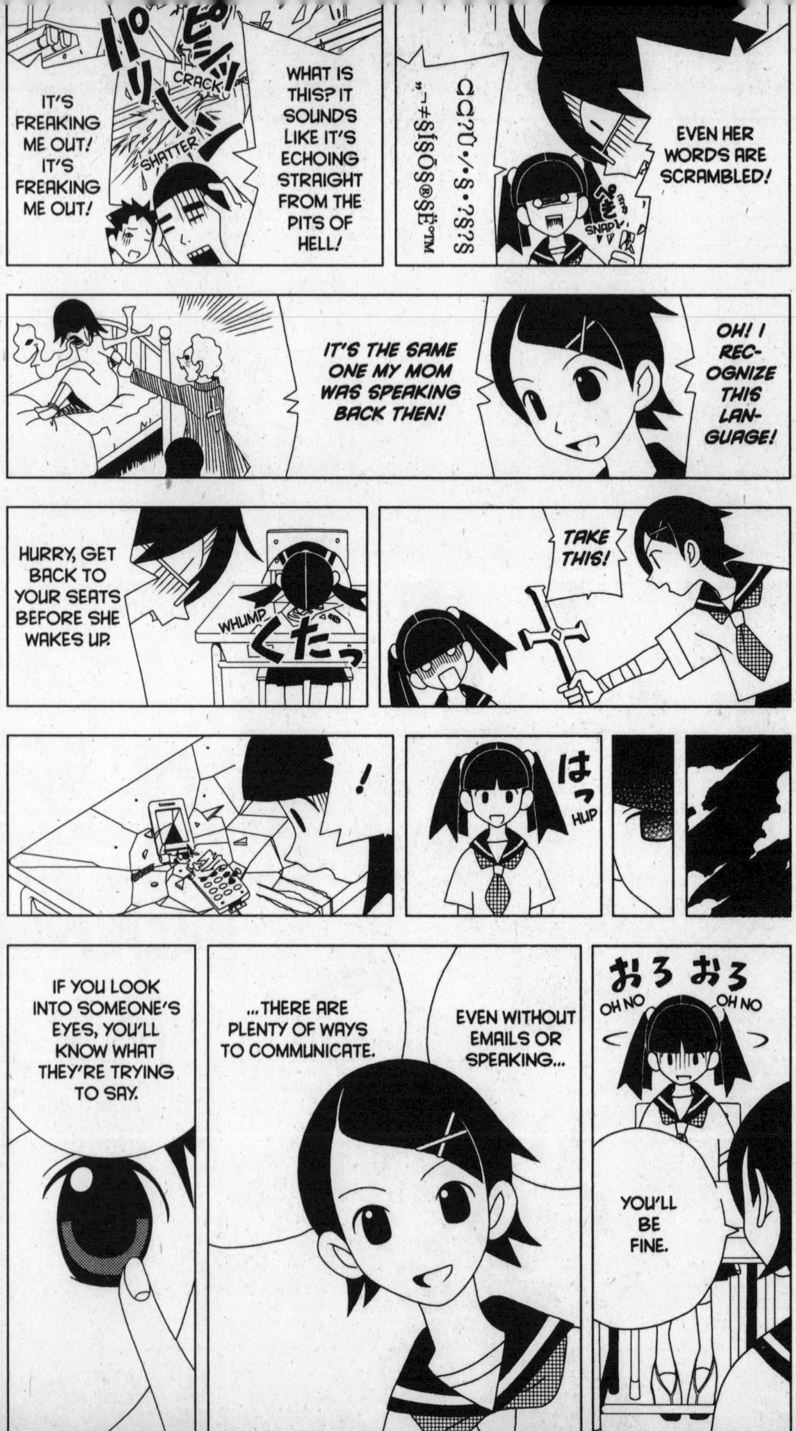
EVEN HER WORDS ARE SCRAMBLED!
SNAP
パリーン
SHATTER
CRACK
WHAT IS THIS? IT SOUNDS LIKE IT'S ECHOING STRAIGHT FROM THE PITS OF HELL!
IT'S FREAKING ME OUT! IT'S FREAKING ME OUT!
OH! I RECOGNIZE THIS LANGUAGE!
IT'S THE SAME ONE MY MOM WAS SPEAKING BACK THEN!
TAKE THIS!
HURRY, GET BACK TO YOUR SEATS BEFORE SHE WAKES UP.
くたっ
WHUMP
はっ
HUP
!
おろ おろ
OH NO OH NO
YOU'LL BE FINE.
EVEN WITHOUT EMAILS OR SPEAKING...
...THERE ARE PLENTY OF WAYS TO COMMUNICATE.
IF YOU LOOK INTO SOMEONE'S EYES, YOU'LL KNOW WHAT THEY'RE TRYING TO SAY.

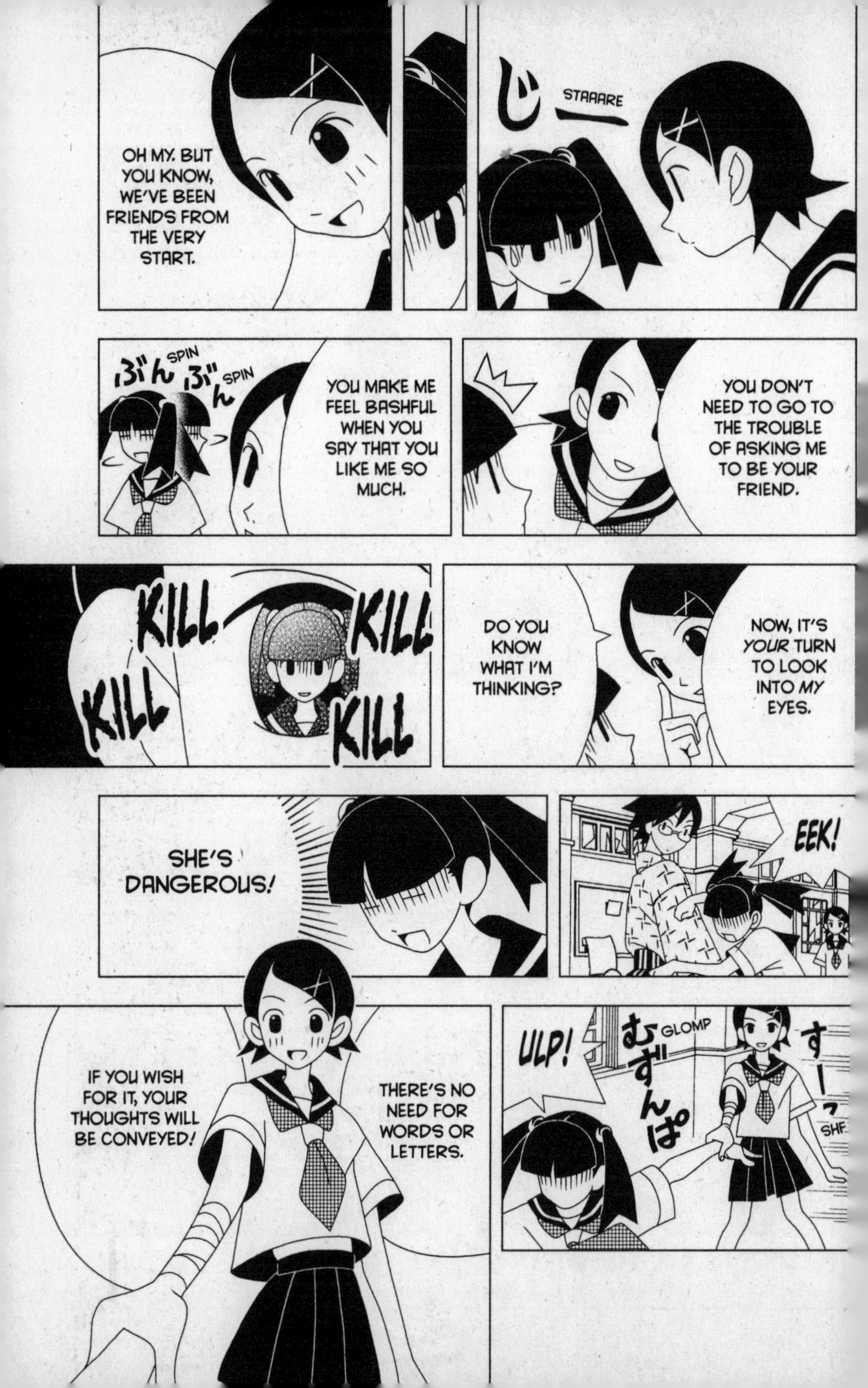
じー STAAARE
OH MY. BUT YOU KNOW, WE'VE BEEN FRIENDS FROM THE VERY START.
YOU DON'T NEED TO GO TO THE TROUBLE OF ASKING ME TO BE YOUR FRIEND.
ぶん SPIN ぶん SPIN
YOU MAKE ME FEEL BASHFUL WHEN YOU SAY THAT YOU LIKE ME SO MUCH.
NOW, IT'S *YOUR* TURN TO LOOK INTO *MY* EYES.
DO YOU KNOW WHAT I'M THINKING?
KILL
KILL
KILL
KILL
EEK!
SHE'S DANGEROUS!
すー SHF
むずんぱ GLOMP
ULP!
THERE'S NO NEED FOR WORDS OR LETTERS.
IF YOU WISH FOR IT, YOUR THOUGHTS WILL BE CONVEYED!

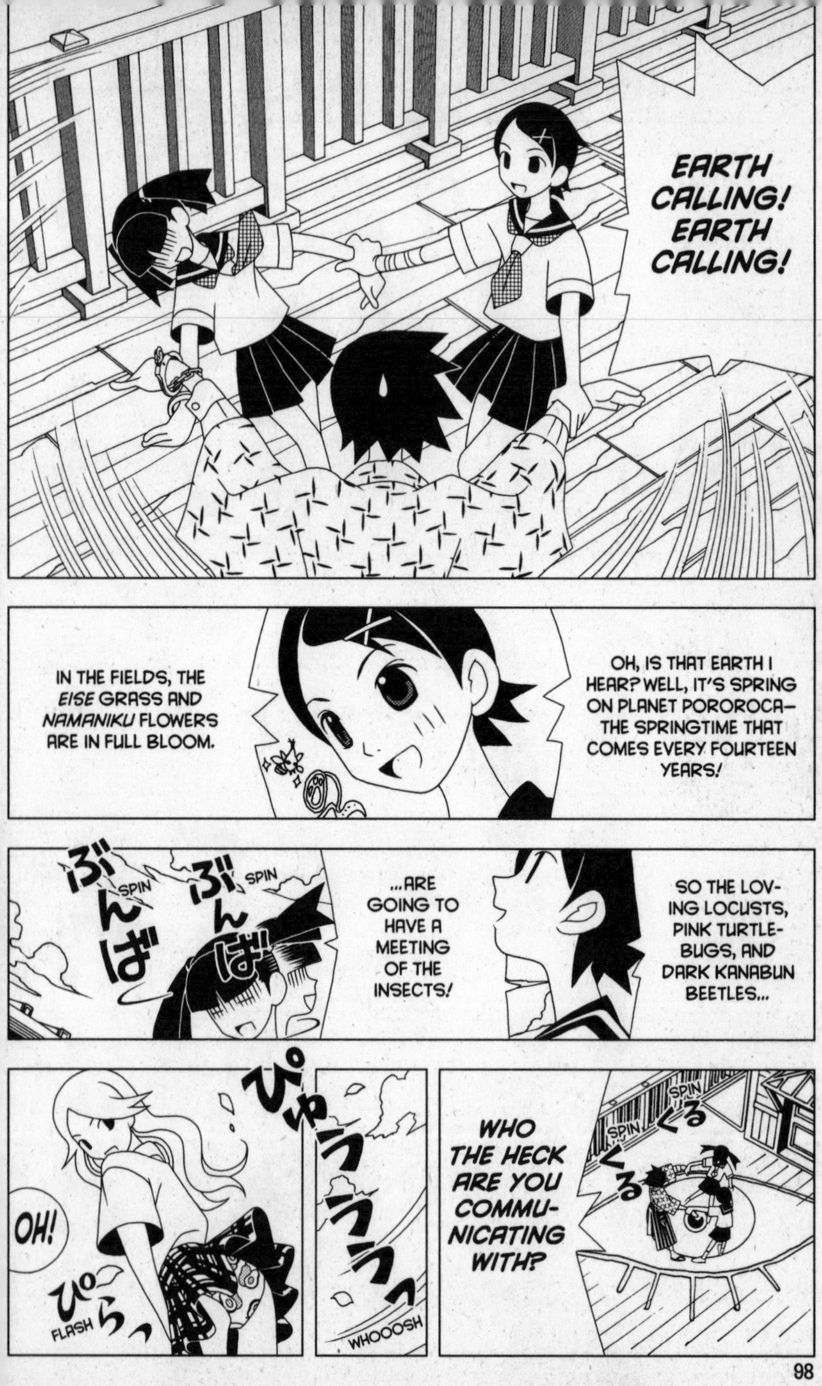
EARTH CALLING! EARTH CALLING!
OH, IS THAT EARTH I HEAR? WELL, IT'S SPRING ON PLANET POROROCA—THE SPRINGTIME THAT COMES EVERY FOURTEEN YEARS!
IN THE FIELDS, THE *EISE* GRASS AND *NAMANIKU* FLOWERS ARE IN FULL BLOOM.
SO THE LOVING LOCUSTS, PINK TURTLE-BUGS, AND DARK KANABUN BEETLES...
...ARE GOING TO HAVE A MEETING OF THE INSECTS!
SPIN
SPIN
くる SPIN
くる SPIN
WHO THE HECK ARE YOU COMMUNICATING WITH?
WHOOOSH
OH!
ぴらっ FLASH

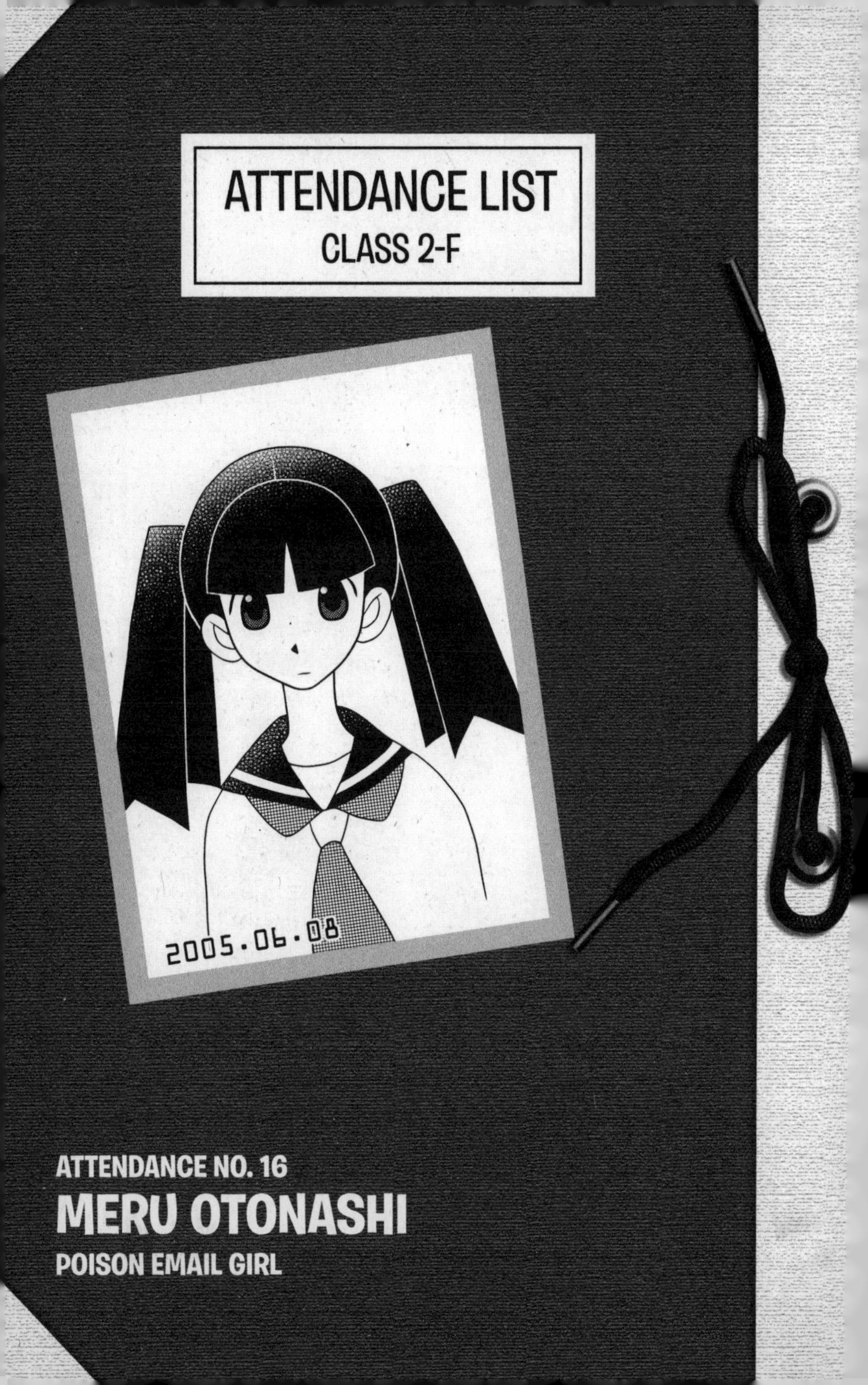
ATTENDANCE LIST
CLASS 2-F
2005.06.08
ATTENDANCE NO. 16
MERU OTONASHI
POISON EMAIL GIRL

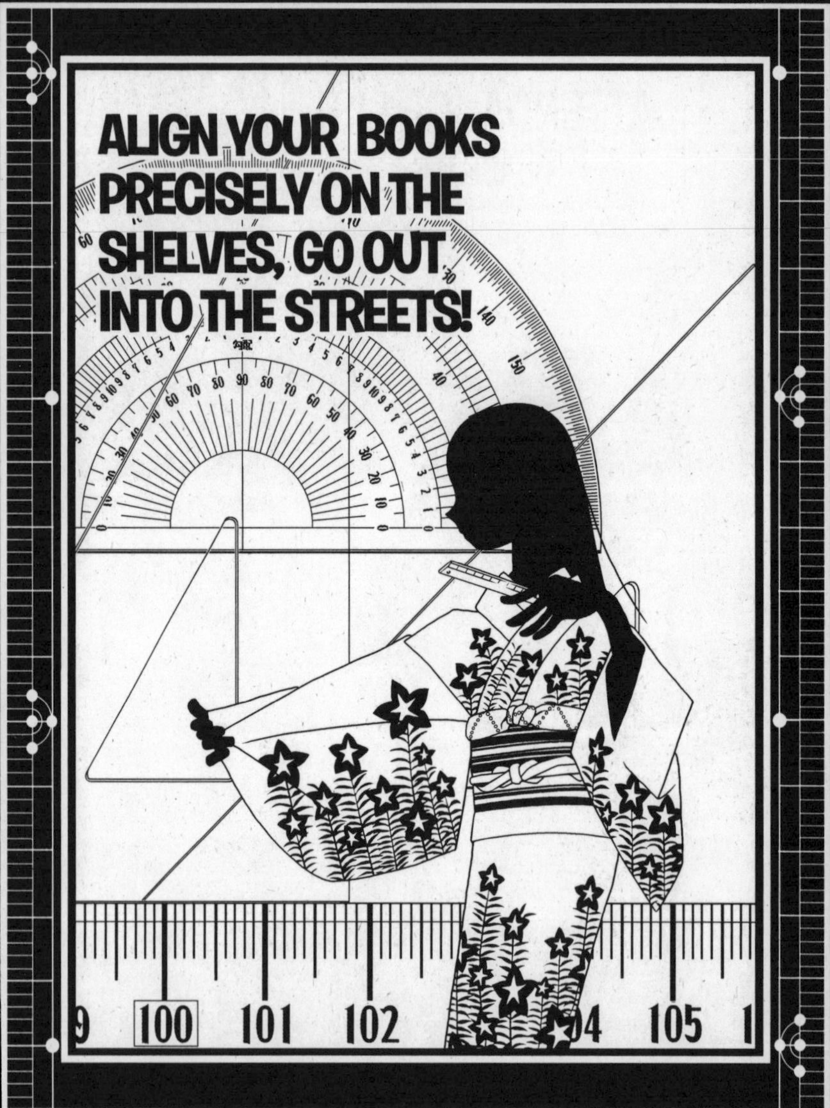
ALIGN YOUR BOOKS PRECISELY ON THE SHELVES, GO OUT INTO THE STREETS!

# CHAPTER 8

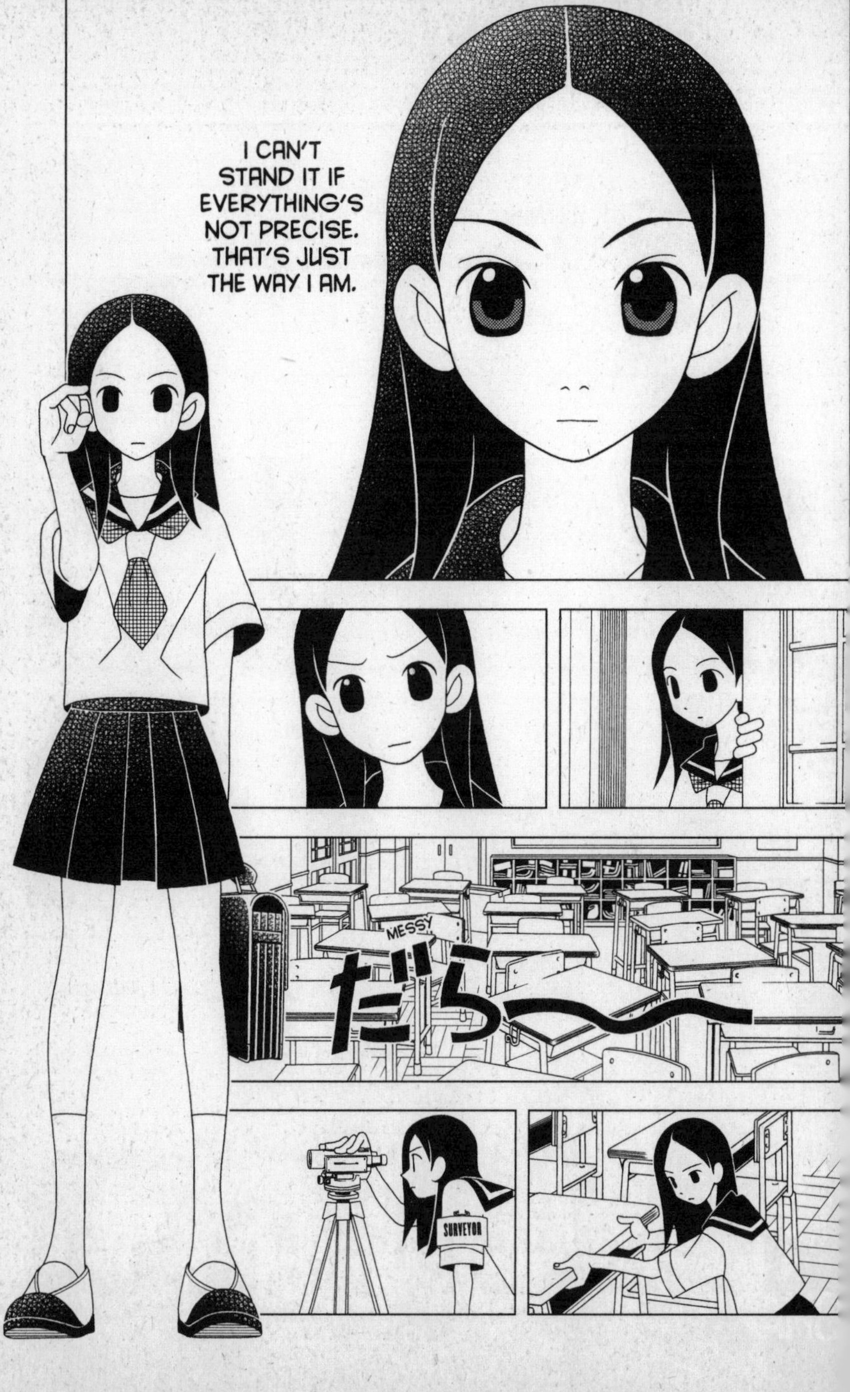
I CAN'T STAND IT IF EVERYTHING'S NOT PRECISE. THAT'S JUST THE WAY I AM.
MESSY
だら～～～
SURVEYOR

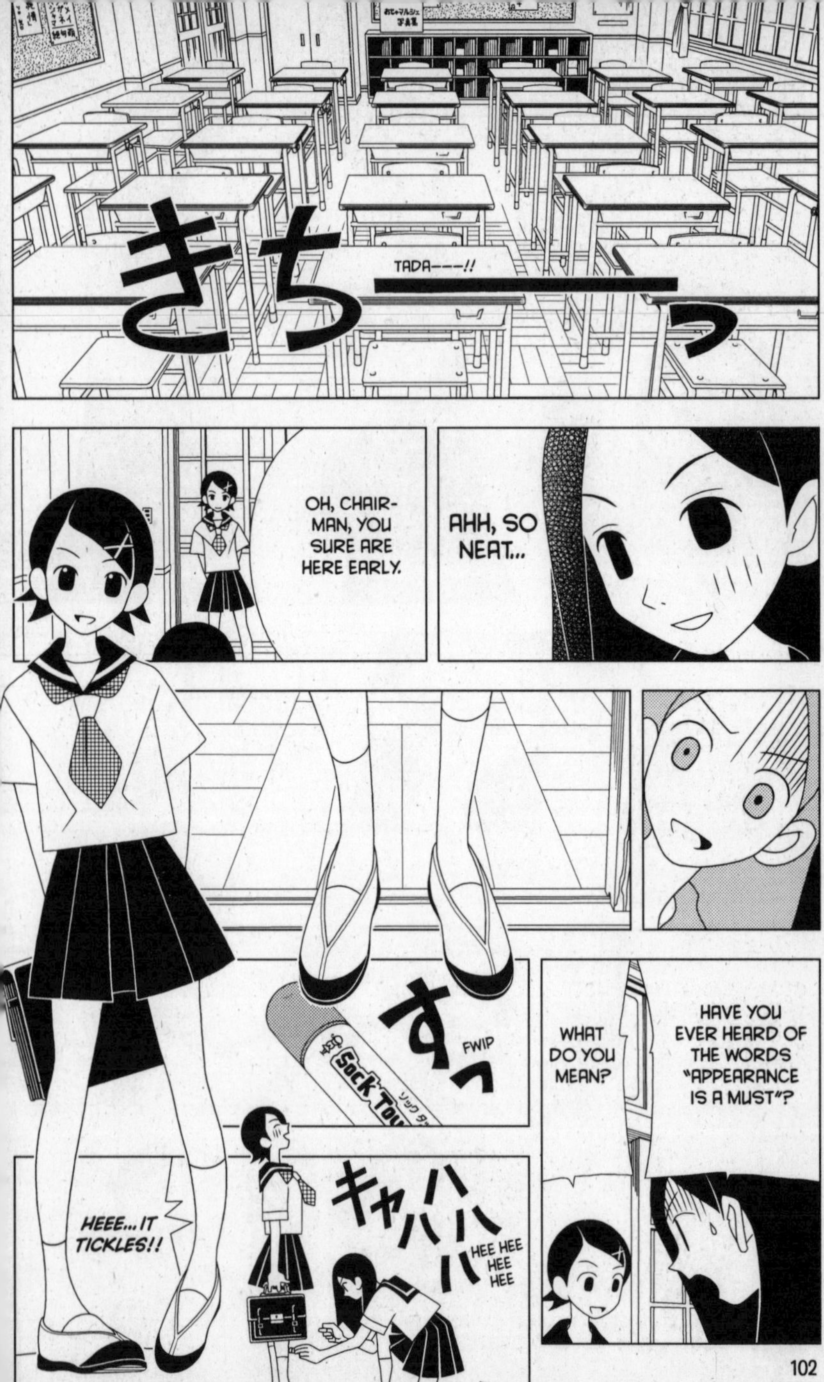
きちーーーっ
TADA---!!
AHH, SO NEAT...
OH, CHAIR-MAN, YOU SURE ARE HERE EARLY.
すっ
FWIP
Sock Touch
ソックタ
HAVE YOU EVER HEARD OF THE WORDS "APPEARANCE IS A MUST"?
WHAT DO YOU MEAN?
キャハハハ
HEE HEE HEE HEE
HEEE... IT TICKLES!!

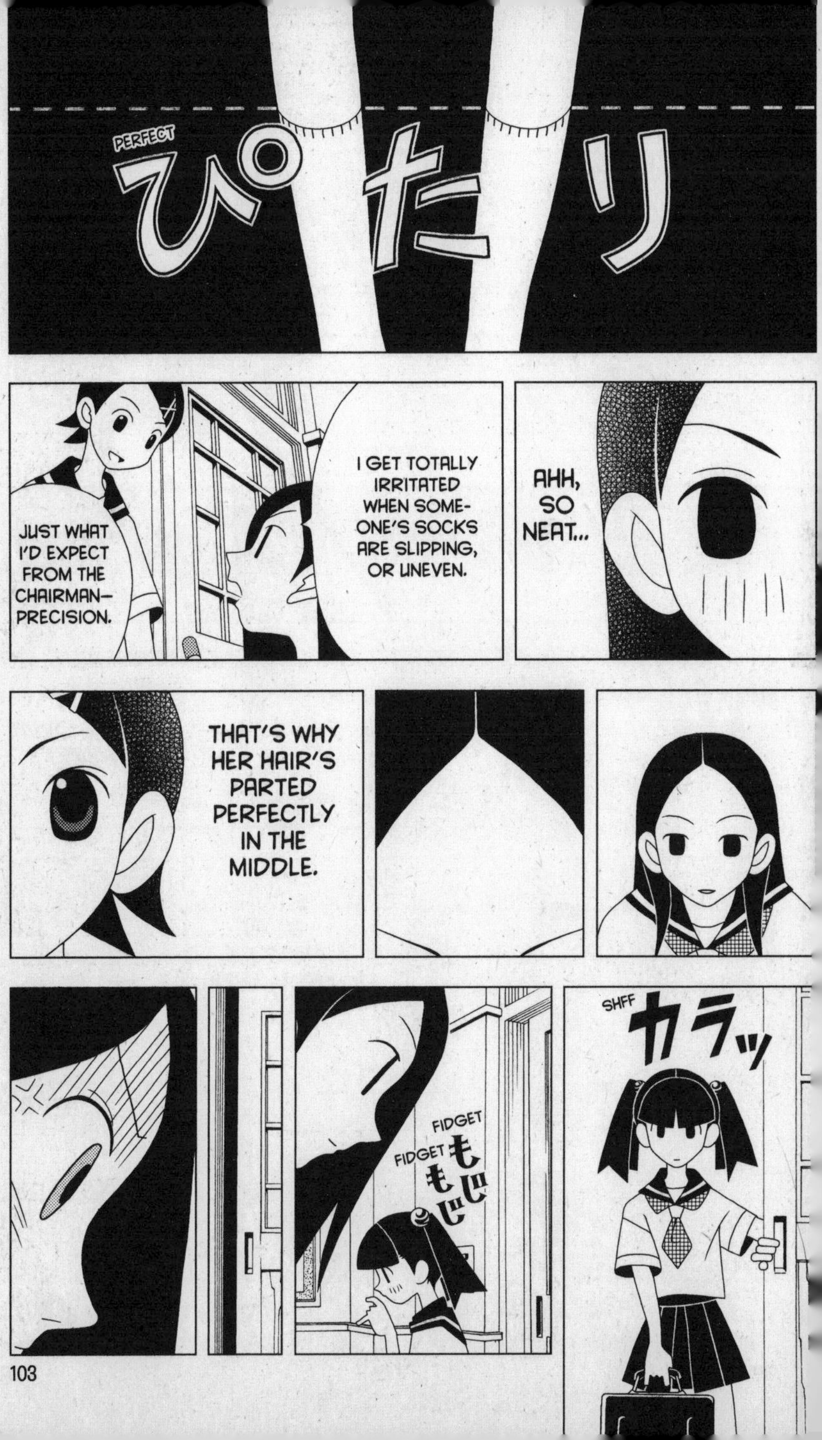
PERFECT
ぴたり
AHH, SO NEAT...
JUST WHAT I'D EXPECT FROM THE CHAIRMAN—PRECISION.
I GET TOTALLY IRRITATED WHEN SOME-ONE'S SOCKS ARE SLIPPING, OR UNEVEN.
THAT'S WHY HER HAIR'S PARTED PERFECTLY IN THE MIDDLE.
SHFF
カラッ
FIDGET
FIDGET
もじもじ

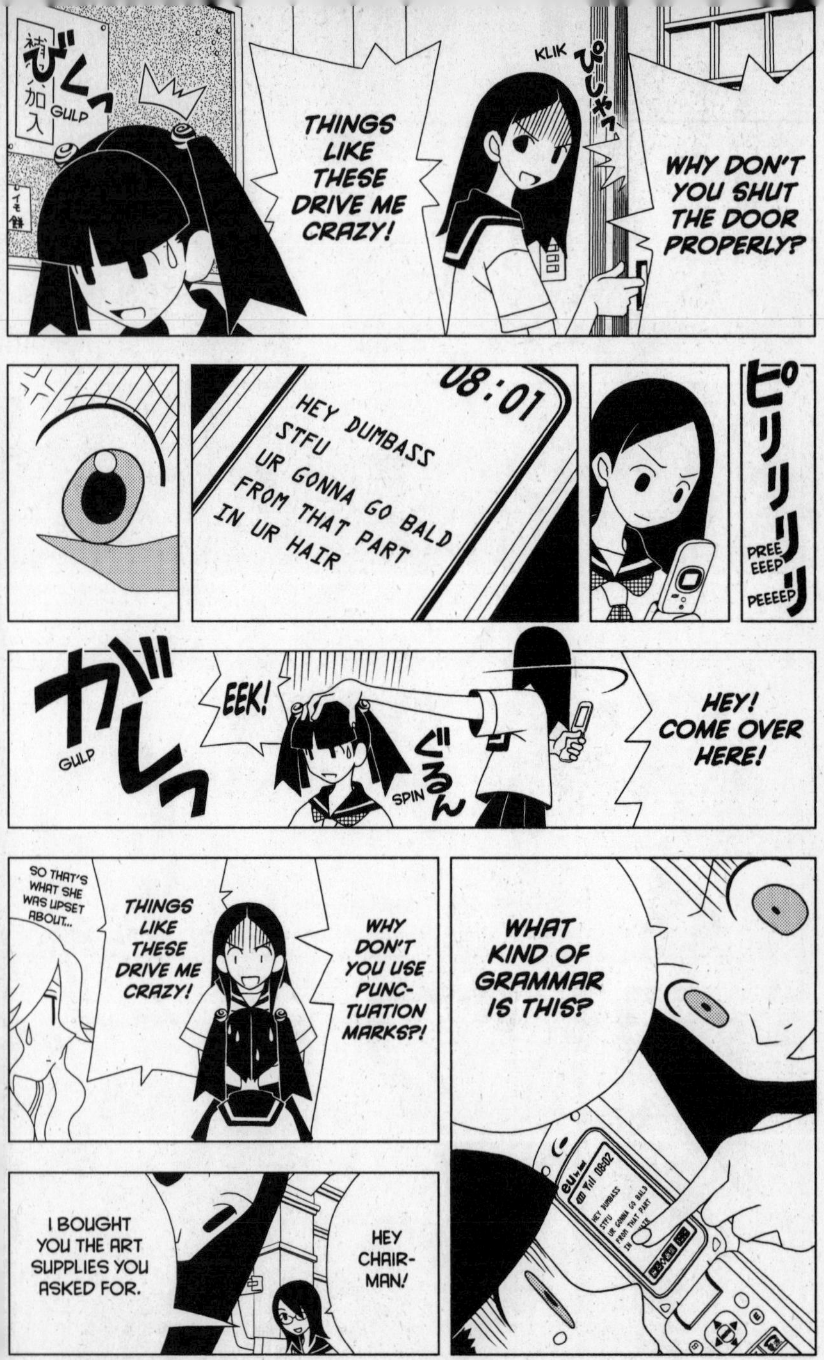
WHY DON'T YOU SHUT THE DOOR PROPERLY?
KLIK
ぴしゃっ
THINGS LIKE THESE DRIVE ME CRAZY!
びくっ
GULP
ピリリリ
PREE EEEP
PEEEEP
08:01
HEY DUMBASS
STFU
UR GONNA GO BALD
FROM THAT PART
IN UR HAIR
HEY! COME OVER HERE!
ぐるん
SPIN
EEK!
ガしっ
GULP
WHAT KIND OF GRAMMAR IS THIS?
WHY DON'T YOU USE PUNC-TUATION MARKS?!
THINGS LIKE THESE DRIVE ME CRAZY!
SO THAT'S WHAT SHE WAS UPSET ABOUT...
HEY CHAIR-MAN!
I BOUGHT YOU THE ART SUPPLIES YOU ASKED FOR.

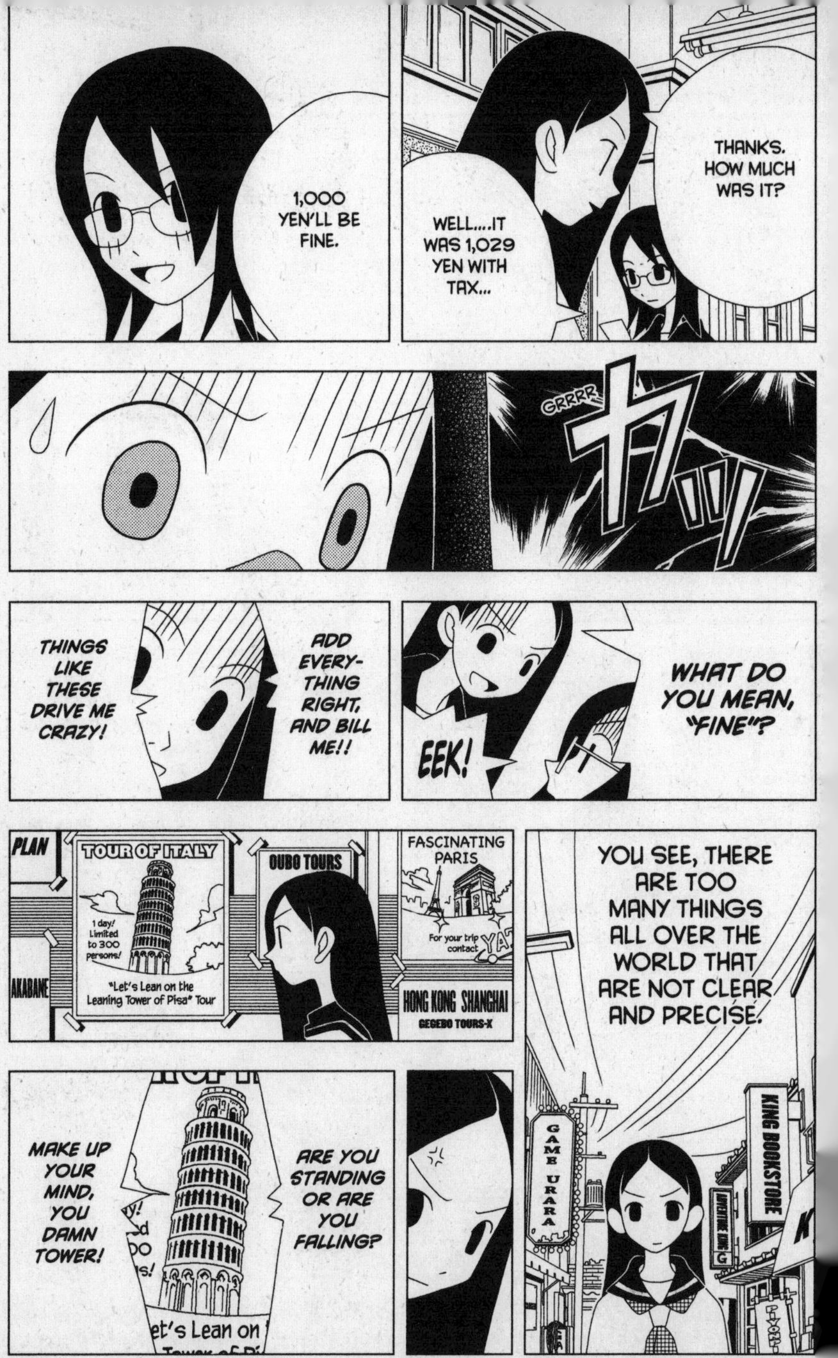
THANKS. HOW MUCH WAS IT?
WELL....IT WAS 1,029 YEN WITH TAX...
1,000 YEN'LL BE FINE.
GRRRR
カッ
WHAT DO YOU MEAN, "FINE"?
EEK!
ADD EVERY-THING RIGHT, AND BILL ME!!
THINGS LIKE THESE DRIVE ME CRAZY!
YOU SEE, THERE ARE TOO MANY THINGS ALL OVER THE WORLD THAT ARE NOT CLEAR AND PRECISE.
GAME URARA
KING BOOKSTORE
FASCINATING PARIS
For your trip contact
HONG KONG SHANGHAI
GEGEBO TOURS-X
OUBO TOURS
TOUR OF ITALY
1 day! Limited to 300 persons!
"Let's Lean on the Leaning Tower of Pisa" Tour
PLAN
AKABANE
ARE YOU STANDING OR ARE YOU FALLING?
MAKE UP YOUR MIND, YOU DAMN TOWER!

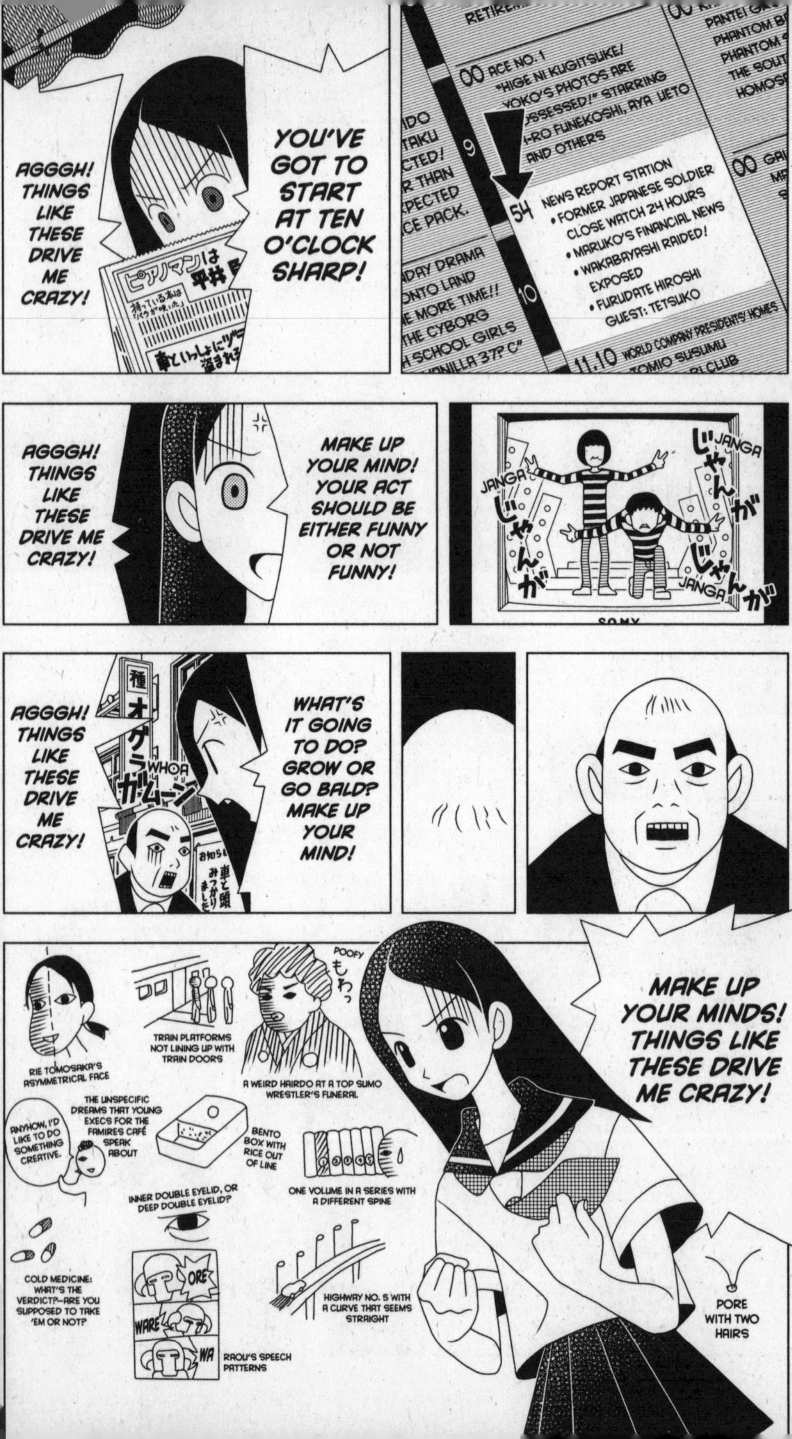
00 ACE NO. 1
"HIGE NI KUGITSUKE/ YOKO'S PHOTOS ARE POSSESSED!" STARRING
AYA UETO AND OTHERS
54 NEWS REPORT STATION
• FORMER JAPANESE SOLDIER CLOSE WATCH 24 HOURS
• MARUKO'S FINANCIAL NEWS
• WAKABAYASHI RAIDED! EXPOSED
• FURUDATE HIROSHI
GUEST: TETSUKO
11.10 WORLD COMPANY PRESIDENTS' HOMES
TOMIO SUSUMU
THE CYBORG
YOU'VE GOT TO START AT TEN O'CLOCK SHARP!
AGGGH! THINGS LIKE THESE DRIVE ME CRAZY!
ピアノマンは平井
持っている本は「ぐりとぐら」が咲いた
JANGA じゃんが
JANGA じゃんが
JANGA じゃんが
MAKE UP YOUR MIND! YOUR ACT SHOULD BE EITHER FUNNY OR NOT FUNNY!
AGGGH! THINGS LIKE THESE DRIVE ME CRAZY!
WHAT'S IT GOING TO DO? GROW OR GO BALD? MAKE UP YOUR MIND!
WHOA
AGGGH! THINGS LIKE THESE DRIVE ME CRAZY!
MAKE UP YOUR MINDS! THINGS LIKE THESE DRIVE ME CRAZY!
PORE WITH TWO HAIRS
POOFY もわっ
A WEIRD HAIRDO AT A TOP SUMO WRESTLER'S FUNERAL
TRAIN PLATFORMS NOT LINING UP WITH TRAIN DOORS
RIE TOMOSAKA'S ASYMMETRICAL FACE
BENTO BOX WITH RICE OUT OF LINE
THE UNSPECIFIC DREAMS THAT YOUNG EXECS FOR THE FAMIRES CAFÉ SPEAK ABOUT
ANYHOW, I'D LIKE TO DO SOMETHING CREATIVE.
ONE VOLUME IN A SERIES WITH A DIFFERENT SPINE
INNER DOUBLE EYELID, OR DEEP DOUBLE EYELID?
HIGHWAY NO. 5 WITH A CURVE THAT SEEMS STRAIGHT
ORE
WARE
WA
RAOU'S SPEECH PATTERNS
COLD MEDICINE: WHAT'S THE VERDICT?—ARE YOU SUPPOSED TO TAKE 'EM OR NOT?

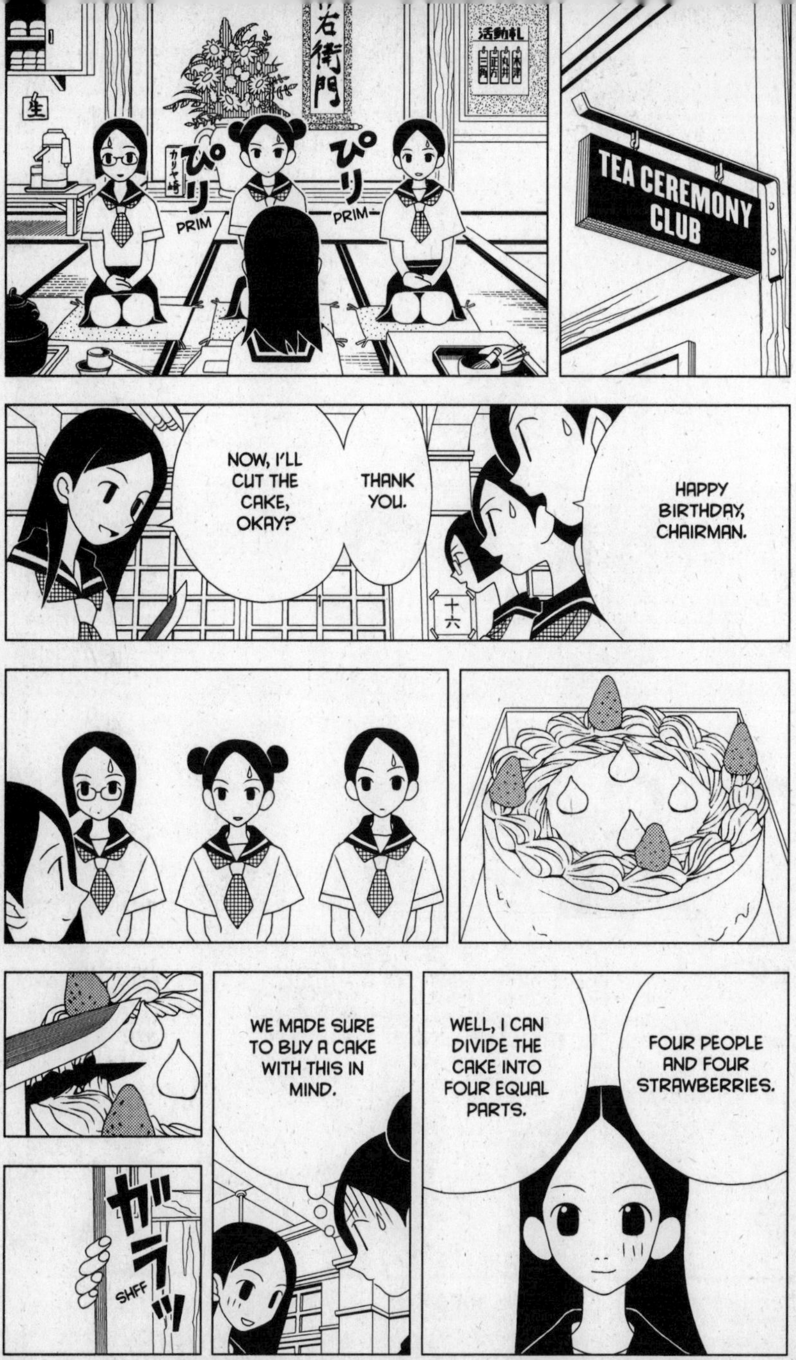
TEA CEREMONY CLUB
ぴり
PRIM
ぴり
PRIM
HAPPY BIRTHDAY, CHAIRMAN.
THANK YOU.
NOW, I'LL CUT THE CAKE, OKAY?
FOUR PEOPLE AND FOUR STRAWBERRIES.
WELL, I CAN DIVIDE THE CAKE INTO FOUR EQUAL PARTS.
WE MADE SURE TO BUY A CAKE WITH THIS IN MIND.
ガラッ
SHFF

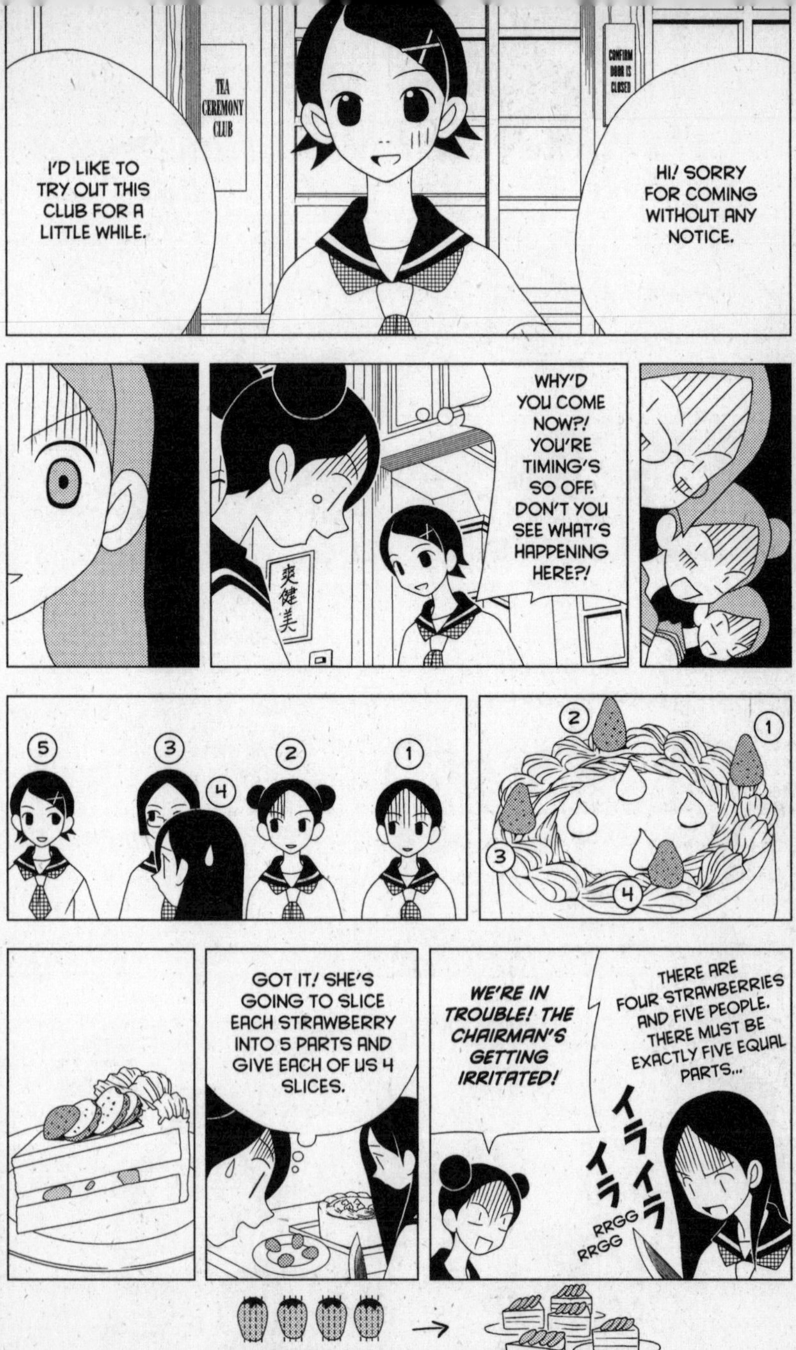
CONFIRM DOOR IS CLOSED
TEA CEREMONY CLUB
HI! SORRY FOR COMING WITHOUT ANY NOTICE.
I'D LIKE TO TRY OUT THIS CLUB FOR A LITTLE WHILE.
WHY'D YOU COME NOW?! YOU'RE TIMING'S SO OFF. DON'T YOU SEE WHAT'S HAPPENING HERE?!
爽健美
1
2
3
4
5
1
2
3
4
THERE ARE FOUR STRAWBERRIES AND FIVE PEOPLE. THERE MUST BE EXACTLY FIVE EQUAL PARTS...
イライラ
イライラ
RRGG
RRGG
WE'RE IN TROUBLE! THE CHAIRMAN'S GETTING IRRITATED!
GOT IT! SHE'S GOING TO SLICE EACH STRAWBERRY INTO 5 PARTS AND GIVE EACH OF US 4 SLICES.
EACH DIVIDED INTO 5 PARTS;
PLACE 4 SLICES ON EACH PIECE.

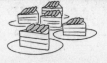

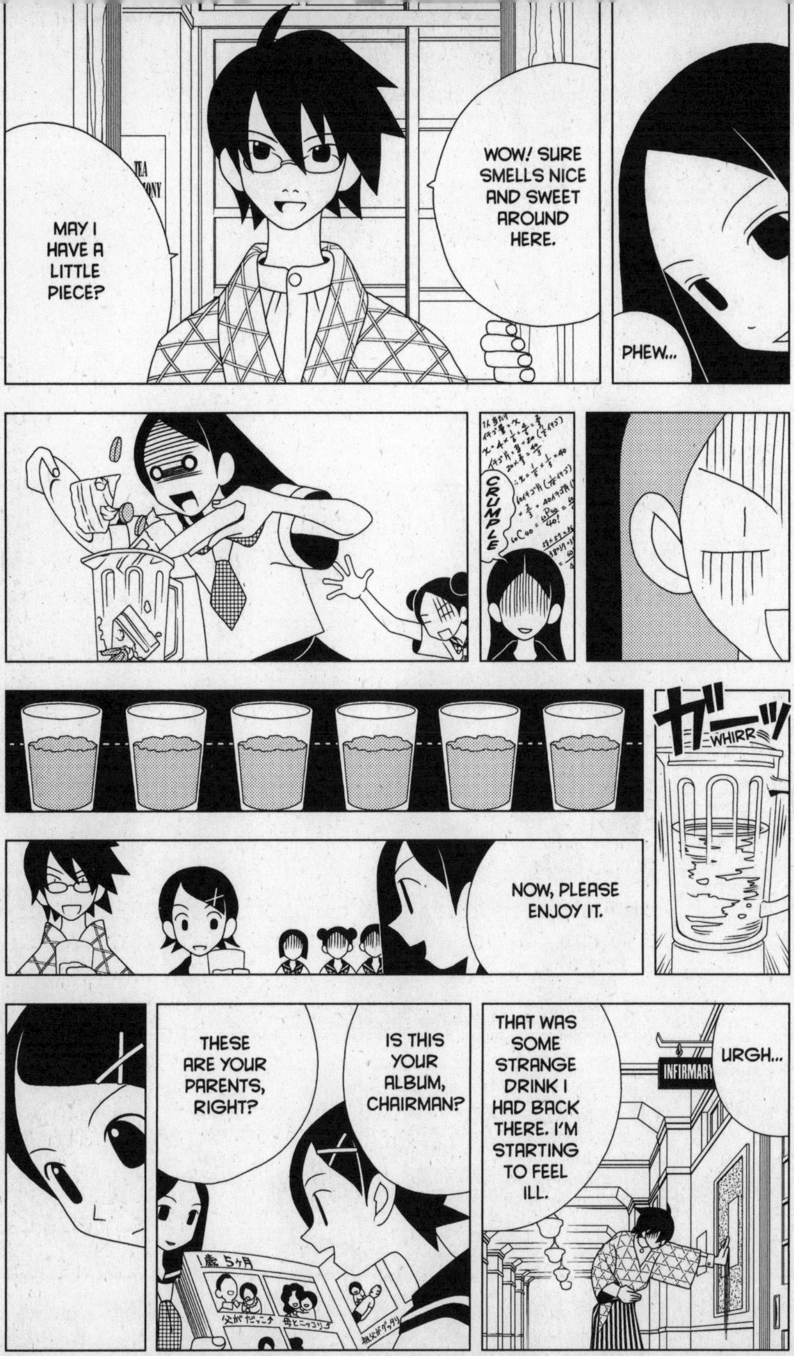
PHEW...
WOW! SURE SMELLS NICE AND SWEET AROUND HERE.
MAY I HAVE A LITTLE PIECE?
CRUMPLE
ガーッ
WHIRR
NOW, PLEASE ENJOY IT.
URGH...
INFIRMARY
THAT WAS SOME STRANGE DRINK I HAD BACK THERE. I'M STARTING TO FEEL ILL.
IS THIS YOUR ALBUM, CHAIRMAN?
THESE ARE YOUR PARENTS, RIGHT?
1歳 5ヶ月

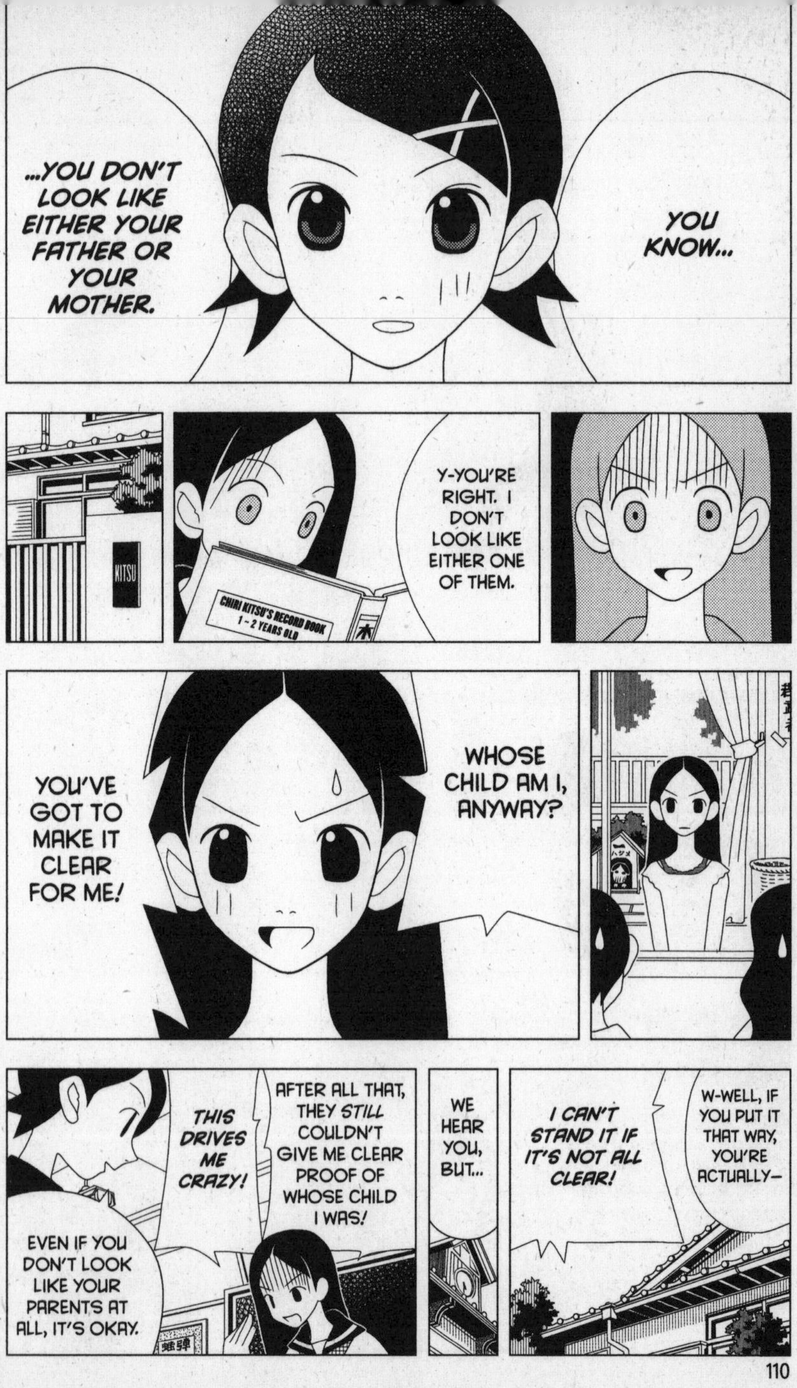
YOU KNOW...
...YOU DON'T LOOK LIKE EITHER YOUR FATHER OR YOUR MOTHER.
Y-YOU'RE RIGHT. I DON'T LOOK LIKE EITHER ONE OF THEM.
CHIRI KITSU'S RECORD BOOK 1 ~ 2 YEARS OLD
KITSU
WHOSE CHILD AM I, ANYWAY?
YOU'VE GOT TO MAKE IT CLEAR FOR ME!
W-WELL, IF YOU PUT IT THAT WAY, YOU'RE ACTUALLY—
I CAN'T STAND IT IF IT'S NOT ALL CLEAR!
WE HEAR YOU, BUT...
AFTER ALL THAT, THEY STILL COULDN'T GIVE ME CLEAR PROOF OF WHOSE CHILD I WAS!
THIS DRIVES ME CRAZY!
EVEN IF YOU DON'T LOOK LIKE YOUR PARENTS AT ALL, IT'S OKAY.

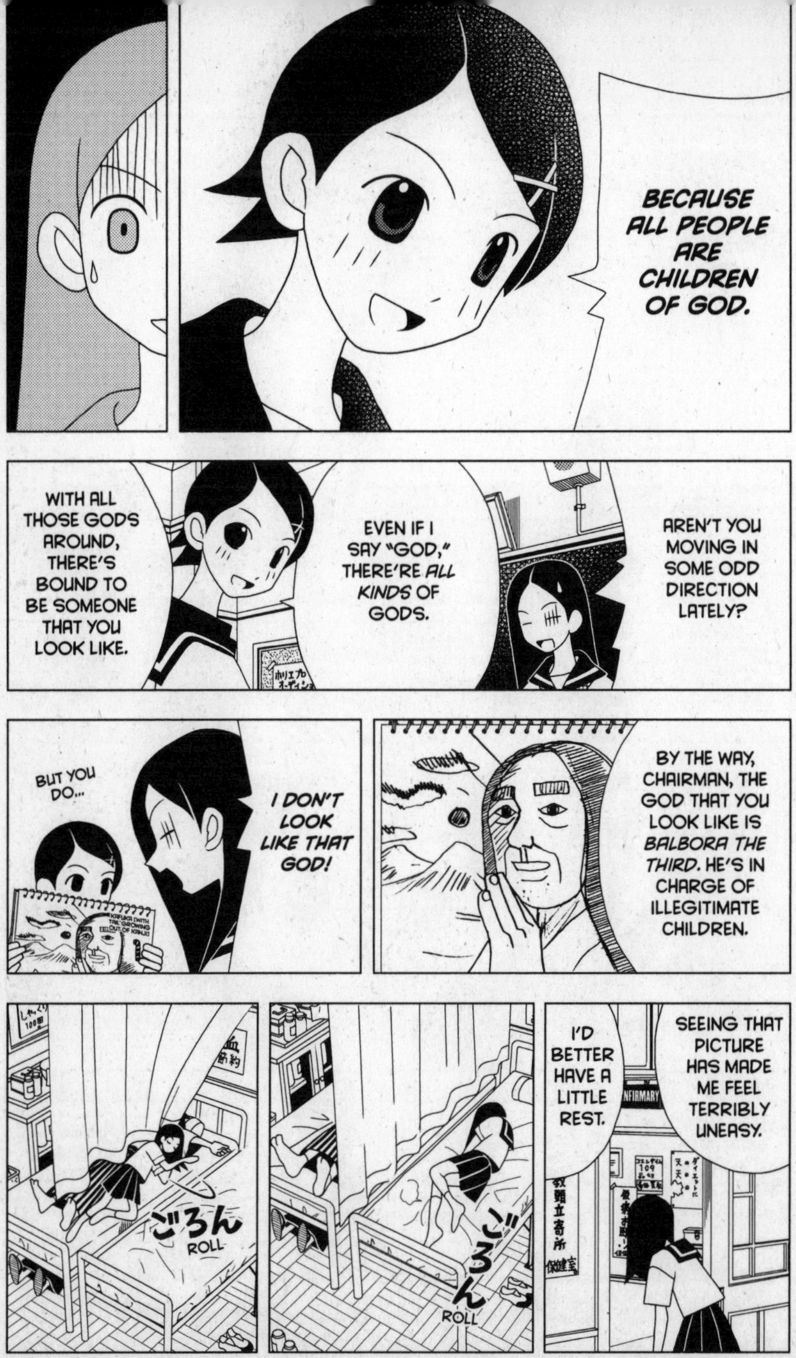
BECAUSE ALL PEOPLE ARE CHILDREN OF GOD.
AREN'T YOU MOVING IN SOME ODD DIRECTION LATELY?
EVEN IF I SAY "GOD," THERE'RE *ALL KINDS* OF GODS.
WITH ALL THOSE GODS AROUND, THERE'S BOUND TO BE SOMEONE THAT YOU LOOK LIKE.
BY THE WAY, CHAIRMAN, THE GOD THAT YOU LOOK LIKE IS *BALBORA THE THIRD*. HE'S IN CHARGE OF ILLEGITIMATE CHILDREN.
I DON'T LOOK LIKE THAT GOD!
BUT YOU DO...
SEEING THAT PICTURE HAS MADE ME FEEL TERRIBLY UNEASY.
I'D BETTER HAVE A LITTLE REST.
INFIRMARY
保健室
ごろん
ROLL
ごろん
ROLL

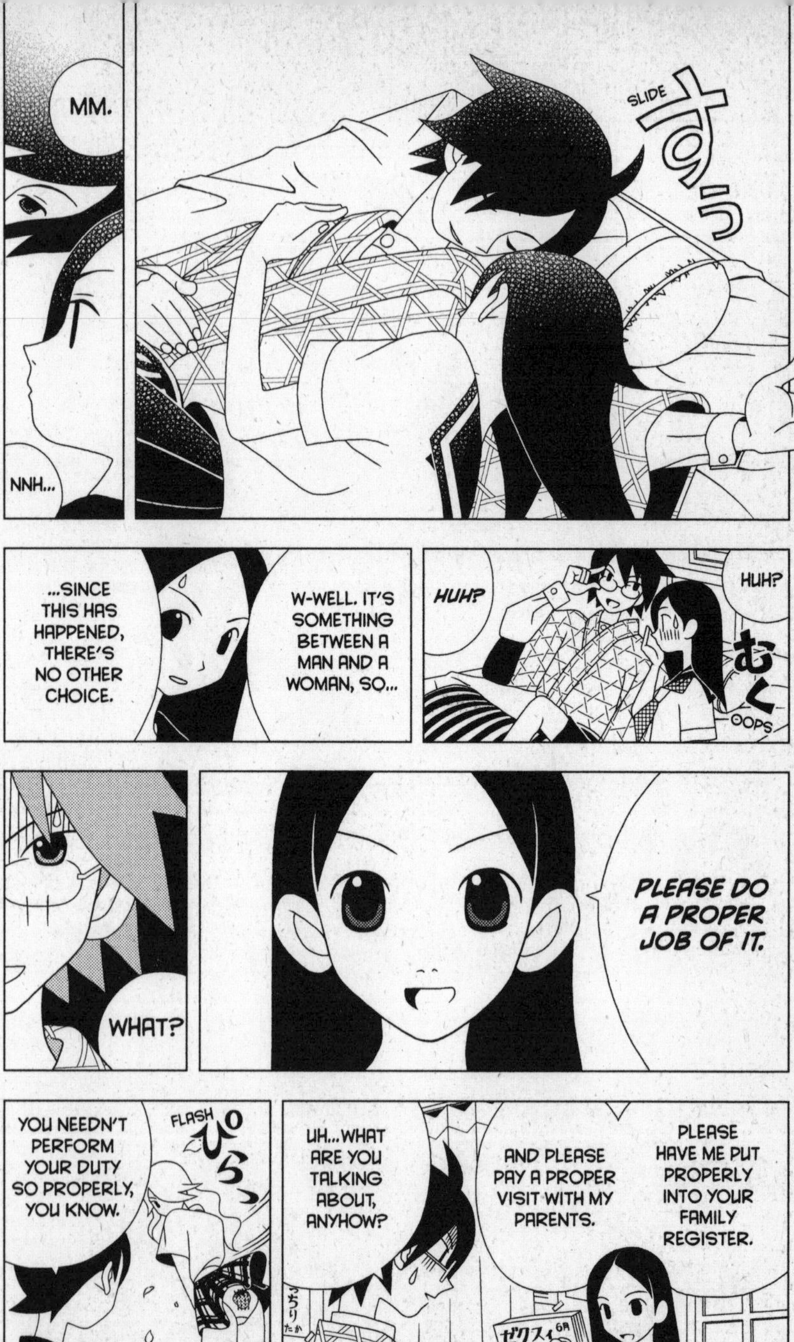
SLIDE
すう
MM.
NNH...
HUH?
HUH?
むく
OOPS
W-WELL. IT'S SOMETHING BETWEEN A MAN AND A WOMAN, SO...
...SINCE THIS HAS HAPPENED, THERE'S NO OTHER CHOICE.
PLEASE DO A PROPER JOB OF IT.
WHAT?
PLEASE HAVE ME PUT PROPERLY INTO YOUR FAMILY REGISTER.
AND PLEASE PAY A PROPER VISIT WITH MY PARENTS.
UH...WHAT ARE YOU TALKING ABOUT, ANYHOW?
ゼクスィ 6月
FLASH
ぴらっ
YOU NEEDN'T PERFORM YOUR DUTY SO PROPERLY, YOU KNOW.

# ATTENDANCE LIST
## CLASS 2-F

2005·06·15

**ATTENDANCE NO. 17**
# CHIRI KITSU
**METHODICAL AND PRECISE GIRL**

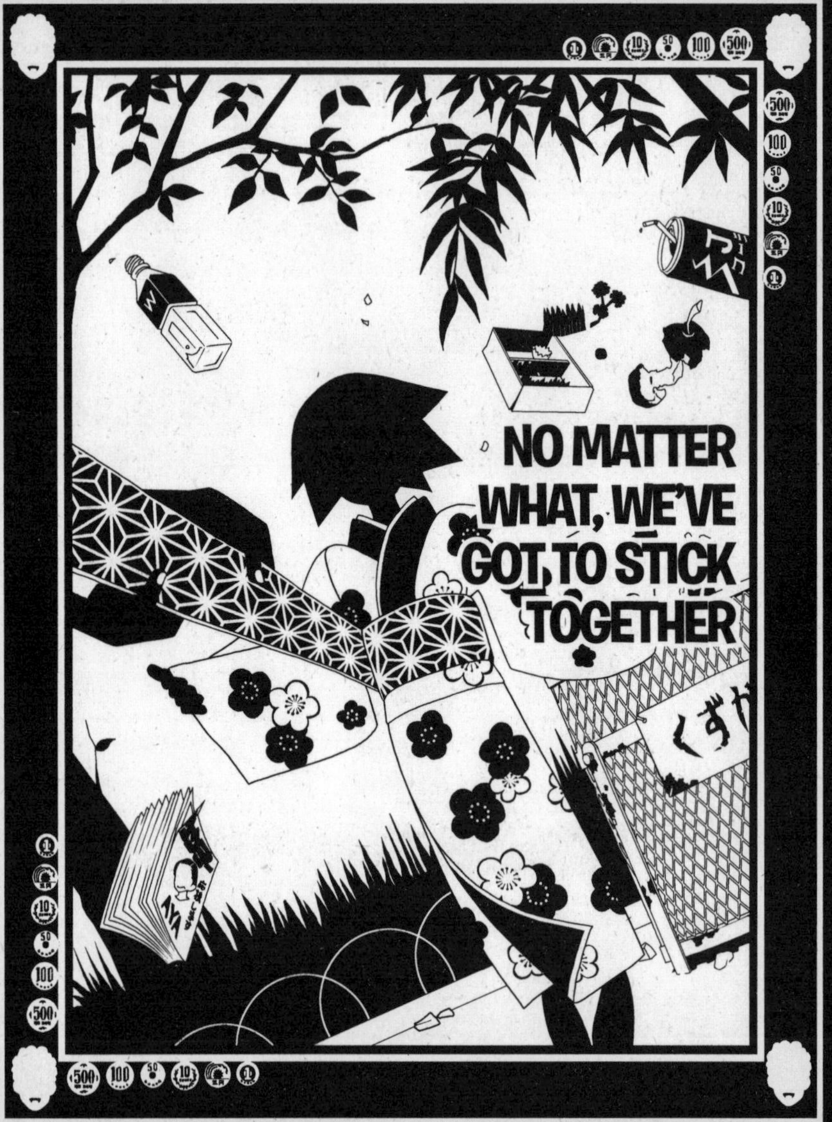
NO MATTER WHAT, WE'VE GOT TO STICK TOGETHER

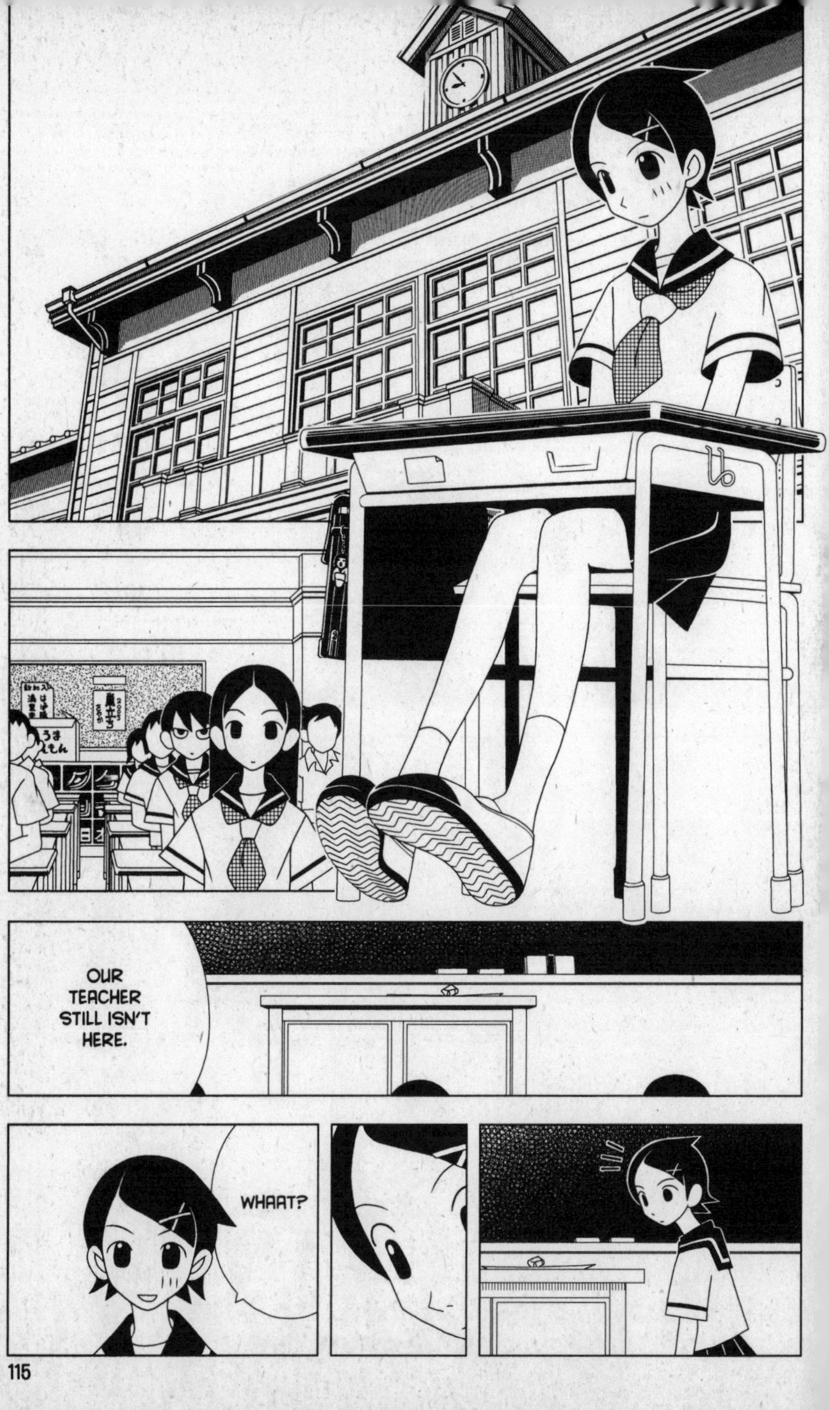
OUR TEACHER STILL ISN'T HERE.
WHAAT?

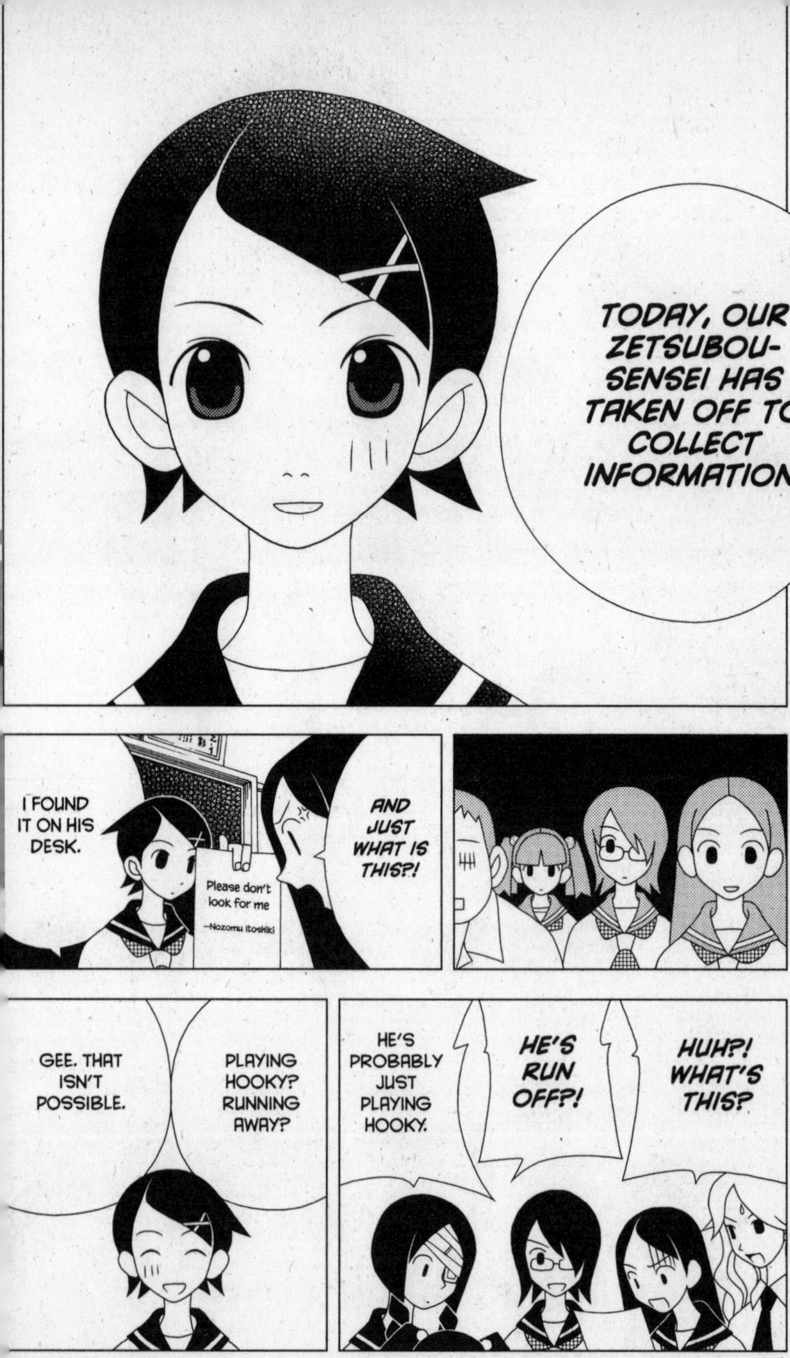
TODAY, OUR ZETSUBOU-SENSEI HAS TAKEN OFF TO COLLECT INFORMATION.
AND JUST WHAT IS THIS?!
I FOUND IT ON HIS DESK.
Please don't look for me
—Nozomu Itoshiki
HUH?! WHAT'S THIS?
HE'S RUN OFF?!
HE'S PROBABLY JUST PLAYING HOOKY.
PLAYING HOOKY? RUNNING AWAY?
GEE. THAT ISN'T POSSIBLE.

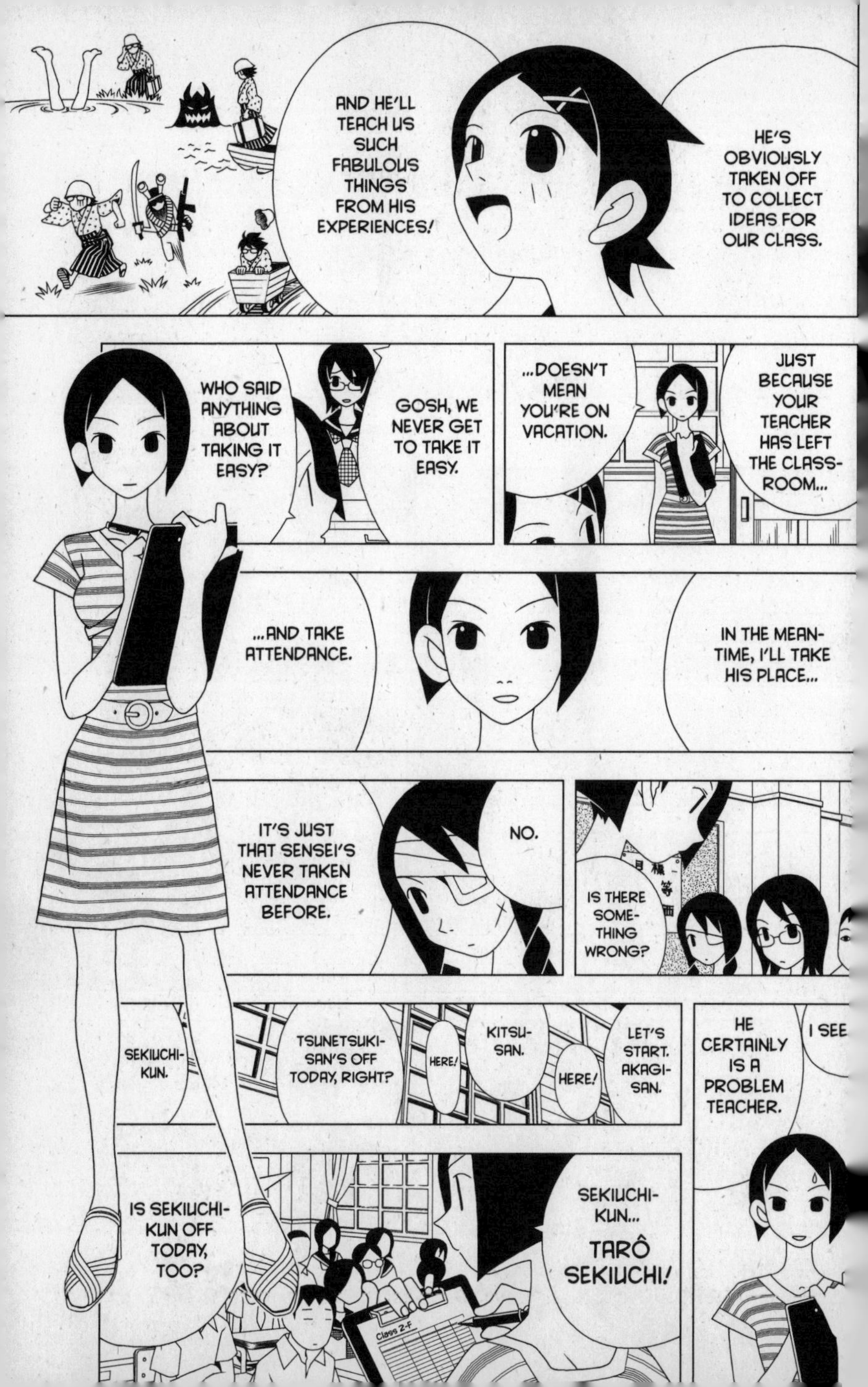

HE'S OBVIOUSLY TAKEN OFF TO COLLECT IDEAS FOR OUR CLASS.
AND HE'LL TEACH US SUCH FABULOUS THINGS FROM HIS EXPERIENCES!
JUST BECAUSE YOUR TEACHER HAS LEFT THE CLASS-ROOM...
...DOESN'T MEAN YOU'RE ON VACATION.
GOSH, WE NEVER GET TO TAKE IT EASY.
WHO SAID ANYTHING ABOUT TAKING IT EASY?
IN THE MEAN-TIME, I'LL TAKE HIS PLACE...
...AND TAKE ATTENDANCE.
IS THERE SOME-THING WRONG?
NO.
IT'S JUST THAT SENSEI'S NEVER TAKEN ATTENDANCE BEFORE.
I SEE
HE CERTAINLY IS A PROBLEM TEACHER.
LET'S START. AKAGI-SAN.
HERE!
KITSU-SAN.
HERE!
TSUNETSUKI-SAN'S OFF TODAY, RIGHT?
SEKIUCHI-KUN.
SEKIUCHI-KUN... TARÔ SEKIUCHI!
Class 2-F
IS SEKIUCHI-KUN OFF TODAY, TOO?

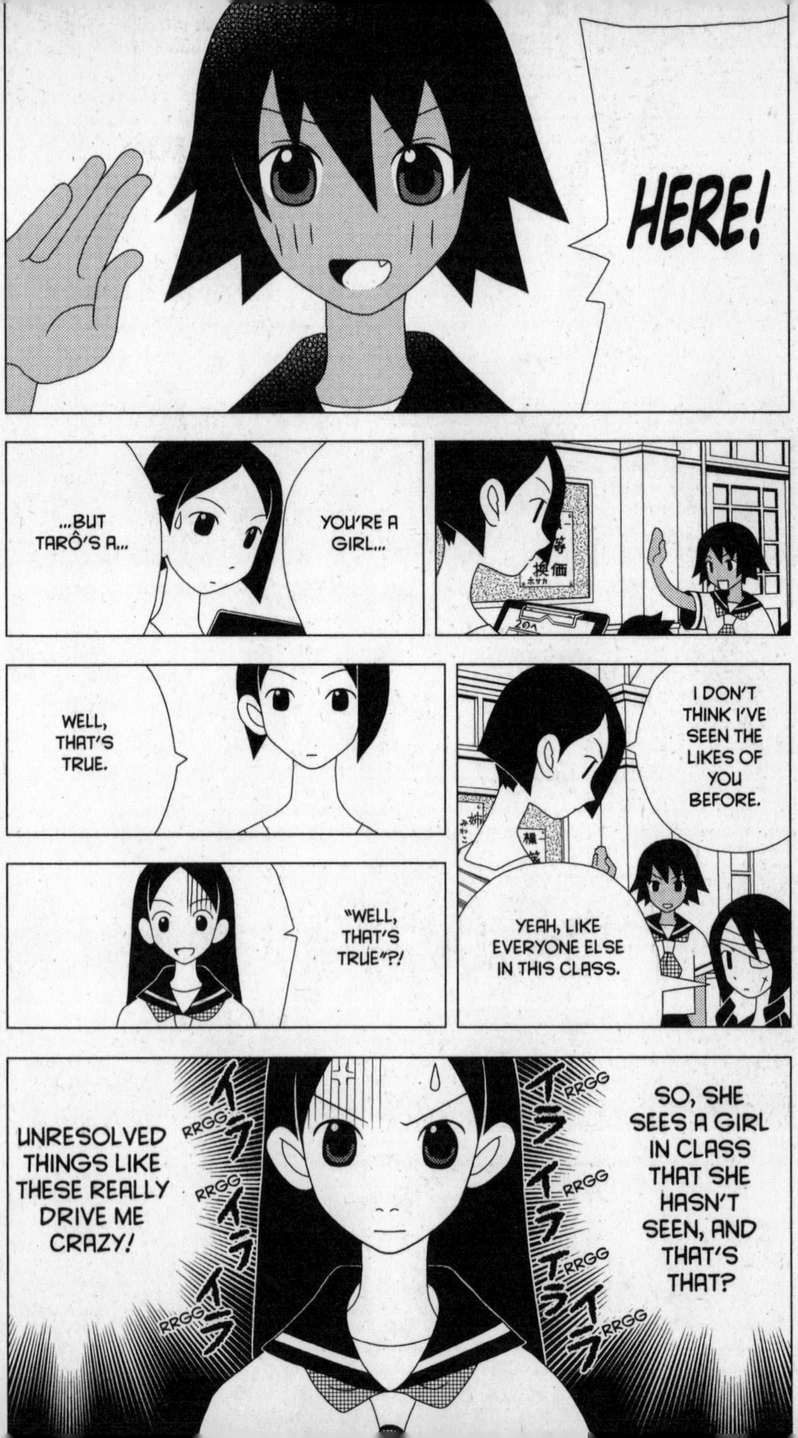
HERE!
YOU'RE A GIRL...
...BUT TARÔ'S A...
I DON'T THINK I'VE SEEN THE LIKES OF YOU BEFORE.
YEAH, LIKE EVERYONE ELSE IN THIS CLASS.
WELL, THAT'S TRUE.
"WELL, THAT'S TRUE"?!
SO, SHE SEES A GIRL IN CLASS THAT SHE HASN'T SEEN, AND THAT'S THAT?
イライラ RRGG RRGG RRGG
イライラ RRGG RRGG RRGG
UNRESOLVED THINGS LIKE THESE REALLY DRIVE ME CRAZY!

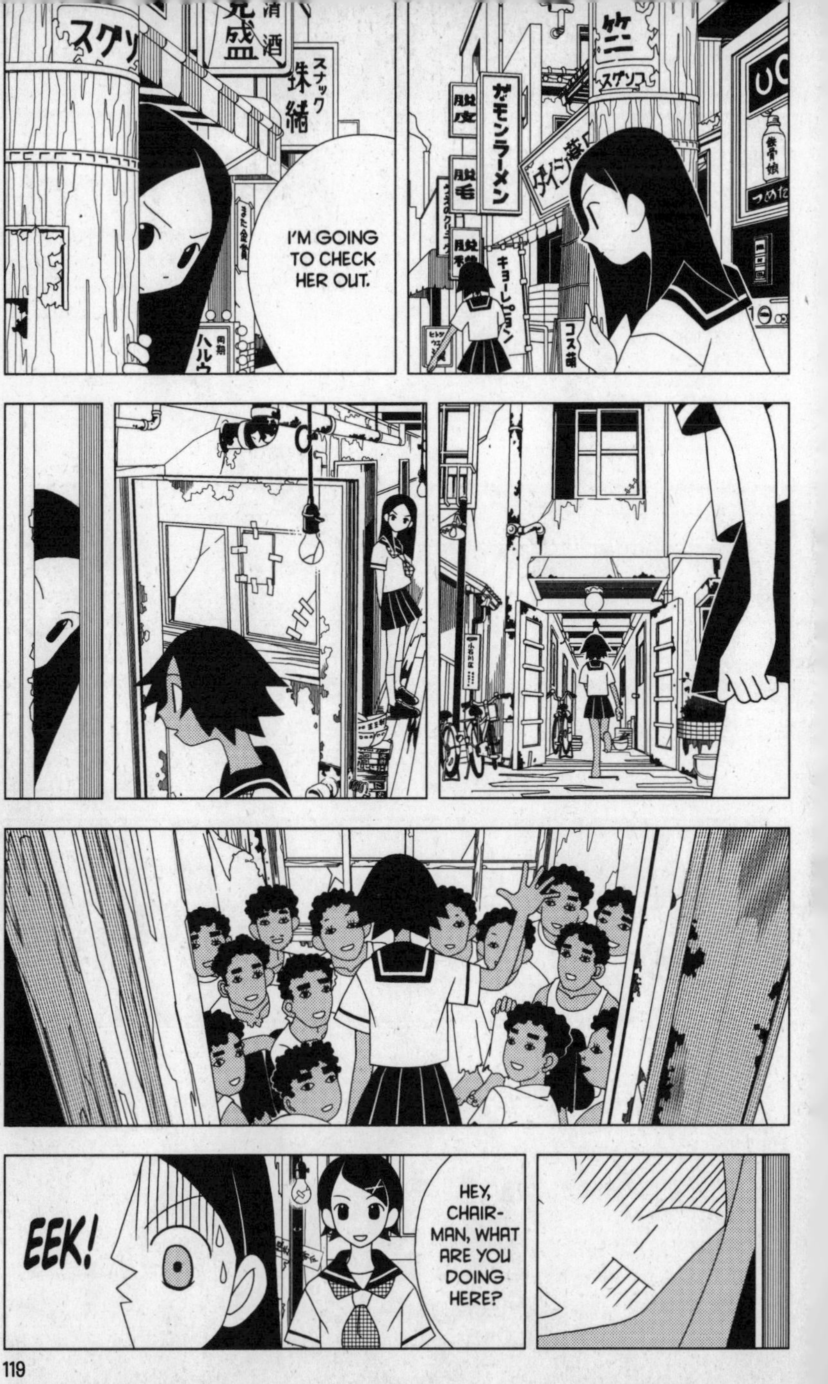
I'M GOING TO CHECK HER OUT.
HEY, CHAIR-MAN, WHAT ARE YOU DOING HERE?
EEK!

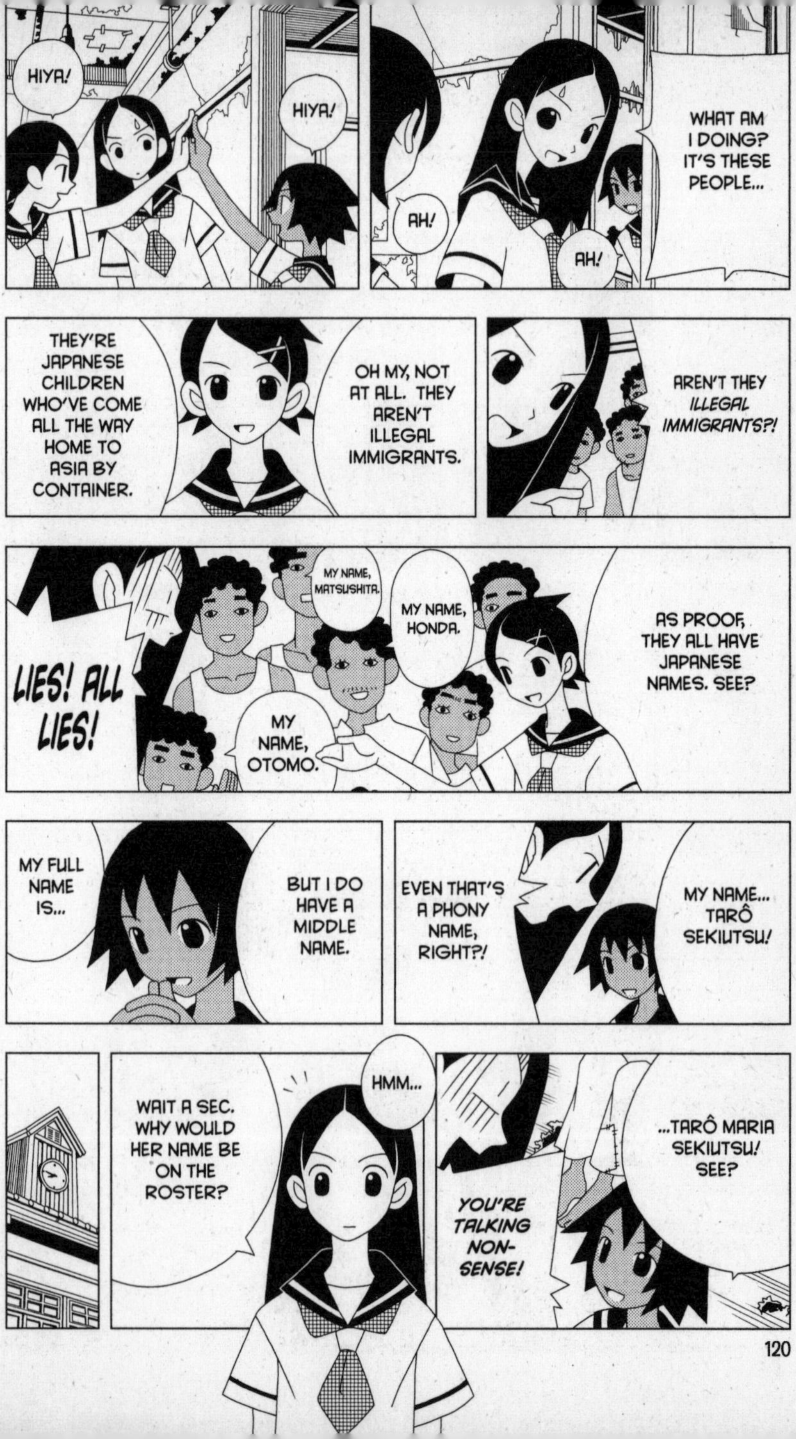
WHAT AM I DOING? IT'S THESE PEOPLE...
AH!
AH!
HIYA!
HIYA!
AREN'T THEY *ILLEGAL IMMIGRANTS?!*
OH MY, NOT AT ALL. THEY AREN'T ILLEGAL IMMIGRANTS.
THEY'RE JAPANESE CHILDREN WHO'VE COME ALL THE WAY HOME TO ASIA BY CONTAINER.
AS PROOF, THEY ALL HAVE JAPANESE NAMES. SEE?
MY NAME, HONDA.
MY NAME, MATSUSHITA.
MY NAME, OTOMO.
LIES! ALL LIES!
MY NAME... TARÔ SEKIUTSU!
EVEN THAT'S A PHONY NAME, RIGHT?!
BUT I DO HAVE A MIDDLE NAME.
MY FULL NAME IS...
...TARÔ MARIA SEKIUTSU! SEE?
YOU'RE TALKING NON-SENSE!
HMM...
WAIT A SEC. WHY WOULD HER NAME BE ON THE ROSTER?

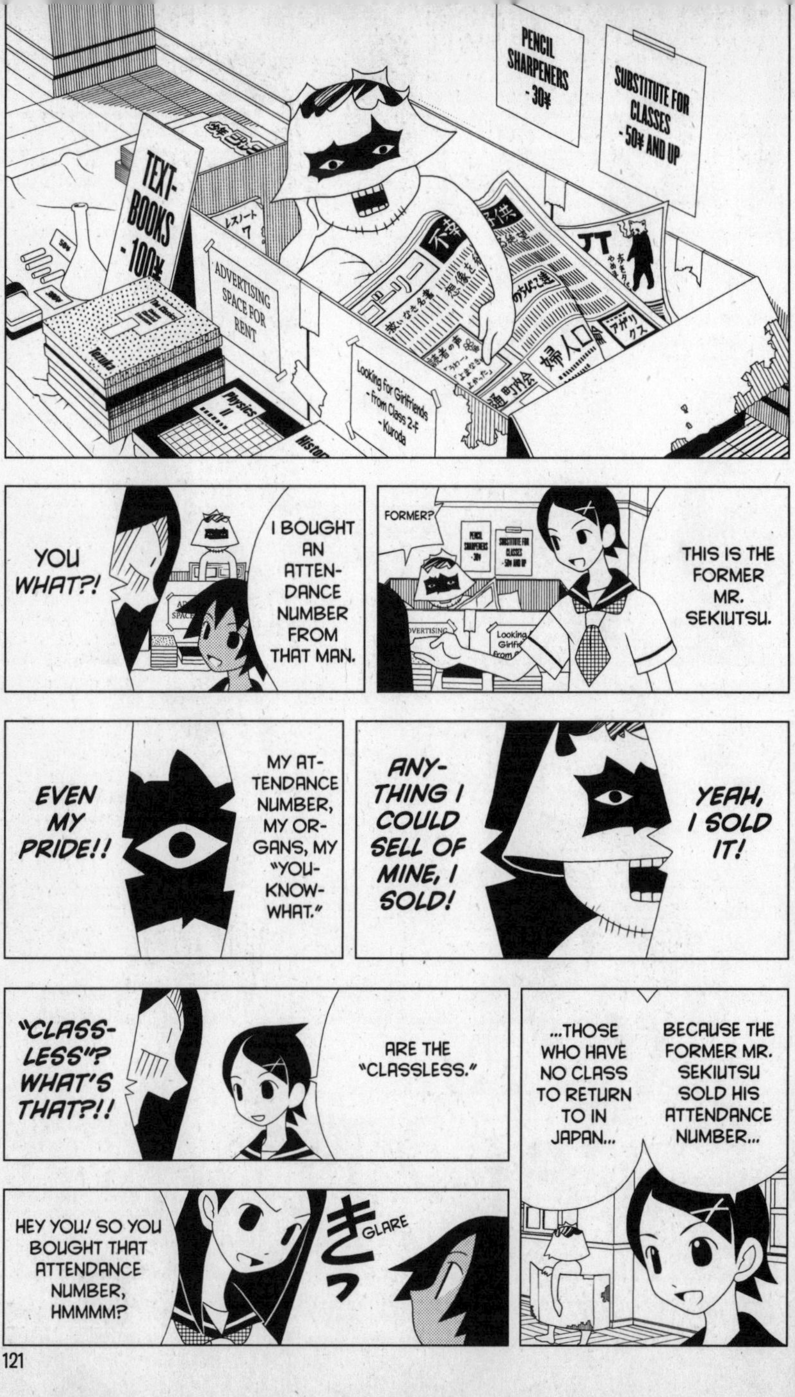
SUBSTITUTE FOR CLASSES - 50¥ AND UP
PENCIL SHARPENERS - 30¥
TEXT-BOOKS - 100¥
ADVERTISING SPACE FOR RENT
Looking for Girlfriends - from Class 2-F - Kuroda
Physics II
THIS IS THE FORMER MR. SEKIUTSU.
FORMER?
I BOUGHT AN ATTEN-DANCE NUMBER FROM THAT MAN.
YOU WHAT?!
YEAH, I SOLD IT!
ANY-THING I COULD SELL OF MINE, I SOLD!
MY AT-TENDANCE NUMBER, MY OR-GANS, MY "YOU-KNOW-WHAT."
EVEN MY PRIDE!!
BECAUSE THE FORMER MR. SEKIUTSU SOLD HIS ATTENDANCE NUMBER...
...THOSE WHO HAVE NO CLASS TO RETURN TO IN JAPAN...
ARE THE "CLASSLESS."
"CLASS-LESS"? WHAT'S THAT?!!
きっ GLARE
HEY YOU! SO YOU BOUGHT THAT ATTENDANCE NUMBER, HMMMM?

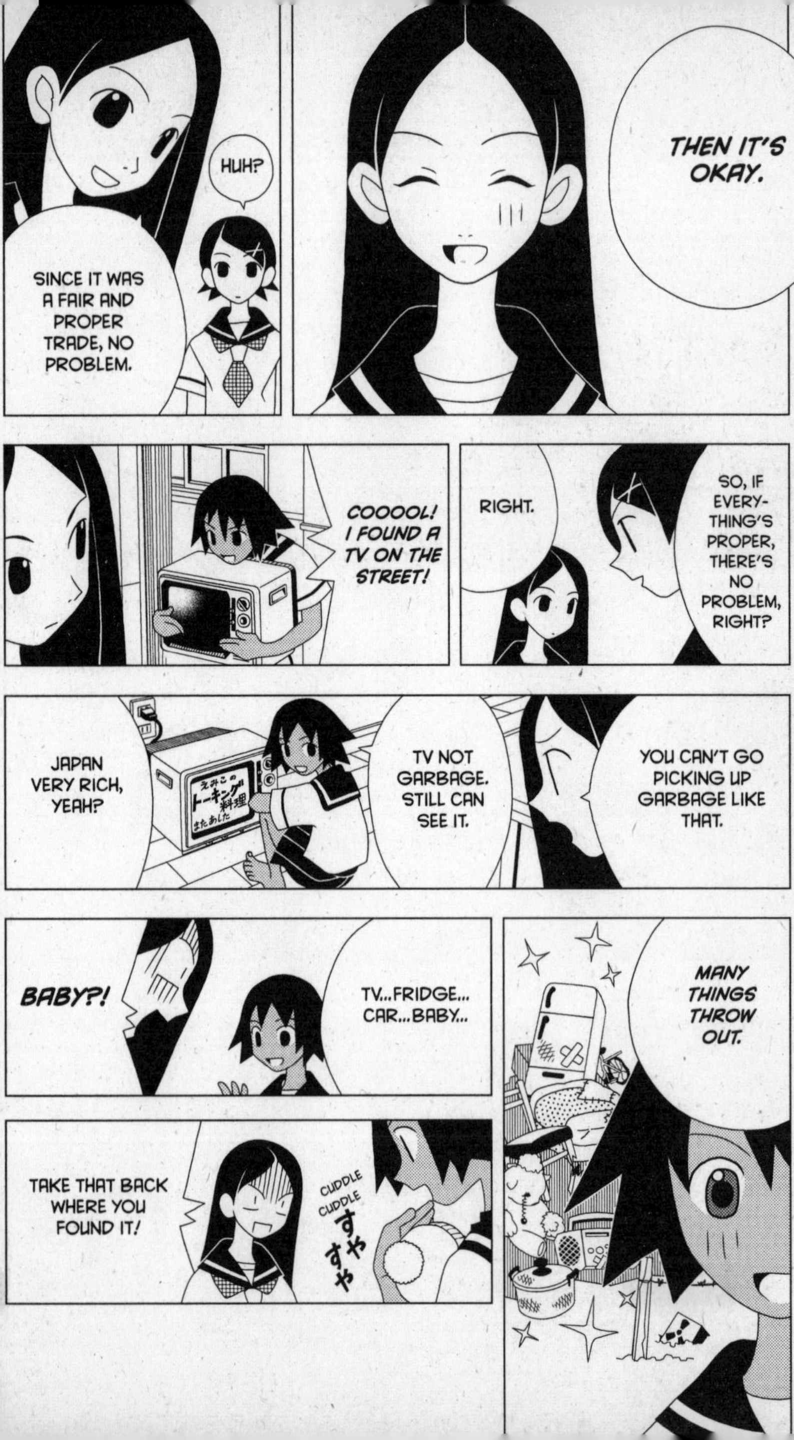
THEN IT'S OKAY.
HUH?
SINCE IT WAS A FAIR AND PROPER TRADE, NO PROBLEM.
SO, IF EVERYTHING'S PROPER, THERE'S NO PROBLEM, RIGHT?
RIGHT.
COOOOL! I FOUND A TV ON THE STREET!
YOU CAN'T GO PICKING UP GARBAGE LIKE THAT.
TV NOT GARBAGE. STILL CAN SEE IT.
えみこの
トーキング料理
またあした
JAPAN VERY RICH, YEAH?
MANY THINGS THROW OUT.
TV...FRIDGE... CAR...BABY...
BABY?!
CUDDLE CUDDLE
すやすや
TAKE THAT BACK WHERE YOU FOUND IT!

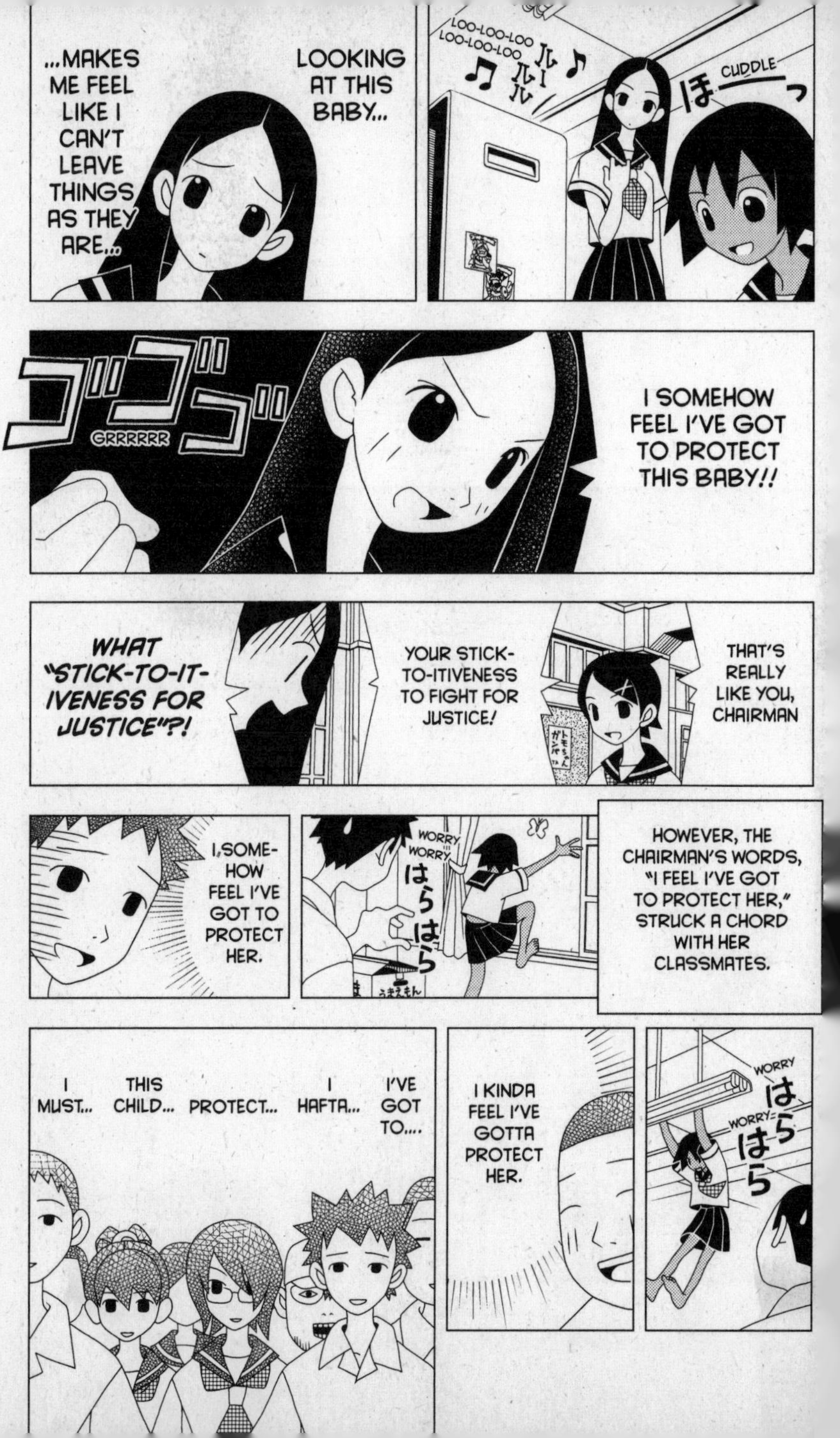
LOO-LOO-LOO
LOO-LOO-LOO
CUDDLE
ほーっ
LOOKING AT THIS BABY...
...MAKES ME FEEL LIKE I CAN'T LEAVE THINGS AS THEY ARE...
I SOMEHOW FEEL I'VE GOT TO PROTECT THIS BABY!!
ゴゴゴ
GRRRRRR
THAT'S REALLY LIKE YOU, CHAIRMAN
YOUR STICK-TO-ITIVENESS TO FIGHT FOR JUSTICE!
WHAT "STICK-TO-IT-IVENESS FOR JUSTICE"?!
HOWEVER, THE CHAIRMAN'S WORDS, "I FEEL I'VE GOT TO PROTECT HER," STRUCK A CHORD WITH HER CLASSMATES.
WORRY WORRY
はらはら
I, SOME-HOW FEEL I'VE GOT TO PROTECT HER.
WORRY
はら
WORRY
はら
I KINDA FEEL I'VE GOTTA PROTECT HER.
I'VE GOT TO....
I HAFTA...
PROTECT...
THIS CHILD...
I MUST...

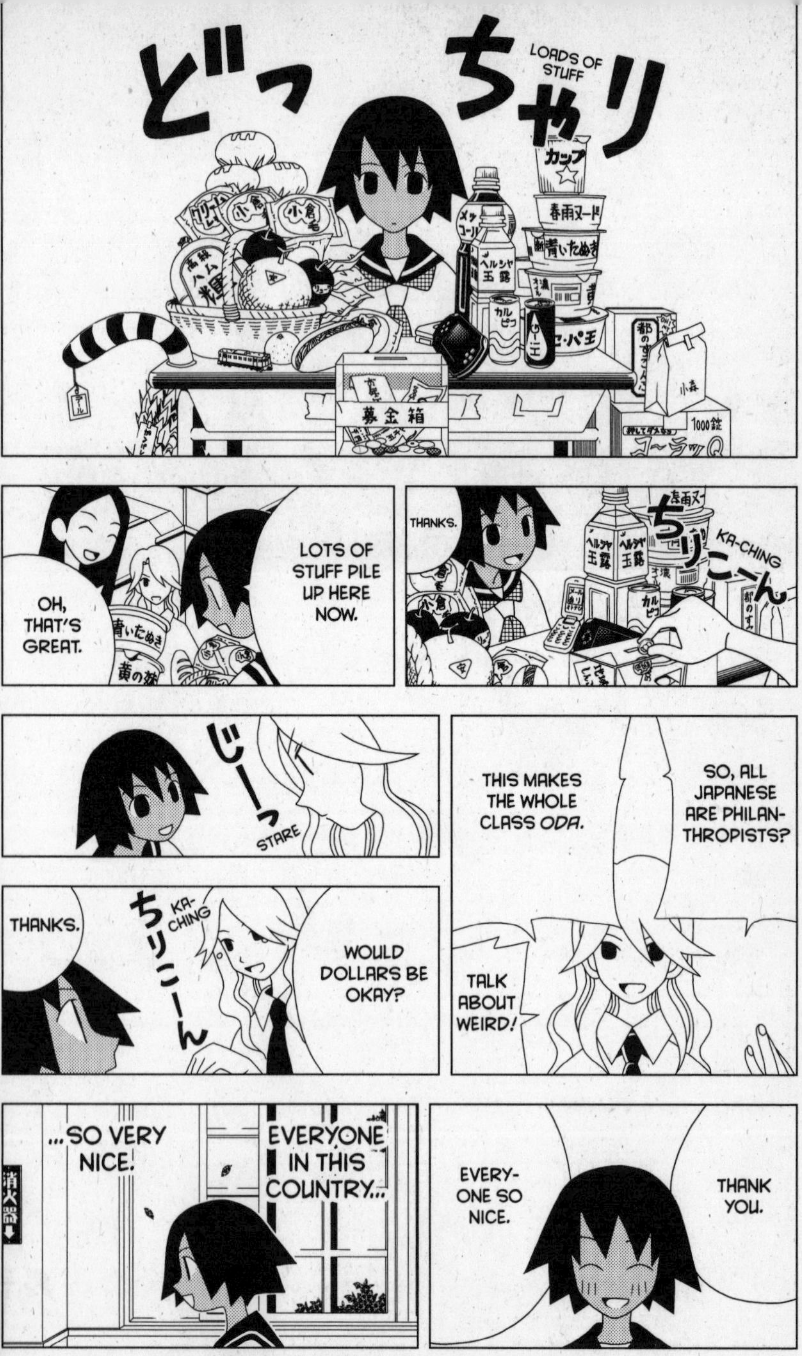
どっちゃり
LOADS OF STUFF
カップ
春雨ヌード
募金箱
THANKS.
ちりこーん
KA-CHING
LOTS OF STUFF PILE UP HERE NOW.
OH, THAT'S GREAT.
SO, ALL JAPANESE ARE PHILANTHROPISTS?
THIS MAKES THE WHOLE CLASS *ODA*.
TALK ABOUT WEIRD!
じーっ
STARE
WOULD DOLLARS BE OKAY?
ちりこーん
KA-CHING
THANKS.
THANK YOU.
EVERY-ONE SO NICE.
EVERYONE IN THIS COUNTRY...
...SO VERY NICE.
消火器

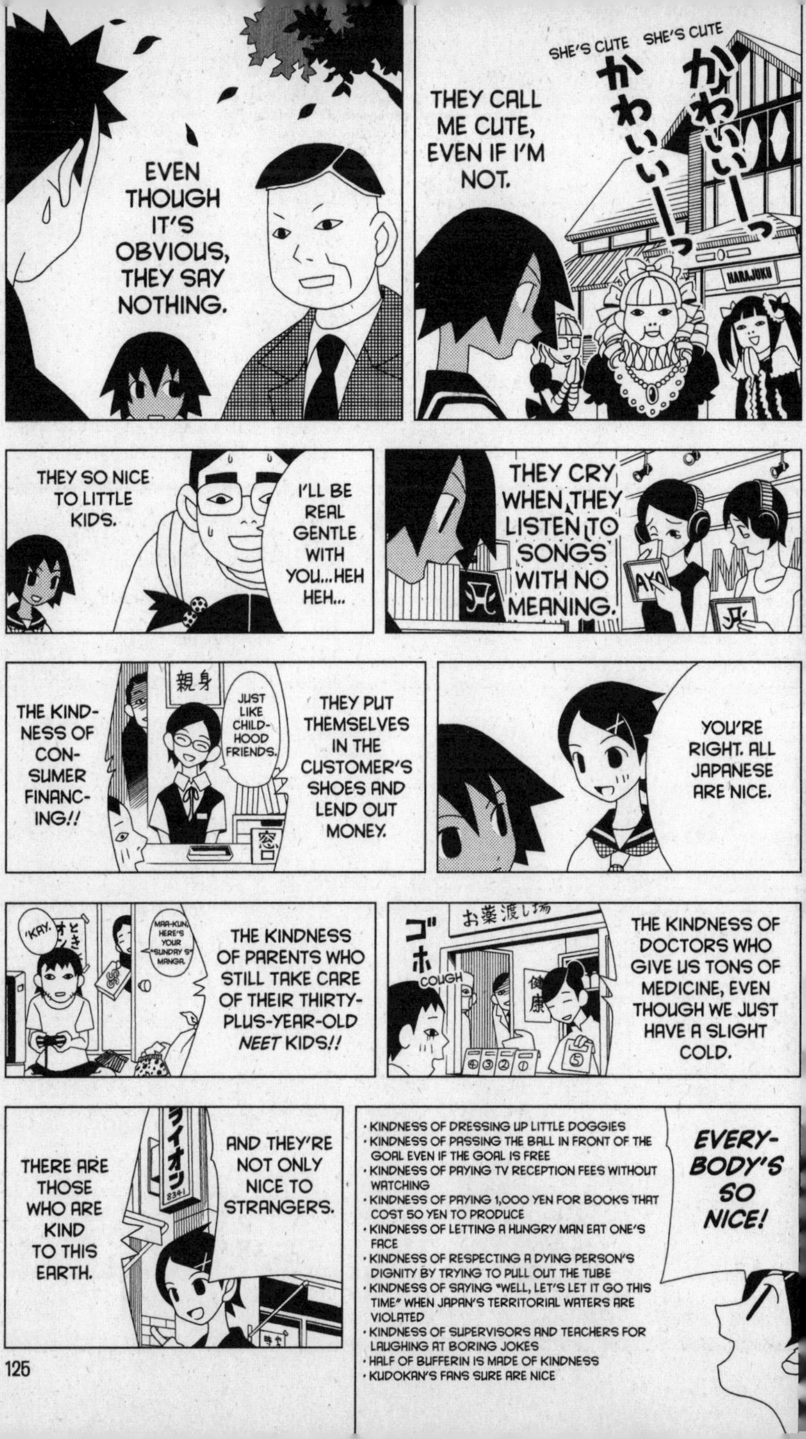
かわいいーっ
SHE'S CUTE
かわいいーっ
SHE'S CUTE
THEY CALL ME CUTE, EVEN IF I'M NOT.
HARAJUKU
EVEN THOUGH IT'S OBVIOUS, THEY SAY NOTHING.
THEY CRY WHEN THEY LISTEN TO SONGS WITH NO MEANING.
I'LL BE REAL GENTLE WITH YOU...HEH HEH...
THEY SO NICE TO LITTLE KIDS.
YOU'RE RIGHT. ALL JAPANESE ARE NICE.
THEY PUT THEMSELVES IN THE CUSTOMER'S SHOES AND LEND OUT MONEY.
親身
JUST LIKE CHILDHOOD FRIENDS.
THE KINDNESS OF CONSUMER FINANCING!!
お薬渡し場
THE KINDNESS OF DOCTORS WHO GIVE US TONS OF MEDICINE, EVEN THOUGH WE JUST HAVE A SLIGHT COLD.
ゴホ
COUGH
健康
THE KINDNESS OF PARENTS WHO STILL TAKE CARE OF THEIR THIRTY-PLUS-YEAR-OLD *NEET* KIDS!!
MAA-KUN, HERE'S YOUR "SUNDAY S" MANGA.
'KAY.
EVERYBODY'S SO NICE!
• KINDNESS OF DRESSING UP LITTLE DOGGIES
• KINDNESS OF PASSING THE BALL IN FRONT OF THE GOAL EVEN IF THE GOAL IS FREE
• KINDNESS OF PAYING TV RECEPTION FEES WITHOUT WATCHING
• KINDNESS OF PAYING 1,000 YEN FOR BOOKS THAT COST 50 YEN TO PRODUCE
• KINDNESS OF LETTING A HUNGRY MAN EAT ONE'S FACE
• KINDNESS OF RESPECTING A DYING PERSON'S DIGNITY BY TRYING TO PULL OUT THE TUBE
• KINDNESS OF SAYING "WELL, LET'S LET IT GO THIS TIME" WHEN JAPAN'S TERRITORIAL WATERS ARE VIOLATED
• KINDNESS OF SUPERVISORS AND TEACHERS FOR LAUGHING AT BORING JOKES
• HALF OF BUFFERIN IS MADE OF KINDNESS
• KUDOKAN'S FANS SURE ARE NICE
AND THEY'RE NOT ONLY NICE TO STRANGERS.
ライオン
THERE ARE THOSE WHO ARE KIND TO THIS EARTH.

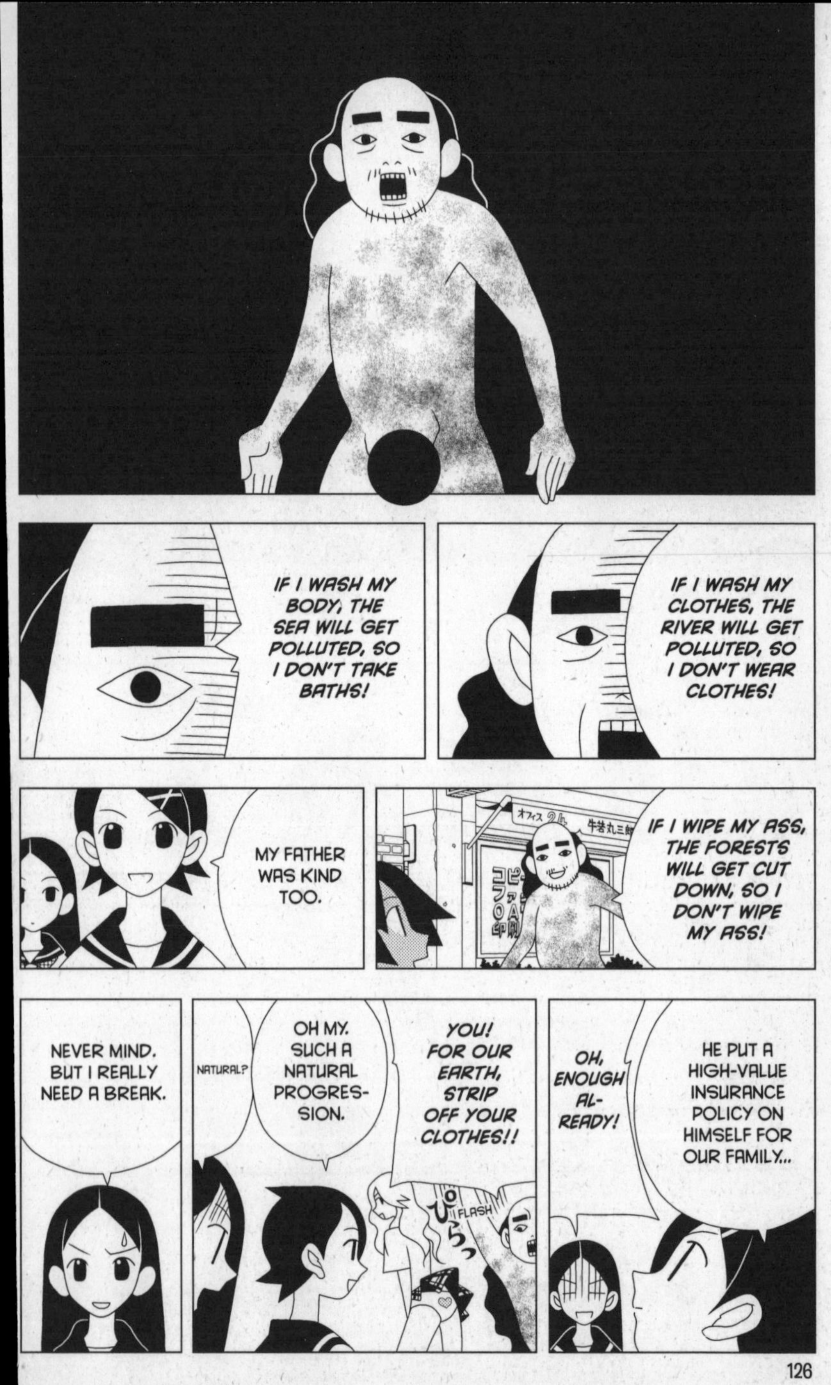
IF I WASH MY CLOTHES, THE RIVER WILL GET POLLUTED, SO I DON'T WEAR CLOTHES!
IF I WASH MY BODY, THE SEA WILL GET POLLUTED, SO I DON'T TAKE BATHS!
IF I WIPE MY ASS, THE FORESTS WILL GET CUT DOWN, SO I DON'T WIPE MY ASS!
MY FATHER WAS KIND TOO.
HE PUT A HIGH-VALUE INSURANCE POLICY ON HIMSELF FOR OUR FAMILY...
OH, ENOUGH AL-READY!
YOU! FOR OUR EARTH, STRIP OFF YOUR CLOTHES!!
FLASH
OH MY. SUCH A NATURAL PROGRES-SION.
NATURAL?
NEVER MIND. BUT I REALLY NEED A BREAK.

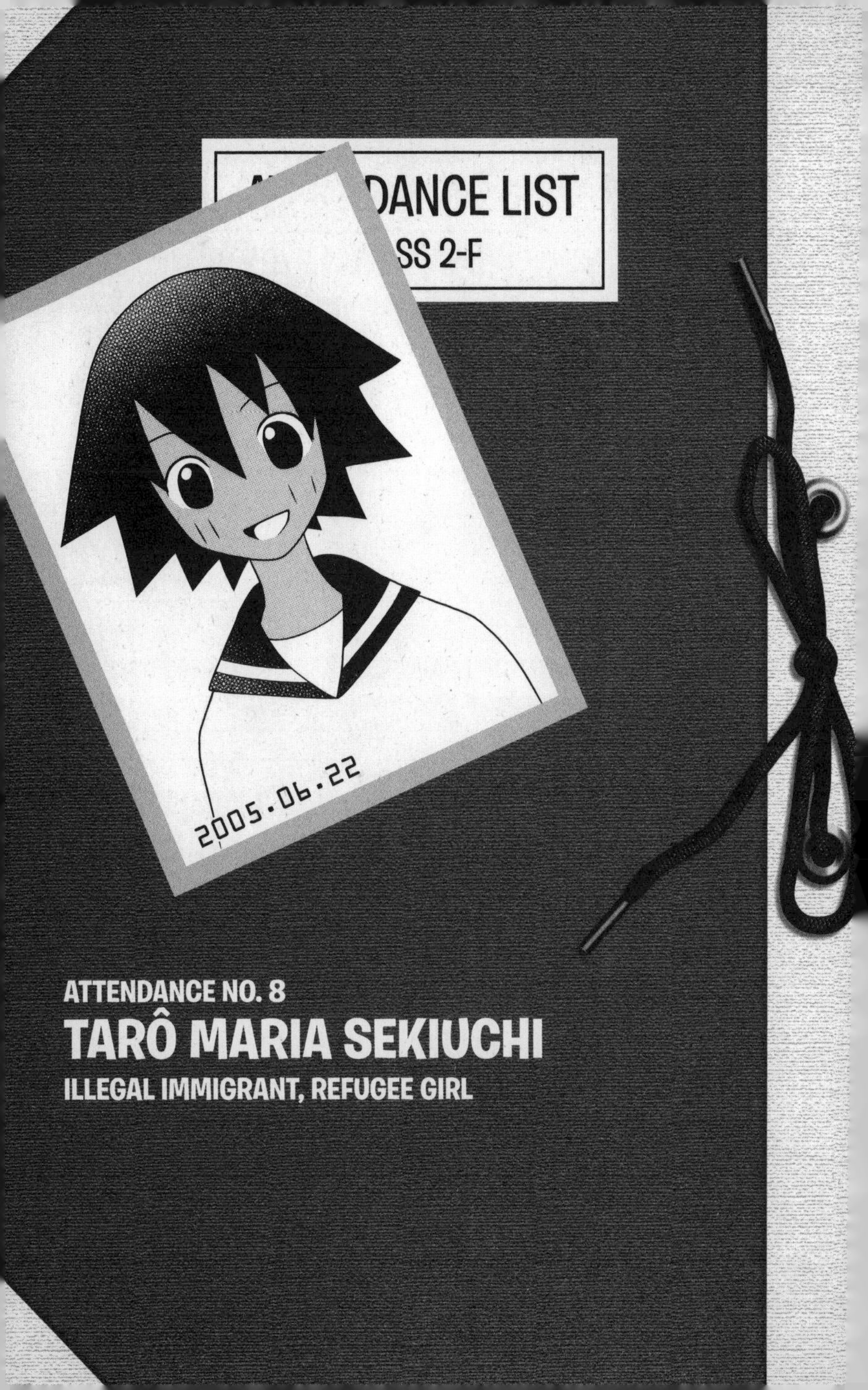
DANCE LIST
SS 2-F
2005.06.22
ATTENDANCE NO. 8
TARÔ MARIA SEKIUCHI
ILLEGAL IMMIGRANT, REFUGEE GIRL

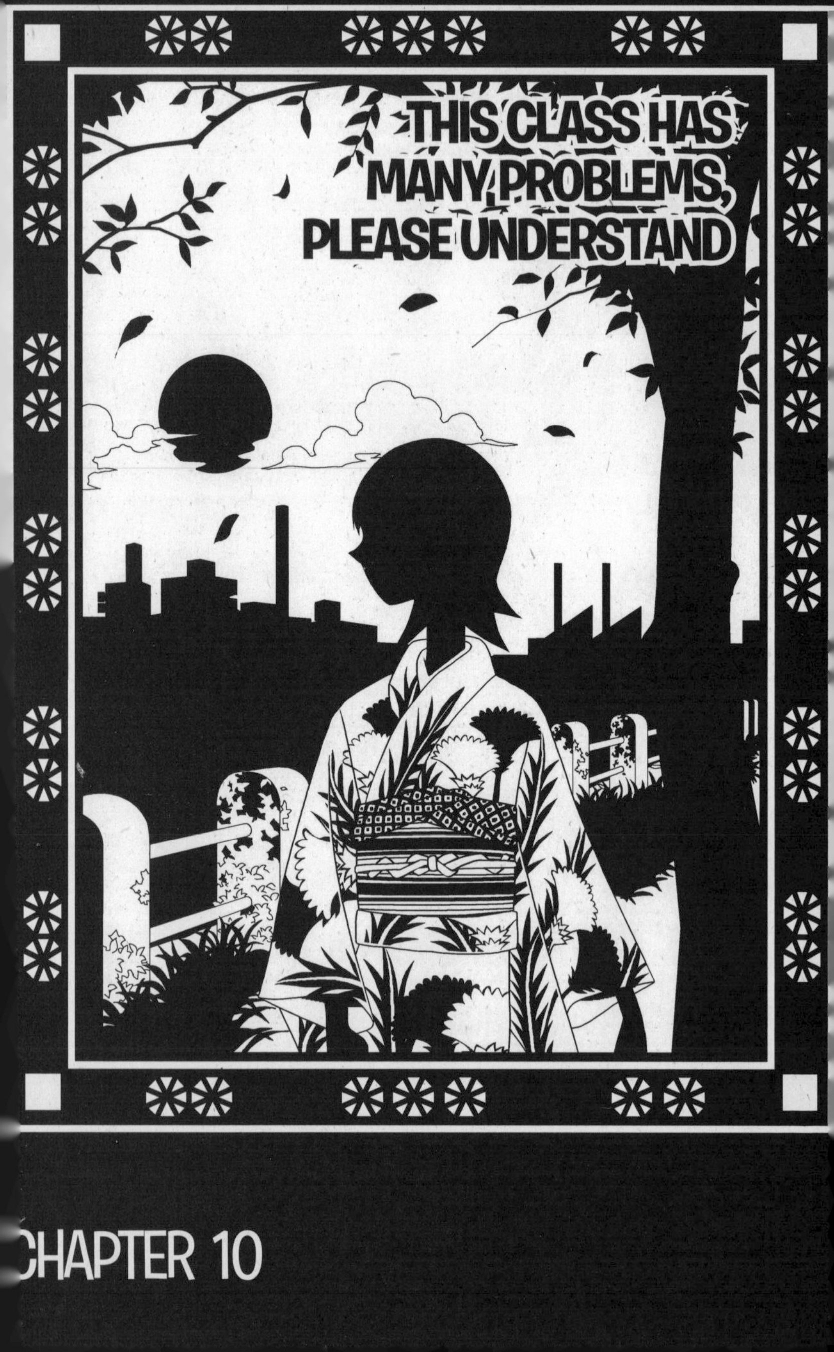
THIS CLASS HAS MANY PROBLEMS, PLEASE UNDERSTAND

# CHAPTER 10

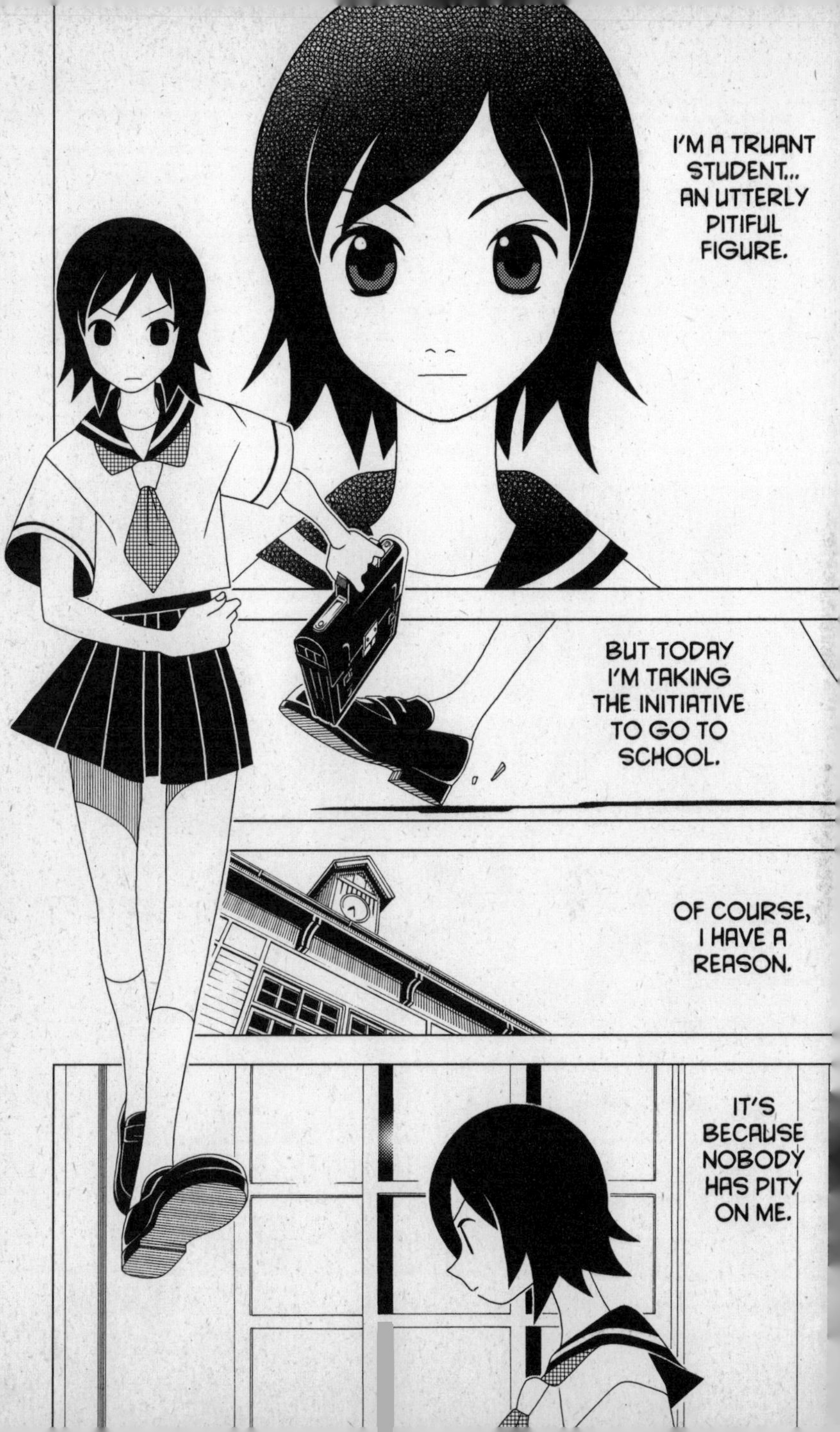
I'M A TRUANT STUDENT... AN UTTERLY PITIFUL FIGURE.
BUT TODAY I'M TAKING THE INITIATIVE TO GO TO SCHOOL.
OF COURSE, I HAVE A REASON.
IT'S BECAUSE NOBODY HAS PITY ON ME.

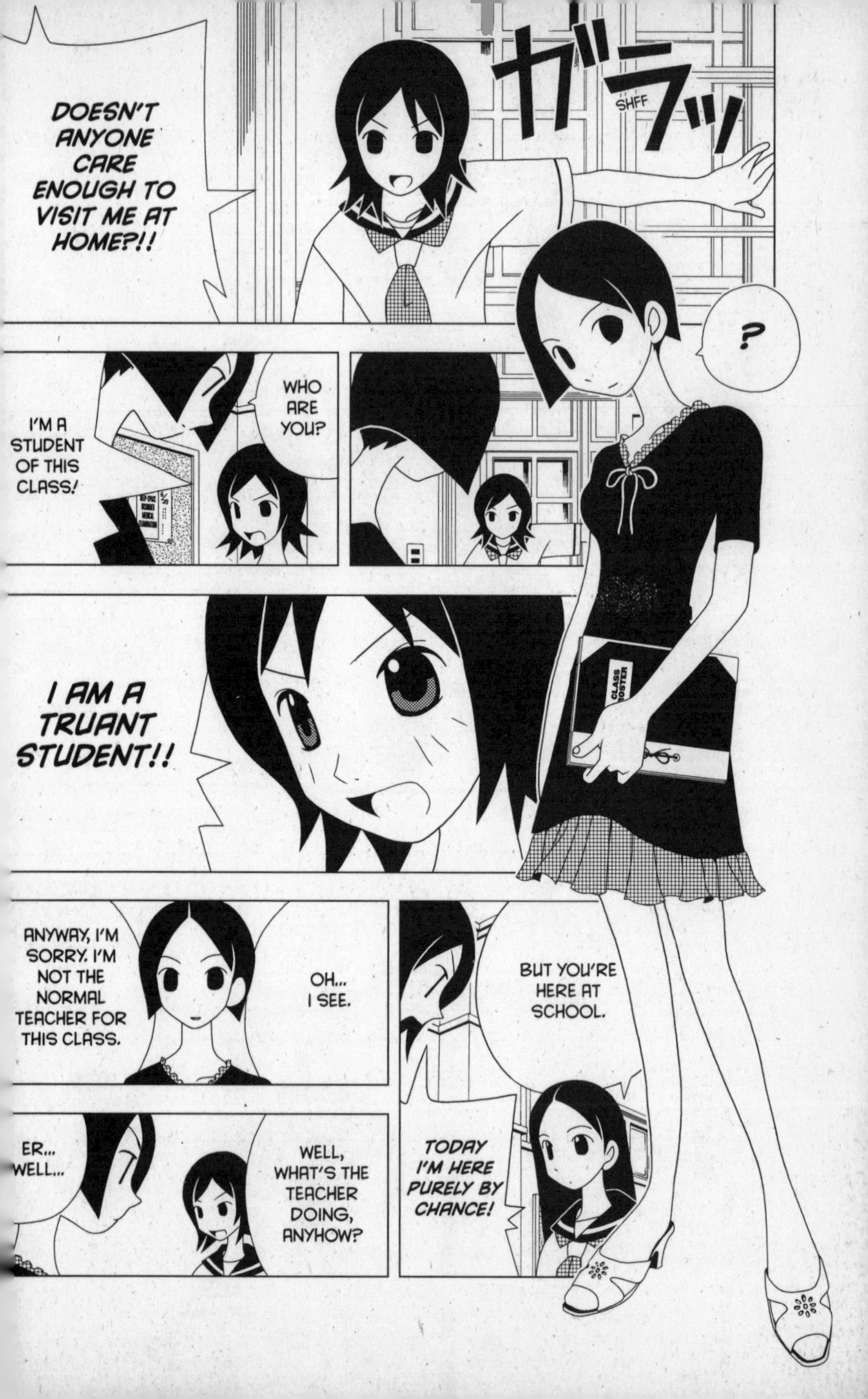
ガラッ
SHFF
DOESN'T ANYONE CARE ENOUGH TO VISIT ME AT HOME?!!
?
CLASS ROSTER
WHO ARE YOU?
I'M A STUDENT OF THIS CLASS!
I AM A TRUANT STUDENT!!
BUT YOU'RE HERE AT SCHOOL.
TODAY I'M HERE PURELY BY CHANCE!
OH... I SEE.
ANYWAY, I'M SORRY. I'M NOT THE NORMAL TEACHER FOR THIS CLASS.
WELL, WHAT'S THE TEACHER DOING, ANYHOW?
ER... WELL...

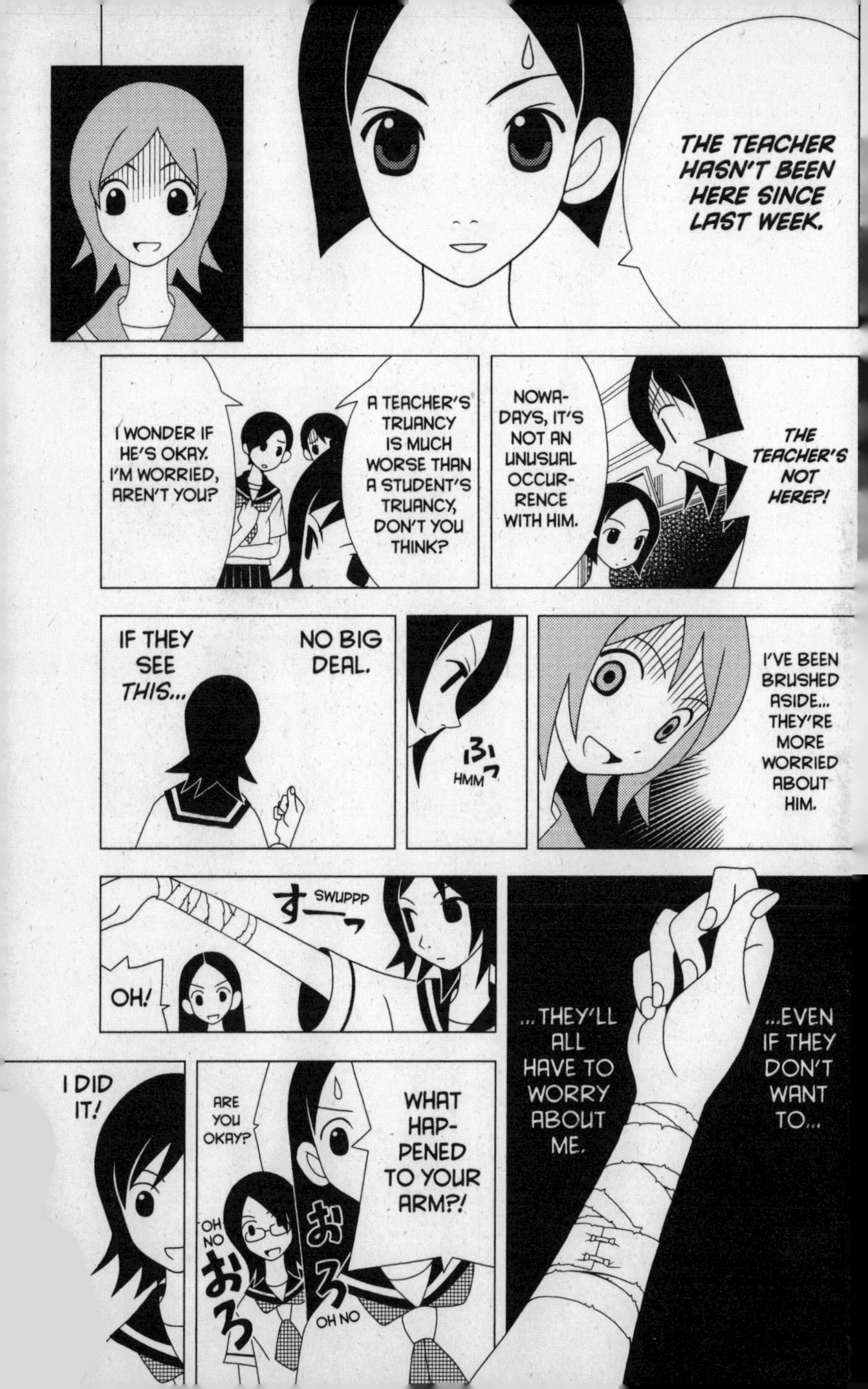
THE TEACHER HASN'T BEEN HERE SINCE LAST WEEK.
THE TEACHER'S NOT HERE?!
NOWA-DAYS, IT'S NOT AN UNUSUAL OCCUR-RENCE WITH HIM.
A TEACHER'S TRUANCY IS MUCH WORSE THAN A STUDENT'S TRUANCY, DON'T YOU THINK?
I WONDER IF HE'S OKAY. I'M WORRIED, AREN'T YOU?
I'VE BEEN BRUSHED ASIDE... THEY'RE MORE WORRIED ABOUT HIM.
ふー
HMM
NO BIG DEAL.
IF THEY SEE THIS...
...EVEN IF THEY DON'T WANT TO...
...THEY'LL ALL HAVE TO WORRY ABOUT ME.
すー
SWUPPP
OH!
WHAT HAP-PENED TO YOUR ARM?!
ARE YOU OKAY?
おろ
OH NO
おろ
OH NO
I DID IT!

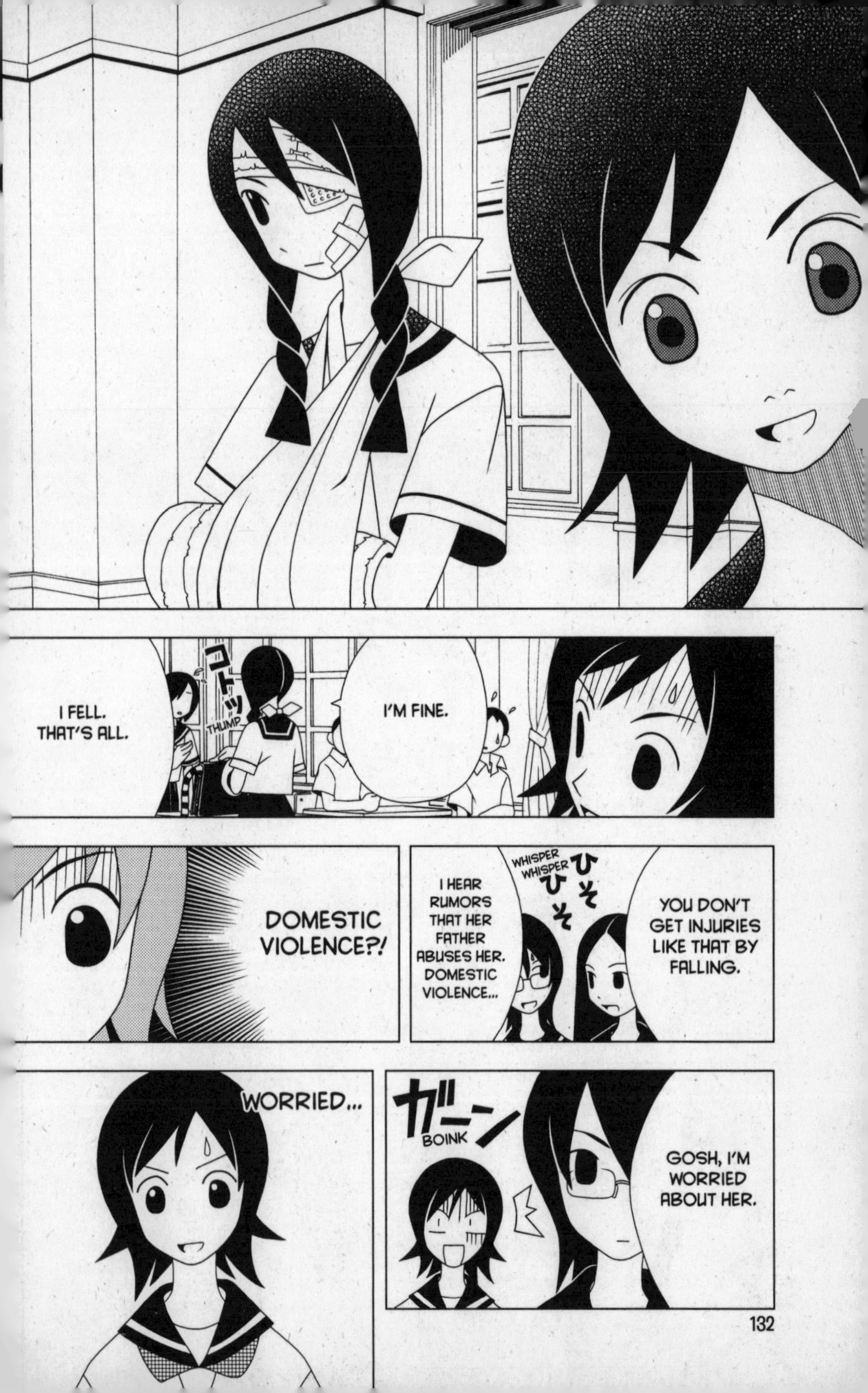
I'M FINE.
コトッ
THUMP
I FELL. THAT'S ALL.
YOU DON'T GET INJURIES LIKE THAT BY FALLING.
ひそひそ
WHISPER WHISPER
I HEAR RUMORS THAT HER FATHER ABUSES HER. DOMESTIC VIOLENCE...
DOMESTIC VIOLENCE?!
GOSH, I'M WORRIED ABOUT HER.
ガーン
BOINK
WORRIED...

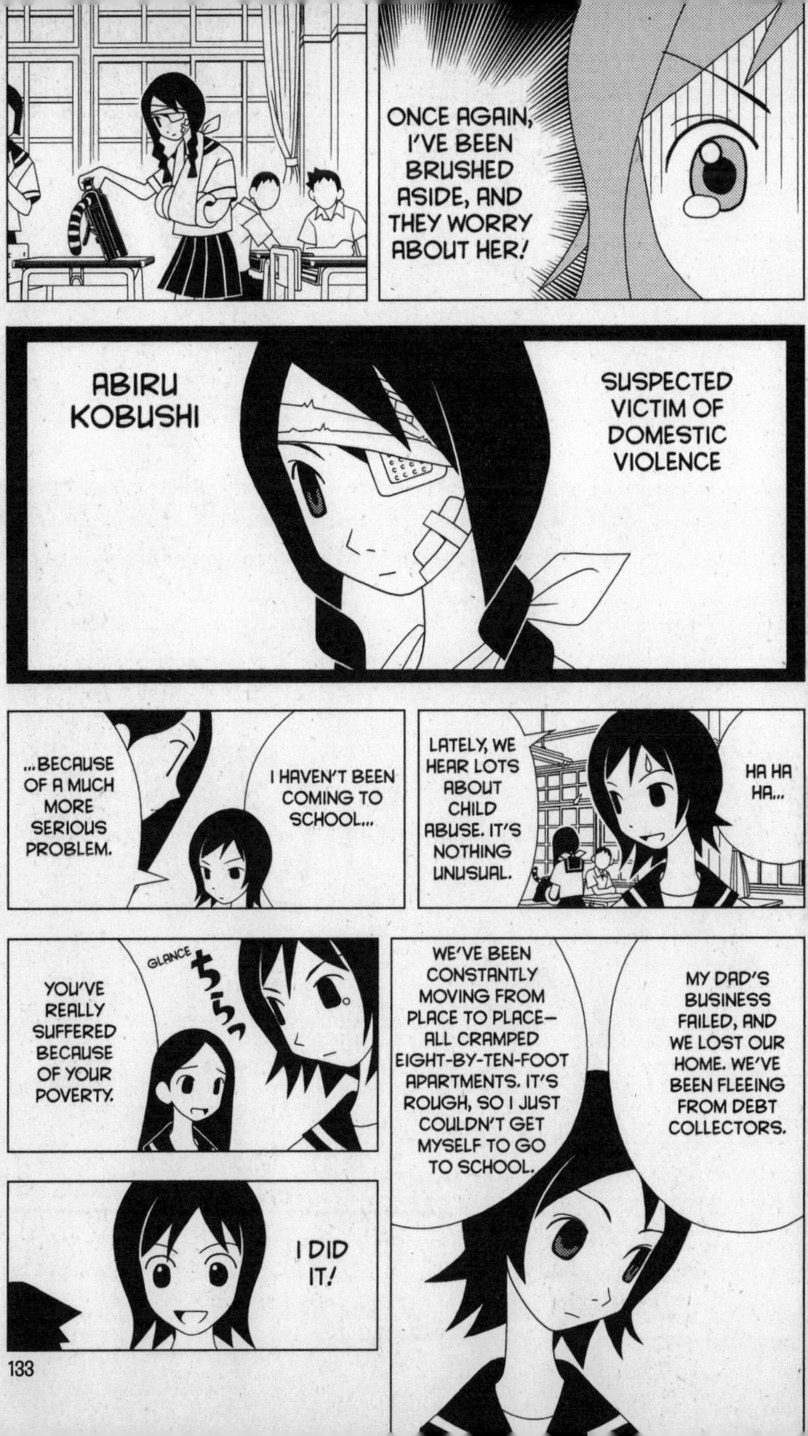
ONCE AGAIN, I'VE BEEN BRUSHED ASIDE, AND THEY WORRY ABOUT HER!
SUSPECTED VICTIM OF DOMESTIC VIOLENCE
ABIRU KOBUSHI
HA HA HA...
LATELY, WE HEAR LOTS ABOUT CHILD ABUSE. IT'S NOTHING UNUSUAL.
I HAVEN'T BEEN COMING TO SCHOOL...
...BECAUSE OF A MUCH MORE SERIOUS PROBLEM.
MY DAD'S BUSINESS FAILED, AND WE LOST OUR HOME. WE'VE BEEN FLEEING FROM DEBT COLLECTORS.
WE'VE BEEN CONSTANTLY MOVING FROM PLACE TO PLACE—ALL CRAMPED EIGHT-BY-TEN-FOOT APARTMENTS. IT'S ROUGH, SO I JUST COULDN'T GET MYSELF TO GO TO SCHOOL.
GLANCE
ちらっ
YOU'VE REALLY SUFFERED BECAUSE OF YOUR POVERTY.
I DID IT!

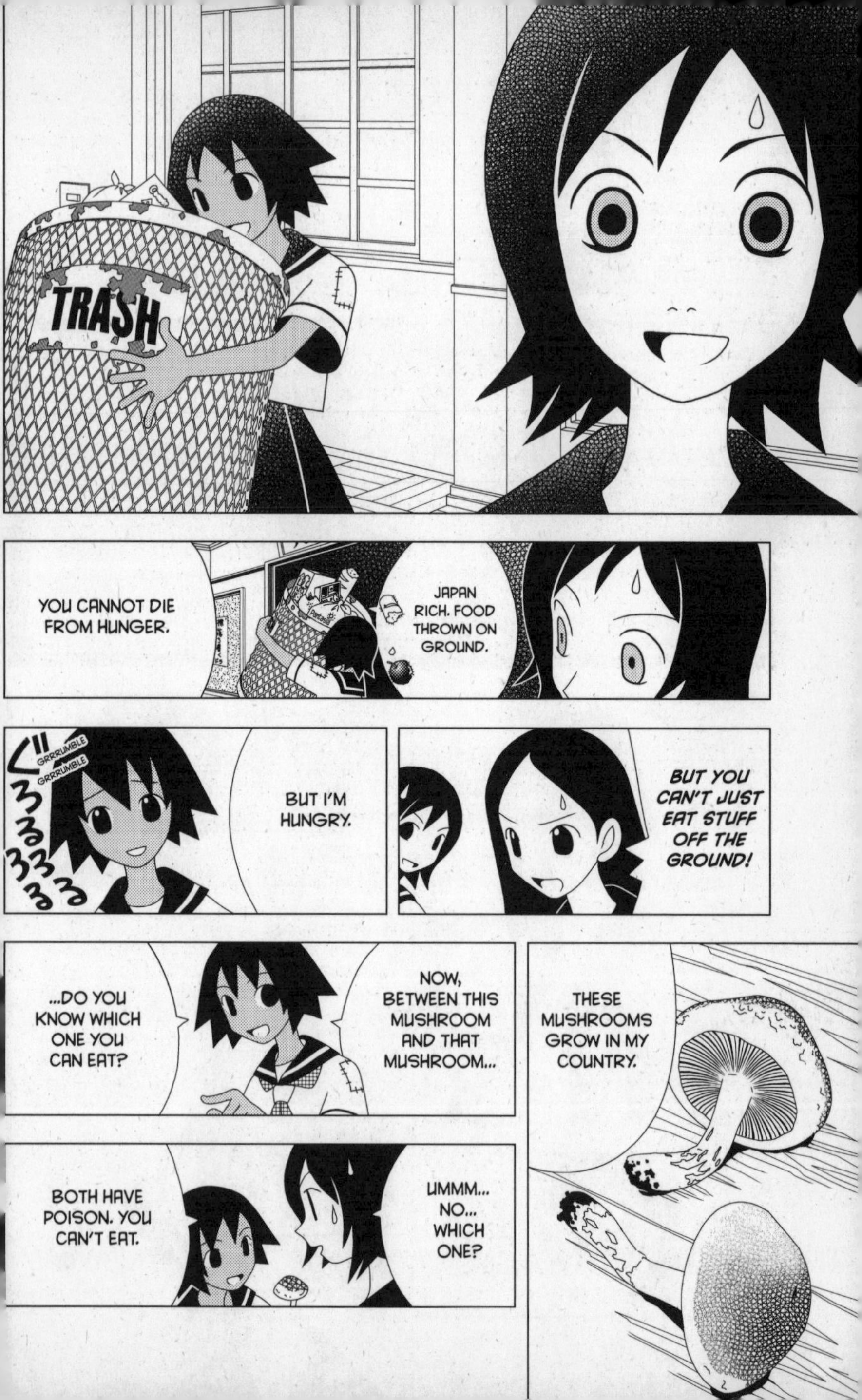
TRASH
JAPAN RICH. FOOD THROWN ON GROUND.
YOU CANNOT DIE FROM HUNGER.
BUT YOU CAN'T JUST EAT STUFF OFF THE GROUND!
GRRRUMBLE GRRRUMBLE
BUT I'M HUNGRY.
THESE MUSHROOMS GROW IN MY COUNTRY.
NOW, BETWEEN THIS MUSHROOM AND THAT MUSHROOM...
...DO YOU KNOW WHICH ONE YOU CAN EAT?
UMMM... NO... WHICH ONE?
BOTH HAVE POISON. YOU CAN'T EAT.

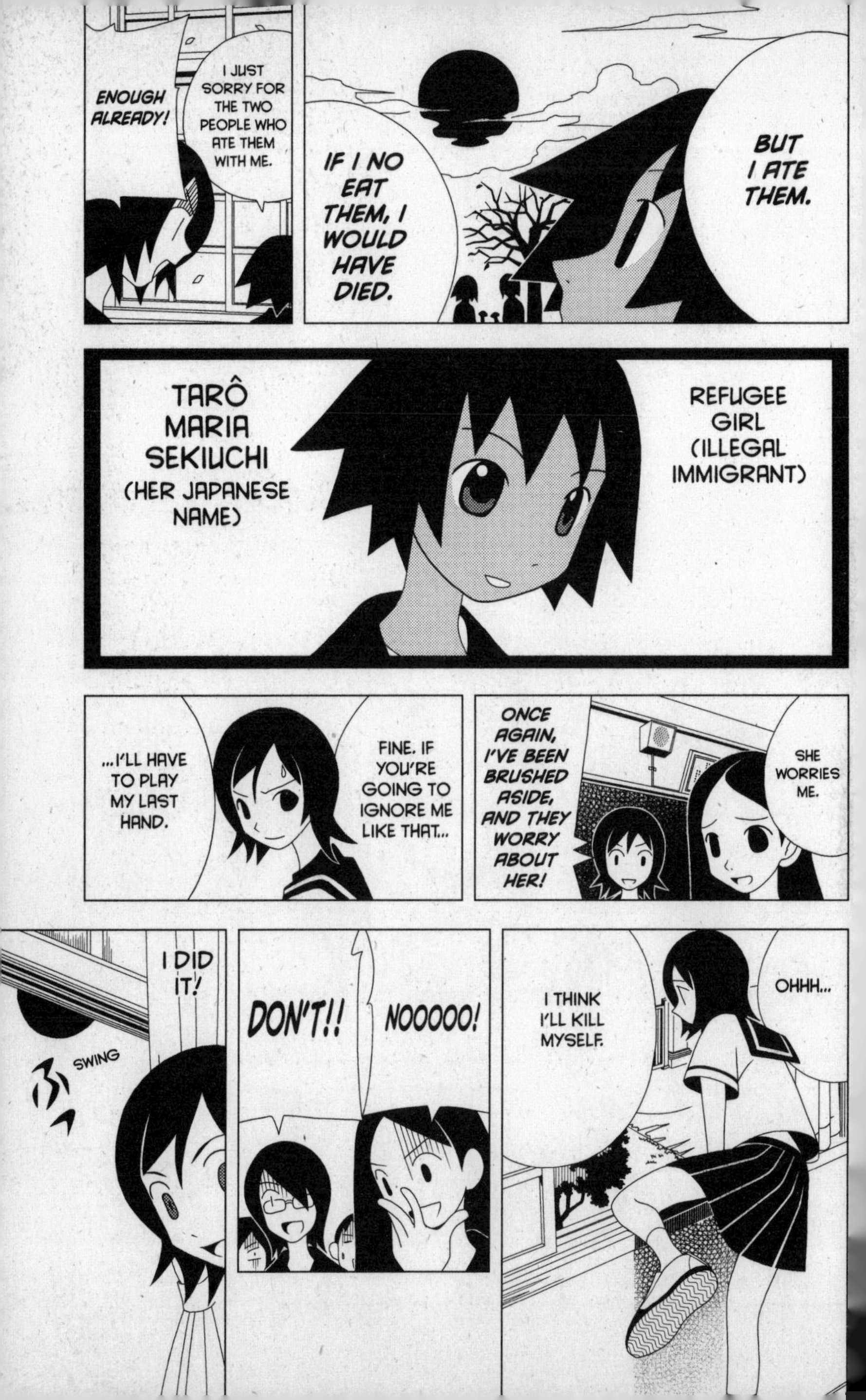
BUT I ATE THEM.
IF I NO EAT THEM, I WOULD HAVE DIED.
I JUST SORRY FOR THE TWO PEOPLE WHO ATE THEM WITH ME.
ENOUGH ALREADY!
REFUGEE GIRL (ILLEGAL IMMIGRANT)
TARÔ MARIA SEKIUCHI (HER JAPANESE NAME)
SHE WORRIES ME.
ONCE AGAIN, I'VE BEEN BRUSHED ASIDE, AND THEY WORRY ABOUT HER!
FINE. IF YOU'RE GOING TO IGNORE ME LIKE THAT...
...I'LL HAVE TO PLAY MY LAST HAND.
OHHH...
I THINK I'LL KILL MYSELF.
NOOOOO!
DON'T!!
I DID IT!
SWING

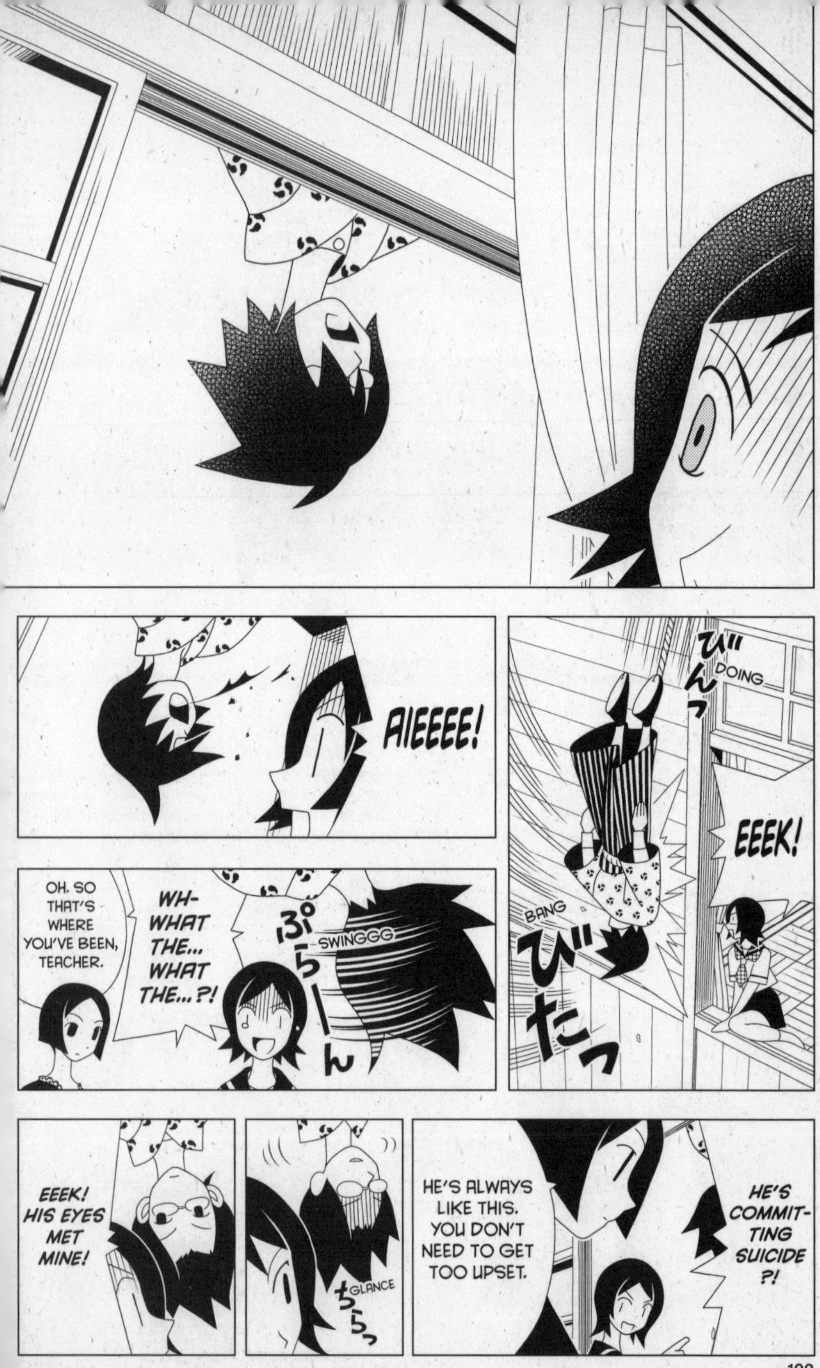

びんっ
DOING
EEEK!
BANG
びたっ
AIEEEE!
ぶらーん
SWINGGG
WH- WHAT THE... WHAT THE...?!
OH. SO THAT'S WHERE YOU'VE BEEN, TEACHER.
HE'S COMMITTING SUICIDE?!
HE'S ALWAYS LIKE THIS. YOU DON'T NEED TO GET TOO UPSET.
ちらっ
GLANCE
EEEK! HIS EYES MET MINE!

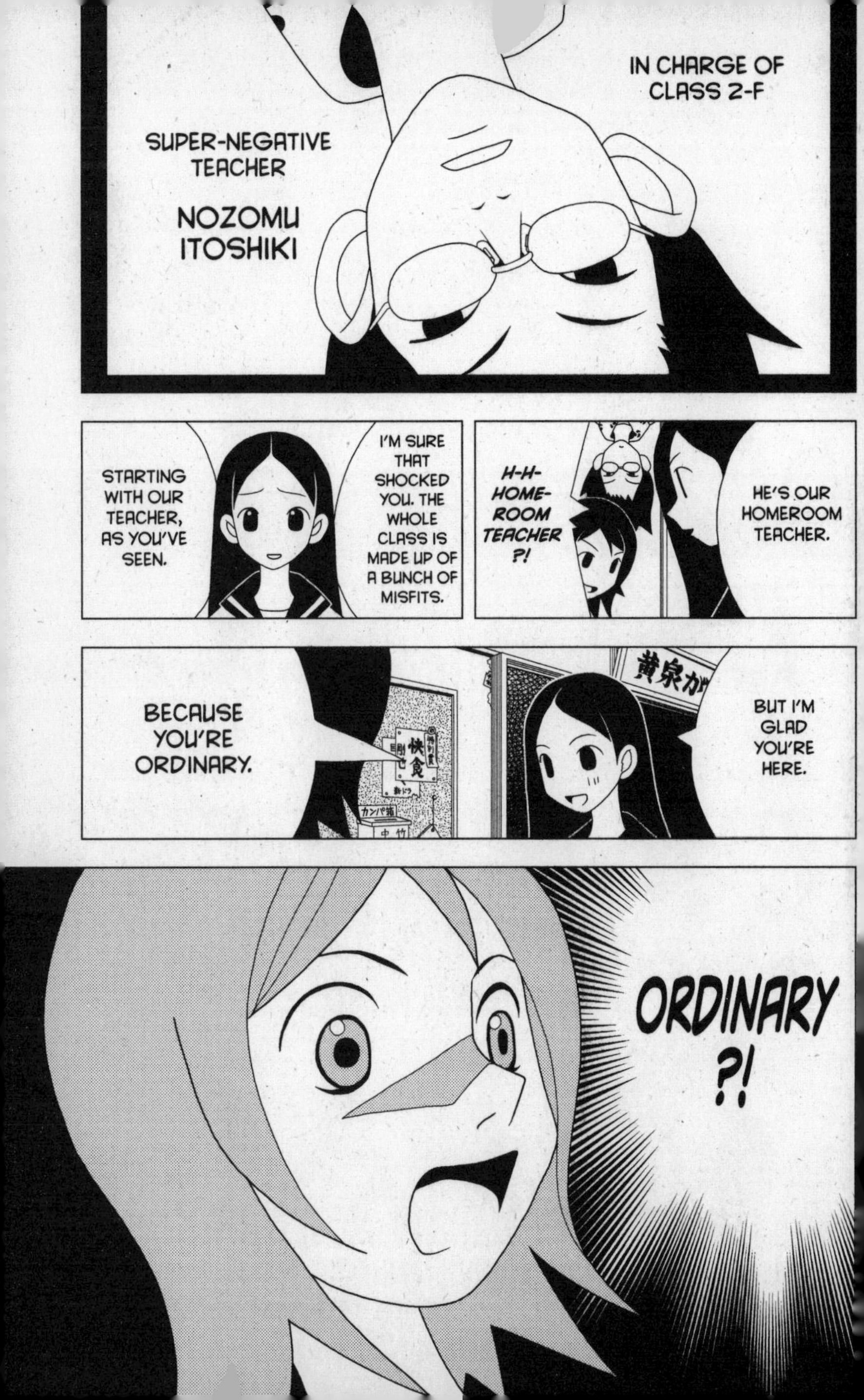
IN CHARGE OF CLASS 2-F
SUPER-NEGATIVE TEACHER
NOZOMU ITOSHIKI
HE'S OUR HOMEROOM TEACHER.
H-H-HOME-ROOM TEACHER?!
I'M SURE THAT SHOCKED YOU. THE WHOLE CLASS IS MADE UP OF A BUNCH OF MISFITS.
STARTING WITH OUR TEACHER, AS YOU'VE SEEN.
BUT I'M GLAD YOU'RE HERE.
BECAUSE YOU'RE ORDINARY.
ORDINARY?!

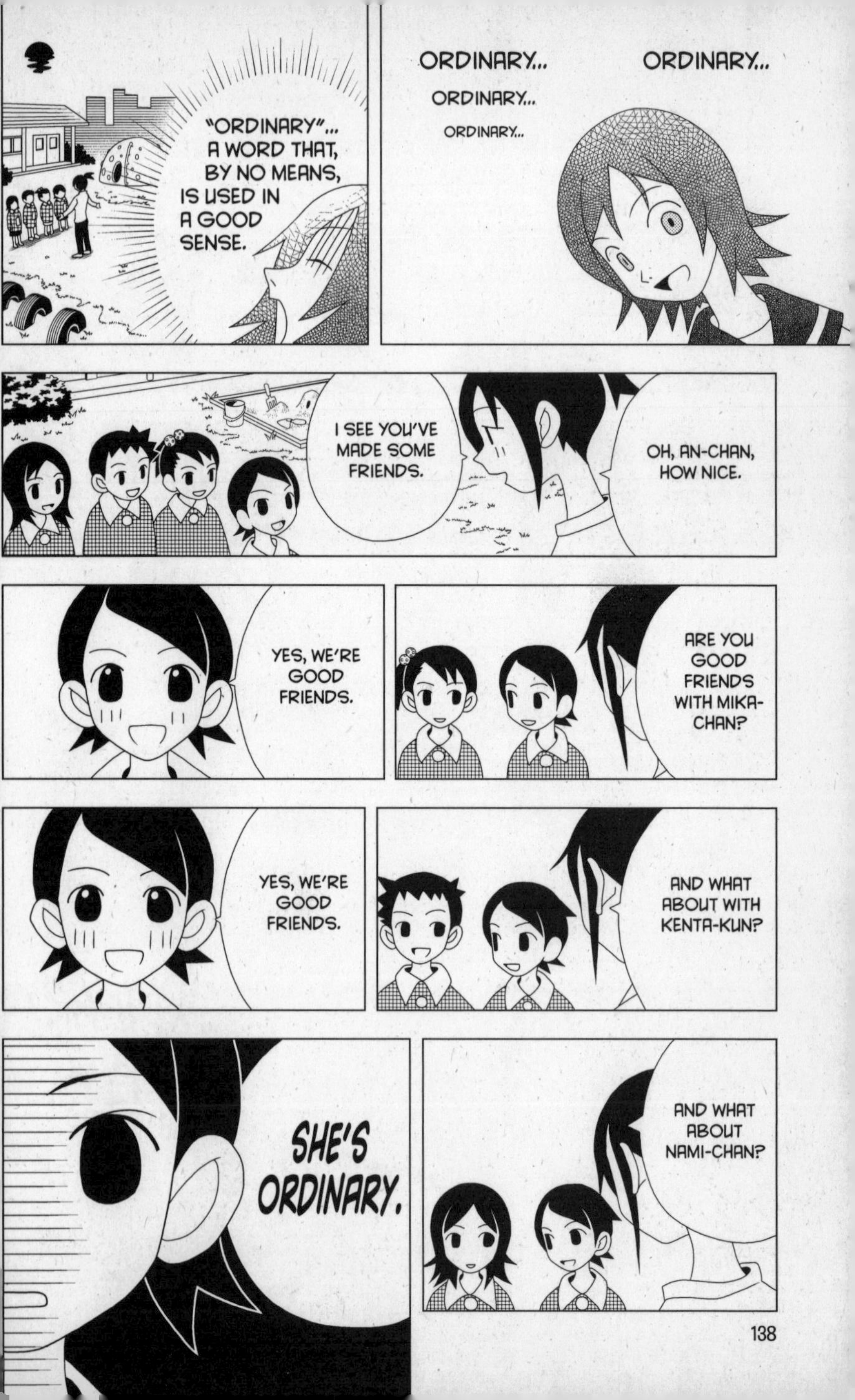
ORDINARY...
ORDINARY...
ORDINARY...
ORDINARY...
"ORDINARY"... A WORD THAT, BY NO MEANS, IS USED IN A GOOD SENSE.
OH, AN-CHAN, HOW NICE.
I SEE YOU'VE MADE SOME FRIENDS.
ARE YOU GOOD FRIENDS WITH MIKA-CHAN?
YES, WE'RE GOOD FRIENDS.
AND WHAT ABOUT WITH KENTA-KUN?
YES, WE'RE GOOD FRIENDS.
AND WHAT ABOUT NAMI-CHAN?
SHE'S ORDINARY.

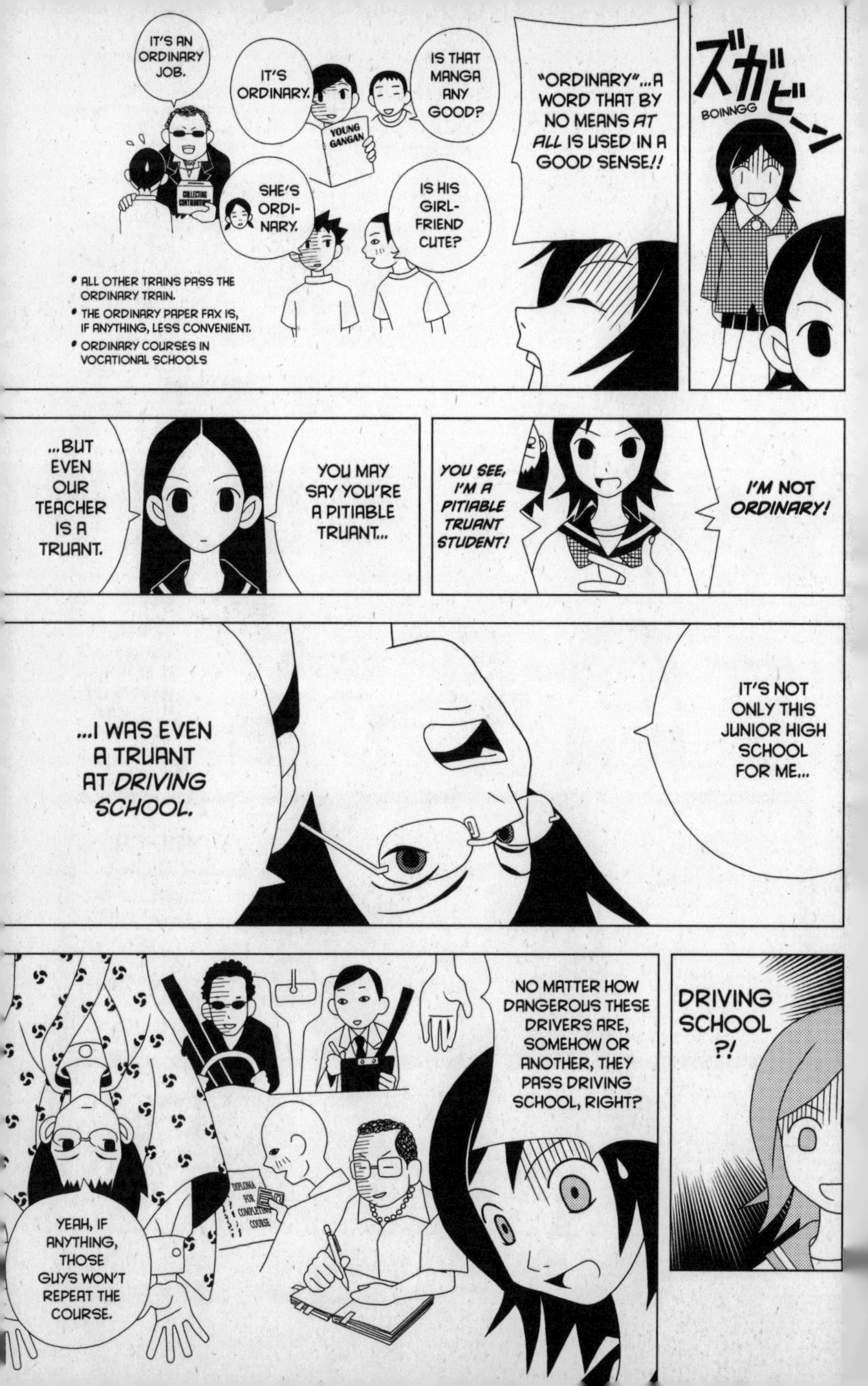
ズガビーン
BOINNGG
"ORDINARY"...A WORD THAT BY NO MEANS AT ALL IS USED IN A GOOD SENSE!!
IS THAT MANGA ANY GOOD?
IT'S ORDINARY.
YOUNG GANGAN
IT'S AN ORDINARY JOB.
COLLECTING
IS HIS GIRLFRIEND CUTE?
SHE'S ORDINARY.
• ALL OTHER TRAINS PASS THE ORDINARY TRAIN.
• THE ORDINARY PAPER FAX IS, IF ANYTHING, LESS CONVENIENT.
• ORDINARY COURSES IN VOCATIONAL SCHOOLS
I'M NOT ORDINARY!
YOU SEE, I'M A PITIABLE TRUANT STUDENT!
YOU MAY SAY YOU'RE A PITIABLE TRUANT...
...BUT EVEN OUR TEACHER IS A TRUANT.
IT'S NOT ONLY THIS JUNIOR HIGH SCHOOL FOR ME...
...I WAS EVEN A TRUANT AT DRIVING SCHOOL.
DRIVING SCHOOL ?!
NO MATTER HOW DANGEROUS THESE DRIVERS ARE, SOMEHOW OR ANOTHER, THEY PASS DRIVING SCHOOL, RIGHT?
DIPLOMA FOR COMPLETING COURSE
YEAH, IF ANYTHING, THOSE GUYS WON'T REPEAT THE COURSE.

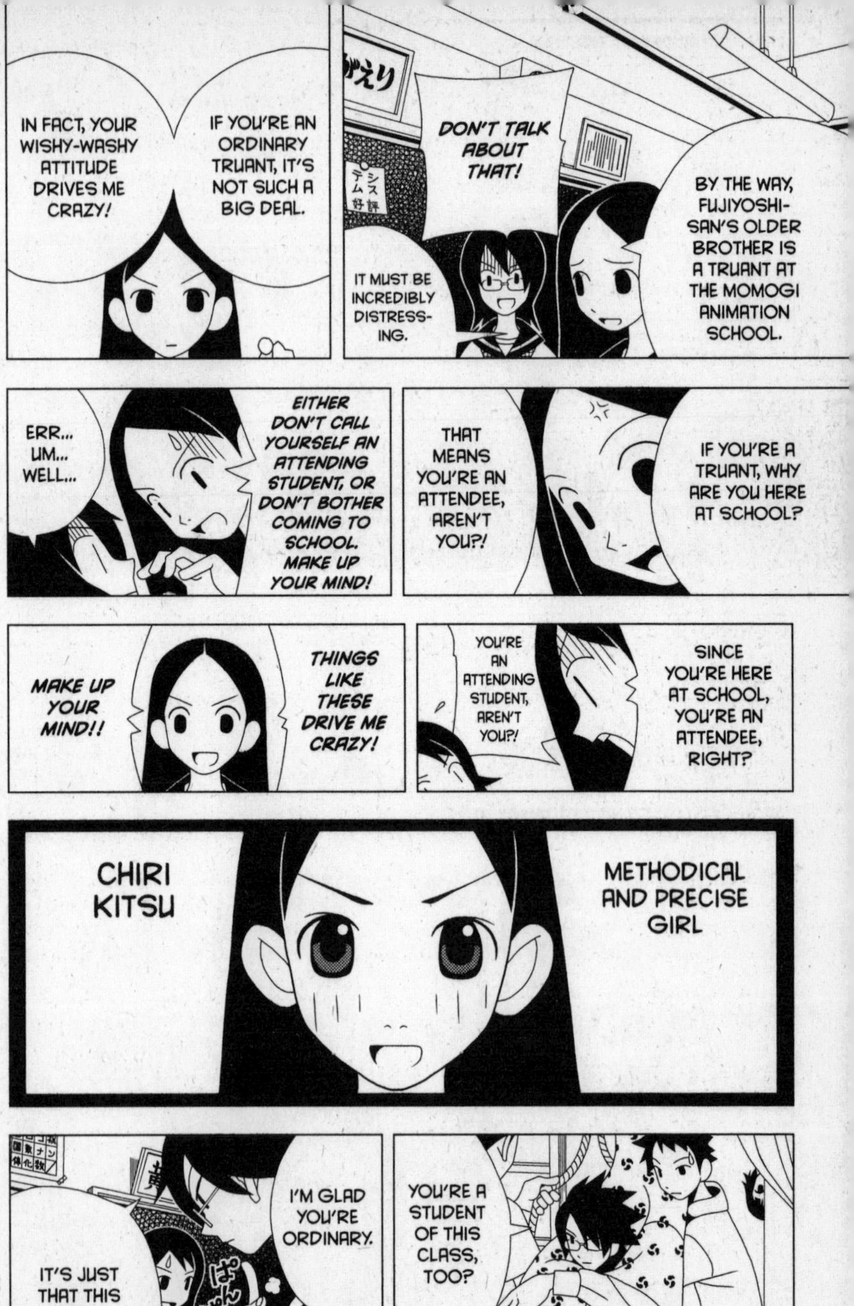
BY THE WAY, FUJIYOSHI-SAN'S OLDER BROTHER IS A TRUANT AT THE MOMOGI ANIMATION SCHOOL.
DON'T TALK ABOUT THAT!
IT MUST BE INCREDIBLY DISTRESSING.
IF YOU'RE AN ORDINARY TRUANT, IT'S NOT SUCH A BIG DEAL.
IN FACT, YOUR WISHY-WASHY ATTITUDE DRIVES ME CRAZY!
IF YOU'RE A TRUANT, WHY ARE YOU HERE AT SCHOOL?
THAT MEANS YOU'RE AN ATTENDEE, AREN'T YOU?!
EITHER DON'T CALL YOURSELF AN ATTENDING STUDENT, OR DON'T BOTHER COMING TO SCHOOL. MAKE UP YOUR MIND!
ERR... UM... WELL...
SINCE YOU'RE HERE AT SCHOOL, YOU'RE AN ATTENDEE, RIGHT?
YOU'RE AN ATTENDING STUDENT, AREN'T YOU?!
THINGS LIKE THESE DRIVE ME CRAZY!
MAKE UP YOUR MIND!!
METHODICAL AND PRECISE GIRL
CHIRI KITSU
YOU'RE A STUDENT OF THIS CLASS, TOO?
I'M GLAD YOU'RE ORDINARY.
ぱんぱん
PAT PAT
IT'S JUST THAT THIS CLASS...

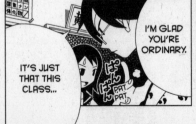

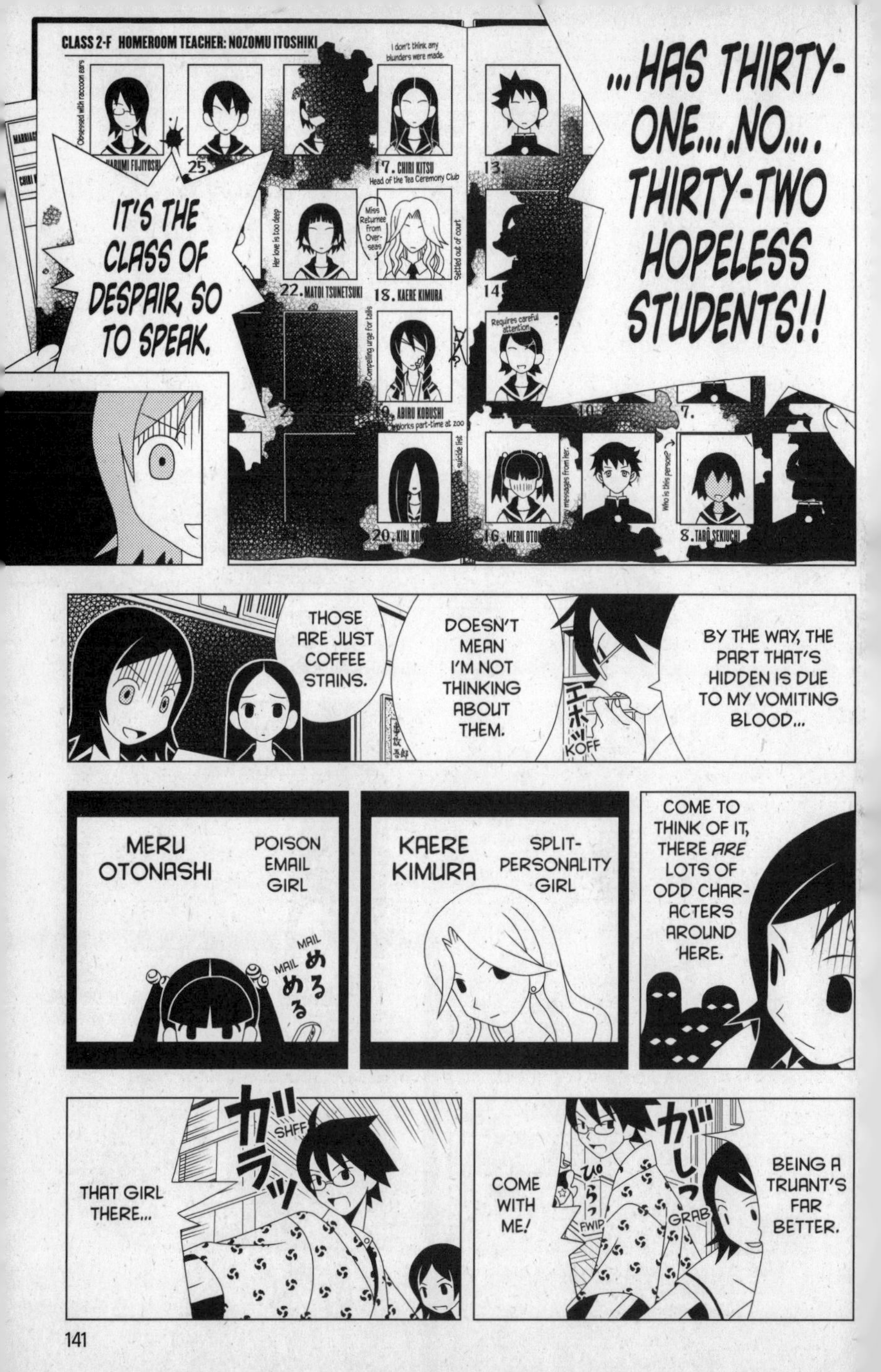
CLASS 2-F HOMEROOM TEACHER: NOZOMU ITOSHIKI
...HAS THIRTY-ONE....NO..... THIRTY-TWO HOPELESS STUDENTS!!
I don't think any blunders were made.
13.
17. CHIRI KITSU
Head of the Tea Ceremony Club
Settled out of court
Miss Returnee from Over-seas
18. KAERE KIMURA
Requires careful attention
Compelling urge for tails
19. ABIRU KOBUSHI
Works part-time at zoo
Her love is too deep
22. MATOI TSUNETSUKI
Obsessed with raccoon ears
HARUMI FUJIYOSHI
25.
Who is this person?
8. TARÔ SEKIUCHI
7.
16. MERU OTO
20. KIRI KO
IT'S THE CLASS OF DESPAIR, SO TO SPEAK.
BY THE WAY, THE PART THAT'S HIDDEN IS DUE TO MY VOMITING BLOOD...
エホッ KOFF
DOESN'T MEAN I'M NOT THINKING ABOUT THEM.
THOSE ARE JUST COFFEE STAINS.
COME TO THINK OF IT, THERE ARE LOTS OF ODD CHARACTERS AROUND HERE.
KAERE KIMURA
SPLIT-PERSONALITY GIRL
MERU OTONASHI
POISON EMAIL GIRL
めるめる MAIL MAIL
BEING A TRUANT'S FAR BETTER.
がしっ GRAB
COME WITH ME!
ぴらっ FWIP
ガラッ SHFF
THAT GIRL THERE...

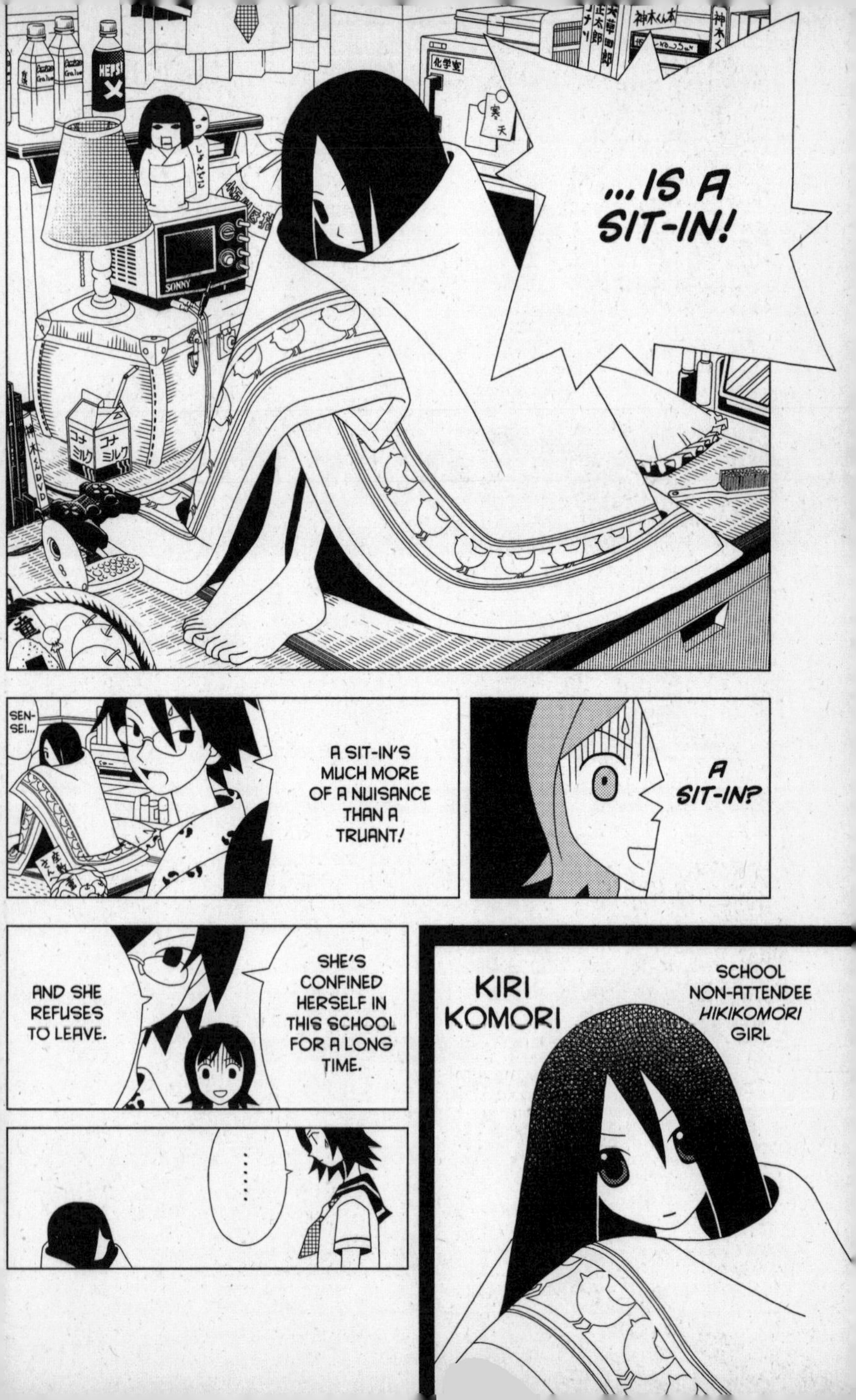
...IS A SIT-IN!
A SIT-IN?
A SIT-IN'S MUCH MORE OF A NUISANCE THAN A TRUANT!
SEN-SEI...
SCHOOL NON-ATTENDEE *HIKIKOMORI* GIRL
KIRI KOMORI
SHE'S CONFINED HERSELF IN THIS SCHOOL FOR A LONG TIME.
AND SHE REFUSES TO LEAVE.
......

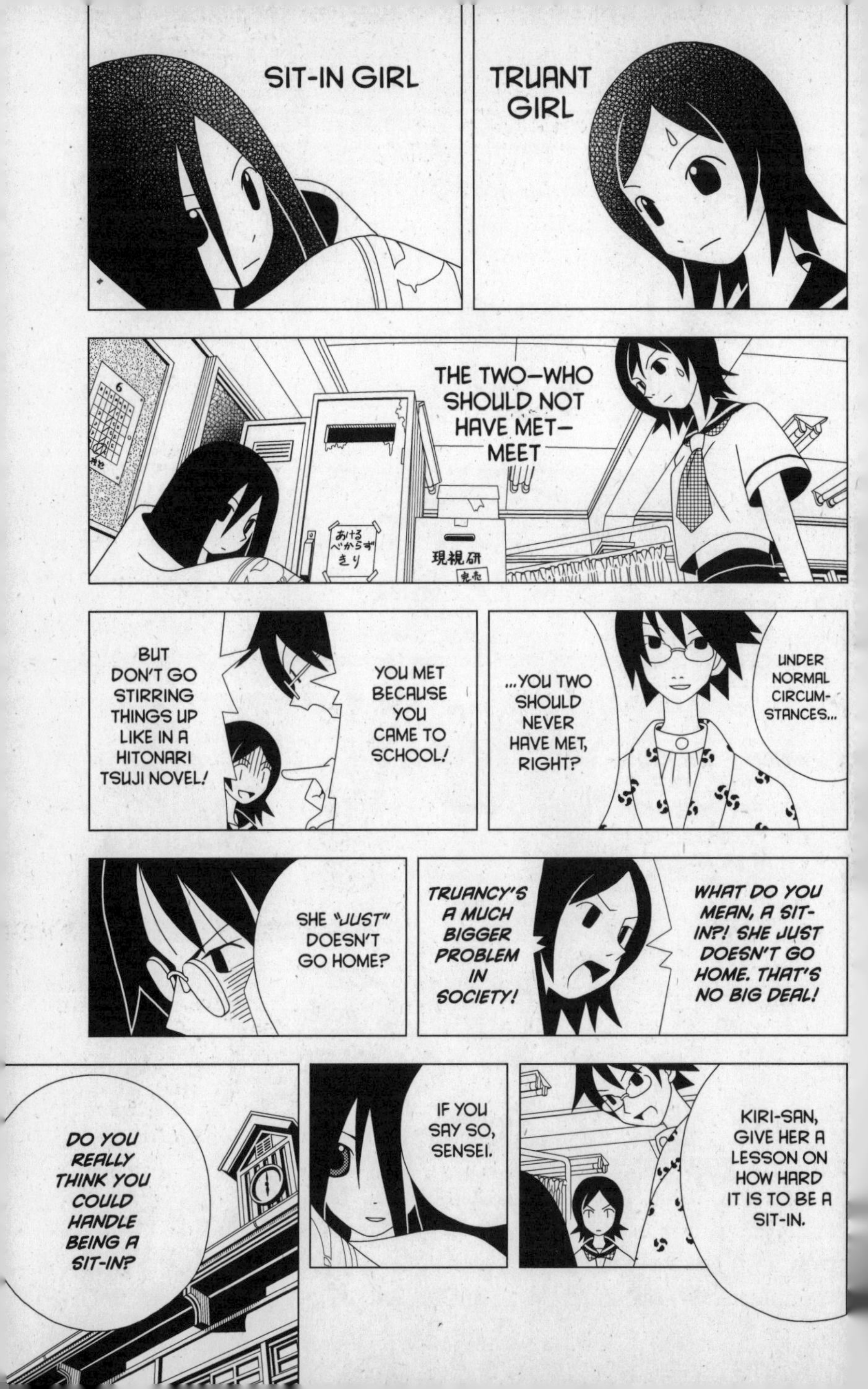
TRUANT GIRL
SIT-IN GIRL
THE TWO—WHO SHOULD NOT HAVE MET—MEET
あけるべからず きり
現視研
UNDER NORMAL CIRCUM-STANCES...
...YOU TWO SHOULD NEVER HAVE MET, RIGHT?
YOU MET BECAUSE YOU CAME TO SCHOOL!
BUT DON'T GO STIRRING THINGS UP LIKE IN A HITONARI TSUJI NOVEL!
WHAT DO YOU MEAN, A SIT-IN?! SHE JUST DOESN'T GO HOME. THAT'S NO BIG DEAL!
TRUANCY'S A MUCH BIGGER PROBLEM IN SOCIETY!
SHE "JUST" DOESN'T GO HOME?
KIRI-SAN, GIVE HER A LESSON ON HOW HARD IT IS TO BE A SIT-IN.
IF YOU SAY SO, SENSEI.
DO YOU REALLY THINK YOU COULD HANDLE BEING A SIT-IN?

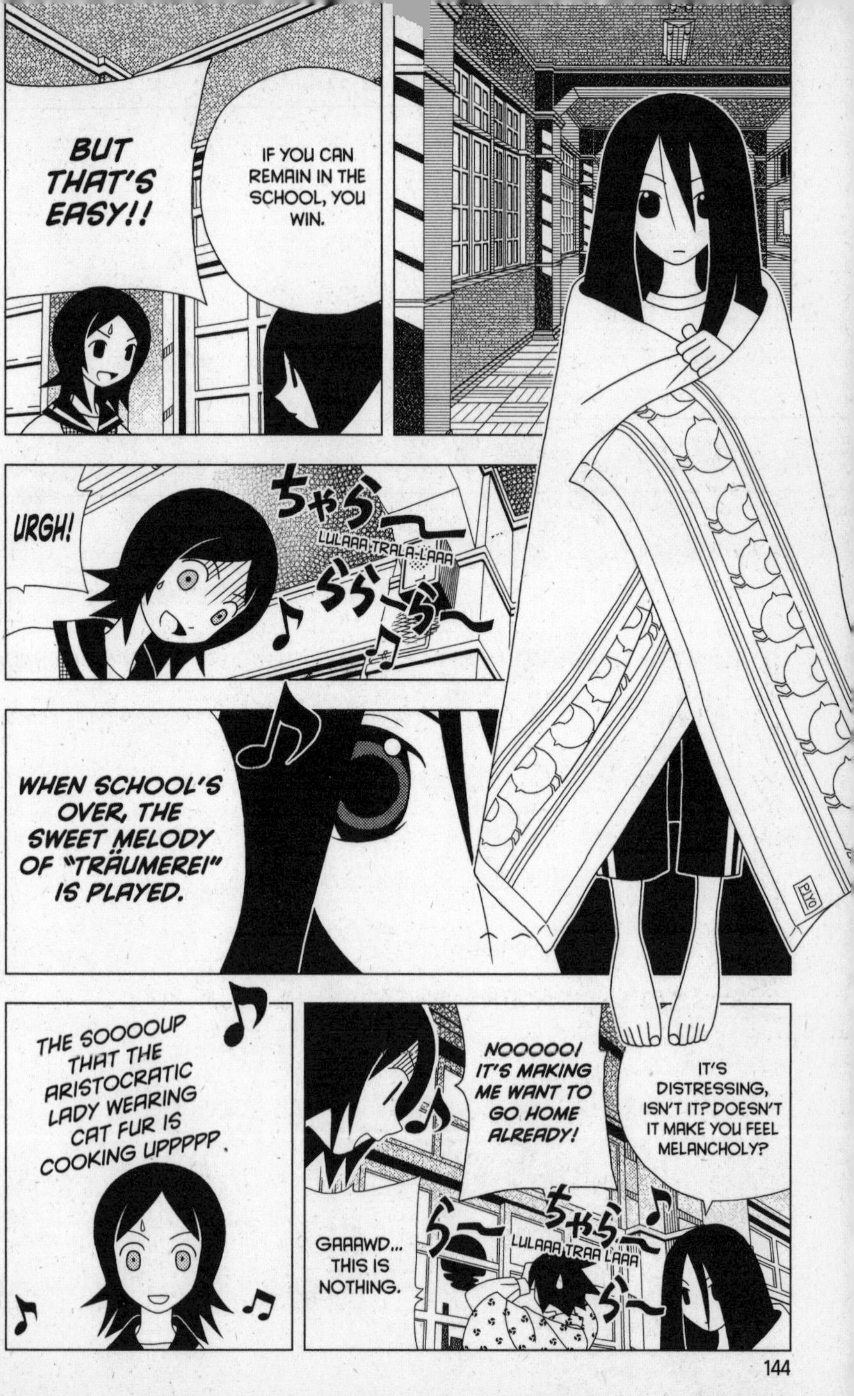
IF YOU CAN REMAIN IN THE SCHOOL, YOU WIN.
BUT THAT'S EASY!!
ちゃら〜
LULAAA TRALA-LAAA
ららら〜ら〜
URGH!
WHEN SCHOOL'S OVER, THE SWEET MELODY OF "TRÄUMEREI" IS PLAYED.
IT'S DISTRESSING, ISN'T IT? DOESN'T IT MAKE YOU FEEL MELANCHOLY?
NOOOOO! IT'S MAKING ME WANT TO GO HOME ALREADY!
ちゃら〜
ら〜
LULAAA TRAA LAAA
ら〜
GAAAWD... THIS IS NOTHING.
THE SOOOOUP THAT THE ARISTOCRATIC LADY WEARING CAT FUR IS COOKING UPPPPP

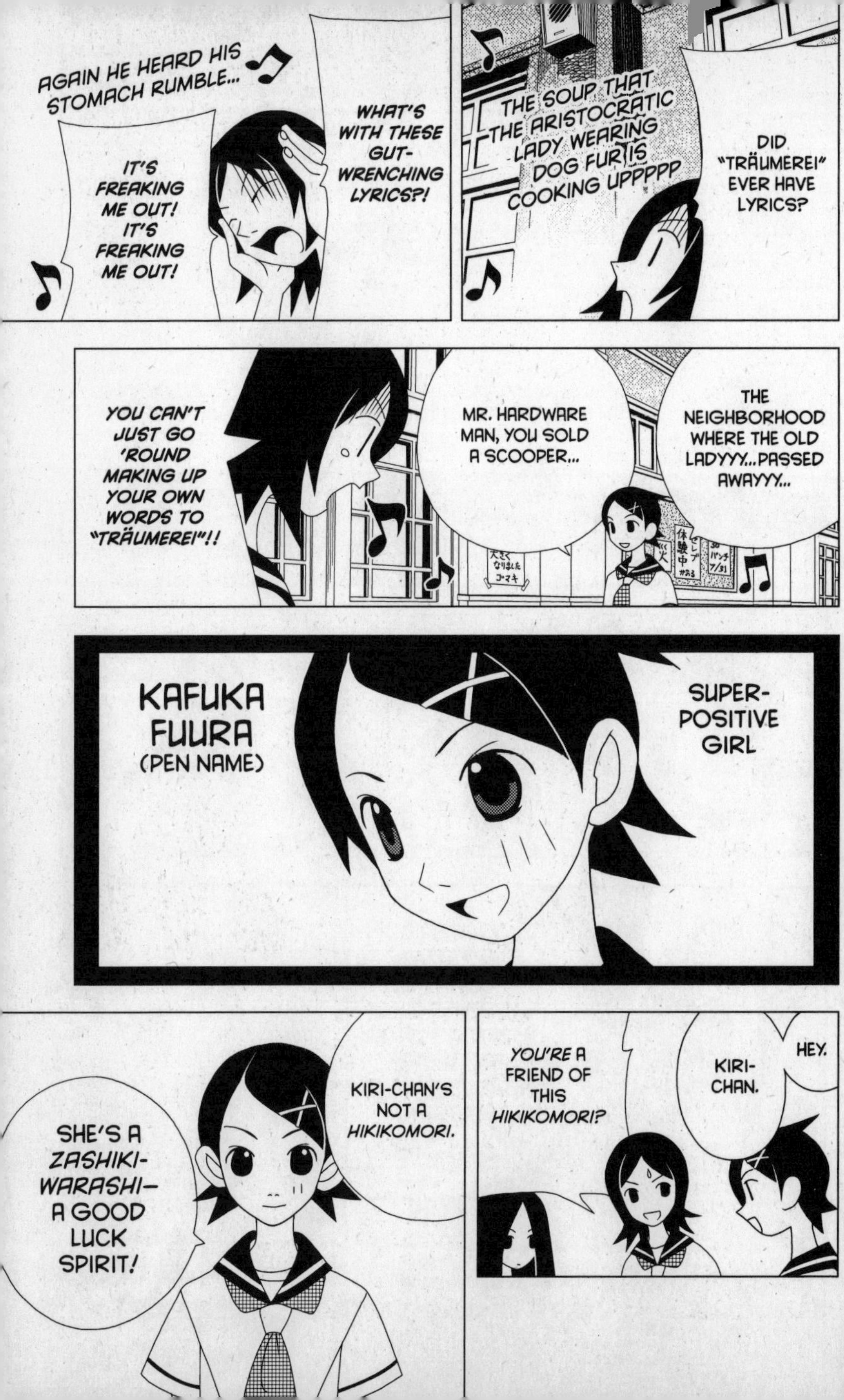
THE SOUP THAT THE ARISTOCRATIC LADY WEARING DOG FUR IS COOKING UPPPPP
DID "TRÄUMEREI" EVER HAVE LYRICS?
AGAIN HE HEARD HIS STOMACH RUMBLE...
WHAT'S WITH THESE GUT-WRENCHING LYRICS?!
IT'S FREAKING ME OUT! IT'S FREAKING ME OUT!
THE NEIGHBORHOOD WHERE THE OLD LADYYY...PASSED AWAYYY...
MR. HARDWARE MAN, YOU SOLD A SCOOPER...
YOU CAN'T JUST GO 'ROUND MAKING UP YOUR OWN WORDS TO "TRÄUMEREI"!!
SUPER-POSITIVE GIRL
KAFUKA FUURA (PEN NAME)
HEY.
KIRI-CHAN.
YOU'RE A FRIEND OF THIS HIKIKOMORI?
KIRI-CHAN'S NOT A HIKIKOMORI.
SHE'S A ZASHIKI-WARASHI—A GOOD LUCK SPIRIT!

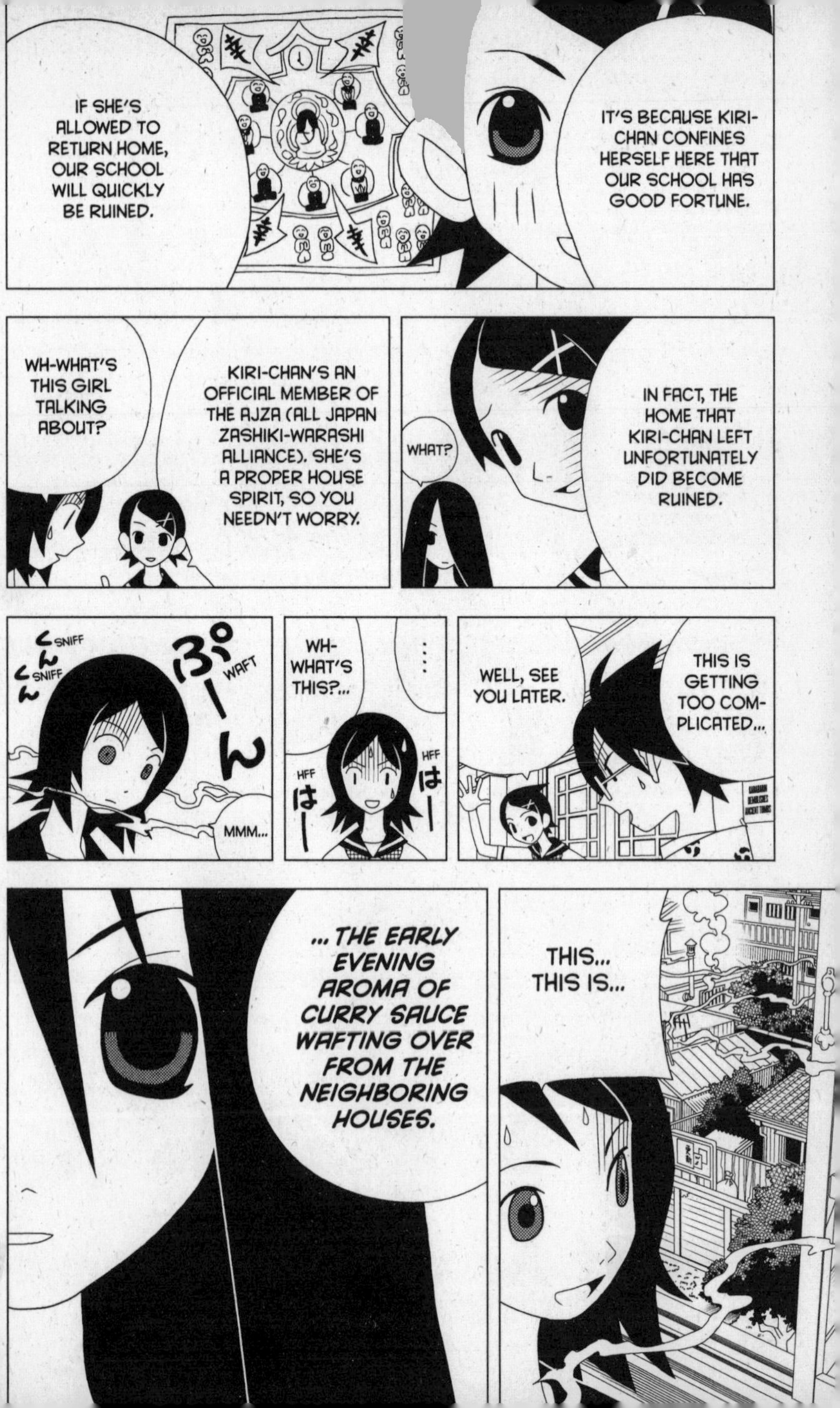
IT'S BECAUSE KIRI-CHAN CONFINES HERSELF HERE THAT OUR SCHOOL HAS GOOD FORTUNE.
IF SHE'S ALLOWED TO RETURN HOME, OUR SCHOOL WILL QUICKLY BE RUINED.
IN FACT, THE HOME THAT KIRI-CHAN LEFT UNFORTUNATELY DID BECOME RUINED.
WHAT?
KIRI-CHAN'S AN OFFICIAL MEMBER OF THE AJZA (ALL JAPAN ZASHIKI-WARASHI ALLIANCE). SHE'S A PROPER HOUSE SPIRIT, SO YOU NEEDN'T WORRY.
WH-WHAT'S THIS GIRL TALKING ABOUT?
THIS IS GETTING TOO COMPLICATED...
WELL, SEE YOU LATER.
......
WH- WHAT'S THIS?...
はー HFF
はー HFF
ぷーん WAFT
くん SNIFF
くん SNIFF
MMM...
THIS... THIS IS...
...THE EARLY EVENING AROMA OF CURRY SAUCE WAFTING OVER FROM THE NEIGHBORING HOUSES.

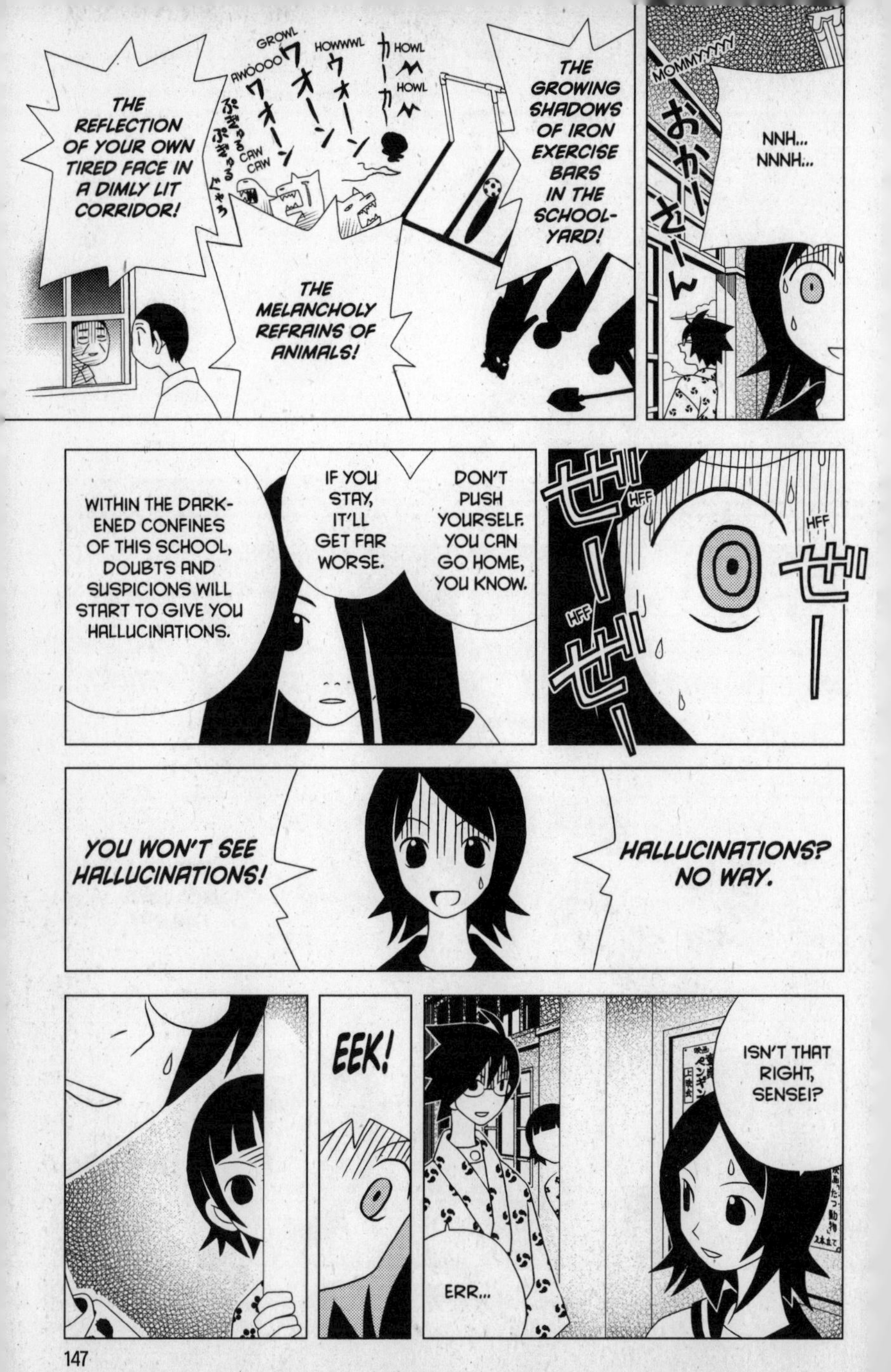
MOMMYYYY
おかーさーん
NNH... NNNH...
THE GROWING SHADOWS OF IRON EXERCISE BARS IN THE SCHOOL-YARD!
HOWL
HOWL
カーカー
HOWWWL
ウォーン
ウォーン
GROWL
AWOOOO
ワオーン
ワオーン
CAW CAW
THE MELANCHOLY REFRAINS OF ANIMALS!
THE REFLECTION OF YOUR OWN TIRED FACE IN A DIMLY LIT CORRIDOR!
HFF
ぜー
HFF
ぜー
HFF
ぜー
DON'T PUSH YOURSELF. YOU CAN GO HOME, YOU KNOW.
IF YOU STAY, IT'LL GET FAR WORSE.
WITHIN THE DARK-ENED CONFINES OF THIS SCHOOL, DOUBTS AND SUSPICIONS WILL START TO GIVE YOU HALLUCINATIONS.
HALLUCINATIONS? NO WAY.
YOU WON'T SEE HALLUCINATIONS!
ISN'T THAT RIGHT, SENSEI?
ERR...
EEK!

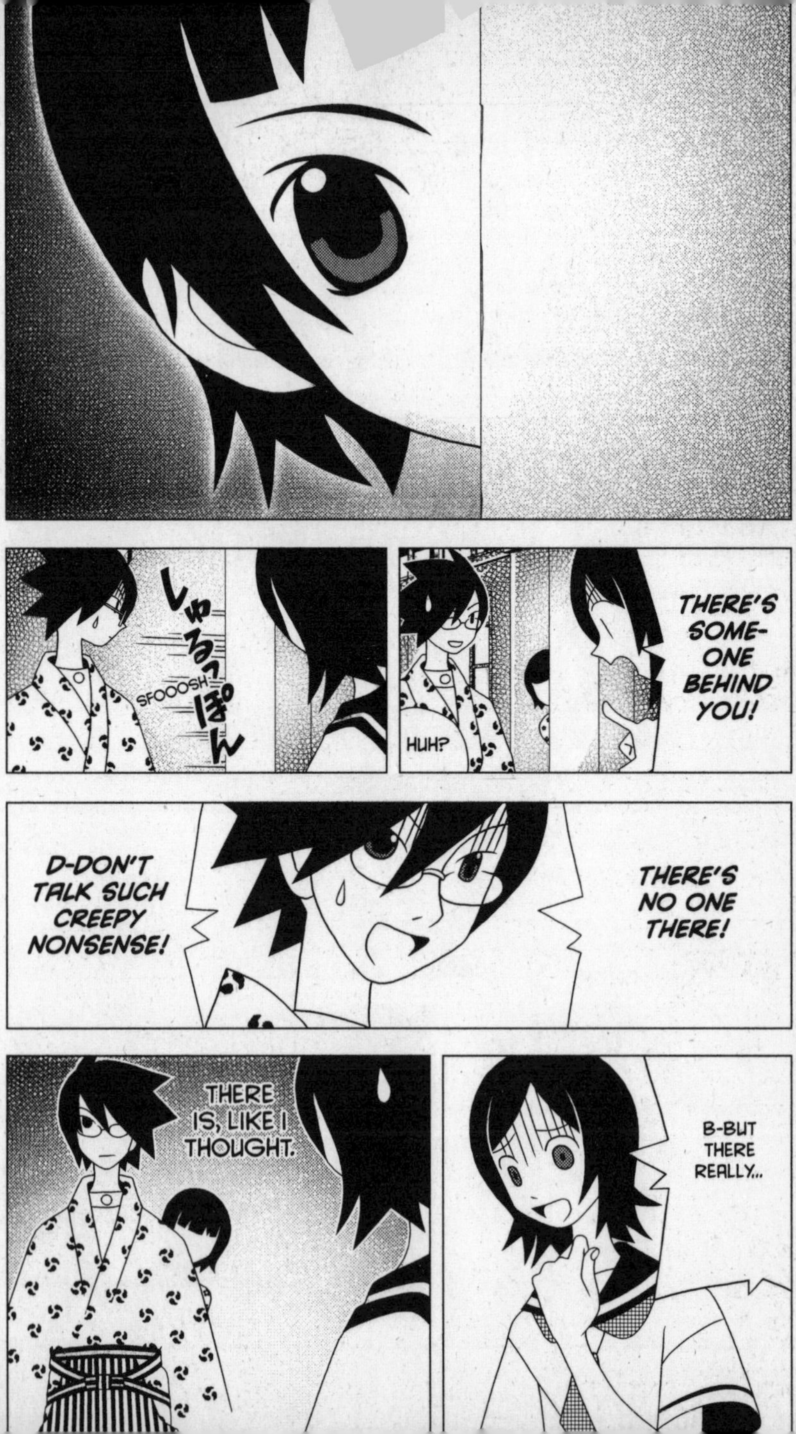

THERE'S SOME-ONE BEHIND YOU!
HUH?
しゅるっぽん
SFOOOSH
THERE'S NO ONE THERE!
D-DON'T TALK SUCH CREEPY NONSENSE!
B-BUT THERE REALLY...
THERE IS, LIKE I THOUGHT.

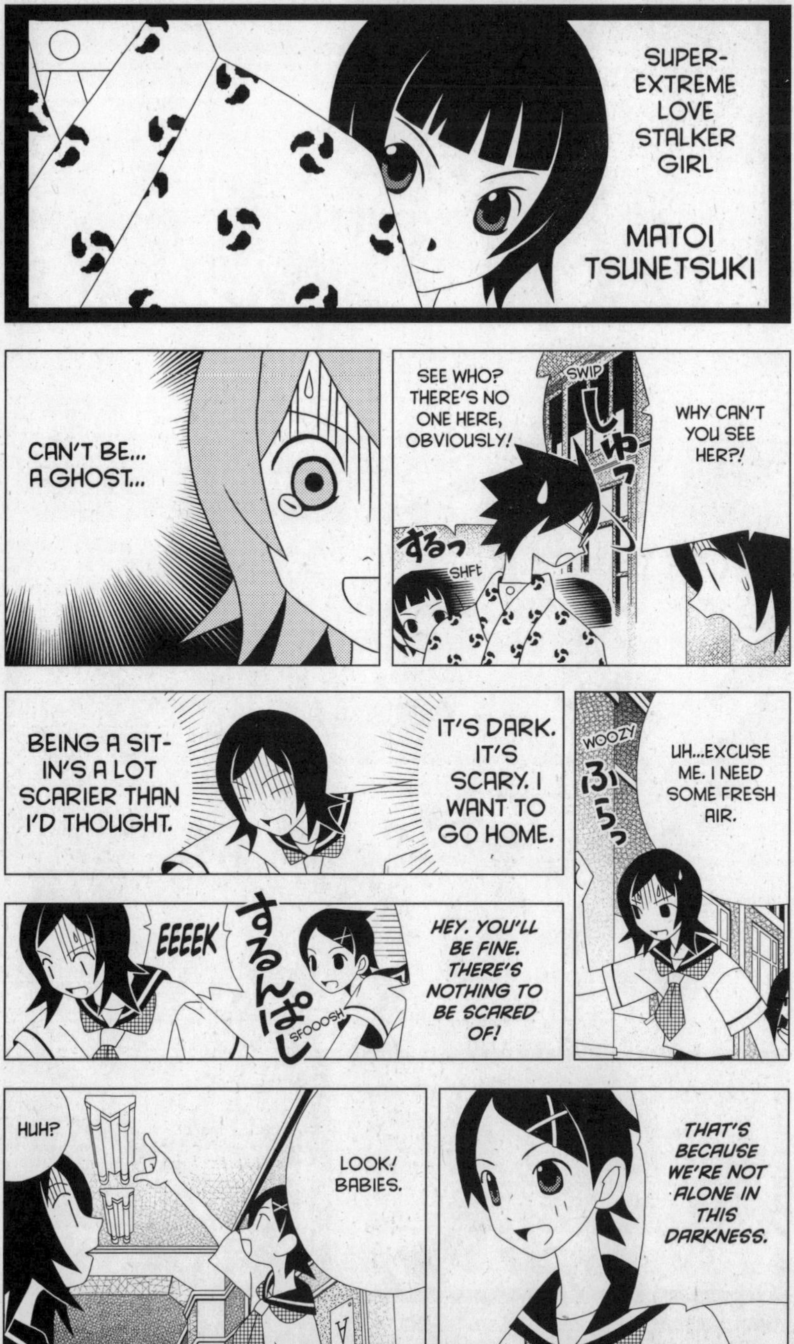
SUPER-EXTREME LOVE STALKER GIRL
MATOI TSUNETSUKI
WHY CAN'T YOU SEE HER?!
SWIP
しゅっ
SEE WHO? THERE'S NO ONE HERE, OBVIOUSLY!
するっ
SHFt
CAN'T BE... A GHOST...
UH...EXCUSE ME. I NEED SOME FRESH AIR.
WOOZY
ふらっ
IT'S DARK. IT'S SCARY. I WANT TO GO HOME.
BEING A SIT-IN'S A LOT SCARIER THAN I'D THOUGHT.
HEY. YOU'LL BE FINE. THERE'S NOTHING TO BE SCARED OF!
するんぱし
SFOOOSH
EEEEK
THAT'S BECAUSE WE'RE NOT ALONE IN THIS DARKNESS.
LOOK! BABIES.
HUH?

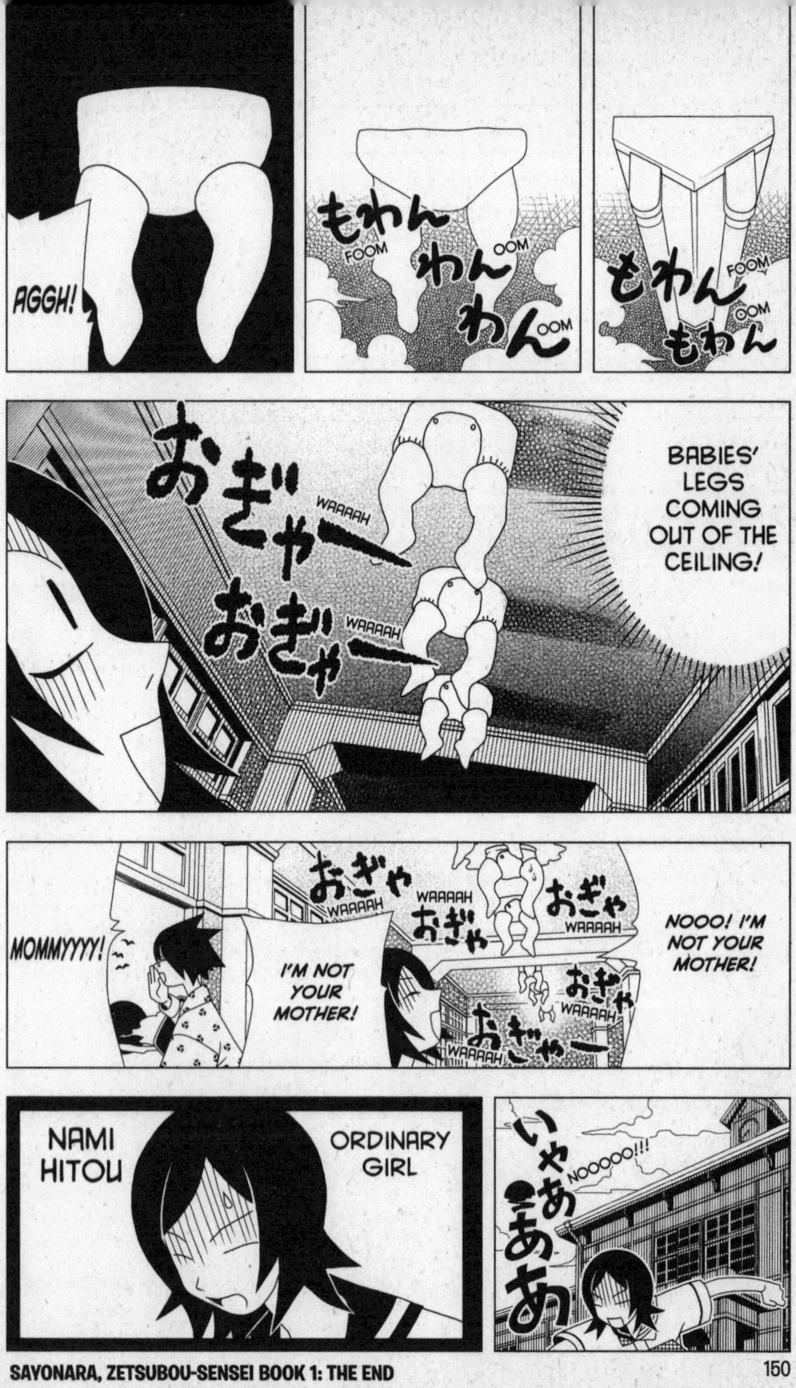
もわん
FOOM
もわん
OOM
もわん
FOOM
わん
OOM
わん
OOM
AGGH!
BABIES' LEGS COMING OUT OF THE CEILING!
おぎゃー
WAAAAH
おぎゃー
WAAAAH
NOOO! I'M NOT YOUR MOTHER!
おぎゃ
WAAAAH
おぎゃ
WAAAAH
おぎゃ
WAAAAH
おぎゃ
WAAAAH
おぎゃー
WAAAAH
I'M NOT YOUR MOTHER!
MOMMYYYY!
いやぁぁぁ
NOOOOO!!!
ORDINARY GIRL
NAMI HITOU

SAYONARA, ZETSUBOU-SENSEI BOOK 1: THE END

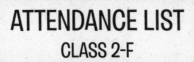

# ATTENDANCE LIST
## CLASS 2-F

**ATTENDANCE NO. 28**
## NAMI HITOU
### ORDINARY GIRL

# SAYONARA, ZETSUBOU-SENSEI

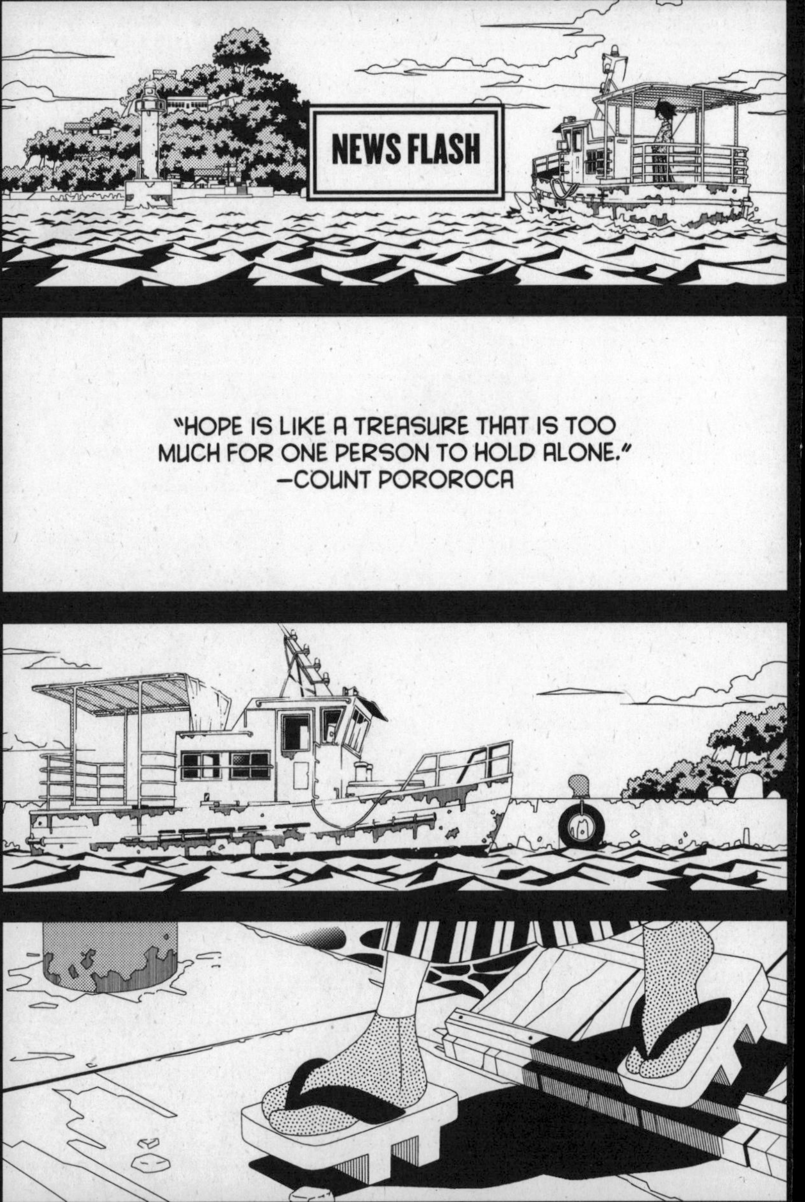
NEWS FLASH
"HOPE IS LIKE A TREASURE THAT IS TOO MUCH FOR ONE PERSON TO HOLD ALONE."
—COUNT POROROCA

Preview

# SAYONARA, ZETSUBOU-SENSEI

Koji Kumeta

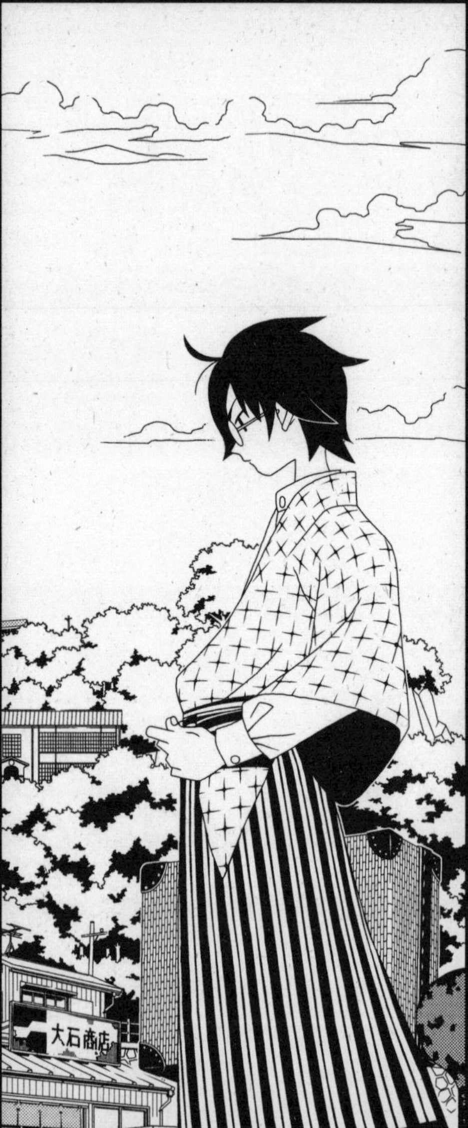
大石商店

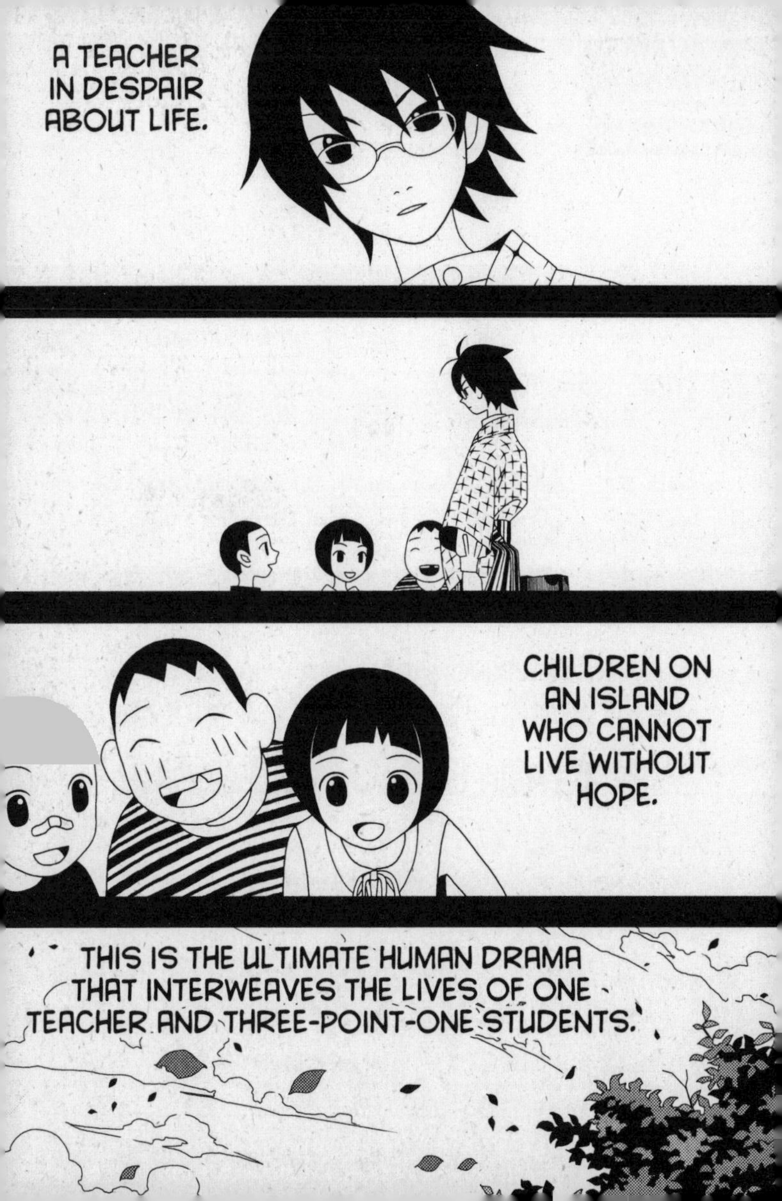
A TEACHER IN DESPAIR ABOUT LIFE.
CHILDREN ON AN ISLAND WHO CANNOT LIVE WITHOUT HOPE.
THIS IS THE ULTIMATE HUMAN DRAMA THAT INTERWEAVES THE LIVES OF ONE TEACHER AND THREE-POINT-ONE STUDENTS.

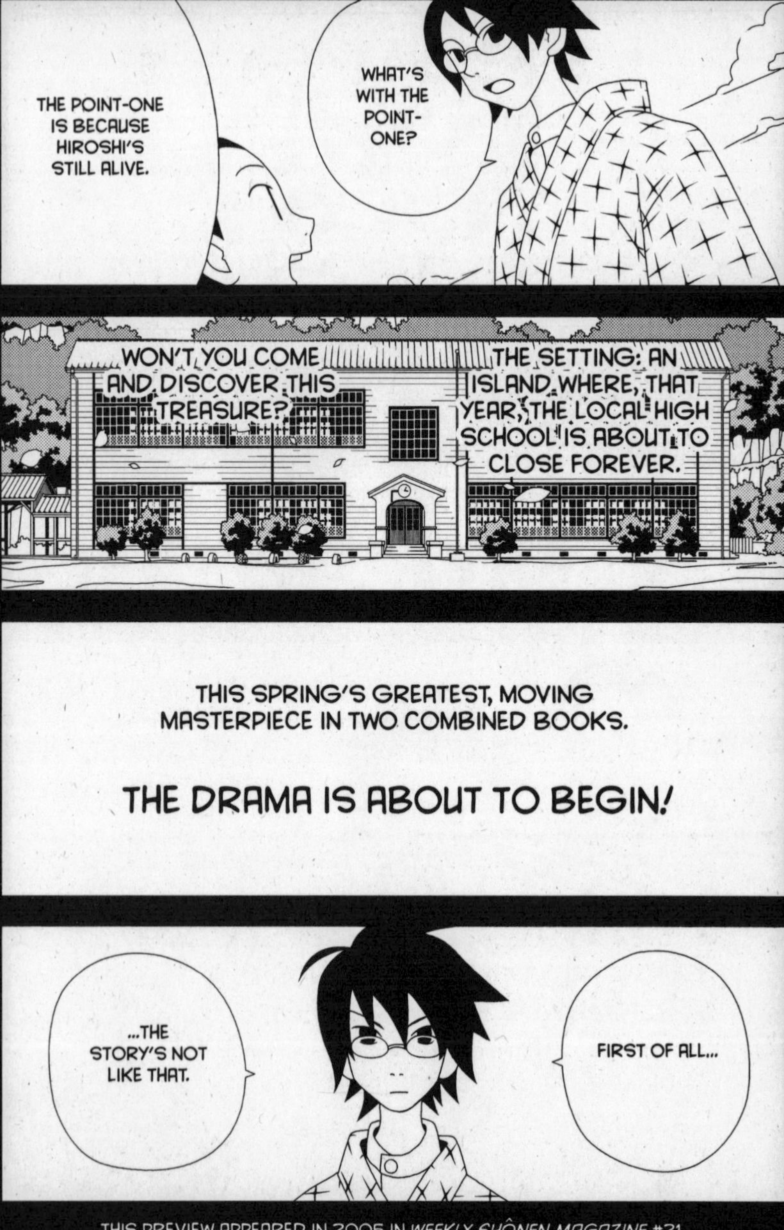
WHAT'S WITH THE POINT-ONE?
THE POINT-ONE IS BECAUSE HIROSHI'S STILL ALIVE.
THE SETTING: AN ISLAND WHERE, THAT YEAR, THE LOCAL HIGH SCHOOL IS ABOUT TO CLOSE FOREVER.
WON'T YOU COME AND DISCOVER THIS TREASURE?
THIS SPRING'S GREATEST, MOVING MASTERPIECE IN TWO COMBINED BOOKS.
THE DRAMA IS ABOUT TO BEGIN!
FIRST OF ALL...
...THE STORY'S NOT LIKE THAT.

THIS PREVIEW APPEARED IN 2005 IN *WEEKLY SHÔNEN MAGAZINE* #21, BEFORE *SAYONARA, ZETSUBOU-SENSEI* BEGAN PUBLICATION.

# PAPER BLOGS

**PREAMBLE** | NEGATIVE | POSITIVE | RECLUSE | STALKER

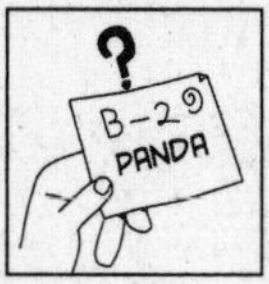
?
B-2@
PANDA

LUCKILY, I WAS SOMEHOW PICKED UP AT OTOWA (WHERE THE PUBLISHER KODANSHA IS LOCATED). EIGHT MONTHS HAVE GONE BY. WHEN YOU HEAR ABOUT THE LIFE OF A BATTERY, IT ALL SOUNDS GOOD, BUT NO MATTER HOW MUCH YOU TRY TO CHARGE A WORN-OUT BATTERY, IT DOESN'T DO MUCH GOOD. MY RICKETY CARTOON ROBOT BATTERY DOESN'T HAVE MUCH POWER LEFT IN IT. EIGHT MONTHS. I HARDLY HAVE ANY MEMORIES OF THAT TIME. OR RATHER, THERE'S NOT MUCH TO REMEMBER THAT'D BE WORTH TALKING ABOUT TO OTHERS. NOT ONE THING. THERE WAS A PUZZLING MEMO I FOUND IN A COAT I WAS WEARING OVER THE WINTER, "B-2@PANDA." I COULDN'T FOR THE LIFE OF ME FIGURE OUT WHAT THAT WAS. THE NEXT DAY, I REMEMBERED. IT WAS A MEMO TO REMIND ME WHERE I PUT MY CAR IN THE PARKING LOT. I FELT LIKE DYING. THEN, FROM ANOTHER JACKET, WAS ANOTHER MEMO. (IT SAID "A 7-CM STICK, BY THE THIRD..."). I DON'T THINK I'LL GET MYSELF TO TRY TO REMEMBER WHAT THAT WAS.

PREAMBLE | **NEGATIVE** | POSITIVE | RECLUSE | STALKER

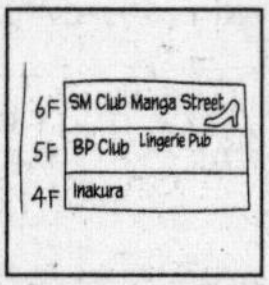
6F SM Club Manga Street
5F BP Club Lingerie Pub
4F Inakura

FOR SOME REASON, I FEEL THAT READERS ARE DISAPPOINTED THAT I'M NOT DEAD. A LONGER LIFE MEANS MORE DISGRACE. "PLAN TO DIE BEFORE THE AGE OF FORTY" IS A WELL-KNOWN PASSAGE IN AN ESSAY FROM *TSUREZUREGUSA (ESSAYS IN IDLENESS)*, BY THE AUTHOR KENKÔ YOSHIDA. I'M SAYING THAT FROM THIS POINT ON, MY LIFE HISTORY GETS THE FINAL COATING OF HUMILIATION. IT'S THE BEGINNING WHEREBY THE MORE I DRAW, THE GREATER THE SERIES OF HUMILIATIONS I'LL RECEIVE. INCIDENTALLY, THE AKASAKA SM CLUB (MANGA STREET) IS LOOKING FOR "S" PEOPLE. THE ENTRANCE FEE IS 410 YEN (INCLUDING TAX). THIS CLUB CAN CLOSE WITHOUT NOTICE ON ORDERS OF THE AUTHORITIES. JUST WANTED TO LET YOU KNOW THAT IN ADVANCE.

PREAMBLE | NEGATIVE | **POSITIVE** | RECLUSE | STALKER

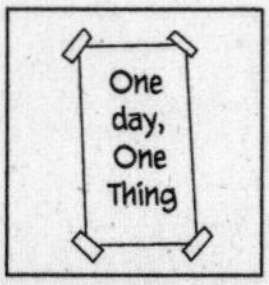
One day, One Thing

FOR EIGHT MONTHS, I TRIED TO MAKE SURE THAT I GOT OUTSIDE, SINCE IT'S NOT GOOD TO CONSTANTLY STAY AT HOME. BUT, SINCE I'M NOT USED TO GOING OUT, I COULD ONLY DO ONE THING A DAY. TODAY, I WENT TO THE BANK, SO THAT'S IT. TODAY, I WENT TO BIC CAMERA, SO I'M DONE. TODAY, I WENT OUT TO THROW OUT THE GARBAGE, SO THAT'S IT. IF I WENT TO THE CONVENIENCE STORE, I'D NEVER PICK UP MY LAUNDRY ON THE WAY HOME. ONE DAY, WHEN IT WAS EXTREMELY HOT, I STEPPED INTO THREE COFFEESHOPS ON MY WAY TO SHINJUKU STATION, WHICH IS A NINE-MINUTE WALK AWAY. THAT WAS JUST TO BE CHARMING. COME TO THINK OF IT, MY DAYS WERE BUSY AND FULFILLED.

PREAMBLE | NEGATIVE | POSITIVE | **RECLUSE** | STALKER

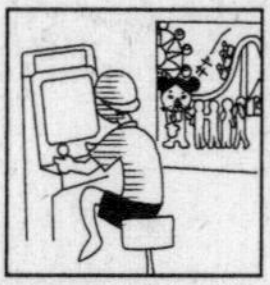

I THINK I'VE HAD PLENTY OF OPPORTUNITIES TO BECOME A *HIKIKOMORI*. IN THE SIXTH GRADE, ALL MY REPORT CARDS HAD THE REMARK "UNCOOPERATIVE" ON THEM. IT'S TRUE THAT WHEN THE CLASS WOULD GO TO THE PARK ON A FIELD TRIP, I WOULDN'T PLAY WITH THE OTHER KIDS' GROUPS, I WOULDN'T RIDE THE RIDES, I'D PLAY IN GAME ARCADES ALONE, SO I GUESS WHAT THE TEACHER SAID WAS TO BE EXPECTED. BUT EVEN I WANTED TO PLAY WITH OTHERS. WHEN KIDS WHO LIKED ONE ANOTHER GOT TOGETHER TO FORM A GROUP, I ENDED UP IN A GROUP WITH THE REJECTS AND OUTCASTS. IT WAS TOUGH BEING IN A GROUP OF PEOPLE WHO DIDN'T LIKE ONE ANOTHER. OUT OF THE FOUR OF US, TWO WERE ALWAYS ABSENT. IT WAS JUST THE TWO OF US, S-KUN AND I, WHO WENT TO SCHOOL. TEACHER, PLEASE UNDERSTAND. I HAD MY REASONS.

PREAMBLE | NEGATIVE | POSITIVE | RECLUSE | **STALKER**

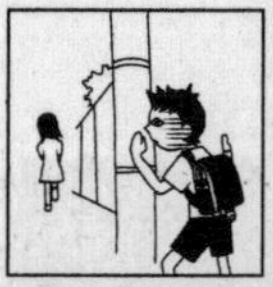

WHEN I WAS IN ELEMENTARY SCHOOL, IN ADDITION TO PLAYING SPY GAMES, SECRETLY FOLLOWING GIRLS FROM OUR CLASS WAS POPULAR. YOU TAIL THE GIRL HOME, MAKING SURE YOU AREN'T DETECTED, AND ALWAYS MAKE SURE TO CHECK OUT THE SURROUNDINGS. THE NEXT DAY, YOU'D ANNOUNCE YOUR FINDINGS TO THE TARGET. LIKE "YOU'VE GOT A BLACK DOG, RIGHT?" OR "YOUR ROOF IS RED," ETC. THE GIRL WOULD ANSWER, "HEY, HOW'D YOU KNOW THAT?," WHICH WAS SO HILARIOUS. ONE DAY, K-KUN, N-KUN, AND I DECIDED TO FOLLOW Y-SAN, WHO WAS A POPULAR GIRL IN SCHOOL. BUT Y-SAN HAD GREAT INSTINCTS AND FOUND OUT WHAT WE WERE DOING HALFWAY THROUGH OUR GAME. TO US GUYS, WHO WERE JUST CLOWNING AROUND, Y-SAN SAID, "ENOUGH ALREADY. WHAT'RE YOU DOING? AND TWO DAYS IN A ROW, TOO!" K-KUN AND N-KUN LOOKED REALLY PUZZLED. THAT'S RIGHT. I'D TAILED HER BY MYSELF FOR TWO DAYS. IF IT HAD HAPPENED TODAY, I'D BE ARRESTED.

**ANIMALS** | GO BACK TO YOUR COUNTRY | MAIL | PRECISION | ILLEGAL IMMIGRATION | ORDINARY

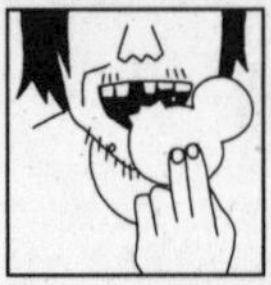

I WAS A GENTLE CHILD; THE KIND WHO'D EAT ANIMAL CRACKERS FROM THEIR TAILS. I EVEN ATE *TAIYAKI, HATO SABLE,* AND MUSHROOMS FROM THEIR TAILS. ONE DAY, MY DAD RETURNED FROM A BUSINESS TRIP TO AOMORI AND BROUGHT ME BACK SOME BADLY-SHAPED ANIMAL COOKIES; I COULDN'T TELL WHICH SIDE WAS THE HEAD AND WHICH WAS THE TAIL. SINCE I DIDN'T KNOW WHERE TO START, I ATE 'EM FROM THEIR BELLIES. THAT NIGHT, I CRIED. I CRIED BECAUSE I FELT I DID SOMETHING CRUEL. I WAS A KID THAT LOVED BENDING THE TABS ON THOSE PETIT PUDDING CUPS. NOW, I'VE GROWN INTO A MEAN ADULT WHO EATS MICKEY COOKIES BY THEIR EARS.

ANIMALS | **GO BACK TO YOUR COUNTRY** | MAIL | PRECISION | ILLEGAL IMMIGRATION | ORDINARY

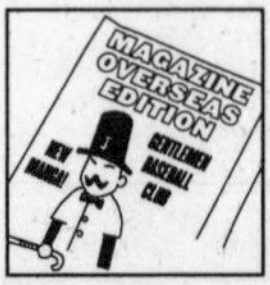
MAGAZINE OVERSEAS EDITION
NEW MANGA!
GENTLEMEN BASEBALL CLUB

I CAN'T SAY THIS OUT LOUD, BUT *SHÔNEN MAGAZINE* HAS AN OVERSEAS EDITORIAL DEPARTMENT AND, AS TO BE EXPECTED, *SHÔNEN MAGAZINES* OF A HIGH QUALITY ARE BEING PRODUCED THERE. THE GROUP OF AUTHORS IN THE OVERSEAS GROUP ARE REALLY AMAZING, AND WHEN THEY RETURN TO JAPAN, WE'RE INEVITABLY SHUNTED FARTHER AND FARTHER INTO THE BACKGROUND. THE MOST POPULAR WORK FROM THE OVERSEAS GROUP IS "ALPS DETECTIVE LENO." IT'S A REALLY FUNNY HARD-ACTION STORY ABOUT CONFRONTATIONS WITH A CHEESE SMUGGLING ORGANIZATION, THE "MELTY SNOW CHEESE GANG." (I RECOMMEND IT.) AS FOR THE GAG COMICS, I HEAR THAT "MONMARUTORU-CHAN" IS GOING TO BE TURNED INTO AN ANIMATED FILM. THE NEW COMIC "WE'RE THE GENTLEMEN BASEBALL CLUB" IS NOW APPEARING SERIALLY BY POPULAR DEMAND. (THE FIRST STORY'S TITLE: "THE HIDDEN PRIZE IS... THE DEATH PENALTY!")

ANIMALS | GO BACK TO YOUR COUNTRY | **MAIL** | PRECISION | ILLEGAL IMMIGRATION | ORDINARY

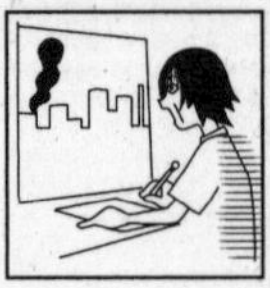

I'M NOT THE KIND OF GUY WHO CARRIES A CELL PHONE WITH ME, SO I REALLY DON'T NEED ONE. THERE'S NOT MUCH THAT I'D WANT TO CONVEY THROUGH EMAILS, SO THE NECESSITY'S NOT QUITE THERE. SOME SAY IT'S STRANGE THAT I DON'T CARRY A CELL PHONE, BUT IT MAKES ME WANT TO ASK THEM IF THEY'D CARRY ALL THE CELL PHONE STRAPS IN THE HOUSE AROUND WITH THEM. WE'RE EVEN AT THE POINT OF NOT CARRYING PORTABLES, SO WE'RE MUTUALLY STRANGE. BY THE WAY, I DO ATTACH JUST THE CELL PHONE STRAP OF *NAYABASHI MANJU* ON MY BAG. I'M ALWAYS WORKING OUT OF THE HOUSE SO A REGULAR CORD PHONE IS PLENTY FOR ME. IT'D BE MORE CONVENIENT FOR ME IF THERE WEREN'T ANY PHONES AT ALL. SMOKE SIGNALS WOULD BE ENOUGH FOR CONTACTS WITH THE EDITOR. WHEN MY ORIGINAL BOOK IS FINISHED, A RED SMOKE SIGNAL GOES UP. WHEN IT IS ACCEPTED, A GREEN SMOKE SIGNAL GOES UP. IF YOU'RE CANCELING ME, PUT UP A BLACK SMOKE SIGNAL, OKAY? I ASK FOR YOUR COOPERATION.

ANIMALS | GO BACK TO YOUR COUNTRY | MAIL | **PRECISION** | ILLEGAL IMMIGRATION | ORDINARY

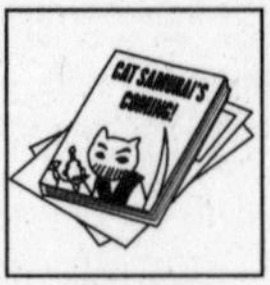
CAT SAMURAI'S COMING!

EVEN I CAN'T STAND IT UNLESS THINGS ARE IN ORDER. MY LIFE PLANS ARE ALSO IN ORDER. THE OTHER DAY, I BOUGHT MY GRAVE. I'VE ALSO RECEIVED MY POSTHUMOUS BUDDHIST NAME IN ADVANCE. SOME OF YOU MAY ALREADY KNOW IT, BUT IT'S "MANGA INKURA YAMINOSUKE." ANYHOW, EXCUSE ME, BUT I'D LIKE TO TALK ABOUT MY NEXT LIFE. I'M THINKING OF APPLYING FOR THE HOP STEP AWARD FOR NEW MANGA ARTISTS. THE TITLE OF MY WORK'LL BE *CAT SAMURAI'S COMING.* OF COURSE, MY PEN NAME WOULD BE HIROSHI YUME.

ANIMALS | GO BACK TO YOUR COUNTRY | MAIL | PRECISION | **ILLEGAL IMMIGRATION** | ORDINARY

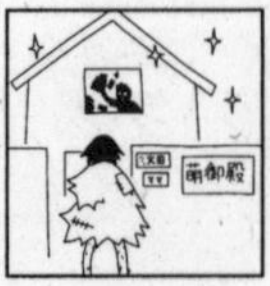

I CAN'T SAY THIS OUT LOUD, BUT THIS IS AN ILLEGAL COMIC SERIES. IT DIDN'T PASS THE MAGAZINE INSPECTION INTO THE COUNTRY. KEEP THIS HUSH-HUSH TO THE EDITOR. DON'T TIP ME OFF. I'D BE FORCIBLY DEPORTED. WHEN I WAS DEPORTED, MY HOME WAS TAKEN OVER BY SOME OTHER PERSON SO, NOW, SOMEONE ELSE IS LIVING THERE. THE NAMEPLATE SAID "HIDA." I WONDER WHAT THE PERSON'S LIKE? MY PLACE IN THIS NEW COUNTRY IS SMALLER THAN MY LAST ONE. I'D LIKE TO LIVE HERE PERMANENTLY. ARE THE PEOPLE IN THIS COUNTRY KIND?

ANIMALS | GO BACK TO YOUR COUNTRY | MAIL | PRECISION | ILLEGAL IMMIGRATION | **ORDINARY**

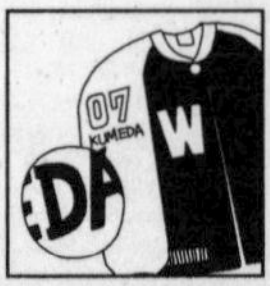
07
KUMEDA
W

I THOUGHT I'D TRY TO BE NORMAL. LIKE THE STUDENTS OF THAT TIME, I TRIED TO BE PRETENTIOUS. I JOINED A PRETENTIOUS CIRCLE. TENNIS IN SUMMER, SKIING AND HOT SPRINGS IN WINTER—IT WAS PRETTY PRETENTIOUS. I HAD A LETTERMAN JACKET LIKE EVERYONE ELSE. ON THE BACK WAS MY NAME AND NUMBER. 07 * KUMEDA...I JUST DIDN'T CARE ANYMORE. BEFORE THE SUMMER, I STOPPED HANGING WITH THE CIRCLE. I'D THOUGHT I HADN'T CARED ABOUT THE DISTINCTIONS BETWEEN THE *D* AND THE *T*. THE OTHER DAY, THAT JACKET APPEARED. IT LOOKED AS IF THE LETTER *D* HAD BEEN SCRAPED WITH MY NAILS. SURE ENOUGH, I'D BEEN CONCERNED ABOUT THAT ALL ALONG.

**SAYONARA,
ZETSUBOU-SENSEI**

# CURRENT CHARGES FROM THIS ISSUE

LETTER OF ACCUSATION

PLAINTIFF:
OCCUPATION: STUDENT
NAME: KAERE KIMURA

DEFENDANT:
OCCUPATION: STUDENT
NAME: MERU OTONASHI

DATE: JUNE 8
ATTN: CHIEF OF POLICE

- PURPOSE OF ACCUSATION
THE ACTS BY THE DEFENDANT AS STATED BELOW ARE CONSIDERED TO FALL UNDER CRIMINAL LAW, ARTICLE 231 (CRIME OF INSULT), AND THIS COMPLAINT IS MADE TO PURSUE SEVERE PUNISHMENT TO BE HANDED OUT TO THE DEFENDANT.

- FACTS OF THE ACCUSATION
AT ABOUT 1:00 PM, WHILE CLASS WAS IN SESSION, THE DEFENDANT OPENLY CARRIED OUT INSULTING ACTS, BY TEXTING MY CELL PHONE WITH MESSAGE CONTENTS SUCH AS, "UR JUST A PANTY CHARACTER."

THE AFOREMENTIONED ACTS ARE CONSIDERED TO FALL UNDER CRIMINAL LAW, ARTICLE 231 (CRIME OF INSULT) AND, IN ORDER FOR THE DEFENDANT TO BE GIVEN STRICT PUNISHMENT, I HEREBY MAKE MY CHARGES.

EVIDENCE
1. EVIDENTIARY WITNESS: CLASSMATE A
2. CELL PHONE COMPANY: DOCUMENTS SUBMITTED BY THE INFORMATION MANAGEMENT DIVISION

SUPPLEMENTARY DOCUMENTS
WRITTEN DOCUMENTATION OF ABOVE-MENTIONED TEXT MESSAGE – 1 DOCUMENT

---

LETTER OF ACCUSATION

PLAINTIFF:
OCCUPATION: STUDENT
NAME: KAERE KIMURA

DEFENDANT:
OCCUPATION: HIGH SCHOOL TEACHER
NAME: NOBORU ITOSHIKI

DATE: JUNE 1
ATTN: CHIEF OF POLICE

- PURPOSE OF ACCUSATION
THE ACTS BY THE DEFENDANT AS STATED BELOW ARE DEEMED TO COME UNDER CRIMINAL LAW, ARTICLE 176 (FORCIBLE ACT OF LEWDNESS), AND THIS COMPLAINT IS MADE TO PURSUE SEVERE PUNISHMENT TO BE HANDED OUT TO THE DEFENDANT.

- FACTS OF THE ACCUSATION
AT ABOUT 2:00 PM, WHILE I WAS PASSING BY THE KONAN BRIDGE, THE DEFENDANT CALLED OUT, "THIS IS MY PLACE," AND PURSUED ME TO BRIDGE'S RAILING.

I FELT THE DANGER OF FALLING OFF THE BRIDGE, AND ATTEMPTED TO GET AWAY FROM THE DEFENDANT. SUBSEQUENTLY, THE DEFENDANT COMMITTED A LEWD ACT BY GRABBING BOTH MY ANKLES, HANGING ME UPSIDE DOWN, AND LEERING AT MY UNDERWEAR. AT THAT TIME, I SUSTAINED A HEAD INJURY.

THE ACT BY THE DEFENDANT IS CONSIDERED TO FALL UNDER CRIMINAL LAW, ARTICLE 176, CRIME OF FORCIBLE ACT OF LEWDNESS, SO I HEREBY FILE A COMPLAINT SO THAT SEVERE PUNISHMENT MAY BE HANDED TO THE DEFENDANT.

EVIDENCE
1. WITNESS: PASSERBY A
2. HEAD OF UNIVERSITY HOSPITAL—PREPARED MEDICAL REPORT

SUPPLEMENTARY DOCUMENTS
ABOVE-MENTIONED DOCUMENT – 1 DOCUMENT

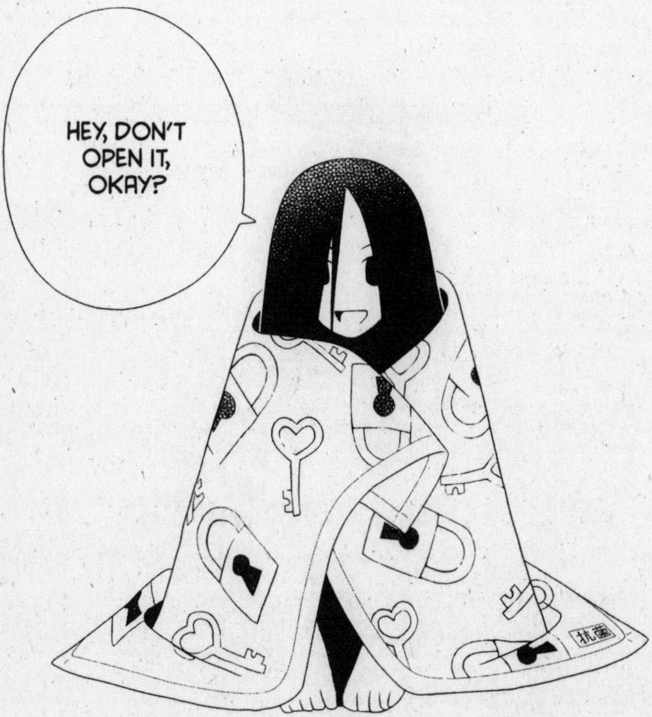
HEY, DON'T OPEN IT, OKAY?
抗菌

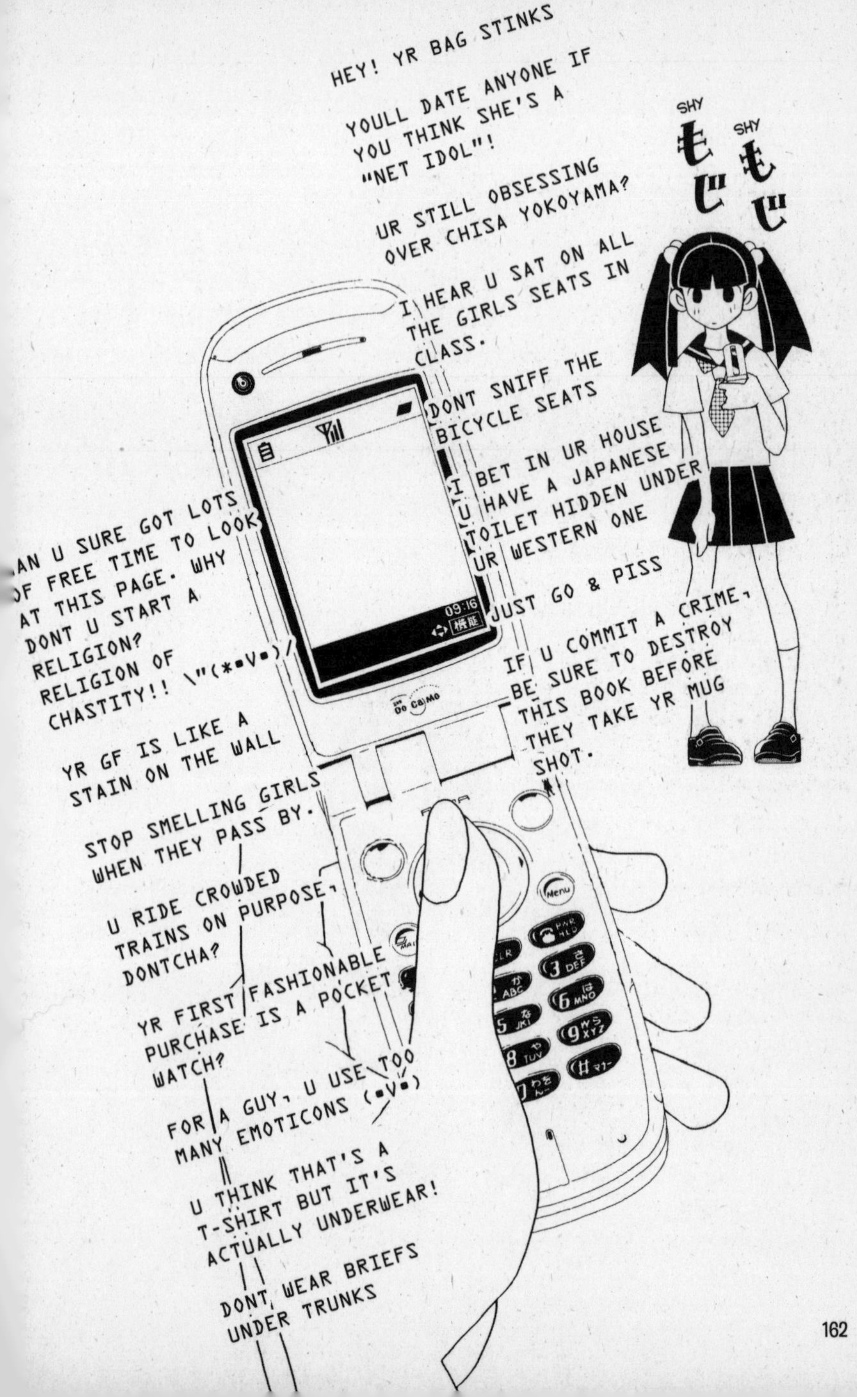
HEY! YR BAG STINKS
YOULL DATE ANYONE IF YOU THINK SHE'S A "NET IDOL"!
UR STILL OBSESSING OVER CHISA YOKOYAMA?
I HEAR U SAT ON ALL THE GIRLS SEATS IN CLASS.
DONT SNIFF THE BICYCLE SEATS
I BET IN UR HOUSE U HAVE A JAPANESE TOILET HIDDEN UNDER UR WESTERN ONE
JUST GO & PISS
IF U COMMIT A CRIME, BE SURE TO DESTROY THIS BOOK BEFORE THEY TAKE YR MUG SHOT.
SHY
SHY
AN U SURE GOT LOTS OF FREE TIME TO LOOK AT THIS PAGE. WHY DONT U START A RELIGION? RELIGION OF CHASTITY!! \"(*▪V▪)/
YR GF IS LIKE A STAIN ON THE WALL
STOP SMELLING GIRLS WHEN THEY PASS BY.
U RIDE CROWDED TRAINS ON PURPOSE, DONTCHA?
YR FIRST FASHIONABLE PURCHASE IS A POCKET WATCH?
FOR A GUY, U USE TOO MANY EMOTICONS (▪V▪)
U THINK THAT'S A T-SHIRT BUT IT'S ACTUALLY UNDERWEAR!
DONT WEAR BRIEFS UNDER TRUNKS

## ZETSUBOU LITERARY COMPILATION

## DEATH COUNTRY

AFTER PASSING THROUGH THE TUNNEL WAS ANOTHER TUNNEL.
AFTER PASSING THROUGH THAT TUNNEL THERE WAS, AGAIN, ANOTHER TUNNEL.
ENDLESS AND FOREVER, TUNNEL AFTER TUNNEL, EVERLASTING TUNNELS INTO THE DISTANCE IS MY LIFE.
AFTER PASSING THROUGH THE TUNNEL WAS ANOTHER TUNNEL.

# About the Author

**Koji Kumeta** (1967– ) is the creator of numerous humor manga, including *Ike! Nangoku Ice Hockey Bu* ("Go! Southern Ice Hockey Club"), *Katte ni Kaizô,* and *Taiyo no Senshi Pokapoka* ("Pokapoka, Soldier of the Sun"). Although his early work shares similarities with other love comedy manga, Kumeta soon developed a distinctive style of black humor and satire. His latest work, *Sayonara, Zetsubou-sensei,* began in *Weekly Shônen Magazine* in 2005. Kenjiro Hata (*Hayate the Combat Butler*) once served as Kumeta's assistant.

# Translation Notes

Japanese is a tricky language for most Westerners, and translation is often more art than science. In the case of a text-dense manga like *Sayonara, Zetsubou-sensei*, it's a delicate art indeed. Although most of the jokes are universal, Koji Kumeta is famous for filling his manga with references to Japanese politics, entertainment, otaku culture, religion, and sports. Unless you're a true Japanophile, it's difficult to understand it all without some serious background knowledge of current events at the time when the manga was running. Kumeta also uses references to foreign literature and politics, so even Japanese readers probably don't get all the humor. For your reading pleasure, here are notes on some of the more obscure references and difficult-to-translate jokes in *Sayonara, Zetsubou-sensei*.

# General Notes

## *Sayonara, Zetsubou-sensei* (title)

The title *Sayonara, Zetsubou-sensei* literally translates to "Good-bye, Mr. Despair." It's a possible reference to James Hilton's 1934 novel of a beloved teacher, *Good-bye, Mr. Chips* (known in Japan as *Chips-sensei, Sayonara*). The Del Rey edition preserves the original Japanese title, with *The Power of Negative Thinking* as a subtitle to express Itoshiki's philosophy. (The English subtitle is itself a reference to Norman Vincent Peale's 1952 self-help book *The Power of Positive Thinking*.)

## Signs

Koji Kumeta's highly detailed and realistic renderings of modern Japanese life present one special challenge to the letterer. Kumeta fills his panels with all the ephemera of everyday life—street signs, product labels, magazine covers, newspaper pages, and so on. It's difficult to replace this text with English lettering without interfering with the integrity of the original illustrations. Out of respect for Kumeta's unique artwork, many signs have retained their original Japanese lettering.

# Page Notes

## Kafuka's tree names, page 11

Kafuka's tree names are all based on various elaborate titles. The "*Udaijin*," the "Minister of the Right," was a government position in ancient Japan. "*Daimaoh*," "Great Demon King," is a title used by villains in many manga, including *Dragon Ball*.

## **Naming rights,** page 12

Yahoo! BB, Livedoor, Ajinomoto, Rakuten, and Docomo are major Japanese companies.

## **Dense forests around Mt. Fuji,** page 14

Aokigahara, the dense woodland around Mt. Fuji, is infamous throughout Japan as a popular spot for suicides. In 2002, seventy-eight dead bodies were found within, beating the previous record of seventy-three suicides in 1998.

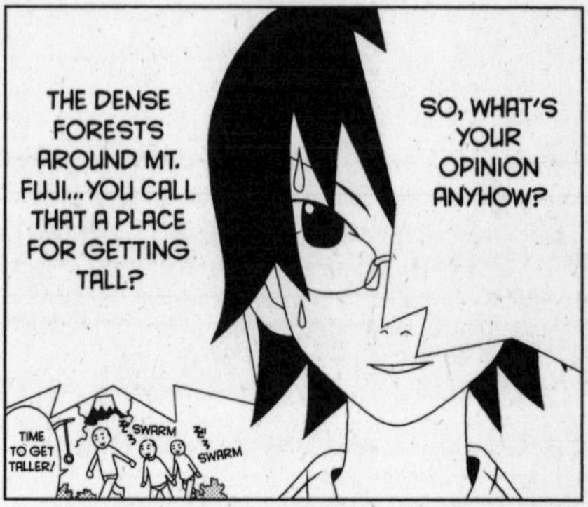
SO, WHAT'S YOUR OPINION ANYHOW?
THE DENSE FORESTS AROUND MT. FUJI...YOU CALL THAT A PLACE FOR GETTING TALL?
TIME TO GET TALLER!
SWARM
SWARM

## **Inauspicious characters,** page 17

In Japan, serious thought is given when choosing name a name for a child. When kanji (Chinese characters) are combined to create a name, they convey meanings, so great care is taken to select kanji with auspicious meanings, pleasing sounds, as well as an overall aesthetic balance. Just by looking at a written name, one can begin to imagine the characteristics in the person (e.g., strength, beauty, kindness), so it's important to have one that positively reflects one's character. Sometimes, a person will change his/her name in adulthood, believing that it will bring more luck.

## **Hiro★Tsunoda,** page 17

Hiro★Tsunada (1949–) is a singer, composer, and renowned drummer. Several of his songs became megahits in the 1970s. He also composed songs for many singers, started a drumming school, and has competed with musicians from all over the world. Since the name "Hiro Tsunoda" didn't have a particularly pleasing sound, and it was difficult to distinguish where his first and last names started, he changed it by inserting a star between the names. For a while, he was called Tsunoda Hoshihiro, with "*hoshi*" meaning "star." Now he's Hiro Tsunoda again, and the star is silent.

## Zetsubou, page 18

Nozomu Itoshiki's family name is the combination of two innocuous characters, *ito* (thread) and *shiki* (color). Grouped together into one kanji, however, the same characters read *zetsubou* (despair). It's a terrible humiliation for him to be confronted with it before the whole class.

## Hair, page 22

*Ke*, the kanji for "hair," looks a lot like the stylized *E* with wings on the baseball cap (especially if you have a cynical mind). Nozomu's distracted mind can only see the irony of the kanji "hair" on the cap of the bald baseball player.

## "The Chuo train stopped running again today, didn't it?" page 23

The Chuo line is infamous for fatal accidents, which often result in train delays. It's a typically pessimistic statement from Nozomu.

## Post-Graduation Career Hopes Survey, page 23

These surveys actually exist in Japan. They're intended to get the students thinking about the companies they'd like to work for, or universities they'd like to attend.

## Post-Graduation Career Despair Survey, page 25

This is a more obvious pun in Japanese than in English. In Japanese, *kibou* means "hope." It's made up of the kanji *ki* and *bou*, which taken individually, also mean "hope." However, since *zetsu* means "to sever, cut off, shut off, die out," etc., the word *zetsubou* means "despair" or "hopelessness." Both words use the same root, *bou*.

## Momogi Animation School, page 26

A possible reference to an actual school, Yoyogi Animation Film School.

## Celebrities' examples, page 26

As sometimes happens in *Sayonara, Zetsubou-sensei,* the references are so thick and obscure here it's questionable whether anyone but Kumeta gets them all. The "strawberry panties" may be a reference to the manga *Strawberry 100%* (see page 63), which, coincidentally, also involves big-breasted teenage girls. *Fusafusa* is a way of reading the numbers 2-3-2-3, and also has the meaning of "fluffy."

## Planet Pororoca, page 28

The word *pororoca* may refer to the *pororoca* tidal phenomenon at the mouth of the Amazon river, a strong tide known as a "tidal bore" or "adverse tide." It might also have been chosen because it sounds funny.

## Kafuka Fura, page 29

Kafuka's name is a reference to Franz Kafka (1883–1924), a famous writer known for his themes of alienation, absurdity, and the pointlessness of existence. It's an ironic name for the cheerful Kafuka. The P.N. stands for "pen name."

## Beyond the Tunnel Was Whiteness, page 30

This chapter title is based on a line from the famous book *Yukiguni* ("Snow Country") by Nobel Prize–winning author, Yasunari Kawabata.

## Street signs, page 31

The signs on this page are, for the most part, ordinary street signs.

## Hikikomori, page 34

*Hikikomori* is a Japanese term for individuals who have chosen to withdraw from society and not leave their homes. The word comes from the verb *hikikomoru* which means "stay indoors" or "be confined indoors." It is considered a serious social problem in Japan. Often it is the intense pressures of school and the feeling of being unable to fulfill expected goals that trigger this withdrawal from society. Bullying at school and family problems such as ineffective parenting, are also contributing factors. To the *hikikomori*, it is easier to stay alone in the confines of one's room than to have to cope with others on the outside. Komori's name comes from the *hikikomori* phenomenon.

## Zashiki-warashi, page 36

"*Zashiki-warashi*" literally means "Japanese tatami-floored room-child." A *zashiki-warashi* is a special spirit that's said to bring fortune to a home, provided it stays there. However, if it leaves, misfortune will befall the home.

## Hinouma, page 40

*Hinouma*, the "fire horse," is a Chinese astrological sign which comes round once every sixty years (1906, 1966, and 2026). Women born in the year of the fire horse are considered unlucky and dangerous to men and are still occasionally subject to prejudice.

## Double Suicide Notes, page 42

The large text on Itoshiki-sensei's book can be read as either "Double Suicide Notes" or "Notes of Innermost Thoughts." The phrase "Death Note" is probably a reference to the famous manga.

## Before Me, There's No One; Behind Me, There's You, page 44

This is a reference to the line "Before me, there's no road; behind me, a road is formed" from Kotaro Takamura's poetry anthology *Journey*.

## Street signs, page 45

The signs on this page are ordinary street signs (an advertisement for a loan company, etc.).

## Schoolgirl prostitution, page 48

In the original Japanese this is *enko*, short for *enjo kôsai* (literally, "compensated dating"). It's a euphemism for various kinds of escort services and prostitution, not specifically involving schoolgirls, although much of the Japanese media coverage of *enjo kôsai* has focused on scandalous stories of prostitution among middle-class teenagers.

## Newspaper and TV, page 51

The text on the newspaper and TV screen is mostly ordinary news or obscure references. There is, however, one particularly unusual headline: "Pomegranate 100%? Hooray!" It's a reference to the manga *Strawberry 100%*.

## Text on blackboard, page 52

The text on the blackboard is a quotation from the famous Japanese author Natsume Sôseki (1867–1916).

## Boy's Love Club, page 53

The original Japanese text on the poster reads "Boy's La-Bu," with the *Bu* meaning "club" (as in *Ouran High School Host Club*). Together, it makes a pun on "Boy's Love."

## *Manga Michi*, page 54

*Manga Michi*, or "The Way of Manga," is a famous manga about the struggle of becoming a manga artist, by the artistic duo Fujiko Fujio.

## Not Losing to Elbows, Not Losing to Knees, page 58

This is a reference to the poem "Ame ni mo Makezu" ("Not Losing to the Rain") by Kenji Miyazawa.

## *Sambo*, page 59

This could be a reference to the infamous children's book *Little Black Sambo* (in Japanese, *Chibikuro Sambo*), which has been controversial for its racism in both the United States and Japan.

## Domestic violence, page 59

In the original Japanese, the abbreviation "DV" is used for "domestic violence." It's a not uncommon abbreviation in Japan.

## Street signs, pages 60-65

The signs on these pages are ordinary street signs and store signs.

## Kyoko Hamaguchi, page 67

Kyoko Hamaguchi (1978– ) is a female wrestler trained by her father, "Animal" Hamaguchi (real name Heigo Hamaguchi, 1947– ) a former heavy-weight class wrestler and body-building trainer. Her father had her train with boys, and she started amateur wrestling at the age of fourteen. In his wrestling days, "Animal" Hamaguchi would enter the ring wearing his trademark Tarzan outfits, while his entrance theme song was "Matador." So, like Kyoko, Abiru is getting "animal" therapy.

## *Saint Tail,* page 67

*Saint Tail,* about a ponytailed girl, is the name of a manga by Megumi Tachikawa.

## Tail signs, page 68

Abiru's collection of tails includes a tiger, an African wild dog, an armadillo, a lion, a sand fox, a tortoiseshell cat, a chihuahua, and an okojo. Okojo is the ferret-like hero of *Okojo-san,* a *shojo* manga by Ayumi Uno.

## Street signs, page 70

The signs on this page are ordinary street signs.

## *Faithful Elephants,* page 70

*Faithful Elephants* (literally "The Poor Elephants," *Kawaiiso na Zô,* in the original Japanese) is a famous children's book by Yukio Tsuchiya. It takes place during World War II, when Japan was being bombed, and there was the fear that the animals in Ueno Zoo would escape amid all the destruction. The zoo keepers killed the animals one by one, until only three faithful elephants remained. In the end, although the elephants resisted various poisons and tried to please the humans by doing tricks, they too died of starvation.

## Fly Over That Country to Come Here, page 72

This is a parody of the line "jump over the fire to come here" from the climax of Yukio Mishima's novel *Sound of the Waves.*

## Watching fireworks, page 73

Itoshiki-sensei's speech is a reference to the 1993 Japanese movie *Uchiage hanabi, shita kara Miruka? Yoko kara Miruka?* ("Fireworks, Should We See It from the Side or the Bottom?"). At the end, the heroine flies off in a helicopter and presumably sees the fireworks from above.

## Rakuten and Shidax, page 74

The Rakuten Golden Eagles and the Shidax Baseball Club are two Japanese baseball teams. Both were managed at different times by the notoriously cranky manager and ex-baseball-player Katsuya Nomura.

## *eki-in,* page 77

*Eki-in* are train station officials. Trains are well-known in Japan as "a groper's paradise" where perverts (*chikan*) harass and sexually assault female commuters. Many male commuters have even resorted to carrying an item such as a book in both hands to ensure that they have an alibi if wrongly accused. This is why Nozomu yelled, "You're the type to scream '*Pervert!*' and turn me over to the *eki-in!*" to make his case. Incidentally, the large number of *chikan* has led to the creation of special commuter cars reserved for women only.

## Dejima Island, page 78

Dejima Island is a tiny, man-made island (170 meters by 75 meters) in the Bay of Nagasaki, used as the only contact point with the outside world during Japan's self-imposed isolation during the Edo Period (seventeeth/eighteenth centuries). Here, Nozomu likens his classroom to Dejima Island, for it is the only place where his students are allowed to make contact with him.

## Kaere, page 79

Kaere Kimura's first name "Kaere" is homonymous with the words "leave, go back, or return." So, chanting "Kaere! Kaere!" here, is not only shouting out her name, but they're also shouting threats for her to go back to her country.

## "I'm at my limits as a Japanese girl!" page 82

In the original, Kaera says "I'm at my limits as a *Yamato Nadeshiko!*" "*Yamato Nadeshiko*" is an old expression for the ideal Japanese woman.

## Signs in lower right panel, page 82

All the signs in this panel are references to obscolete computers and computer programming. "Ba-Maga" is short for *Mycom Basic Magazine*, a computer programming magazine that ceased publication in 2003. It was known as a bible for programmers. N88-BASIC was a programming language. The Sharp X68000 was a Japanese home computer. Pokekon is short for "pocket computer," portable computers popular in Japan in the 1980s.

## Konan Bridge and Shini Rurubu, page 83

Konan Bridge (*Konan-bashi*) literally means "Old Calamity Bridge" or "Old Misfortune Bridge." Nozomu obviously selects his suicide spots with detailed research and planning. Perhaps it's with his handy copy of Shini Rurubu, *Rurubu for Dying*, a parody of the actual *Rurubu* series of Japanese travel guidebooks.

## Sign on wall, page 84

The kanji *"shou"* (meaning "righteous" or "correct") is used to count in Japan, because it takes five strokes to make the kanji. The sign shows a count of twenty three—presumably the number of days that the illegal immigrants have been in the container box.

## The Antenna Is Rising...We Must Attempt to Live! page 86

This is a parody of the line "The wind is rising...we must attempt to live" by the French poet and author Paul Valéry. It was also quoted at the beginning of Hori Tatsuo's novel *The Wind Has Risen*.

## Meru, page 87

The name "Meru" is derived from the Japanese pronunciation of the English word "mail," as in "email."

## Genshiken, page 88

The box (which reappears in the seventh panel on page 89) is labeled with the name of Kio Shimoku's manga *Genshiken,* about a college club of manga, anime, and video game *otaku*. Fittingly, the box is full of *dôjin* (from *dôjinshi,* fan-produced goods, generally small-press manga).

## Famous quotations, page 89

The list of quotations goes from the famous (Marie Antoinette's famous quote "Let them eat cake," and the insult that started the Incident of the 47 Ronin) to the obscure. "Players should know their place. They are just players" is a quote attributed to Tsuneo Watanabe, the blustering former owner of the Yomiuri Giants baseball team. "Ami's pay is lower than SPEED's" is a quote attributed to the father of singer Ami Suzuki, who complained that his daughter was getting less pay than other musicians in the same age group. The complaint led to Suzuki being ostracized from the music world. "I'm the very first negotiator for the Police Agency" is a reference to a movie starring Yusuke Santamaria. "From the sovereign..." is part of the famous historical message from Prince Shôtoku of Japan to the Sui Dynasty emperor of China. "Parapunte" is an unpredictable spell in the *Dragon Quest* video game series. "Balse" is a magic word in the Miyazaki movie *Laputa: Castle in the Sky*.

## Store signs, page 89

The signs in this panel are ordinary store signs.

## hazukashigariyasan@dacam, page 90

*Hazukashigaryasan* is Japanese for "shy girl."

## Dacamo, page 94

Dacamo is a take-off on the popular Docomo brand of cell phones.

### *eise* grass and *namaniku* flowers, page 98

*Eise* grass means "reincarnation grass," while *namaniku* flowers literally means "raw meat flowers." It's hard to know what may be growing on other planets way out there in the universe. But Kafuka, perhaps, has "otherworldly" sensibilities.

### Align Your Books Precisely on the Shelves, Go Out into the Streets! page 100

This title is a reference to the 1971 film *Throw Away Your Books, Go Out into the Streets!* directed by Shôji Terayama.

### Famires Café, page 106

The Japanese language abounds in combination words and this is one of them. "Famires" is a Japanese combo term for a family-style restaurant, such as Denny's. It is also the name of a specific restaurant.

### Raou's speech patterns, page 106

Raou is the chief antagonist of the manga series *Fist of the North Star*. In Japanese, there are many different pronouns for "I," which one can use based on one's attitude, and Raou uses several of them. Chiri takes this as an example of inconsistency.

### A weird hairdo at a top sumo wrestler's funeral, page 106

When the sumo wrestler Koji Takanohana attended the funeral of his father, the late great sumo wrestler Kenshi Takanohana, the press commented that his hair looked inappropriate. It had a permed, tousled, "bed-head" look.

### Family register, page 112

In Japan, the family register is an important government document. It officially registers immediate family members with their name, date of birth, permanent place of residence, etc. It serves as a legal document that gives official recognition and status to an individual. Chiri, being extremely precise, wants to be registered properly as a member of the family so that her status can't be disputed.

### No Matter What, We've Got to Stick Together, page 114

This is a reference to Jules Verne's 1888 novel *Two Years' Vacation*, which was made into an anime in 1987.

### Tarô Sekiuchi, page 117

Translating Tarô's language is challenging, because sometimes it's grammatically correct, and other times it's broken (like how a foreigner would speak English, sometimes with a bit of "Me Tarzan, you Jane" exaggeration). Given the difficulty of Japanese, she often misinterprets, or reinterprets, the harder compound words. Incidentally, Tarô is usually a boy's name.

## **Street signs,** page 119

The signs on this page are ordinary street signs.

## **Food,** page 124

Although most of the snack food donated to Tarô is just ordinary food, there are a few in-jokes in the Japanese brand names. *Cream Lemon* is the name of an infamous 1984 adult anime. Fans of the manga *Death Note* may catch the reference in Ryuk brand apples.

## ***ODA*****,** page 124

ODA stands for "Official Development Assistance," a category of development aid provided to poor countries by rich ones (not only by Japan).

## ***NEET*** **kids,** page 125

"*NEET*" stands for "Not currently engaged in employment, education, or training." It's a growing social problem in Japan.

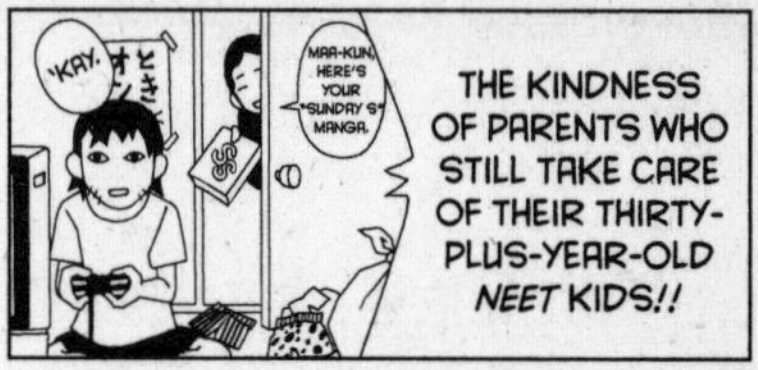
THE KINDNESS OF PARENTS WHO STILL TAKE CARE OF THEIR THIRTY-PLUS-YEAR-OLD *NEET* KIDS!!
MAA-KUN, HERE'S YOUR "SUNDAY S" MANGA.
'KAY.

## **List of kindnesses,** page 125

Some of Kafuka's examples of "kindness" are universal, but others are specifically Japanese. The "kindness of allowing a hungry man to eat one's face" is a complicated reference to a comment by Takashi Yanase, the creator of the manga *Anpanman* and the children's book *Yasashii Lion* ("The Gentle Lion"). (Incidentally, the phrase "Lion 8341" used in panel 10 is also a reference to *Yasashii Lion,* since "8341" can be read as "Yasashii" in Japanese.) The "kindness of paying TV reception fees without watching" refers to the Japanese law that each household with a television must have a broadcast receiver license and pay for TV reception fees, although enforcement is lax. The line about "territorial waters" refers to incidents when Chinese nuclear submarines and North Korean ships have entered Japanese territorial waters, but the Japanese Self Defense Forces, being forbidden to use arms, did nothing. "Half of Bufferin is made of kindness" is a phrase from a Bufferin TV commercial. Kudokan (short for Kudô Kankurô) is a screenwriter/actor/director.

## **This Class Has Many Problems, Please Understand,** page 128

This is a reference to a line ("This restaurant gets many orders, please understand") from Kenji Miyazawa's novel *The Restaurant with Many Orders*.

## Pantasia, page 134

Pantasia is the name of the bakery in Takashi Hashiguchi's manga *Yakitate!! Japan*.

## "Ordinary?!" page 137

The Japanese word *futsû* translates as "average," "ordinary," "common," "medium," or "standard." There's no one English word that covers all the meanings on panel 139.1.

## Nami, page 138

Nami is a female name, but it is also a homonym with the word "ordinary" or "normal" (although the written characters used are different).

## Signs and books, page 142

The signs and books on this page are mostly ordinary. One exception is the basket of offerings that is dedicated "To Zashiki-warashi-san."

## Hitonari Tsuji, page 143

Hitonari Tsuji (1959– ), also known as Jinsei Tsuji, is a Japanese writer, composer, and film director.

## "Träumerei," page 144

*Träumerei* ("Reverie") is one of the best-known classical pieces by the nineteenth-century German composer Robert Schumann. As a romantic composition, *Träumerei* is a particularly gentle and sensitive piece, but it can sound hauntingly beautiful or a bitspooky, depending on your mood and time of day. It'll never sound the same for me after Kafuka put in her lyrics.

WHEN SCHOOL'S OVER, THE SWEET MELODY OF "TRÄUMEREI" IS PLAYED.

## Assorted references, page 158

*Taiyaki* are fish-shaped cakes filled with bean jam. Hato Sable are dove-shaped cookies, and Petit Pudding comes in little plastic cups with tabbed lids. The "Melty Snow Cheese Gang" is a reference to the Japanese product Snow Brand Melty Cheese. Nayabashi Manju is a famous brand of *manju*, a Japanese confection. The process of getting a posthumous Buddhist name is a real custom in Asian cultures, although in Japan it is normally reserved for the emperor and a few extremely wealthy individuals who can pay a lot of money for the honor.

## Death Country, page 163

"Death Country" is written in Japanese as *Yukiguni*, a pun on the famous book *Yukiguni* ("Snow Country") by Nobel Prize–winning author Yasunari Kawabata.

# Sayonara, Zetsubou-sensei
## Volume 2

# Preview

We're pleased to present you with a preview of volume 2.
Please check our website (www.delreymanga.com) to see
when this volume will be available in English. For now, you'll
have to make do with Japanese!

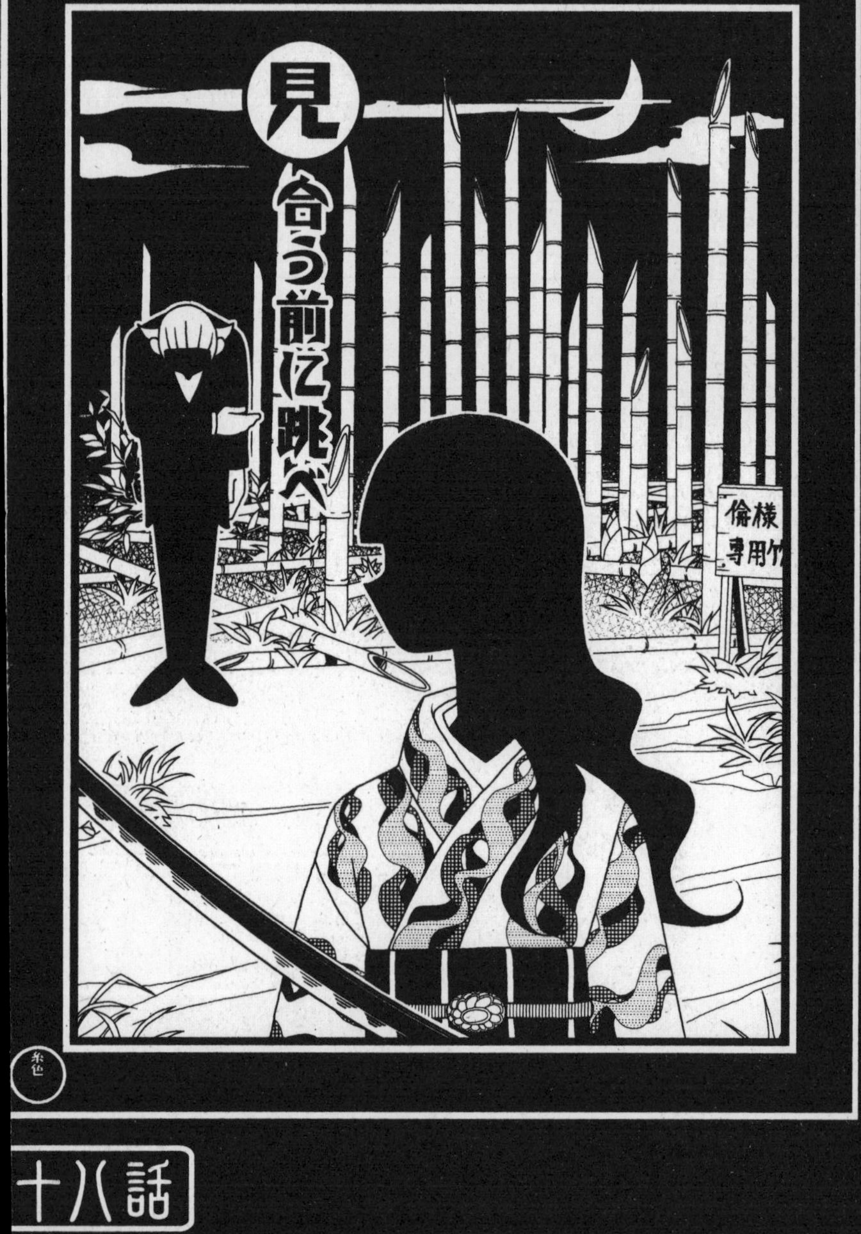
見合う前に跳べ
倫様
専用竹

糸色

# 十八話

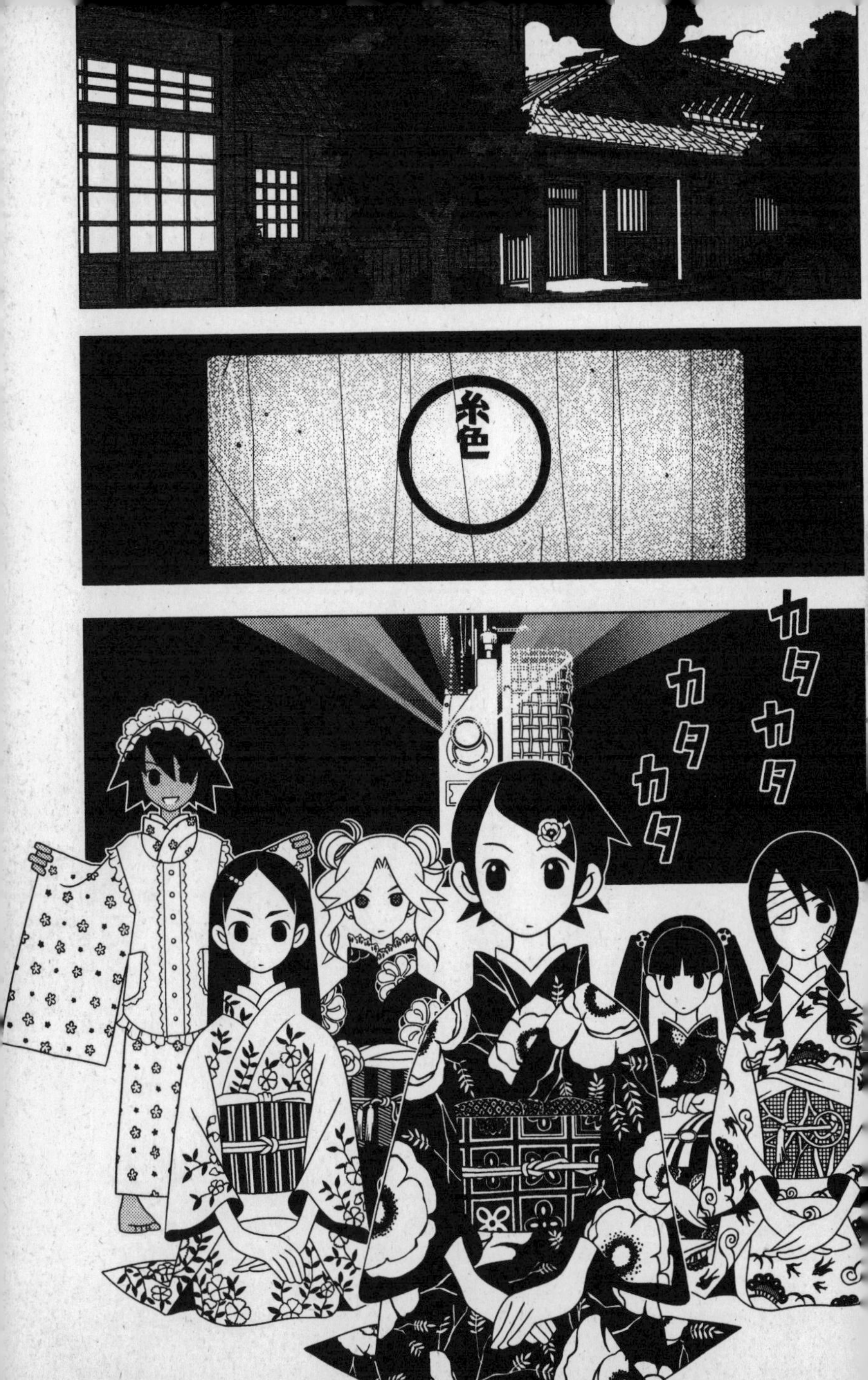
糸色
カタカタ
カタカタ

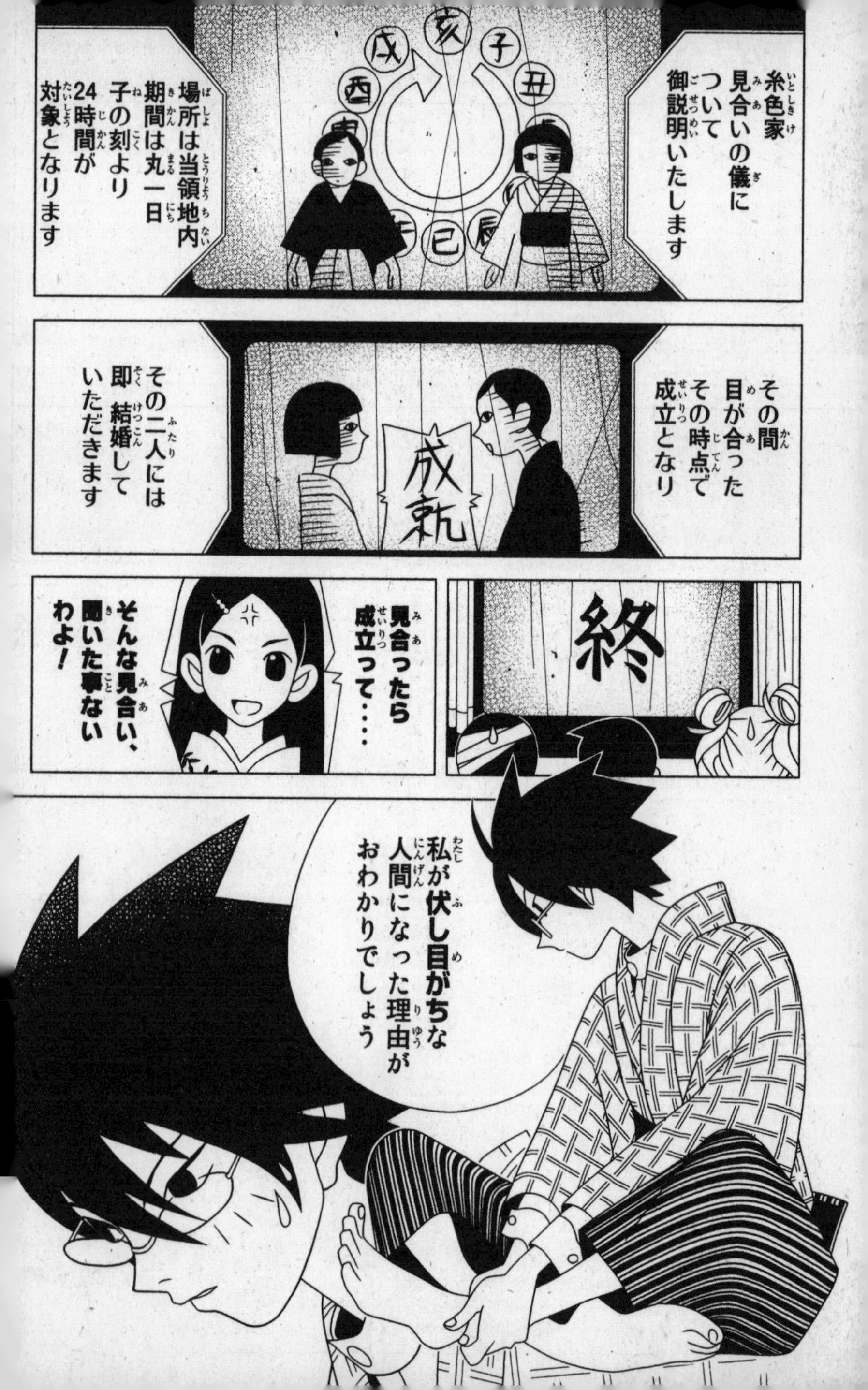

糸色家見合いの儀についてご説明いたします
場所は当領地内 期間は丸一日 子の刻より24時間が対象となります
その間目が合ったその時点で成立となり
成就
その二人には即結婚していただきます
終
見合ったら成立って……
そんな見合い、聞いた事ないわよ!
私が伏し目がちな人間になった理由がおわかりでしょう

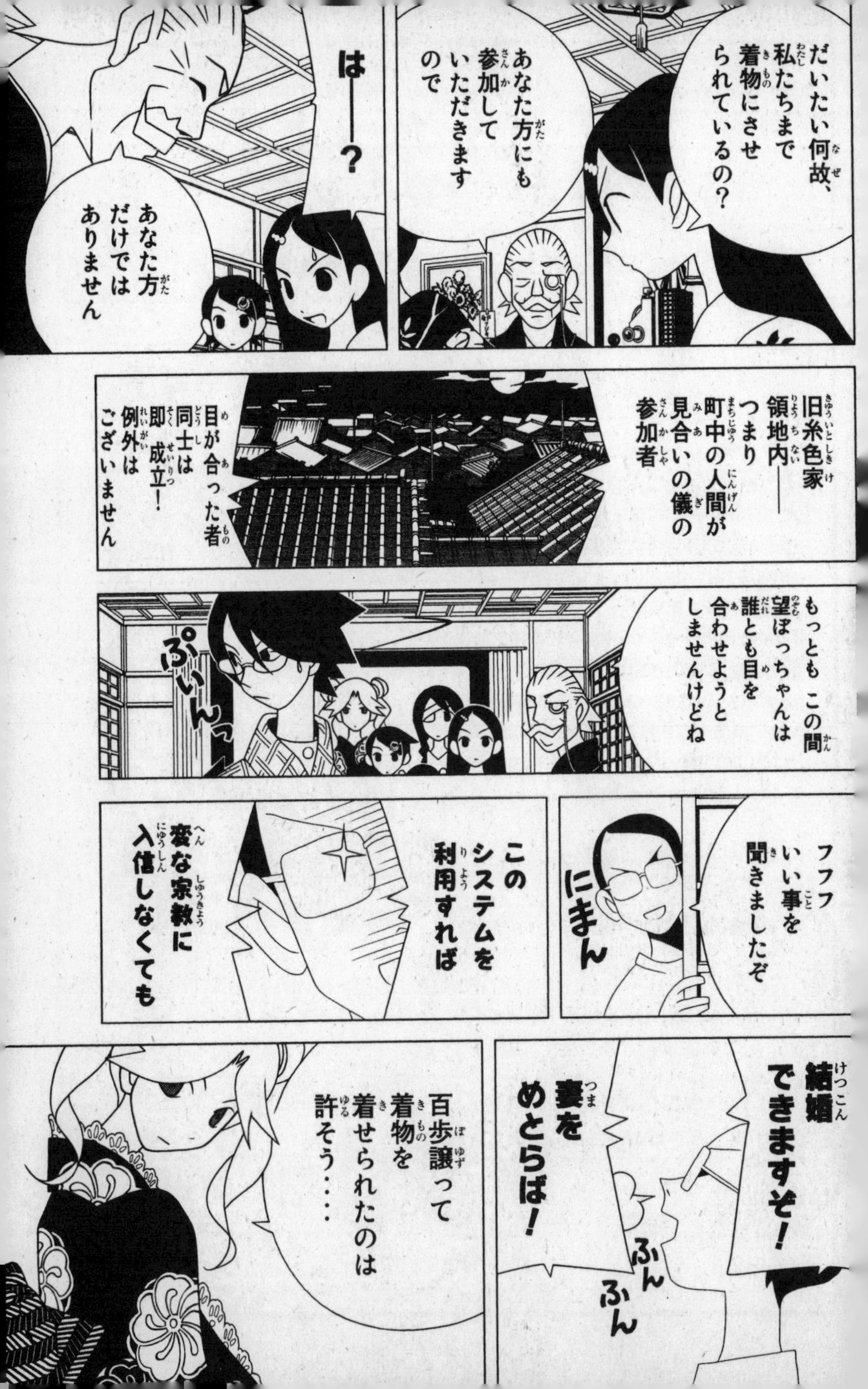
だいたい何故、私たちまで着物にさせられているの？
あなた方にも参加していただきますので
は――？
あなた方だけではありません
旧糸色家領地内――つまり町中の人間が見合いの儀の参加者
目が合った者同士は即成立！例外はございません
もっとも この間望ぼっちゃんは誰とも目を合わせようとしませんけどね
ぷいんっ
フフフ いい事を聞きましたぞ
にまん
このシステムを利用すれば
変な宗教に入信しなくても
結婚できますぞ！
妻をめとらば！
ふん ふん
百歩譲って着物を着せられたのは許そう…

# PARASYTE

## BY HITOSHI IWAAKI

### THEY DESCEND FROM THE SKIES.
### THEY HAVE A HUNGER FOR HUMAN FLESH.

They are parasites and they are everywhere. They must take control of a human host to survive, and once they do, they can assume any deadly form they choose.

But they haven't taken over everyone! High school student Shin is resisting the invasion— battling for control of his own body against an alien parasite committed to thwart his plans to warn humanity of the horrors to come.

- *Now published in authentic right-to-left format!*
- *Featuring an all-new translation!*

## Special extras in each volume! Read them all!

## BY KEN AKAMATSU

**N**egi Springfield is a ten-year-old wizard teaching English at an all-girls Japanese school. He dreams of becoming a master wizard like his legendary father, the Thousand Master. At first his biggest concern was concealing his magic powers, because if he's ever caught using them publicly, he thinks he'll be turned into an ermine! But in a world that gets stranger every day, it turns out that the strangest people of all are Negi's students! From a librarian with a magic book to a centuries-old vampire, from a robot to a ninja, Negi will risk his own life to protect the girls in his care!

Ages: 16+

*Special extras in each volume! Read them all!*

VISIT WWW.DELREYMANGA.COM TO:
- View release date calendars for upcoming volumes
- Sign up for Del Rey's free manga e-newsletter
- Find out the latest about new Del Rey Manga series

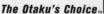